Lectures on Developing Economies

Lectures on Developing Economies

Japan's Experience and Its Relevance

Kazushi Ohkawa and Hirohisa Kohama

UNIVERSITY OF TOKYO PRESS

Publication of this volume was supported in part by grants from the Japan Foundation and the Suntory Foundation.

HC
462.9
033
1989

ISBN 0–86008–438–8
ISBN 4–13–047044–2

Printed in Japan

Contents

v

Part II   Major Factors and Activities

Preface

The lectures in this book are addressed to government officials and private business people engaged in practical implementation of economic development and to university and college students of development economics. The lecture materials are the actual texts used for economic development training courses at the International Development Center of Japan (IDCJ) in collaboration with the Economic Development Institute (EDI), the World Bank, and the United Nations Industrial Development Organization (UNIDO). The results of research on developing economies carried out at IDCJ are also incorporated.

Economic historians often try to elucidate the unique features of the Japanese experience, emphasizing particularly its sociocultural characteristics. Our approach, in contrast, aims at clarifying the Japanese experience through the language of standard economics common and comparable to any developing economy. Empirical evidence to test hypotheses is given priority over abstract theoretical propositions. When an academic approach seems necessary, it is footnoted to focus the text on an applied field close to the real problem.

The scope is not comprehensive but selective—a problem-oriented approach wherein some of the subjects are illustrated by examples. Japan's sociopolitical features, for example, can be explained more systematically in comparison with those of other countries. The problem of different political regimes is outside our scope. For centrally planned developing economies, for instance, the possible relevance of Japan's experience would depend upon the perspective, and it certainly would require special explanation.

Studies on the long-term growth path of Japan were comprehensively quantified by the Institute of Economic Research, Hitotsubashi University, Tokyo, and published in fourteen volumes as *Long-Term Economic Statistics* (LTES). The empirical evidence in the lectures depends heavily upon the LTES data, particularly because of our methodology, and we are indebted to the authors of each of the LTES volumes. The books and papers published by our academic friends and colleagues, cited in the lectures, including comments received when we were revising an earlier draft, were also sources of inspiration.

We are much obliged to the staff members of IDCJ—beginning with Saburo Kawai, chairman, and Hideo Monden, president—who are engaged in project surveys, research, and training pertaining to developing countries. In particular, Tamiko Sakatani and Kenji Tahara were of great help in typing all the drafts and computing and arranging the data. Without their contribution this book could not have been published.

KAZUSHI OHKAWA
HIROHISA KOHAMA

Introduction

This volume contains eight lectures on economic development based on Japan's experience. It does not attempt to describe Japan's history of economic development by emphasizing its uniqueness. Instead, in each lecture, historical materials are used to analyze problems common to all developing economies. The possible points of similarity of Japan's economic growth to contemporary developing economies are identified, while dissimilarities due to different circumstances are duly qualified.

Today Japan is one of the industrial market economies. In the North-South context it is undoubtedly one of the influential members of the North. Its economic growth—in particular its postwar performance—has often been compared with that of other industrialized countries. Analytically, it is attractive and fruitful to compare Japan's long-term economic growth and postwar economic performance with Western models of development.[1] An earlier study attempted another kind of analysis that compared Japan with contemporary developing countries[2]; the analytical focus there was to treat Japan as a latecomer to the North and to the Western development process. Japan's case thus can and should be observed from two perspectives that complement rather than contradict each other. This volume extends, in a sense, the latter approach, although comparative analysis is not explicitly carried out by subject as in the earlier work.

The main text consists of two parts. Lectures on phases of development are contained in Part I. Part II consists of lectures on major factors and activities. The phase approach forms the framework for dealing with the process of development. In each development phase,

[1] One example of such a comprehensive approach is Angus Maddison, *Phases of Capitalist Development* (Oxford: Oxford University Press, 1982).
[2] Kazushi Ohkawa and Gustav Ranis, eds., *Japan and the Developing Countries* (Oxford: Basil Blackwell, 1985).

major factors and activities operate differently, requiring a thorough and consistent observation throughout the entire development process. Parts I and II thus are intended to be an interwoven set.

Our concept of the way to distinguish phases of development is explained in Lecture 1. The relevance of Japan's experience can only be assessed with reference to such phases because the major problems and concerns vary in developing economies according to their different orientations on the path of development.

Japan is a country poor in natural resources, so that industrialization was its major means of development; but this is not true in all developing economies. Modification of the phasing is thus an important requirement in the context of relevance.

Academic models of phasing require the application of intermediary links for the treatment of the actual process of development. We try to provide these intermediary links. One major link is the actual relationship between trade structure and domestic industrial structure, which have hitherto been approached independently.

Primary and secondary phases of development are each divided into subphases, depending upon the major pattern and mechanism of industrialization. The primary phase is the topic of Lecture 1, section II. Its relevance is particularly stressed for countries at an early stage of development, even though their places in the international environment and demographic patterns differ. Lectures 2 and 4 are designed to analyze in depth the performance of import substitution and export substitution in the secondary phase. In the former, the emphasis is on clarifying the performance of the simultaneous process of primary export substitution and secondary import substitution relative to the reality of today's developing economies. More attention is given to the operation of the competitive market in the domestic private economy than usual and to the government's role in promoting the "early start" of strategic industries. In the latter, emphasis is on analyzing technological advance in manufacturing (particularly in the machinery industry) to clarify its relationship to augmenting international competitiveness. Organizational changes are also an important topic pertaining to the problem of medium- and small-scale enterprises, particularly in the context of the subcontracting system.

Lecture 3 aims at explaining a basic concept which we term Factor Input Ratio (FIR), and its application to the data provided by the Manufacturing Survey or the like. The FIR reveals a sharp distinction in the technological properties of industries—for instance, textiles, machinery, and iron and steel. In demarcating phases and analyzing a shift from one phase to another, FIR plays an important role. In

Lecture 2 its preliminary use is discussed, and in Lecture 4 it is more fully applied.

In Part II, Lecture 5, by analyzing Japanese long-term investment data, we attempt to illustrate our concept of capital formation analysis and take a simple quantitative approach to the problem of investment efficiency and criteria. Development is grasped as an innovative process *à la* Shumpeter's concept of innovation. The conventional approach of "growth accounting" is used for quantifying the innovative process. The incremental residual per investment unit is the core term. Its path of augmentation over time is identified through phases in Japan's economic growth. The conventional term capital-output ratio (or the incremental capital-output ratio, ICOR) is decomposed into relevant terms to be used as an indicator of investment efficiency, and its validity and limitations are tested for use in development planning. The criteria of the investment terms ICOR and incremental FIR are discussed in overall and sectoral settings. Thus ICOR is applied conditionally with a certain type of technology. Special attention is paid to investment allocation between the public and the private sectors, and detailed discussion of infrastructure is in the Appendix.

The discussion of human resources in Lecture 6 proceeds from the hypothesis of borrowed technology and our basic concept of social capability. The effort to conduct technology transfer in a way that efficiently meets local requirements is essential for all latecomers to economic development. Japan is a typical case. We believe that efficient technology transfer depends upon the level and rate of enhancing social capability measured in human and institutional terms. The problem of human resources is assessed from this conceptual framework. Human capability is enhanced by formal education and "learning by doing." The role of on-the-job training is important, but our analysis has focused mostly on formal education because of the availability of data. Education in Japan seems similar to that in contemporary developing countries, and almost nothing unique has been identified in its early developing process. Estimates of education's costs and benefits, linked to the measured residual increase mentioned above, provide important guidelines for allocating resources to education. The pattern of sectoral reallocation and the rate at which human resources are used are also examined.

Lecture 7 focuses on industrial policy from the historical perspective of its interaction with the private sector. An industry promotion policy was inaugurated in the initial years of Japan's development. From the postwar years to the present, the government's so-called industrial policy has drawn international attention to Japan's noteworthy growth and export performance. These policies—including those distorted by military expansion in the secondary phase—are investigated to elucidate the real function of policies relative to the competitive market mechanism in the private sector. For latecomers to economic development to succeed in catching up to the forerunners, government participation is indispensable, though policies and types of administrative guidance may vary. This view implies that efficient operation of the market mechanism is highly significant for the innovative process of development. The other side of the coin is to note that overparticipation by a government will have the negative effect of obstructing the vigor of private enterprises.

In Lecture 8, after presenting a critical review of the notion of an export-led economy, which is misapplied in Japan's case, observation of structural changes in industry and trade is extended to focus on the postwar period of rapid economic growth. The fast shift from capital-intensive heavy industry to technology-intensive industry is analyzed. The indicator of a Net Export Ratio is used to indicate successive shifts of comparative advantages among industries. Following a review of Japan's institutions, systems, and organizations for export promotion, the concluding remarks aim at clarifying their relevance for developing countries, on the basis of a legitimate understanding of the public function of industrial policies and private sector activities in enhancing international competitiveness.

The post-development phase is beyond our scope, but brief comments on Japan's recent economic performance are included in the Epilogue to Lecture 8. It is our view that the significant role to be played by expanding exports should not be underestimated, and the importance of a new policy of enhancing imports of manufactured goods should be emphasized: such is our perspective on the restructuring process in Japan's final steps toward full industrialization at the end of this century.

The eight lectures as a whole are presented from three points of view:

1. Japan's experience is not a unique but a common process of latecomer economic development. Its relevance to contemporary developing economies can be drawn from the transferable knowledge not only of successes but also of failures. The patterns and mechanisms of economic growth of latecomers can be broadly clarified by applying the conventional concepts of economics, but emphasis on intensive analysis is required because of the characteristics of the development process, particularly with regard to the possibility of technological-organizational advance. How to realize what we call the "telescoping effects" of advancement is the essential problem for latecomers.

2. An essential problem for all developing economies is productivity enhancement vs. employment augmentation. More attention is drawn to investment efficiency rather than just to labor productivity increases, but creating employment is important as well. The so-called trade-off between the two objectives can be solved, or at least decreased, through innovative technological-organizational progress based on enhancing human capability. The conventional classification based on the dichotomy between capital-intensive and labor-intensive production cannot be advocated as investment criteria. Investment criteria should be both capital-efficient and employment-enhancing to optimize sectoral resource allocation. The conditions required for doing so may differ according to a country's phases of development.

3. Regarding development plans and policies, the role of industrial policy seems to be more significant than is usually thought—particularly for technological advance by sector. A macro approach on the one hand and micro approach (individual projects) on the other may not be satisfactory without filling the gap in between by an intensified sectoral and subsectoral approach. Optimum policy options depend heavily upon exact knowledge of these sectors in each country analyzed.

Part I

The Phases of Development

Economic Development in Historical Perspective:

The Phases of Industrialization

A century of Japan's economic development will be discussed with the hope of contributing to clarifying the problems of developing economies. The century is divided into segments that are demarcated by phases; the phase is a conceptual means of understanding the pattern of long-term economic development in historical perspective. In identifying development phases, however, no assumption is made *a priori* that the path of shifting phases should be uniform and inevitable for all developing economies. Dissimilarities for the initial historical conditions, for the typologies as well as the political regimes, are all constituents that influence formation of the pattern and mechanism of economic development.

A phase is defined as a segment of the development process, characterized by a certain pattern and mechanism that distinguish it from other segments. With respect to the method and criteria for phase identification and demarcation, however, no uniformity should be assumed. Depending upon the standpoint and purpose of analysis, we may be able to choose different standards or criteria. For example, changes in government strategies and policies can be one such criterion. Any change in the pattern of industrialization will be a major factor. For historical reasons, however, the transformation of the relationship between the modern and the traditional sectors will also be significant. This particular aspect may be relevant to those developing countries which have long histories.

We will pay attention to the typological features, but we will not attempt to discuss the initial conditions except in the context of human capability in Lecture 6. The reasons are twofold. First, if we ask why Japan could start its economic modernization in the mid-nineteenth century—much earlier than other Asian countries—then the initial conditions become the major subject of analysis. However, for our phase approach, what is important is the process instead of its genesis.

The sociocultural and historical system substantially affected the pattern and mechanism of subsequent development. As reflected in economic activities, this system will be dealt with by stressing the importance of its traditional elements and sectors. Second, Japan's initial economic level, as seen in per capita income, agricultural productivity, and industrial structure, was almost as low as that of other East and Southeast Asian countries in the early postwar years. Economists and historians often argue that Japan's economic level at the start must have been much higher than those of other Asian countries, but this conjecture is refuted by our empirical research.[1] Therefore, we are not concerned about the influence of differences of income-productivity levels when we discuss the possible relevance of Japan's experience to that of contemporary developing countries.

Two major phases are demarcated: the primary phase, 1868–1919, and the secondary phase, 1920–75.[2] The mid-1970s, when Japan became a developed country, is outside the scope of our inquiry. Each major phase consists of two subphases. The initial subphase and the second subphase demarcated at around the turn of the century are for the major primary phase; the first subphase and the second subphase demarcated at around 1960 are for the major secondary phase. Another demarcation will sometimes be used for the prewar and postwar periods. Identification of these phases, however, is not our primary purpose. Our primary purpose is to find out how a shift is made from one phase to the next, thereby clarifying the required conditions and mechanism of development from an analysis of past experience.

A century of Japan's economic development was first analyzed by demarcating phases[3]; with emphasis on international trade, a similar phase analysis was applied to East Asia—Japan, South Korea, and

---

[1] Kazushi Ohkawa, "Initial Conditions: Economic Level and Structure," in *Papers and Proceedings of the Conference on Japan's Historical Development Experience and the Contemporary Developing Countries: Issues for Comparative Analysis* (Tokyo: International Development Center of Japan, 1978). For example, Japan's estimated per capita GNP for 1876–87 is 154. Although such measures cannot be precise, this figure is comparable with the estimates of per capita GDP in 1953–57 for some Asian countries: the Philippines 136, Thailand 95, South Korea 158, Taiwan 175 (all in 1965 U.S.$). Agricultural output (measured by wheat unit-equivalent to one ton of wheat) per worker is 2.50 for Japan in 1880 and 2.33 on average for Southeast Asia in 1963.

[2] The term "semi-industrialized phase" has been used in previous papers and will also be used in this volume. It is equivalent to what we call the secondary phase here.

[3] Kazushi Ohkawa and Henry Rosovsky, "A Century of Japanese Economic Growth," in W. W. Lockwood, ed., *The State and Economic Enterprise in Japan* (Princeton: Princeton University Press, 1965).

Taiwan.[4] The lectures in Part I will be given in the framework of development phases, depending heavily upon these two previous works, although certain aspects of some phases will be emphasized. In this lecture, a conceptual explanation is given for the framework of phasing; an empirical approach is made to linking the transformation of domestic industrial structure with that of international trade, and several important aspects of application of the phase approach are noted. Section I outlines these topics, and in section II the major primary phase is discussed substantively.

I. Conceptual Framework and the Problems of Application

Trade Approach
Let us begin by summarizing phase demarcation from the viewpoint of changes in trade structure. This approach not only is widely accepted in the field of academic analysis based in principle on the concept of comparative advantage, but also is closely related to the policy debates on the developing economies such as inward-looking vs. outward-looking or import substitution vs. export promotion. A simple framework of phases and their shifts is as follows: (1) traditional product export, (2) primary import substitution of nondurable consumer goods, (3) primary export substitution of light manufactured goods for agricultural products, (4) secondary import substitution of durable goods for producers and consumers by further development of domestic manufacturing, and (5) secondary export substitution in which export of nondurables is replaced by durable goods export.

The series of shifts from one phase to another, $(1) \rightarrow (2) \rightarrow (3) \rightarrow (4) \rightarrow (5)$, was empirically observed through the entire process of industrialization in East Asia, although some modifications in the sequence were made for individual countries. For example, in the case of Japan, phase 2, primary import substitution, was brief, and is treated together with phase 1 for 1870–1900; for Taiwan and Korea, following phase 1 traditional export expansion, phase 2 primary import substitution can be demarcated separately for 1950–62 (Taiwan) and 1953–64 (Korea). Phase 3 primary export substitution, however, can be identified distinctly for all: 1900–19 in Japan, 1962–70 in Taiwan, and 1964–72 in

[4] John C. H. Fei, Kazushi Ohkawa, and Gustav Ranis, "Economic Development in Historical Perspective: Japan, Korea and Taiwan," in Kazushi Ohkawa and Gustav Ranis, eds., *Japan and the Developing Countries* (Oxford: Basil Blackwell, 1985).

Korea. For Japan, phase 4 of secondary import substitution is demarcated for 1920–60, followed by phase 5, secondary export substitution, 1960–75.[5] For Taiwan and Korea, phase 4 can be identified after the beginning of the 1970s, but it is still too early to demarcate the dates of a shift to phase 5.

The concepts involved in the phase demarcations as well as their relation to our phase identification will be discussed later. We believe that a detailed analysis of modern economic growth in the Kuznets sense will be facilitated if sets of countries can be grouped around basic affinities, as in the three cases of Japan, Taiwan, and Korea. In the subsequent lectures, the examination and observation will be focused on Japan; however, attention will always be drawn to the possible relevance for other developing countries. Affinity or disaffinity is a problem for which a clear-cut solution is impossible. Initial conditions (inheritance from a premodern epoch of feudalism or colonialism; high level of social capability), typologies (including natural resource endowments and country size), the strategies and policies of a government, and the international environment all may affect the pattern of phase formation and mechanism of its shift in the long-term process of a developing economy.

The phase performance of an oil-producing country, for example, may bear little relation to that of Japan. Countries rich in natural resources for agriculture (for example, some of the Latin American countries) may, as a result of their sustained export expansion of farm products, skip phase 3 primary export substitution by the development of light industries.[6] A faster shift from phase 2 to 3 and from 3 to 4 in Taiwan and Korea than in Japan certainly was supported by a more favorable international environment. Nevertheless, it is our view that Japan's case can be a good framework of reference, if not a standard, for a great number of other developing countries, if and when the phases are appropriately demarcated to take into account the relevant considerations mentioned above.

From this point of view, phase identification through changes in

---

[5] Phases 4 and 5 and their dating will be discussed in Lectures 2 and 4.

[6] The percentage share of manufactured goods in total merchandise exports (1) is a simple indicator of typological difference, if compared with the share percentage of manufacturing output in GDP (2). For example, in 1982, (1):(2) is 92:27 for South Korea, 47:25 for the Philippines, 39:27 for Brazil, and 24:28 for Argentina. Japan is 87:24 for the phase of secondary import substitution. These country comparisons illustrate a wide difference in (1) despite the similar value of (2). No doubt two very different patterns, such as a sustained export expansion of agricultural products (the Latin American pattern) vs. an export concentration to manufacturing goods (the East Asian pattern), cannot be treated by an application of our phasing.

the trade structure would need amplification. In the words of a comparative study of Asian economies:

This evolutionary view complements the more traditional analysis of shifts in the sectoral composition of output and labor allocation among the agricultural, industrial, and services sectors. As has been pointed out by Colin Clark and, more rigorously, by Kuznets, we usually encounter in the course of development a relatively shrinking agricultural sector, an expanding industrial sector and a fairly stable (if markedly changing in composition) services sector. Such structural changes reflect changes in demand as well as in capacity, or—in an open economy—in changing comparative advantage, as per-capita income rises. The phasing developed in this essay focuses on the same question, the underlying issue being how increases in productivity are allocated among sectors as income rises.[7]

Actually, analysis along this line for Japan's case reveals a pattern similar to those of Western countries regarding changes in output, labor, and output per worker, but with some differences that will be explained in the lectures that follow.[8] First, however, we wish to clarify the relationship between the two approaches, one focused on the trade structure and the other on the domestic industrial structure. The problem in historical perspective is the same, but there is a conceptual difference in the method of approach: the former aims at identifying phases —certain intervals or segments of a long-term process, each being distinguished from others in changing comparative advantage—while the latter intends to clarify the long-term trend of structural transformation in response to changes in productivity and income level.

Manufacturing, for example, is a core sector of industry and one in which technological change is most notable. In a normal path of development its growth rate of output (Y_M) is sustained to be greater than that of GDP (Y). Therefore, its share (Y_M/Y) has a long-term trend of increase. This share percentage is often used as a simple indicator of industrialization. Japan's share for selected years is 10.8% (1885), 17.4% (1904), 23.4% (1919), 29.1% (1938), 18.0% (1955), 24.2% (1960), and 36.4% (1976). The drop from 1938 to 1955 is clearly

[7] Fei, Ohkawa, and Ranis, "Economic Development," p. 36.

[8] For example, see Kazushi Ohkawa,"Changes in Industrial Structure," in Kazushi Ohkawa and Miyohei Shinohara, eds., *Patterns of Japanese Economic Development: A Quantitative Appraisal* (New Haven: Yale University Press, 1979).

Table 1.1
Japan's Trade Development

Period	Development Phase	Manufacturing Share of GDP Y_M/Y (%)
1870–1900	Traditional product export and primary import substitution	10.8–17.4[a]
1900–19	Primary export substitution	17.4–23.4
1919–60	Secondary import substitution	23.4–24.2
1960–75	Secondary export substitution	24.2–36.4

[a] Some differences in dating contribute to the spread of these data, which will be discussed in greater detail below.

a distortion caused by World War II. Otherwise, a straightforward increasing trend would have been observed.

A demarcation of segments corresponds to the phases identified by a trade approach (Table 1.1).

The shift of phases corresponds with industrialization, although the pace of the share (Y_M/Y) changes is not necessarily uniform (the abnormally small change from 1919 to 1960 was caused in part by World War II). Therefore, these shares, if adequately normalized, can be indicative of phase demarcation because the increase in Y_M/Y implies an advance in a comparative advantage for manufacturing. From our knowledge of the pattern of changes in the share itself, we know that the trend changes in the domestic industrial structure do not necessarily coincide with changes in the comparative advantage between either agriculture and manufacturing or nondurable and durable production sectors within manufacturing. Typological features may be the best explanation for the discrepancies.

Industry Approach
Let us clarify the content of an industry approach in relation to a trade approach. The changes in the share (Y_M/Y) have their own significance in the industrial transformation when they are used with output growth rate (expressed by G): a weighted growth rate for manufacturing $GY_M \cdot Y_M/Y = \Delta Y_M/Y$ and for agriculture $GY_A \cdot Y_A/Y = \Delta Y_A/Y$. First, the over-time changes in the weighted growth rate between manufacturing and agriculture provide useful information on the dating and nature of the initial phase of industrialization. Second, the changes may indicate important information for demarcating the terminal dates of long-term transition as discussed by Kuznets.

For a normal path of industrialization, starting with the initial condition $Y_A/Y > Y_M/Y$ and a dynamic process of $GY_A < GY_M$, the difference of weighted growth rate between agriculture and manufacturing tends to narrow to a point where the difference eventually disappears ($\Delta Y_A = \Delta Y_M$), implying that the sectoral contribution to GDP growth rate is equal between agriculture and manufacturing ($\Delta Y_A/Y = \Delta Y_M/Y$) and marking the point where the economic development of the economy achieves its initial phase of preparation for accelerating further industrialization. After arriving at this point, the economy will be characterized by a sustained path of $\Delta Y_M > \Delta Y_A$ if the driving force of industrialization continues.[9]

The dates of arrival at this point may differ among countries mostly because of rich or poor natural endowments for agriculture. In Japan's case, $\Delta Y_M > \Delta Y_A$ occurred around the turn of the century, almost coinciding with the year of shift in phases from traditional agricultural exports to primary export substitution by light manufacturing, illustrating consistent performance between a trade-structure-focused and domestic-industrial-structure-focused approach. The average weighted growth rate of manufacturing in India from 1976 to 1982 was still lower than that of agriculture (0.7% vs. 1.0%) because its richer natural resources created more sustained agricultural growth.[10]

A second topic pertains to the terminal dates of the industrialization process. When and how does economic development end? The answer basically is a notion of the end of transition growth in the Kuznets sense. Such terms as "full industrialization" and "economic maturity" have often been used for demarcating the terminal point. The problem of dating the terminal point needs clarification both conceptually and

---

[9] Of course a ratio of simple shares Y_M/Y_A or $(Y_M/Y)/(Y_A/Y)$ has its own meaning. Today's developing countries adopt various indicators or targets of industrialization in their development plans. For example, the Fifth Plan of Thailand, 1982–86, adopted a simple share ratio, setting the year of equality between Y_A/Y and Y_M/Y as the landmark for turning from an agriculture-based to an inudstrialized country (actually, for 1983, $Y_M/Y = 19\%$, $Y_A/Y = 23\%$).

[10] A number of latecomers still locate themselves in the initial phase of development, not yet having arrived at the initial point defined above. If the performance of agricultural development is normal, this evaluation is natural because of very late participation in economic development. However, for many of these countries, the rate of growth of agriculture is too low, such as for sub-Sahara African countries in the 1970s and onward. The weighted growth rate of agriculture was 0.5% vs. 0.3% for manufacturing in the 1970s, and 1.1% vs. 0.4% in the 1960s. These rates are estimated as a simple average of 24 countries, excluding several countries with favorable growth performance. The problem for these countries is to have a realistic perspective for reaching the initial phase for increasing industrialization by enhancing agricultural development.

empirically. In our view, the point demarcated by an industrial structure approach cannot coincide with that demarcated by a trade structure approach. Conceptually it is quite natural to apply the notion of contributed share to the entire process of industrialization and to identify the terminal point as the beginning of a decrease in the weighted growth rate of manufacturing. The terminal point also can be defined as the point of full industrialization in the sense that the driving force of the industrial sector eventually ends there. Many people believe the process of development also ends there, but we do not share this view. The end of development is defined as the point at which the final phase of secondary export substitution, as defined in the trade structure approach, is completed. These two terminal points do not necessarily coincide.

Let us examine the empirical facts. Regarding Japan's prewar development, a long-term trend of increase in the contribution share of manufacturing is clearly identified in sub-phase averages: 1887–1904, 19.5%; 1904–19, 27.0%; 1919–30, 39.6%; 1931–38, 46.3%.[11] The shape of the trend may differ among developing economies. Japan's trend was artificially accelerated toward the end of the 1930s with military mobilization. Nevertheless, the trend of increase is universally observed through developing economies except for some Latin American countries.

In Japan's postwar period, the contribution share of manufacturing for shorter intervals (Table 1.2, column 5) appears not necessarily to show the pattern of performance expected. Until 1966–70, it continues to increase, following the prewar trend (the numerical levels are not comparable because of differences in data and calculation), and does decrease, as expected, from 1971 to 1975. However, the share again increases from 1976 to 1980 and 1981 to 1985.

The decrease in manufacturing growth rate from 1966 to 1975 was a result of the first oil crisis and thus was temporary. However, Japan's manufacturing share did continue to increase as a trend throughout the postwar years, despite a distinct shift from high to slower growth intervals.[12] The ratio GY_M/G_Y demarcates the earlier interval of high growth rates and the later interval of slow growth rates. World Bank data for 1973 and 1984, which will be discussed in detail later, rough-

[11] LTES (Long-term Economic Statistics of Japan), Vol. 1, National Income, Table 3–3, p. 50.

[12] As is well known, a decrease in the labor force of the manufacturing sector is a general part of the employment structure of industrialized economies. Japan's labor force slightly decreased through the 1970s but somehow has been increasing in the 1980s.

Table 1.2
Postwar Japan's Growth: Contribution Share Percentage of Manufacturing

	GDP Share of Manufacturing	Growth Rates			Weighted Growth Rate of Manufacturing	Contribution Share
		Manufacturing	GDP	Ratio		
Period	Y_M/Y	GY_M	G_Y	GY_M/G_Y	$\Delta Y_M/Y$	$(\Delta Y_M/Y)/G_Y$
1956–60	15.9	16.8	9.7	1.73	2.69	27.7
1961–65	20.0	13.4	9.3	1.44	2.68	28.8
1966–70	24.7	18.0	13.3	1.35	4.65	34.9
1971–75	26.5	4.4	4.0	1.10	1.17	29.2
1976–80	28.1	7.5	5.0	1.25	2.10	42.0
1981–85	32.6	7.5	3.9	1.92	2.45	62.8

Source: Economic Planning Agency, Annual Reports on National Accounts.
Note: Five-year averages of the annually calculated series in constant prices, 1980 base.

ly correspond to the slow-growth interval. We believe this shift is a structural phenomenon, and that the point of completing the secondary export-substitution is demarcated around the mid-1970s (to be confirmed in Lectures 4 and 7), and not the terminal point of industrialization.

Some readers may wonder whether Japan's case is atypical. Japan's limited natural resources make it strategically important to enhance the comparative advantage of manufacturing through shifting phases of development. Even after completion of secondary export substitution this trend has been sustained. In Lecture 8 we will investigate this performance in detail in relation to the recent export expansion of manufactures. Other developing economies—particularly newly industrializing Asian economies—may perform similarly in the future.

A brief look at the postwar performance of other industrialized economies may be useful to indicate their performance toward the terminal point of full industrialization. According to the classification of "industrial market economies" in the World Bank World Development Report, for the latest interval, 1973–84, these countries show a common pattern of sectoral output growth: $GY_i < GY_s$ (i, industrial sector; s, services sector).[13] The only exception among the fourteen

[13] Since the services sector share in GDP(Y_s/Y) is becoming greater and the number of countries for which the data of Y_M is available is limited, $GY_i \gtrless GY_s$ is used to approximate the contribution share of manufacturing.

countries listed is Japan. This anomaly appears to support treating Japan as an atypical case. However, in the earlier postwar interval—for instance, between 1960 and 1970—the picture was quite different: the dominant performance was $GY_i > GY_s$, and the only exception was the United Kingdom. All other industrial economies, including the United States, have reversed the industrial sector inequality at a certain point between 1960 and 1970 to arrive at the terminal point of industrialization. Such performance supports our view that the concept of the terminal point of full industrialization can and should be treated quite independently from that of the terminal point of the development process, implying that in the future Japan will also certainly arrive at the terminal point of full industrialization. Thus we can conceive a "final subphase toward full industrialization" demarcated between the two terminals. This conception is a natural way of bridging the trade structure approach and industrial structure approach consistently (see the Epilogue to Lecture 8).

One more relevant aspect of our "phase approach" is its relationship with the "industry approach," represented by the "flying-geese pattern" thesis developed by Akamatsu, Kojima, and Yamazawa. This thesis has greatly contributed to clarifying the long-term changes in Japan's international trade structure by examining the cycle (import substitution—induced domestic production—export expansion), industry by industry. Taking these together—for example, textiles, steel, and automobiles—the shape looks like flying geese.[14]

The two approaches complement each other in dealing with the problem, but the emphasis differs. Taking the phase of secondary import substitution, for example, the ratio of domestic production to total demand sharply increases for durables, represented by steel, but is still under the level of unity. But the export of textiles shows a high level of the ratio (about 1.8 to 1.6 according to Yamazawa) from 1919 to 1935. Our phase identification is represented by imports and does not refer explicitly to exports, although of course we do not ignore their importance. The simultaneous process of industry growth of machinery and textiles will be the major subject of Lecture 2. Our approach essentially aims at elucidating an evolutionary process of development and the performance of innovative industries, as emphasized in phasing.

Another example is the phase of primary export substitution. The ratio of domestic production to total demand for textiles (mainly yarn)

[14] Ippei Yamazawa, *Nihon no Keizai Hatten to Kokusa iBungyo* [Japan's Economic Development and International Trade] (Tokyo: Toyo Keizai Shimposha, 1983).

made a sharp increase from the end of the 1890s to the end of World War I. Light manufacturing goods could be substituted for agricultural goods in export, but at the same time, the productivity expansion in agriculture was substantial. Although an import substitution policy for sugar failed, the sustained productivity growth in rice cultivation and sericulture was notable. Here again the simultaneous growth of the textile industry and traditional agriculture is clearly shown.[15] This growth will be discussed in some detail later in Section III. Viewed from its evolutionary nature, the phase is called "primary export substitution," but the importance of agriculture should not be underestimated.

The policy implications of the phase thesis will be dealt with in Lecture 7. However, regarding the implications of simultaneous growth, in the context of debates on the policy option of "inward looking vs. outward looking" for today's developing economies, the phase thesis is often misunderstood as indicating an *alternative* option between export promotion and import substitution, as discussed with regard to exchange rate policy. The overlapping sequence of the phases does not indicate the possibility of one replacing the other. The simultaneous growth sequence implies both inward- and outward-looking policy for different phases. As a matter of fact, in most developing countries, policy efforts have been made for both export promotion and import substitution simultaneously regarding selected industries. The real point is whether the selection of industries can be based on the long-term perspectives of evolutionary process of a country facing the pressures of current resource shortages.

Sectoral Reallocation of the Labor Force

Thus far, phasing has been discussed relative to output in either international trade or the domestic industrial structure. Basically, however, shifts of phases imply changes in the proportion of production, prices, and the technological advances involved. These aspects also can be consistently dealt with conceptually in phasing.

The original idea of development phasing stems from recognizing basic changes in the pattern and mechanism of employment-wage performance in a certain period during the long-term process of industrialization. The analytical concept of the "turning point" (TP) is widely

---

[15] This specific growth has been called "concurrent growth," disproving the notion that agricultural development is the precondition for industrialization. Kazushi Ohkawa, "Concurrent Growth of Agriculture with Industry," Part III, in *Differential Structure and Agriculture*, Economic Research Series No. 13 (Tokyo: Kinokuniya; Institute of Economic Research, Hitotsubashi University, 1972).

used in this regard not only in academic writing but also in discussions of actual development planning from a long-term perspective. The thesis is that in the primary phase, the economy is characterized by a virtually unchanged level of the real wages of unskilled labor. The economy, however, increases its real wage level when the "unlimited supplies" of unskilled labor are exhausted at a certain point—the TP. The rise of the real wage level is a result of changes in the demand for labor as well as the supply of labor. The unchanged wage level is assumed to be determined by the people's traditional standard of living historically given as the initial condition. In this sense, the wage level rises in the modern sectors. The level at the TP, therefore, is directly caused by labor demand enhancement brought forth by industrialization. From that level onward the economy comes to have a competitive mechanism for wage-employment determination throughout the entire economy.

This theoretical framework has been applied by a number of economists to the cases of East Asian development—for example, it has been a valid framework for Japan, Korea, and Taiwan[16]—and yet, apart from disagreement with the neoclassical thought that denies the emergence of TP, the most controversial analytical debates arise from interpretation of TP's applied results for Japan. Our viewpoint is that the TP emerged around 1919, that is, toward the end of the subphase of secondary import substitution.[17]

The essential aspect should be not the interpretation of Japan's economic history itself but its possible relevance to developing economies: surplus labor should be the core concept. From this standpoint our view is that there were not one but two turning points in Japan's case: at the first investment spurt and later again at the postwar investment spurt. The interval between the two turning points is the unstable interwar period, and the years directly affected by the war are included. "Surplus labor"—defined as labor that can be released from present employment without causing a substantial decrease in output—was re-created during this interval of a downward swing of the Japanese economy. Underemployment accumulated in the services sector. The agricultural labor force, which had been decreasing, began to increase again. Immediately after World War II, the great number of repatriated workers exacerbated the situation of surplus labor.

---

[16] Fei, Ohkawa, and Ranis, "Economic Development."

[17] For example, Ryoshin Minami, *The Turning Point in Economic Development: Japan's Experience* (Tokyo: Kinokuniya, 1973).

The drastic expansion of demand for labor brought forth by investment spurts, we believe, is the major explanation for the double occurrence of TP. As will be explained in Lecture 5, during the entire process of industrialization, Japan experienced three investment spurts. The second spurt occurred in the 1930s, but it was greatly affected by the forces toward military mobilization and is quite different from the other two, since it did not have an effect on the demand for labor. The concept of "spurt" originates in Gerschenkron's theory of economic backwardness. He argued that, in light of European economic history, "one big spurt" is necessary for latecomers to be successful in industrialization.[18] For latecomers in general, however, we think there is no reason for a spurt to occur only once.

Sectoral reallocation of labor during industrialization has a pattern of a net outflow from the traditional to the modern sectors. This long-term tendency, however, does not proceed smoothly. The major reason for its variation is the rate of capital accumulation in the modern sector. For this reason Japan's investment spurts cause drastic upsurges in labor demand. In general, the reallocation process of labor (L) can be represented as a two-sector model wherein subscript 1 represents the modern sector; subscript 2 is the traditional sector; L_1/L and L_2/L are sectoral shares; and Δ stands for the incremental increase: $\Delta L/L = \Delta L_1/L_1 \cdot L_1/L + \Delta L_2/L \cdot L_2/L$. An increase in L_1/L by capital accumulation in sector 1 and a decrease in L_2/L are normal. This norm is equivalent to $\Delta L = \Delta L_1 + \Delta L_2$, where ΔL is incremental supply and, for simplicity, is assumed to be determined demographically. The difference $(\Delta L - \Delta L_1)$ yields ΔL_2, the source of surplus labor. No visible unemployment is assumed for the sake of simplicity.

The surplus labor is analytically defined by its lower marginal productivity than the prevailing wage level. However, it is not easy to measure the relationship between the two or to give empirical evidence of either one. As a matter of fact, this lack of analytical data is one reason for the controversies in the TP in Japan's case.[19]

---

[18] Alexander Gerschenkron, *Economic Backwardness in Historical Perspective* (Cambridge: Harvard University Press, 1966). Gerschenkron's original approach did not specifically treat investment; rather, it concerned producer durables and basic goods.

[19] One reason for the controversy on the TP mentioned earlier stems from technical points such as the interpretation of overtime measured in real wages (w) of unskilled labor and measurement of marginal productivity of labor (MP). The central point, however, that needs to be understood pertains to the inequality or equality between w and MP. Even apart from w performance, measured values of MP in agriculture differ from one study to another. One asserts MP<w for the time of first TP, accepting MP=w for the time of second TP; others argue MP<w is

In the primary phase of development, ΔL_1 is much smaller than ΔL_2. Even if its rate of increase is very high, this is inevitable because of its very small share, L_1/L. If industrialization continue successfully, the economy will arrive at a certain point, $\Delta L_1/L_1 \cdot L_1/L = \Delta L_2/L_2 \cdot L_2/L$, where equality can be seen.

This point is equivalent to $\Delta L = 2\Delta L_1$, wherein the incremental magnitude of the labor force employed in the modern sector constitutes one-half of the incremental increase of the total labor force. This point is of substantial significance because it marks two different structures of the labor market: $\Delta L_1 < \Delta L_2$ and $\Delta L_1 > \Delta L_2$. In the latter, the pressure of labor demand in the modern sector operates positively on the traditional sector, while in the former this is not the case.

Neither $\Delta L/L$ nor $\Delta L_1/L$ is constant in the real world. Even though the modern and traditional sectors cannot be precisely classified, the formula is beneficial for grasping a broad change in the long-term pattern of the labor market without depending upon the use of wage data and measurements of marginal product of labor. Since our approach is new, empirical verification is specifically needed. As a rough test, let industry represent the modern sector and agriculture and services mark the traditional sector. The ILO data on "economically active population" are used for the average of three decades: I (1950–1960), II (1960–1970), and III (1970–1980) (Table 1.3).[20]

South Korea's TP has been identified as occurring at the beginning of the 1970s.[21] The rate of increase in its labor force employed in the industrial sector, GL_1, accelerated remarkably from 6.0 in 1950 to 1960 to 10.2% in 1960 to 1970, the highest rate of increase among the selected countries. The ratio, an indicator of $\Delta L_1/\Delta L$, is 53%, over one-half, between 1970 and 1980, following a sustained tendency of

---

the TP both times. As can naturally be expected, MP in agriculture differs widely among different scales of farming (higher for larger scale; lower for smaller scale). Representative MP cannot be judged precisely.

Besides, motivation for the labor flows out of agriculture to nonagricultural sectors cannot be directly linked with the degree of inequality, $MP < w$. Members of farm households may not quickly respond to wage increases in industry. The inequality might exist even in case of wage increases for the majority of farm households. The degree of inequality, we think, might have been greatly narrowed at the second TP, even though its perfect equality cannot be the case. Because of these conditions in Japan, our broad discussion cannot depend solely upon such measurements. Similar measurements for developing economies also need testing.

[20] International Labour Office (ILO), *Economically Active Population Estimates: 1950–1980, Projections: 1985–2025*, Vol. I (Asia), Vol. II (Africa), Vol. III (Latin America).

[21] Fei, Ohkawa, and Ranis, "Economic Development."

Table 1.3

Sectoral Labor Reallocation with Industrialization in Selected Developing Countries, 1950–1980

Country	% of Industrial Sector Share L_1/L			% of Rate of Increase GL_1			% of Weighted Ratio GL_1/GL		
	I	II	III	I	II	III	I	II	III
Asia:									
India	9.7	11.5	12.9	5.1	2.6	2.3	32.4	13.0	17.3
China	5.5	8.2	12.1	4.0	7.1	6.8	25.0	23.2	33.5
Pakistan	15.7	18.3	17.2	3.6	2.5	1.0	73.7	12.7	6.2
Indonesia	7.0	9.0	12.7	3.4	5.1	4.6	15.5	22.9	27.7
Thailand	3.4	5.2	8.2	7.8	6.2	8.0	13.1	11.2	23.2
Malaysia	10.9	13.0	16.7	3.1	4.8	6.8	20.7	23.2	30.9
Rep. of Korea	8.3	15.0	23.3	6.0	10.2	5.9	42.7	48.6	52.9
Latin America:									
Colombia	18.5	21.4	23.4	2.6	4.6	2.6	25.9	36.3	22.9
Cuba	22.1	25.2	27.6	0.9	2.2	3.8	13.8	55.5	34.2
Brazil	17.5	20.1	24.2	3.8	1.3	5.5	24.6	8.5	38.7
Mexico	18.1	21.9	26.6	3.9	5.1	6.2	30.7	40.7	37.6
Argentina	29.3	34.2	34.1	2.0	1.5	0.9	44.8	36.1	31.6
Africa:									
Kenya	4.4	5.1	6.2	4.5	5.0	4.4	6.0	7.8	7.5
Zimbabwe	6.8	7.8	9.2	5.1	5.5	4.9	30.2	31.7	24.9
Nigeria	8.7	10.2	11.2	5.3	3.3	3.6	19.7	12.6	13.0
Egypt	12.5	14.5	18.1	1.9	4.7	3.6	13.8	28.8	31.4

Source: International Labour Office (ILO), *Economically Active Population Estimates: 1950–1980*.

I: 1950–60; II: 1960–70; III: 1970–80.

Note: GL is calculated directly from the original estimates. GL_1 is calculated from the absolute number estimated by averaging each the decade. The share is the average of the first and last years of a decade: for exa mple, I is the average of 1950 and 1960. All the figures are rounded off to the nearest one-tenth of a percent.

increase through the preceding two decades. Thus it distinctly endorses the applicability of our formula.

The possibility of arriving at the TP often has been talked about in Malaysia, Brazil, and Mexico. Actually, from 1970 to 1980, the GL_1 of these countries was 6.8%, 5.5%, and 6.2% and, with the exception of Brazil, tends to increase through the three decades. For these countries, it may be too early to talk about the possibility of reaching their TPs.

Beyond specific discussion of the possibility of reaching the TP, the test of our formula presents useful information on the general pattern of changes in the sectoral labor reallocation process. This information is important for countries in earlier phases of industrialization. The criterion for a normal course of industrialization is a sustained trend of increase in the ratio—the crucial term of our formula—as is seen for Malaysia, Indonesia, Egypt, and Korea. Pakistan, Argentina, and Nigeria (almost unchanged between 1960 and 1980) have a reversed course of industrialization. All other countries show intermediate industrialization, the ratio being decreased either between 1950 and 1970 or between 1960 and 1980. Other factors may be responsible for producing such distortions for these countries, but further examination is beyond our scope here.

Japan belongs to the group of countries with distorted performance. Its up-and-down swings of investment, combined with the effects of an unstable international environment during the interwar and World War II years, are responsible for this distortion. The same simple formula can be applied for the intervals corresponding approximately to the phases previously demarcated (see Table 1.4).

The level of the ratio, weighted GL_1/GL, is relatively high even from the early phase. This high level is due to an extremely low rate of the labor force increase (GL), particularly for early subphases. No population explosion took place in Japan. We can say that the rate of increase in the labor employed in the industrial sector is rather moderate in light of its magnitude shown for contemporary developing

Table 1.4
Sectoral Labor Reallocation with Industrialization in Japan, 1890–1970

Period		Percentage			Weighted GL_1/GL
		GL	GL_1	L_1/L	
A	1890–1900	0.5	2.0	15.5	45.3
B	1900–20	0.6	2.4	18.3	71.4
C	1920–40	1.1	2.0	25.9	40.4
D	1950–60	2.1	4.9	28.1	65.3
E	1960–70	1.7	3.4	33.1	62.3

Source: Kazushi Ohkawa and Miyohei Shinohara, eds., Patterns of Japanese Economic Development (PJE) (New Haven: Yale University Press, 1979), Table A.53, pp. 392–93, and Table 14–3, p. 344. For A and B, GL_1 has been modified by us.

Note: The same as for Table 1.3. Because of the abnormality caused by World War II, the period 1940–50 has been eliminated.

countries in Table1.3. Therefore, Japan's case is atypical. Nevertheless, the performance of the ratio is not necessarily atypical. For period B, which includes the first investment spurt, its value is highest, and in the postwar period (D), its value sharply increased from its lowest value in period C. The latter includes the most depressive interval of the Japanese economy; actually, in this period the surplus labor was reproduced. Regarding the conventional two-sector approach (agriculture vs. non-agriculture), Japan's case will be discussed in section II of this lecture.

In the development planning of contemporary developing countries, the problem of labor employment is of utmost importance. This problem needs, however, a long-term perspective, as illustrated by the seventh Indian development plan. Beyond the narrow scope of discussing the TP, we intend to incorporate labor-employment performance in general into the phasing thesis.

Changes in Factor Proportions and Factor Prices

As previously pointed out, with regard to the difference of or change in the rate of the increase in labor demand by development of the industrial sector, two variables are responsible: the pace of capital accumulation and the combination of variables in technological change. Economists differ in their emphasis on these two variables' significance: one view stresses the former and another, the latter. Our view is that the two different dimensions should appropriately be taken up in treating these two variables. The previous emphasis on the role played by the investment spurt represents a dimension of the variation of aggregate demand and demand for industrial labor. Actually, without having a drastic demand surge a shift of phase was impossible. However, in a longer-term dimension of industrial development, the variable combination plays a sustained role in determining the absorbing power of labor. For example, labor-intensive development is more positive than capital-intensive development in advancing technology in the industrial sector. This dimension is often strongly asserted for East Asian countries. But mere emphasis on this aspect alone may be a biased view.

The remarkable differences in Table 1.3 for the rate of increase in the labor employed in the industrial sector among developing countries cannot be explained solely by the technological differences of the combination of variables. For example, India and Korea are often thought to represent examples of capital-intensive vs. labor-intensive industrialization. Actually, in Table 1.3 the widest difference of GL_1 was in the 1960s: 2.6% for India vs. 10.2% for Korea. One cannot attribute this difference solely to variable combination. A much more influential consideration surely stems from the wide difference of the labor demand increase relative to the speed of industrial growth. For example, referring back to Table 1.3, the rate of output growth in the industrial sector created a wide difference: 5.4% (period II) and 4.5% (period III) for India and 17.2% (period II) and 15.4% (period III) for Korea.

On the other hand, a simple indicator such as crude elasticity, $\eta = GL/GY$, has often been used not only in analytical research, but recently in actual compilation of development planning. The value of η is 0.50 for India and 0.48 for Korea on average in the 1960s and 1970s. The difference is amazingly minor, though India's value is greater than usually expected. In talking about capital-intensive technology, Latin America has often been cited. But the value of η in the 1970s is 0.59 (Brazil), 0.69 (Mexico), 0.50 (Argentina), and 0.53 (Colombia). Again the range of difference is not great, though these values appear somehow greater when compared with Asian values.

This observation, however, does not imply that differences in variable combination play no role or are insignificant in determining the labor-absorbing power of the industrial sector. Such a crude elasticity cannot be an appropriate indicator because it does include the negative effects of the speed of neutral technological progress and the crudeness of measurements. For example, the relatively small value of crude elasticity for Korea is negatively influenced, whereas its relatively large value for India is positively influenced. Latin America can be interpreted as the latter example.

Japan will be examined in detail in Lecture 5, but if η is measured similarly for the industrial sector, it is 0.26 to 0.33 for the primary phase, 0.30 for the prewar subphase, and 0.43 for the postwar subphase of the secondary phase. Its relatively small value in international comparison is due to a faster rate of technological progress. A distinct increase from 0.30 to 0.43 during the secondary phase is a development of more labor-intensive technology-industry, particularly in the machinery sector. The suggestion drawn from these observations is that the speed of technological advance is an indispensable variable in discussing the labor reallocation process.

The second topic is the relation of changes in industrial structure and the factor prices in the mechanism of shifting phases of development. According to the thesis of a simplified phasing model, the factor price changes (a relative change in wages to capital prices) must have taken place and have been maintained between the phase before the

TP and the phase after it. In the former, the land—the major source for agriculture—and unskilled labor are the major production variables, although certain amounts of capital and skilled labor are indispensable. In the latter, the requirement of capital and skilled labor becomes much more important. In short, it is often said that the economy makes a shift from a phase of labor-intensive to capital-intensive industries because of the "inducement effects" of factor prices on technology choice. We share this thesis in interpreting the broad line of phase shifting in recognition that the basic forces are sustained in operation through the market mechanism.

However, regarding Japan's historical experience as well as that of contemporary developing economies, what we call the "non-inducement effects" operated to a substantial extent. The government's intervention in the process of industrial transformation is not directly induced by changes in relative factor prices. This aspect will be discussed in detail in the subsequent lectures. What we are concerned with here is its orientation in the phasing approach. Technological-organizational requirements are arranged in advance for new industries to be developed fully in the coming phase; for example, iron-steel and shipbuilding industries in Japan were developed in the phase of primary export substitution, the coming phase being that of secondary import substitution. Regarding the appraisal of such a "non-inducement" performance, economists differ on the merits or demerits being asserted. Our view will be stated in Lecture 7. What is at least clear is that a simplified thesis of a phase shift depending fully on the inducement effects should be broadened by taking into account the interaction between public and private activities based on the market mechanism.

One additional but important aspect pertains to the variable combinations of industries. A simple correspondence is often made by a contrast: labor-intensive technology to the light manufacturing vs. capital-intensive technology to the heavy manufacturing. In our earlier discussion, another simple dichotomy of production of nondurables vs. production of durable goods was used. We will expand upon variable combinations of industries in the lectures that follow, especially in Lecture 3. What we want to emphasize is the machinery industry. This industry produces durables for both producers and consumers, but its capital intensity is distinctly lower than that of heavy industries such as iron-steel and chemicals. Regarding the factor price changes discussed earlier, the performance of this sector cannot be discussed in the same way as for heavy industry: capital and skilled labor should not be taken in a simple unitary combination. With respect to the machinery industry, what matters is the skilled labor and not the capital, because what distinguishes the machinery industry from the textile industry is its heavier dependence on a higher quality labor force.

Shifts of Development Phases

The repeated investment spurts pertain to demarcating phases, as discussed earlier, but this finding does not mean that a certain upgrading in the capital formation proportion (I/Y) causes a shift from one phase to another. W. W. Rostow's well-known notion of take-off[22] is an increase from 5% to 10%. Together with the thesis of a "big push," capital formation enhancement is thought to be a major determinant for demarcating stages of economic development. The concept of stages is less flexible than that of phases. With respect to development, we believe the basic element responsible for a phase shift is an upgrading of what we call the "social capability" of absorbing (borrowing and assimilating) advanced technological knowledge from economically advanced countries. As will be discussed in some detail in Lecture 6, an upgrading of capability means improving both human resources and institutional-organizational structures. To realize technological progress, additional capital is indispensable, but just providing additional capital cannot create the innovative process necessary for technological advance. In the initial phase of development in Japan, in particular, I/Y was low and slow to increase. In short, what distinguishes a higher phase of development from a lower phase is the difference in the level of social capability.

Taking a phase approach to trade, for example, the first shift in phases is from exporting indigenous agricultural products to primary export substitution; the second phase shift is to secondary import substitution; and the third phase shift is secondary export substitution. In Japan's case, all these shifts were possible because of a sustained process of upgrading the social capability to complete both export and import substitution. Social capability is a concept that cannot be directly quantified by statistical measurements. For this reason, economists usually pay more attention to such quantitative variables as capital formation. Improving social capability is usually a gradual, continuous process, seen over time. This characteristic stems from the nature of the process regarding education, training, and learning by doing. Therefore, conceptually, no clear-cut upswings demarcate changes in phases.

---

[22] W. W. Rostow, ed., *The Economics of Take-off into Sustained Growth* (London: Macmillan, 1963).

Another relevant point is "sustained growth," which also was first introduced by Rostow. According to his thesis, if an economy could succeed in its "take-off," it would realize a subsequent process of sustained growth. The implication is that the difficulty is encountered in the initial phase, and during subsequent phases no such difficulties arise. In our view, in contrast, difficulties arise throughout all the phases in any developing process. Japan's experience, we believe, stresses the importance of recognizing the existence of these difficulties, especially in the interaction between the government and private sector (see Lecture 7). The possibility of shifting from one phase to the next is not autonomous, and realization that a shift has occurred may result in difficult internal problems to be resolved, although an unfavorable international environment may often be responsible for aggravating national problems.

A typical example is Japan's prolonged phase of secondary import substitution. As described earlier, this phase continued for more than 40 years, from 1919 to 1960, though with the interruption of World War II. Even if allowance is made for the war, this phase still lasted a long time. The domestic development of heavy and engineering-based industries faced great difficulties, not only financial and technological, but also social. What we call the "differential structure" occurred during the long downswing that eventually led to the next phase of secondary export substitution. This situation is far from one of sustained growth. Today, other developing countries are facing difficulties making a shift from one phase to another. Some of them are still at the initial phase of agricultural product exports because of the difficulty in making a shift to the next phase of primary export substitution. Others face difficulties shifting to secondary export substitution and prolong the second phase shift to secondary import substitution.

The Modern-Traditional (MT) Thesis and Differential Structure
The final topic on phase shifts concerns the historical characteristics unique to Japan. Hitherto phases of development have been defined and marked by economic performance, using concepts that are internationally comparable, such as output, trade, input, and technology. Without a common set of variables, what has been deduced from observation of Japan's development may not be beneficial for understanding the performance of other developing countries. Thus efforts have been directed primarily to present a conceptual framework of a phase approach that fundamentally can be applied to other latecomers.

The development process of every country, however, has its own unique historical and sociocultural context apart from its political system. This unique context is usually stronger and more intensive for countries that have a long history. Japan, after a long seclusion from the rest of the world in the premodern epoch, started toward modern economic growth as a politically unified nation in 1868. Certainly Japan was a latecomer, though its initial economic growth began in the latter half of the nineteenth century. Historical description of Japan's uniqueness compared with other developing economies is not our aim. What we want to concentrate on in our phasing framework is one specific aspect: "dualistic development." The indigenous or traditional elements (T) inherited from the premodern era remained strong and were improved during the early process of development by introducing foreign or modern elements (M). Japan's early development is an MT structure, and other latecomers may have similar MT structures. The two elements, M and T, cover almost all economic performance: people's behavior, technology, production, and institutions.

If we take the MT structure as of the primary significance viewed from a historical, analytical standpoint, what will be its shape in phasing? An answer was given comprehensively by Ohkawa and Rosovsky.[23] What essentially matters pertains to the earlier periods of development referred to by us as transition (1868–85) and initial economic growth (1886–1905).

Japan's initial economic growth almost coincides with the initial phase previously referred to as the first subphase of the primary phase. What we define as transition marks the interval from the political inauguration of economic modernization as a nation to its genuine industrial start (see Lecture 7). The government was intensively involved in establishing basic arrangements, such as liberalizing society from feudal restraints, creating institutions such as banking and currency systems, and combating civil wars and inflation. The normal process of Japan's economic development eventually would start in 1885. Transitional intervals of a similar nature often are seen in contemporary developing countries during the early postwar years of development following their political independence.

The initial phase can now be characterized by the MT thesis, the essential point of which is that the growth of modern sectors depends heavily upon the development of the traditional sectors. Small-scale family farming under the traditional landlordism, small-scale manufacturing that relies on different artisans and craftspeople, and a sus-

[23] Ohkawa and Rosovsky, "A Century of Japanese Economic Growth."

tained traditional preference scale of consumption are examples of traditional elements. The content of the initial phase thus can enrich rather than contradict our previously developed phasing framework.

One more important point indicated by the MT thesis is interpretation of the shift from the initial phase to the next phase:

> The growth potential of the traditional economy was limited. When its growth rate begins to decline, the initial phase of modern economic growth comes to an end. By the time the initial phase comes to an end, the dependence of the modern on the traditional economy has greatly decreased—although it has not disappeared.[24]

This statement clearly explains the shift, emphasizing the performance of the traditional sector, but implies that the initial phase ended soon after the turn of the century. Some economists argue, however, that the growth rate of productivity in agriculture was sustained at a relatively high or even accelerated level until around the end of the phase of primary export substitution. Actually, the initial high productivity growth in agriculture began to decline around 1920, and we are now inclined to share this view. In this case, the MT thesis should cover the entire primary phase instead of being limited to the initial phase, that is, its first subphase, which will be investigated in the following.

What we have earlier called "differential structure" pertains more to the problems of labor employment, poverty, and income distribution. Between growth and equity, there are two major paths of development: one results in an inevitable existence of "trade-offs," while the other seeks possible achievement of both growth and equity. Both in theory and practice, a number of studies have made great efforts to solve this controversial problem. Yet no agreement has been reached.

In the phase approach, this important problem should be given an appropriate place in its general framework. However, at the present level of our knowledge, this is too heroic an attempt. But what can and should be done at present is to examine the historical experience of individual cases of developing economies.

In Japan's case, the problem of labor employment and income distribution in the phase approach, in our view, can be dealt with primarily with the MT thesis developed earlier rather than the direct application of conventional variables such as the rate of unemployment, personal or functional (size or share) distribution coefficients, or the like, for the economy as a whole. These conventional terms are

[24] Ohkawa and Rosovsky, "A Century of Japanese Economic Growth," p. 68.

useful, of course, but qualifications are needed for their use in analyzing the process of dualistic development. An aggregate measure would be obtained by a weighted average of the income distribution coefficient in the modern and the traditional sectors. The differential level of income should be taken into account in the weighted average. Until the economy arrives at the postwar phase, changes in this "intersectoral" income distribution were much more influential than that of the "intrasectoral" income distribution.[25] The notion of differential structure originates in this recognition and pertains primarily to a widening gap in product per worker between the modern and traditional sectors.[26] If we take a simple indicator of the ratio of output per worker in agriculture to that of industry, it shows a distinct decrease throughout the prewar phase of secondary import substitution.[27] This decrease roughly represents the over-time performance of the MT differential (for statistical details, see Lecture 6). Such a distinct differential structure did not take place in the primary phase (its ratio range was 33 to 44), so this is a characteristic of the phase of secondary import substitution.

Changes in both employment and income distribution are involved in the ratio indicator. In dualistic development, the surplus workers not employed in the modern sector are forced to stay in the traditional sector and push the ratio to a lower level. Since the ratio pertains to sectoral averages, the change in income distribution within each sector is not represented. But change in the comparative average occurs if intersectoral distribution does not change substantially. A comparison of current price with constant price series shows the effects of changes in sectoral terms of trade on sectoral income distribution, as singled out from the effects of comparative labor productivity changes. The data shown in footnote 27 indicate both the comparative average and intersectoral distribution increasingly turned unfavorable for agriculture toward the end of the 1930s, thus indicating the considerable effects of relative prices.

---

[25] This is endorsed by the view that "on the assumption . . . the effects of changes in income inequality within the urban and rural sectors cancelled out in the economy as a whole, we submit that changes in the rural-urban income differentials caused the changes in income distribution in prewar Japan." (See Akira Ono and Tsunehiko Watanabe, "Changes in Income Inequality in the Japanese Economy," in Hugh Patrick, ed.' *Japanese Industrialization and its Social Consequences* (Berkeley and Los Angeles: University of California Press, 1976), pp. 363–389.)

[26] Ohkawa and Rosovsky, "A Century of Japanese Economic Growth."

[27] In current prices (1934–36 constant prices in parentheses), the decrease is 32.8% (35.2) for 1917–22; 32.6% (32.1) for 1922–27; 24.0% (26.9) for 1927–32; and 14.8% (21.6) for 1932–37. The industries include manufacturing, mining, construction, public utilities, transportation, and communication.

As the modern sectors tend to increase their employment output weights, income distribution within these sectors becomes more important. The share of income for wage earners in the industrial sector has a general tendency to decrease during the phase under consideration. However, it increased in the postwar period after the economy passed its second turning point.[28] These findings suggest that the disappearance of surplus labor in the postwar phase in contrast to reproduced surplus labor in the prewar phase seems to be crucial to the performance of share distribution, although other organizational-institutional variables such as a trade union movement and a minimum wage system affect the equalized income distribution in the postwar industrial sector (in agriculture, for example, the effects of land reform were influential).

Taking these empirical findings together with the broad dimension of our phases, we can summarize the employment-income distribution as follows: (1) it had almost no distinct change toward unfavorable performance during primary phase; (2) it became unequal during the prewar phase after the first turning point; (3) following the second turning point in the postwar phase, it reversed the tendency toward equalization. One may be reminded of Kuznets's classic hypothetical proposition of "inverse U-shaped curve," and Japan's historical experience seems to endorse its validity. However, we should be cautious to confirm it because Kuznets's scope and method are not the same as ours.

A number of development economists seem to believe that Japan succeeded in growth acceleration at the sacrifice of improving its employment-income distribution. This is not a misunderstanding, but it tells only half the truth.

Comments: Typological Differences

The typological differences among countries are a problem of much wider coverage than our present scope. For the sake of illustration, let us define these differences narrowly to mean natural resource endowments for agriculture, posing a problem that directly concerns our present topic. In countries with rich natural resources, the phase of primary export substitution is skipped. No incentive emerges to substitute industrial goods exports for agricultural goods exports, since comparative advantage is sustained for agriculture because of richer

---

[28] Based on Ryoshin Minami and Akira Ono, "Factor Incomes and Shares," in Ohkawa and Shinohara, eds., *Patterns of Japanese Economic Development*, for the nonagricultural sector.

natural resource endowments. Stronger exchange rates continue to be maintained from the viewpoint of industry. If the surplus that stems from agricultural exports is used for the protection of industry, these countries can make a shift earlier to domestic production of durable goods for producers and consumers. In such a case, the concept of primary phase would be doubtful and of no substantial significance. The actual development path in a number of Latin American countries may be closer to the simplified pattern mentioned here, and a modified hypothesis for phasing would be necessary.

In reality, however, the relation between agriculture and industry cannot be discussed without paying attention to the different options of government policy. For the sake of simplicity, let us assume two categories for agricultural production: consumption-oriented domestic food and export-oriented cash crops. For countries of rich natural resource endowments, there are policy options for what combinations of the two categories can be used in promoting agricultural production. Policies biased to cash crops exist in a number of Latin American countries. A bias for domestic food is found, for example, in India where agricultural resources are relatively richer than those of East Asian countries. India's food self-sufficiency policy is and will continue to be firmly carried out to a long-term perspective plan; Latin American countries, in contrast, usually import food.

The implication of such a different option may be complex, but by analytical simplification, attention is drawn to what follows. If we interpret food self-sufficiency as a policy of import substitution in agriculture in the sense of a projected decrease of food imports for the future, an export-oriented cash crop policy may imply the principle of comparative advantage in promoting exports, without making an effort to advance an import substitution policy against the comparative advantage within agriculture. As noted earlier, Japan's rice self-sufficiency policy during the primary phase did not follow the rationale of comparative advantage from a long-term perspective. If a food self-sufficiency policy needs considerable protection (such as in postwar Japan), the nature of the policy is analogous to a protection policy for industry that does not have a comparative advantage at a particular given time.

We could say a government, following the rationale of comparative advantage, protects agriculture or industry because of a difference in the nation's typology. Such an argument is not acceptable, however, because of the essential nature of the innovative process of development. Comparative advantage should be of a dynamic nature. The technological-organizational progress can create changes in the individual sectors of the economy aimed at producing more competitive industries. In this sense, skipping development of light industry may not necessarily be a distorted growth path.[29] The objective is attaining a shift to the phase of direct (not secondary) export substitution of agricultural goods by durable industrial goods regardless of the advantage or disadvantage of rich natural resource endowments.

Taking comparative advantage into account is a very simple suggestion for modifying our framework of the phase-shift sequence. Japan's modified sequence was applied for primary import substitution. We are not inclined, however, to build a completely different framework of phasing for each nation. Economists point out that the process of labor reallocation by shifting it from agriculture to industry is retarded when the phase of primary export substitution is skipped. We share this view. Actually, the problem of surplus labor has not yet been resolved, for instance, in Brazil. Why then do some economists assume that the phase of secondary import substitution should entirely be dominated by capital-intensive industries? In light of Japan's experience, and in our view, the possibility of developing a relatively labor-intensive type of machinery industry should draw more attention.

II. The Primary Major Phase and Its Two Subphases

Having discussed the analytical framework in the preceding section, we now want to turn our attention to the historical sequence of the development process. First, let us summarize our previous proposals regarding the demarcation of the two major phases: primary and secondary. If we date the first investment spurt, 1919 is the year demarcating these two major phases. Substantially, this demarcation implies three aspects: (1) Historically, the relationship between the modern and traditional sectors had distinguished characteristics of the two sectors. (2) The performance of the real wages of unskilled labor created a basic change in the sectoral labor reallocation process. (3) Changes in the trade structure led to a distinction between "primary" and "secondary" imports and exports of the two major phases. In Japan's case, these three aspects have roughly the same dating; but the coincidence may not necessarily be expected for all developing economies because of dissimilar conditions. Let us keep these points in mind in the following discussion of the primary major phase.

The primary major phase seems to be consistent with what Kuznets,

---

[29] See, for example, Akio Hosono, *Latin America no Keizai* [Economies of Latin America] (Tokyo: University of Tokyo Press, 1983).

criticizing Rostow's concept of take-off and stages of economic development, specifies as the "early phase of modern growth." We believe the following citation is beneficial for a more precise and deeper understanding of our phasing framework:

> The firm point in this [phase] approach is the feasibility of dating the beginning of modern economic growth by some "hard" data, relating to one or several characteristics that are constituent elements in the very definition of modern economic growth. In doing this, all that we specify is the *early* phase of the segment of the long record of modern economic growth on which we wish to concentrate. The termination of the period is then to be decided on the basis of any substantive hypotheses concerning the distinctive characteristics of the early phases, although one would assume that since the span of modern economic growth in most countries is not much over a hundred years, there are narrow limits to the length of the early growth phase that an economist *of today* can set.[30]

As mentioned earlier, each major phase is eventually framed into two subphases, although the plausibility of phases and subphases has not yet been confirmed by actual historical experience. With respect to the primary major phase, the pattern of changes in the relationship between the modern and the traditional sectors is crucial to demarcate the two subphases. From the standpoint of changes in the trade structure, however, an unclear pattern of primary import substitution remains to be integrated into the framework of two subphases, although the phases of traditional products export and primary export substitution can be integrated into the framework.

To test our framework, we will try the following: (1) select a few representative sectors (the silk-reeling industry, cotton textile industry, and agriculture), (2) clarify changes in the relationship between modern and traditional activities in each sector, and (3) pay particular attention to technological changes in each sector.

The Silk-Reeling Industry

The silk-reeling industry is a typical case of an industry that developed with traditional production. Viewed from a phasing approach focused on changes in the trade structure, traditional export expansion is the

---

[30] Simon Kuznets, "Notes on the Take-off," in W. W. Rostow, ed., *The Economics of Take-off into Sustained Growth*, pp. 42–43.

initial subphase of the primary phase. Until around the turn of the century, traditional goods such as silk cocoons, tea, and other agricultural goods were exported. However, these were not the only major source for financing imports of producer goods and manufactured nondurable consumer goods. As a matter of fact, simultaneously, exports of textiles (first raw silk, then cotton yarns) also began to show initial profits. Primary import substitution proceeded slowly. For example, maximum cotton yarn imports (¥37 million, in 1934–36 prices) decreased to almost zero at the turn of the century, and from then onward, import substitution by cotton fabrics continued until World War I— that is, during the phase of primary export substitution. A clear pattern of phase shift from traditional exports to primary import substitution did not occur.

One of the reasons that the pattern is unclear is the strong role played by the traditional elements: substitution of imported manufactured goods by domestic manufactures was limited. Another reason is that silk reeling played a significant role in the initiation of manufacturing expansion. The silk-reeling industry is based on an expansion of sericulture by improving the methods of mulberry cultivation and cocoon raising. Traditional silk reeling (*zakuri*) was improved, and mechanized silk reeling was introduced. Together they expanded domestic production until around the turn of the century—though the export proportion of machine-reeled silk was greater than that of hand-reeled silk— when traditional silk reeling was increasingly replaced by its mechanized counterpart. The replacement (or substitution) was between the traditional and modern production, not between importation and domestic production.

The conditions responsible for the remarkable growth of the raw silk industry in Japan have been clarified by a number of economists, who are in almost perfect agreement on the following: (1) Private-sector activities were the driving force; the government played the leading role in establishing a model factory and setting up experiment and inspecting systems. (2) Technological advances contributed a great deal toward augmenting Japan's international competitive power, even though the original selection of this industry was based on comparative advantage. (3) This industry is a typical case of a late-developing country's successful technological progress attained by borrowing technological knowledge from advanced countries, modifying and adapting it to local conditions under a domestic price relationship (expensive capital vs. cheap labor). (4) Improvements in sericulture, which included adding newly introduced summer-fall cocoons to the original spring cocoon reeling,[31] better quality, standardized sizes, and even distribution of the supply of the cocoons, were great contributions to improving the production efficiency of silk reeling.

Depending heavily upon Ono's comprehensive analysis,[32] we will focus on technological advance in our brief discussion of the performance of this industry. French technology (steel reeling machinery) was introduced to the Tomioka model silk-reeling factory built by the Japanese government. This technology contributed to the initial incentive to develop the silk-reeling industry, yet failed to be assimilated widely in Japan. Steel reeling machines were too expensive, so private enterprises tried replacing steel parts with wooden counterparts. Despite a certain deterioration in precision and quality, the new technology had the advantages of much lower prices of capital goods and faster retooling of the reeling machines, and similar power equipment was being adopted throughout the industry.

Such production modification, however, cannot be pursued for all industries. As will be discussed in Lecture 2, the story is different for steel mills. No such modification was possible regarding the major process of steel production. The difference stems essentially from the nature of the technology. It is often asserted that the gap in the technological level between improved traditional and modern silk reeling was rather narrow. We share this view and believe silk reeling also implies a narrow gap in the level of human technical capabilities.

The period from 1900 to 1935 covers almost the entire time span for mechanized silk reeling, into the next phase of secondary import substitution (see Table 1.5). Until 1920–25, the rate of output growth was sustained at a high pace. Its slowdown from 1925 to 1935 was affected by a drastic drop in export demand, resulting in particular from the depression in the United States. Because of the industry's heavy dependence on cocoons (the share ranges from 66% to 84%), productivity was greatly affected by the quality of cocoons, which is not revealed by annual growth rate percentages that show only dominant input share.[33] Total productivity growth, GT, is estimated as a residual by a simple conversion formula (see remarks appended to Table 1.5).

[31] Le Thanh Nghiep and Yujiro Hayami, "Mobilizing Slack Resources for Economic Development: The Summer-Fall Rearing Technology of Sericulture in Japan," in *Explorations in Economic History* 16 (1979): 163–71.

[32] Akira Ono, *Seishi-gyo no Seicho Bunseki* [Growth Analysis of the Raw Silk Industry], Part II, "Sen'i kogyo" [Textiles], *LTES*, 11 (1979), pp. 135–220.

[33] The output of raw silk per cocoon (kg) increased from 0.085 in 1900 to 0.140 in 1938. The average annual rate of increase is 1.4%, which may be an overestimation of the efficiency unit. About 1%, at least, is a realistic evaluation.

Table 1.5
Performance of the Mechanized Silk-Reeling Industry, 1900–35

Period	GQ	GM	GK	GL	GT	γGM	αGK	βGL	Total
				Average Annual Rate of Change (%)					
1900–05	7.9	5.4	5.4	3.8	2.6	3.6	1.4	0.3	5.3
1905–10	10.8	10.6	7.8	6.0	1.2	7.6	1.5	0.5	9.6
1910–15	8.9	9.3	5.8	4.2	0.3	7.7	0.5	0.4	8.6
1915–20	8.7	7.9	6.0	4.1	1.3	6.5	0.4	0.4	7.3
1920–25	7.4	6.3	2.2	1.3	1.9	5.2	0.2	0.1	5.5
1925–30	3.9	2.5	4.4	1.6	0.7	2.8	0.2	0.2	3.2
1930–35	3.1	1.6	1.1	−2.5	2.0	1.3	0.1	−0.3	1.1

Source: LTES, vol. 11 (1979), Table 3–11, p. 187, and related tables in Part III.

Note: Q=output amount of production; M=cocoon input; K=capital stock; L=labor; G=rate of growth.
Elasticity of input to output is γ for M, α for K, and β for L. Average input shares for each period are used.

Remarks: The formula is GT=GQ−(γGM+αGK+βGL). All the series are for five-year averages. The average annual rate of change is calculated for each five-year period by linking the beginning and the end years. Some statistical adjustments are made to round off to the nearest one-tenth.

Without exception, all the values of GT are positive and within a broad range of 1.0% to 2.6%. Except for the period 1925–35, the industry is characterized through all the periods by a small value of GK to GL and an increasing rate of capital intensity, ranging from 1.0% to 2.8%, dependent upon intensive use of young female workers. The figures show labor-intensive technological progress, indicated by the crude indicator of GT performance. According to Ono's estimates,[34] the capital-output ratio (K/Y) appears to decline from 1910. We share his view that the decline is due to savings in factory construction, since K/Y for producer-durable equipment is almost unchanged.

The Cotton Textile Industry
The development of the cotton-spinning industry was both similar and dissimilar to that of the silk-reeling industry. It was similar in being based on traditional indigenous technology that used a cotton raw material produced by domestic farming. The government also played an initial role in the introduction to Japan of foreign cotton-spinning technology and organization. The process also had an in-

[34] Ono, Seishi-gyo no Seicho Bunseki.

terval of local competitive coexistence with traditional production until the new technology eventually established its position by dominating the market and increasing the industry's international competitiveness. However, the two industries differ in two respects. First, the gap in the technological level between the traditional and modern production methods was wider for the cotton-spinning industry. Cotton spinning depends much more on a mechanized process and hence more capital investment. Although both industries used young female workers from rural areas, the raw silk industry remained labor-intensive even after being mechanized; hence a large scale of organization (factories and enterprises) was influential in determining the silk-reeling industry's production efficiency. Second, unlike the coordinated development of silk reeling and cocoon production by domestic sericulture, cotton for the modernized cotton-spinning industry shifted completely from local supplies to imported cotton of a quality more suited for mechanized spinning. According to technical experts, Japan's soil and climate were not suitable for remarkable improvements in cotton cultivation. Economists argue that for labor and land use, intensive cotton cultivation was far inferior to sericulture and could not compete with cheap foreign cotton. We share their viewpoint.

Focusing our attention on the phase demarcation for the period from about 1885 to 1919—that is, from the genuine start of modern economic growth to the end of the primary phase—we will describe the characteristics of the development of the cotton-spinning industry. In so doing, we depend heavily on Kiyokawa's analysis and observations.[35]

During the transition interval defined earlier (including construction of the pioneer factory by Kagoshima *han* [feudal domain] in 1867), some twenty cotton-spinning factories were built. Most of them, however, were very small-scale from the conventional point of efficiency and failed to develop: a process of "trial and error" during the transition interval will be discussed in Lecture 7. The initial lead taken by the government, especially its policy of introducing modern technology, was commendable and led to larger-scale factories in subsequent years. Such development was enhanced by a vigorous response from the private sector for assimilating foreign technology by producing Japa-

---

[35] Yukihiko Kiyokawa, "Gijutsu Kakusa to Donyu Gijutsu no Teichaku Katei: Sen'i kogyo no keiken o chushin ni" [Technology Gap and Assimilation of Borrowed Technology: Focusing on the experience of textile industries], Chapter 11 in Kazushi Ohkawa and R. Minami, eds., *Kindai Nihon no Keizai Hatten* [Economic Development of Modern Japan] (Tokyo: Toyo Keizai Shimposha, 1975).

nese versions of foreign industrial machinery adapting modern cotton mixing techniques.

Kiyokawa demarcates the period from around 1887 to 1900 as the time of assimilating the newly introduced modern technology. The number of modern factories increased from 21 in 1887 to 79 in 1900. In 1886, the total capital turnover of yarn (valued in 1934–36 prices) was 11.9 million yen; by 1897, it had increased more than fourteen times, to 176.0 million. The import share of total demand was about 62% in 1886. As mentioned earlier, import substitution was completed in 1902. During this interval, simultaneously, yarn exports began and speedily expanded. In 1897, exports to both Korea and northern China (¥41.2 million) surpassed imports (¥12.6 million). The turn of the century is a landmark point of the cotton textile industry.[36]

Indigenous production was enhanced by so-called treadle spinning, an improved version of traditional methods; this technology spread nationwide because of its small capital investment, convenient availability of power from water wheels, and comparative advantage of using domestically produced cotton. Because of these features, traditional production could develop as off-season work for farm households and compete with the modern technology. Eventually, however, traditional production gave way to the superiority of modern production's quality, uniform grading, strength, and prices. Around the mid-1890s, modern factories became predominant. The dominance of the mechanized production for silk reeling was realized later around the turn of the century.

Two points deserve attention. First, the cotton-spinning industry, unlike the raw silk industry, is a typical case of a clear-cut shift from import substitution to primary export substitution. These two industries, considered together, obscure the phase pattern. Second, however, the phase pattern can be understood consistently when phasing is focused on changes in industrial structure at the end of the initial phase (the first subphase of the primary phase) around the turn of the century. In the MT (modern-traditional) thesis discussed earlier, by that time traditional production was surpassed by modern manufacturing, transferred, and assimilated to Japan's conditions by 1900.

Subsequent development of the cotton-spinning industry and rapid expansion of cotton textile production followed. According to Kiyokawa, 1885 to 1896 was a period for introducing machine loom technology: production of cotton clothing by cotton-spinning enterprises

[36] The figures quoted are from Yamazawa, *Nihon no Keizai Hatten*, appendix tables.

began around 1896.[37] This interval for cotton spinning involved the competitive development of both traditional and newly mechanized technologies. For many small producers of cotton clothing, traditional hand looms, with simple parts of foreign origin, were more attractive than mechanized looms because high capital investment was required for mechanization. Some improved hand-loom parts could be made inexpensively by carpenters, and improved traditional production expanded. Later, more improvements resulted in treadle looms which were widely used in the changeover from the traditional to modern organization of trade and commerce.

After 1900, competitive development continued with the increasing preponderance of modern mechanized looms. By around 1924, the number of power looms had surpassed that of hand looms. Such a prolonged coexistence of mechanized and hand looms resulted from two mutually related facts: the sustained high price of imported machinery and the prevalence of simple, locally improved hand looms. The improved hand looms replaced steel with wood for major parts to make them much cheaper. Despite some sacrifice of precision and durability as compared with the imported steel parts, hand looms were more suited for local production and intensive use of cheap workers. Kiyokawa demarcates 1897 to 1924 as the period of assimilation of power loom technology, during which it also became more efficient.

We believe the cotton textile industry presents a notable example of what we call primary export substitution. Cotton textile exports expanded rapidly at the average annual rate of 38.4%, based on an expansion of production at an average annual rate of 8.0%. Almost simultaneously, import substitution continued—particularly between 1900 (the year of most imports: ¥47.6 million, 57% of domestic production) and 1910, when for the first time exports surpassed imports. Import substitution was completed by 1919.[38]

As seen from the MT thesis, the technological changes in the cotton textile industry appear different from those in silk reeling and cotton spinning. Even after the end of the initial phase, traditional hand loom production continued to play a significant role in development of cotton textile manufacturing. Actually this production is a sort of hybrid category, combining both traditional and modern elements in adapting

[37] Kiyokawa, "Gijutsu Kakusa to Donyu Gijutsu no Teichaku Katei."
[38] All the figures are calculated from Yamazawa, *Nihon no Keizai Hatten*. The tentative treatment of primary import substitution mentioned at the outset of this section now has a substantial explanation. Before 1900, it pertained to yarn and fabrics; thereafter, mostly to fabrics.

to the introduction of foreign technology, that can be integrated into our phasing framework.

The subsequent performance of the cotton-spinning industry—another feature of the subphase of primary export substitution—continued to expand exports at a fairly rapid pace until 1915 (its average annual rate of increase was 7.2%), but then turned the corner and stagnated, although expansion of cotton cloth exports was sustained through the next phase of secondary import substitution (see Lecture 2). The differences in characteristics of this industry between primary export substitution and secondary import substitution deserve mention. In the former phase, remarkable expansion of domestic production was possible through technological advances, assimilating borrowed foreign technology and modifying the production factor combination to fit local factor prices. Major efforts were made to cut capital costs by fuller use of cheap labor and to upgrade product quality. What Kiyokawa calls "the time of establishing local technology" seems to broadly coincide with the end of primary export substitution.

The nature of technological progress during the subsequent years clearly changed. The crucial reason for this change was the substitution of imported machinery by Japanese counterparts in domestic production. Around 1931 the technological base of the cotton-spinning industry was firmly established. Since then this industry has taken new steps toward further modernization by enlarging factory scale, increasing capital investments and rationalization of plants, and boosting production efficiency by intensive use of high-powered electric motors. During the World War I boom, big companies combined weaving and cotton spinning and began to shift from broadcloth looms to automatic power looms. In 1922 the Toyota machine loom was invented and was quickly followed by other prototypes. Further progress was made, and in 1925 the Toyota automatic power loom was completed. Its quality was above the international technological standard. This power loom was quickly and widely used in the weaving factories managed by cotton-spinning companies.

The development of the machinery industry is a major topic of Lecture 2, but a brief explanation of its relationship to the textile industry is necessary. During the phase of primary export substitution, imports of production equipment in general (mostly machinery) were high, though they tended to decrease (the percentage ratio to domestic production is estimated at 46.5 from 1900 to 1904, 40.1 from 1905 to 1919, and 25.4 from 1910 to 1914). Roughly, the decrease is similar to that of contemporary developing economies in Asia at the primary phase; in India, however, the ratio is atypically low owing to the early domestic production of producer durable equipment. During World War I, the ratio abruptly dropped (7.3% from 1915 to 1919) because of the increase in domestic production of this equipment due to import restraints. Expanded production, however, contributed to accelerating import substitution in the subsequent years. The mechanization of the cotton-spinning and cotton-weaving industry occurred congruently with the rise in import substitution of producer durables.

Domestic production of high-quality textile machinery in the early twentieth century deserves particular attention. Exports of textile machinery to China began in 1926. As indicated by a renewed high import-production ratio of 27.4% in 1925 to 1929, nationalization of machinery production was a struggle despite the demand supported by defense expenditures. Japan was still far below the international level in many fields of machinery production. Given this general condition, we contend that growth in textile machinery production was achieved through the long experience of learning by doing to develop this particular industry.

The changes in the textile machinery industry during the phase of secondary import substitution can be quantitatively measured when compared with those of primary export substitution (see Table 1.6).[39] The change over time in the capital-labor ratio (working hours adjusted) has two distinct intervals: between 1896–1905 and 1911–20 it was almost unchanged, tending to increase slowly, whereas between 1916–25 and 1926–35 it increased dramatically. The capital-output ratio was almost unchanged in the former interval, although it increased slightly during the latter interval. The change implies an increase in labor productivity almost corresponding to that of capital intensity. These representative indicators have been discussed earlier regarding the structural changes of the industry. The landmark point of the two subphases surely is between 1911 and 1925. The performance of real wage rates corresponds exactly to this phase. During primary export substitution the level of real wage rates was almost unchanged, whereas it began to increase sharply during secondary import substitution. After a nationalized technology was established, substitution of labor by capital emerged and began to expand.[40]

[39] Shozaburo Fujino and Shiro Fujino, "Menshi Boseki-gyo no Seicho Bunseki" [Growth Analysis of the Cotton-Spinning Industry], Part I, *LTES*, 11 (1979), Table 4–2, p. 31, and related appendix tables.

[40] For an in-depth analysis of this important aspect, comparing Japan's experience with India's, see Gustav Ranis and Gary Saxonhouse, "Determinants of Technology Choice: The Indian and Japanese Cotton Industries," in Ohkawa and Ranis, *Japan and the Developing Countries*, pp. 135–76.

Table 1.6
Performance of the Cotton Textile Industry, 1896–1937 (%)

Period	Ratios[a] K/L+ (yen/hr.)	K/Y	Real Wage Rate (yen/ hr.)	Innovation[b] GY	GK	GL	Weighted GK+GL	GT
1896–1905	0.24	3.6	0.038	9.2	7.3	8.4	7.9	1.3
1901–10	0.26	3.4	0.041	6.7	8.0	6.3	6.7	0.0
1906–15	0.29	3.5	0.043	9.4	9.5	5.6	7.9	1.5
1911–20	0.30	3.3	0.043	6.6	5.5	5.9	4.1	2.5
1916–25	0.36	3.5	0.067	6.8	7.4	6.0	6.9	−0.1
1921–30	0.49	4.0	0.118	4.3	6.6	0.2	3.4	0.7
1926–35	0.76	4.0	0.142	3.7	5.5	−2.0	2.4	1.4
1931–37	0.72	4.4	0.128	8.0*	8.3	−3.0	4.1	3.9

Source: *LTES* 11 (1979), Table 4–2, p. 31, and Table 48 in Part III, p. 287.
Notes: K=capital stock; L=labor input unadjusted by working hours; G=percentage for annual growth rate; GT=total productivity [GY− weighted GK+GL]. Y=amount of added values (1934–36 prices) in a three-year average (*: 1931–36).

[a]K is net capital stock in 1934–36 prices; L+ is labor input adjusted by working hours; real wage rates are deflated by prices of cotton textiles output.

[b]For the weighted sum of GK and GL, adjusted income shares were used under an assumption of $\alpha+\beta=1$ (α=capital; β=labor).

Remarks: The original estimate of β shown in Table 4–2 is 0.3287, an average for 1896 to 1937. According to our measurement, the output elasticity of labor is approximately 0.3943 for 1896 to 1936; its ratio to 0.3287 is around 1.20. As a rough approximation of the cotton textile industry's performance, this ratio is used for all periods of long-term development in a competitive market.

The figures in Table 1.6 are roughly estimated to elucidate the innovative process; the estimates depend on untested assumptions and yet appear realistic and useful for our analysis. The rate of increase in the total productivity (GT) measured, as "residuals," represents acceptable overtime performance. Although its fluctuation is not small from 1896 to 1920, the model magnitude of GT was 1.0–1.5%, suggesting a fairly high rate of technological advance. After passing through fourteen recessive years (1916 to 1930), it showed an increase from 1926–35 to 1931–37. These changes occurred in conjunction with capital intensification, labor cost-saving measures, and a larger production scale aiming at an oligopolistic industrial organization.

Agriculture

The performance of agriculture in the primary phase is particularly important for three reasons. First, agriculture is representative of the traditional sectors, the development of which constituted the basis of the primary phase. Second, agriculture is dissimilar to other traditional sectors because of its sustained or even accelerated growth after the shift to the second subphase. Third, agriculture decreased its growth for the years following the secondary phase (around 1919) to form one of the major elements for demarcating the two major phases.

As noted earlier, Japan's industrialization is characterized by limited land for agriculture, roughly indicated by the small land-man ratio of one hectare per farm household. Despite this limitation, the government adopted a food self-sufficient policy and vigorously encouraged domestic foodstuff production, particularly of rice, after the turn of the century, when rice imports appeared to increase. Landlords and farmers, who were essentially within the frame of a traditional agrarian organization and farming system, responded positively to the government's policy. In other words, the growth potential of traditional agriculture was enhanced by the activities of the public and private sectors despite the view that this sector did not have a comparative advantage from a long-run perspective.

Changes in biochemical technology were "appropriate" for enhancing the growth of traditional agriculture, and these technological changes characterize the farming improvements. For traditional activities in manufacturing and other nonagricultural sectors, technological change was directed more to mechanical improvements, as illustrated by the raw-silk and cotton textile industries. Biochemical technology improvements were made in cocoon production in sericulture, while the domestic cotton supply was eventually replaced by imported cotton.

We believe that these changes were responsible for the sustained development of agriculture, even after the end of the initial phase, and its dissimilarity to nonagricultural traditional activities, which continued to develop during the second subphase but at a pace behind that of the modern sectors.[41]

---

[41] We should be careful not to underestimate the development of these traditional activities. For example, with regard to manufacturing, the output share of nonfac-

Table 1.7
Performance of Agriculture, 1887–1976   (%)

Period	Inputs				GT Weighted Input Total	GY − GB
	GY	GK	GL	GB		
1887–1904	1.42	1.06	0.11	0.49	0.47	0.95	0.93
1904–19	1.93	1.33	−0.72	0.78	0.57	1.36	1.15
1919–38	0.82	0.81	−0.27	0.15	0.15	0.67	0.71
1954–65	2.60	4.61	−2.57	0.24	−0.37	2.97	2.36
1965–76	1.00	7.24	−4.14	−0.74	−0.70	1.80	1.74

Sources: Kazushi Ohkawa and Nobukiyo Takamatsu, "Capital Formation, Productivity and Employment: Japan's Historical Experience and Its Possible Relevance to LDCs," *IDCJ Working Paper Series No. 26* (March 1983), Table 2, p. 18, and Appendix Table 1, p. 36. The original data are from Saburo Yamada and Yujiro Hayami, in Ohkawa and Shinohara, eds., *Patterns of Japanese Economic Development*, and Saburo Yamada, "The Secular Trends in Input-Output Relations of Agricultural Production in Japan, 1878–1978," in Chi-ming Hok and Tzong-shian Yu, eds., *Agricultural Development in China, Japan and Korea* (Seattle and London: University of Washington Press, 1983).

Notes: Table 1.7 does not factor in current input, and the periods correspond to those of the silk-reeling industry (Table 1.5) and cotton textile industry (Table 1.6). The subphases of the secondary phase, however, are included.

1. Data are given in five-year (or three-year when data are limited) averages, and the average annual rate of change is calculated for the periods by a simple bridge method.

2. Annual growth rate GY, the added value of gross capital depreciation, corresponds to K, gross capital stock, and includes perennial crops, livestock, and buildings, but excludes "residentials." The labor force L is not adjusted by working hours. Land area is represented by B. The growth rate of total productivity, GT, is calculated as the residual, GT = GY − (αGK + βGL + γGB), and its output elasticity. Estimates of these output elasticities are made from various sources depending upon the basic data for 1904, 1930, 1938, and 1953–66; for example, the percentage values of α, β, and γ are 11.5, 33.3, 55.5 (1904); 13.8, 17.6, 68.6 (1930); and 15.0, 50.5, 34.4 (1965).

---

tory production is estimated to be 68.5% in 1890, 53.4% in 1900, 47.3% in 1914, and 39.4% in 1919; see Ohkawa and Ranis, eds., *Japan and the Developing Countries*, Table 4.4, p. 81.

Let us first confirm the growth of agriculture and try to explain the important reasons involved by comparing agriculture with the two other sectors at some sacrifice of ignoring agriculture's production characteristics (see Table 1.7). Measurement of growth in agriculture is crude due to the difficulty of quantifying the innovative process of agricultural development. Technological progress was not neutral during the phases demarcated, and input variations should be presented more precisely. Nevertheless, for a broad picture of the long-term performance of this sector, several notable points can be made.

First, regarding the primary phase, the rate of output growth (GY) increases at a fairly rapid pace, accelerating from 1.4% in the initial subphase to 1.9% in the second subphase. The reasons for this growth stem mostly from residual augmentation, since the rate of input growth was moderate. To a certain extent arable land could be expanded, but as will be discussed later, the major reason for growth was the improvement and diffusion of traditional biochemical technology. This variable is roughly but eloquently suggested by an almost parallel augmentation of land productivity growth (GY − GB) with the total factor productivity growth (GT).

The implication of the concurrent growth of agriculture with the raw silk and cotton textile industries reveals that the innovative process of agricultural and industrial development proceeded at almost the same pace, contrary to the common belief that the traditional sector lags behind the modern sector in development. Such an expectation, however, stems from a misunderstanding of output growth rate. It is true that the rate of output growth is much greater for raw silk and cotton textile industries than for agriculture. But this difference results from a much faster rate of increase for conventional inputs in industry than in agriculture. Thus the rate of residual growth is similar.

Regarding the rate of total productivity growth, for mechanized silk reeling, GT ranges from 0.3 to 1.3% for the second subphase (excepting the extraordinary high rate of 2.6 for the beginning years). GT ranges from 0 to 2.5% for cotton textiles during the same subphase. Average total factor productivity growth was 1.4% (including a beginning high) for silk reeling and 1.3% for cotton textiles. The traditional agriculture GT is 1.2% for the same subphase. Because of differences in measuring procedures and the nature of data, comparisons cannot be precise; nevertheless, these figures support what we have stated with respect to the concurrent growth: the innovative process in the two sectors developed in balance.

The technologies that characterized the growth of agriculture are often called "veteran farmers' techniques." Traditional technology represented by veteran farmers provided the source for much technological progress when borrowed technology failed to take root in Japanese soil and research in the newly established agriculture experiment stations was still in its infancy. These farmers developed improved rice varieties by crossbreeding different strains and disseminated them nationwide: the major route for introducing these hybrids was from the western advanced regions to the eastern backward regions. From 1890 to 1920, the rice yield increased nationwide. This trend coincides with the increase in the area planted and a regional pattern of diffusion for these improved varieties. Toward the end of the second subphase, the new varieties developed by the agricultural experiment stations began to partially replace the improved traditional varieties.[42]

These improved rice varieties absorbed more fertilizer, as is indicated by the often-used term "seed-fertilizer innovation" in contemporary discussions on the Green Revolution. This basic improvement helped realize higher yields, and the sustained high rate of fertilizer absorption and other biochemical products such as pesticides characterized Japanese small-scale farming in the subsequent years. This pattern of innovation is common to farming in a number of contemporary developing economies in Asia. During the second subphase, 1900 to 1920, the initial start of augmenting fertilizer distinguished the second from the first subphase. (Detailed statistics are given in LTES.[43])

The average annual percentage rate of increase in fertilizer input and, in parentheses, total current input in agriculture shows a remarkable increase from 1.6 (1.8) between 1886 and 1900 to 7.7 (4.7) between 1900 and 1920. These figures are non-farm inputs and imply that agriculture, though still basically traditional, came to have more intersectoral relationships. Note that among those of other inputs listed in Table 1.7, the increase in non-farm current inputs is outstanding.

Some economists characterize, and overevaluate, Japanese agriculture because of its efficient, widespread irrigation-drainage system inherited from the Tokugawa period. Actually, this system was well developed in the southwestern districts where the improved varieties were introduced, but it was not a nationwide system. As innovations in seed-fertilizers continued, the insufficiency of irrigation and drainage became a major restraint to agricultural efficiency because of the com-

---

[42] The summary presented is based on the estimated data in Yujiro Hayami and Saburo Yamada, "Technological Progress in Agriculture," in Lawrence Klein and Kazushi Ohkawa, eds., *Economic Growth: The Japanese Experience Since the Meiji Era* (Homewood, Illinois: Richard D. Irwin, 1968).

[43] Mataji Umemura et al., "Norin-gyo" [Agriculture and Forestry], *LTES* 9 (1966).

plementarity between seed-fertilizers and water supply. Nevertheless, the government's support of a policy of rice self-sufficiency remained firm:

As early as 1899, public concern about national security, arising from Japan's position as a net importer of rice after the Sino-Japanese War (1894–95), resulted in the enactment of the Arable Land Replotment Law (revised in 1905 and 1909). The law required compulsory participation by farmers and landlords in a land-improvement project if two-thirds of the landlords, together owning two-thirds of the land involved, agreed. This was an institutional innovation, similar to the Enclosure Acts in England.[44]

The ratio of improved land area to the total cultivated area actually did increase during the latter part of the second subphase and continued at an accelerated rate during the next phase. This increase contributed to forming the output growth pattern shown in Table 1.7, although gross capital stock (K) does not adequately represent infrastructure capital formation due to the unavailability of reliable data.

Agricultural development during the primary phase depended heavily on innovation introduced in the premodern Tokugawa period. Combined with modern elements, development continued through the second subphase, but its growth potential was almost exhausted toward the end of the subphase. The rate of output growth decreased distinctly and the innovative process was greatly weakened (GY was 0.8% and GT was 0.7% for 1919 to 1938: see Table 1.7). The major reasons for these changes remain a matter of controversy among experts, but we believe that the following technological and institutional transitions influenced the slowdown.

First, cultivating landlords were replaced in the late nineteenth century by tenants and absentee landlord owners. The postwar land reform reestablished land ownership by cultivating farmers.

Second, an increase in demand for rice and the resulting inflationary rice prices led to the rice riots of 1918. The government's response was to expand rice cultivation in the colonies of Korea and Taiwan, which extended the rice self-sufficiency policy in the yen-circulating sphere and resulted in an increase of imported rice. The Great Depression had a strong discouraging effect on farmers' production incentives.

---

[44] Masao Kikuchi and Yujiro Hayami, "Agricultural Growth Against a Land Resource Constraint: Japan, Taiwan, Korea and the Philippines," in Ohkawa and Ranis, eds., *Japan and the Developing Countries*, pp. 67–90.

In the postwar period, the policy of rice self-sufficiency revived within Japan and kept the rice support price at a level increasingly higher than the international level.

Third, progress in advancing biochemical technology was enhanced by the research in the agricultural experiment stations, and a number of new high-yielding rice varieties were produced: some of these hybrids were even developed for the northern region with its less favorable climate for rice cultivation. Regarding non-farm inputs, the development of the chemical industry greatly contributed to increasing these inputs—particularly chemical fertilizers such as ammonium sulfate. In the postwar years, further faster progress was made along this line (the wide spread of vinyl products is one example). Concerning the performance of current inputs (average annual growth rate weighted by relative share), there is a big difference between 1920 to 1935 and 1955 to 1965. Current inputs are very small (0.35%) from 1920 to 1935 and very big (1.29%) from 1955 to 1965. Since the comparable values of GY are 0.9% (1920–35) and 3.6% (1955–65), a distinct difference of incentives for influencing farmers' behavior in augmenting current inputs emerges.

Fourth, regarding the changes in factor proportions, as biochemical technology replaces land input by non-farm current input, agriculture increasingly depends on industrial development. This chain of events is one of the characteristics of the secondary phase that distinguishes it from the primary phase. Another distinct characteristic of the secondary phase is labor force. In the prewar subphase, the decline in the agricultural labor force—a decline that started early in the second subphase of the primary phase—stabilized to a decrease of only 0.6% a year, whereas in the postwar subphase a drastic decrease in the farming labor sector emerged, a drop of about 2.6% from 1954 to 1965 and 4.1% from 1965 to 1976 (see Table 1.7). Such a structural change emerged in the long-term process of agricultural labor's sectoral reallocation relative to the mechanization of agriculture.

Mechanized farming in the postwar subphase began to increase despite the organizational constraints of small-scale units. Mechanization (M) could have complemented technological advances in biochemicals (BC); instead, however, substitution took place after the second turning point, when the unskilled labor wages became expensive and labor was replaced by capital through mechanization. Note, for example, the dramatic postwar rise in the rate of capital increase (GK) in Table 1.7—a phenomenon not witnessed in the prewar period. After the first turning point, surplus labor was reproduced in the Japanese economy. No attempt was made to convince farmers that technological progress in labor-saving machinery would improve agricultural labor productivity.

The prewar subphase of the secondary phase is characterized by the development of the machinery industry at the import substitution level. Technically the industrial capability of machinery production developed to a certain extent, and, with the right economic incentives, the domestic supply of uncomplicated machinery farming could have increased beyond the limited production of simple cultivators. However, the cost of machinery production at that time was too high to provide machinery substitutes for agricultural labor.

The decrease of farm labor is an important variable for advancing technological progress in agriculture; in contrast, technological progress increases labor employment in manufacturing. In a number of contemporary developing economies, the absolute number of the labor force engaged in agriculture is still increasing. When land resources are severely limited, they face more difficulties than Japan did during the prewar subphase of the secondary phase. A possible development policy would be to accelerate the pace of technological advances.

Concluding Remarks: Characteristics of the Primary Phase
The primary phase is distinguished by the important role of the traditional sector in initiating modern industrialization. Two subphases can be identified. During the first subphase, the traditional sector developed through use of the backlog accumulated before the 1860s. This development corresponds to the phase of traditional products export. In the second subphase light industrialization and improved traditional agriculture grew concurrently. This development is characteristic of the phase of primary export substitution.

A parallel high rate of innovation in industry and agriculture created the core of concurrent growth brought forth by labor-intensive technology in industry and land-saving technology in agriculture. Particular attention was drawn to the sectoral interrelation between the two sectors. The absolute number of the labor force engaged in agriculture tended to decrease around the end of the initial subphase. During the second subphase, the innovative process was given incentive by the labor force decrease, which was created by an increase in industrial labor.

There was a very moderate rate of increase in the capital accumulation in sectors of direct production, although considerable investments were allocated for infrastructure buildup (see Lecture 5). Rostow's thesis of "take-off" through investment acceleration or "big push" is not relevant to the reality of Japan's experience concerning production characteristics of the primary phase. Regarding demand, we can share the view that export expansion was indispensable for industrialization. In the shift from the first to the second subphase, the macro indicator of export ratio to GNP, X/Y, shows a distinct average increase from 8.5% in the first subphase to 14.3% in the second subphase. However, an increase in the domestic demand due to the development of the traditional sector should not be ignored.

Three points were made concerning the potentialities for making a shift to the next phase. First, regarding sectoral reallocation of labor force, toward the end of the primary phase a sign of demand over supply was already apparent. Second, technological advance, as illustrated by the cotton textile industry, needs human and organizational factors of production to complete the assimilation of the borrowed technology and ensure further development through capital intensification. The private sector had largely established the basis for its further development, though its industrial potential was still limited.

Debate over the relevance of Japan's primary phase continues among economists. Disagreements often stem from what aspect one stresses. For example, for some countries—especially those with a colonial background—the significance of the traditional sector may be irrelevant. For the countries whose natural resources are rich enough to export agricultural goods, the phase of primary export substitution by light manufactured goods may not be required, and the variables of the primary phase would need to be modified. However, for countries like Japan whose natural resources are limited, the relationship between technological progress and capital formation is particularly relevant. The primary phase is characterized by an approach toward fuller use of local resources simultaneously with industrialization. Greater attention in this regard is paid to accelerating technological advances than to augmenting capital investments. Such an approach may be handicapped by the greater rate of increase in the labor force for contemporary developing economies. However, the increasing possibility of the "telescoping effect" of the spread of technological advances worldwide may support development more positively than in Japan's case.

2

Semi-Industrialization:

The Secondary Import Substitution Phase

The formation and shift of development phases were described in Lecture 1. In particular, we saw that the secondary major phase of development is characterized by the emergence of secondary import substitution. The distinction between primary and secondary import substitution is conventional. It originates in academic analysis, but now the terms are widely used. As explained earlier, in comparison with nondurable consumer goods (primary goods), substituting imports of durable producer and consumer goods (secondary goods) by developing domestic production is a more difficult problem in all countries' experience. Nevertheless, without achieving the next step, secondary export substitution, as distinguished from primary, a country will not be able to complete the process of development.

Lecture 2 has four themes. First, the secondary phase of development will be discussed in detail by focusing on the pattern and mechanism of secondary import substitution, with examples taken from Japan's economic history. In particular, three aspects will be emphasized in view of their importance in the phasing framework and economic development. These three aspects are (1) production and supply: the competitive growth of import-substituting industries that manufacture capital goods and intermediate goods and major export industries that produce light manufactured goods such as textiles; (2) a comparison of engineering industries and heavy industries, represented by machinery, with metals and chemicals; and (3) an examination of demand and of the role played by the public sector. Change within the machinery industry will be discussed in the Appendix to this lecture. The concept of secondary import substitution is well known. To make the concept more operational to and technically analyze selected aspects of secondary import substitution, we first will clarify the problems and our methods of approaching these problems.

Secondary import substitution was not absent during the primary export substitution phase. The economy depended heavily upon imports of durable goods since domestic production of these goods was quite limited; nevertheless, the ratio of import dependency tended to decrease. Regarding producer durables, the ratio of import dependency (import/domestic production) was about 40% at the beginning of this phase and declined to some 25% immediately prior to World War I (see Table 2.8). During the war, because of import constraints, the ratio temporarily dropped. The high ratio after the war rapidly decreased toward the end of the 1930s. This fluctuation is a characteristic pattern of secondary import substitution, distinguishing it from the prior "early start" during the phase of primary export substitution. The distinction between the two is not only quantitative but also qualitative and is important for conceptual clarification and relevant to industrial policy.

During the entire prewar period, the textile industry had sustained development and retained its dominant role in expanding exports. This industry, which appears to be a continuation of primary export substitution activity, shifted from labor-intensive to capital-intensive production simultaneously with secondary import substitution of durable goods. This important pattern, which we will call a "simultaneous process," requires that an import substitution industry, such as the machinery industry, can become competitive with the textile industry in a domestic market facing constraints on the expansion of its domestic demand. The mechanism for increasing competitiveness will be clarified later.

The second theme is durable goods, which can be defined in two ways: either "by commodity or industry" or "by use." Often in analysis and policy discussion, the two aspects are used interchangeably, thus causing some confusion. Even within each type, a distinction must be made between different components of import substitution activities, such as iron and steel compared with machinery when defined by industry or capital goods compared with intermediate goods when defined by use. These distinctions are indispensable to make our approach operational.

The third theme is technological-organizational advances. In Lecture 1, we stressed the importance of this aspect for the primary export substitution phase. For analyzing the phase of secondary import substitution, our focus is essentially the same, since both phases sustained use of borrowed technology. The process and pattern of assimilation and diffusion of borrowed technology are not the same because secondary import substitution requires more capital-intensive technology. Substitution of capital for labor, which distinguishes this phase from the preceding phase with its labor-intensive technology, also is one of the basic criteria for distinguishing the two subphases and two major phases.[1]

An important modification is necessary to apply this principle: analysis of the role played by labor quality. The machinery industry, for example, is not a heavy industry such as steel or chemicals, and its capital intensity is not much higher than that of the textile industry. Nevertheless, the machinery industry and heavy industry have a common attribute: they both need skilled labor. (Unskilled labor, in contrast, is a characteristic of the textile industry.) The engineering industry is characterized by a higher quality of labor. The change in the quality of labor is an essential factor in our phasing and is a basic criterion. These aspects will be elucidated by empirical studies in this lecture and analyzed further in Lecture 3.

The fourth theme is what we call "noninducement effects." The iron and steel, shipbuilding, and some machinery industries began during the preceding phase in Japan. Similar phenomena are often observed in contemporary developing economies. Does this contradict our phasing framework? We believe it does not if understood within the context of "early start" mentioned earlier.[2] In addition to the inducement effects from the basic market mechanism, nonmarket activity also plays a role—as previously discussed in Lecture 1, section I—in forming the sequence of phase shifts in the innovative process of development. Government stress on strategic defense policies aim to enhance output. Such noninducement activities are desirable if they contribute to raising the level of technical capability required for the next phase. Inducement effects, one might argue, could achieve the same effect, but only if a much longer time is allowed. Thus, in evaluating noninducement effects, their importance is emphasized when considering the longer time span required to increase the supply of skilled labor.

---

[1] The timing and degree of increases in real wages of unskilled labor, together with the emergence of widening wage differentials between unskilled and skilled labor, are problems that have been approached with statistical estimates and analytical research by a number of economists (see Kazushi Ohkawa et al., *LTES* (Long-term Economic Statistics of Japan), Vol. 8, *Prices*, 1967, and Ryoshin Minami and Akira Ono, "Wages," in Kazushi Ohkawa and Miyohei Shinohara, eds., *Patterns of Japanese Economic Development: A Quantitative Appraisal* (New Haven: Yale University Press, 1979). Our analysis by industry (for example, comparing the machinery with the textiles industry) will focus on wage payment costs for enterprisers.

[2] For socialist regimes, the concept of "early start" cannot be directly applied. India's import dependency ratio of the "basic products" was as low as 10% even in the primary phase of industrialization.

An *ex post* observation of historical experience, however, cannot neglect the influence of the government for strategic purposes. In Japan's case, this is important particularly for analyzing the phase of secondary import substitution at the end of this lecture. (A fuller discussion will be given in Lecture 7.)

I. The Simultaneous Process of Import Substitution and Export Expansion

Let us begin with the simultaneous process as it relates directly to the preceding phase. In the phase of secondary import substitution, primary export substitution industries could not stop export expansion. Instead, exports expanded at a fast pace. Textile exports played such a role in eastern Asia. In other Asian countries, in addition to textiles, rubber, wood, and other resource-based industries began exporting their products. Some critics of the phase-shift theory often underestimate one important aspect of the simultaneous process: import substitution and export expansion should develop side by side; otherwise, the foreign exchange required for strengthening import substitution activities cannot be obtained. Without such resources this development phase will lack sufficient capability for producing investment goods and intermediate, capital-intensive products.

An inward- versus outward-looking policy option sometimes leads to an underestimation of the actual importance of the simultaneous process. The outward-looking policy is essential to promote exports, but it should be combined with an inward-looking import-substitution policy of investment goods and capital-intensive intermediate goods, such as basic metals and chemical products. A simultaneous process need not result in such a dichotomy because it emphasizes the importance of keeping both policies in balance.

Simultaneous process does not imply sectoral growth parallel to exports and imports. Export-promoting industries have a comparative advantage because they must be internationally competitive to sustain export expansion. Import-substitution industries, lacking a comparative advantage internationally, have to expand domestic production. Within the domestic economy, however, they must gain competitive power, and various versions of protection policies, including overvaluation of the exchange rate, are often at issue. What we are concerned with here are not the problems of strategy and policy (see section III), but rather the elements and their operation in the process of increasing the competitive power of import-substitution industries in the domestic market vis-à-vis export industries. Without increasing their competitiveness, these industries would prolong and not complete the phase of substituting durable goods imports.

This process faced many difficulties in Japan. For today's less developed nations, telescoping effects may make the process shorter, but they do not eliminate the difficulties to be overcome. "Selective" import substitution is often advocated, but a long-term perspective on how to improve import-substitution industries is necessary to determine the criteria for selection.

The major criteria for selective import substitution are productivity, prices, and wages and their comparative changes in the performance of the selected industry compared with industry that has a comparative international advantage.[3] To improve its competitiveness, the primary requirement of the selected industry is to raise its value productivity at a faster pace than that of the standard industry. Because of the difficulties in realizing this objective, however, maintaining a faster pace often involves raising output prices (or lowering input prices by policy intervention) to increase value productivity. The process thus stems from domestic demand and policy initiative. The major factor on the cost side is the performance of wages. The industry to be selected for promoting import substitution needs more skilled labor than the standard industry because of its higher level of technology. The wage differential between unskilled and skilled labor is crucial. If the shortage of skilled labor tends to make the wage differential wider, there will be pressure on the industry under consideration.

The Machinery vs. Textile Industry

Comparing Japan's machinery and textile industry (1919–38), the prewar interval of the phase under consideration, the performance of the key variables of the machinery industry relative to the textile industry are summarized in Table 2.1, taking the latter as 100. The machinery industry has a great number of subsectors, but Table 2.1 just observes the sector aggregate. Compositional change is discussed in the Appendix.

In the mid-1930s, imports and exports of machinery products became equal. This marked the halfway point toward secondary export substitution. Nevertheless, comparative productivity of the machinery industry shows a decline in 1938 in comparison with 1919—the year

---

[3] If export taxes are substantial, qualification would be required for taking the major export industry as standard. For a more systematic approach to the subject of productivity comparisons, see Lecture 3.

Table 2.1
Japan's Machinery Industries: Key Variables, 1919 and 1938

(textiles = 100)

	Productivity in Real Terms[a]	Value Productivity	Wages
1919	262	172	254
1938	207	273	286

Source: Shinohara data, LTES, Vol. 10, Mining and Manufacturing; Ohkawa et al. data, LTES, Vol. 8, Prices. [a]1934–35 prices.

beginning the phase of secondary import substitution.[4] Comparative value productivity, however, raised its level distinctly, owing no doubt to the increase in relative output prices. The average wage differential also grew, creating pressure on the development of the machinery industry. Therefore, the unfavorable performance of productivity and wages was covered essentially by the output price increase in the domestic market: there was no improvement in productivity. However, improvement in value productivity compared with wages is distinct and greatly favored enterprisers in the machinery industry.

Table 2.2 is arranged to describe long-term and swing variations in productivity in machinery and textiles. The intervals of the preceding phase are also given to show average annual rate of growth between the two overlapping decades.

Machinery shows wide variance in the rate of output growth, whereas textiles maintain a sustained performance. No doubt textiles continued a considerably high rate of growth, and machinery overcame it in upswings, with reversals in the downswing periods (1912–21/1917–26 and 1917–26/1922–31). Higher growth is witnessed in the two periods 1907–16/1912–21 and 1927–36/1931–40—the investment spurt segment of long-term Japanese growth.

In textiles, between the former period (1902–11/1907–16 to 1912–21/ 1917–26) and the latter period (1917–26/1922–31 to 1927–36/1931–40), there is a sharp contrast between a very high rate of employment increase with a low rate of productivity increase (the earlier period) and a zero employment increase with high rates of productivity increase. In comparison, for the machinery industry during the entire period, labor employment had much more influence than productivity on increasing output: the contrast between the two industries became more distinct particularly during the latter period.

[4] Recall, for example, the fast rate of increase in productivity of the cotton textile industry at that time (see Lecture 1, section II).

Table 2.2

Rate of Productivity Growth: The Machinery and Textile Industries in Japan, 1902–40

(average annual rate of growth; %)

Periods	Output (1)		Labor Employed (2)		Productivity (3)	
	Text.	Mach.	Text.	Mach.	Text.	Mach.
1902–11/1907–16	1.7	12.9	4.4	8.2	3.3	4.7
1907–16/1912–21	7.9	18.6	7.2	15.7	0.7	2.8
1912–21/1917–26	6.1	5.1	6.3	7.6	−0.2	−2.5
1917–26/1922–31	5.7	1.4	0.4	5.8	5.3	−4.4
1922–31/1927–36	7.3	10.8	0.01	7.2	7.3	3.7
1927–36/1931–40	4.9	17.4	0.5	15.2	4.4	2.2

Source: Output: Shinohara data in *LTES*, Vol. 10, *Mining and Manufacturing*, Table 1–5, p. 11. Labor: Umemura data in *LTES*, Vol. 2, *Labor Force*.

Notes: 1. Output is gross production in 1934 to 1936 prices. Added value series are not available for comparison over the entire period.

2. The rate of growth in productivity (3) is the difference between (1) and (2). Rounding to the nearest one-tenth may cause some inconsistency.

This finding suggests that the simultaneous process occurred by forming different types of factor combination and through technological progress. Actually, research, including ours described in Lecture 1, has noted that both the raw silk and cotton (spinning and weaving) industries were characterized by labor-intensive development using flexible availability of unskilled labor during the former period (essentially the major part of the primary export substitution phase). During the latter period, when the labor market had changed, labor-saving technological progress began to occur.[5] As will be explained later, real wages pertaining to the enterprisers of this industry actually increased substantially because output prices greatly declined as a result of the depression in the international market. The newly estimated Umemura data on labor employment enabled a sectoral comparison of the productivity for two industries, although the type of factor-combination and technological progress of machinery industry is not yet well

[5] Keijiro Otsuka, "Men Kogyo no Hatten to Gijutsu Kakushin" [Technological Innovation and the Development of the Cotton-textile Industry], chapter 6 in Ryoshin Minami and Yukihiko Kiyokawa, eds., *Nihon no Kogyo-ka to Gijutsu Hatten* [Japan's Industrialization and Technological Progress] (Tokyo: Toyo Keizai Shimposha, 1987).

known. The implications in Table 2.2 are as follows. First, the machinery industry is demand-sensitive, as shown by its distinct fluctuation in growth rate of output, labor, and productivity. This demand sensitivity will be discussed in detail later (including military expenditures) (see section III). Second, the machinery industry is labor-absorbing. Actually the number of workers employed in this industry was only 64,000 from 1902 to 1911 on an annual average as against 535,000 in textiles. In 1940 machinery labor was 1,860,000 compared with 1,580,000 for textiles labor.

After passing through the "turning point" (see Lecture 1), industrial transformation is toward capital-intensive industries, which usually imply the so-called heavy industries. Thus a labor-absorbing industry such as the machinery industry appears not to conform with this pattern. Is Japan's case atypical? We do not think so. Although capital data are not available for the prewar period, from the data of early postwar years, we are convinced that the capital-intensity of the machinery industry must have been much lower than that of heavy industry (see Lecture 3). We believe that the simultaneous process might not result in a capital intensification problem for the machinery industry. Instead, the major problem for the engineering industry was to secure the needed skilled workers and advance technologically, whereas capital intensification was at issue for heavy industry. Therefore, both capital intensification and human resource augmentation should separately be considered for optimum balance in selecting import-substitution industries in the country concerned.

Competition in the Domestic Market

The pattern of changes in output price and wages mentioned earlier needs further explanation. Two approaches are taken in applying our formula: (1) real terms for a long-term approach and (2) nominal terms for specific shorter periods. A long-term approach corresponds to treating productivity in real terms; a short-term approach pertains to the 1930s, when the machinery industry made its last jump to move out of the import substitution phase.

The simple formula is $\pi = Y/K - Lw/K$, in which Y is output, L is labor employed, K is capital stock, w is wages, and π is an indicator comparing the rate of return on capital. (For a detailed explanation, see Lecture 3.) The problem is how to apply this formula approximately, when the data of capital stock is not available—a case often faced for less developed countries.

Comparing the textile (1) and machinery (2) industries, the relative competitive power in the domestic market is judged by $\pi_1 \gtrless \pi_2$. Starting with a situation of $\pi 1 > \pi 2$, the improvement process of machinery should narrow the degree of this inequality of two components: Lw/K and Y/Lw; that is, $L_1w_1/K_1 \gtreqless L_2w_2/K_2$ and $Y_1/L_1w_1 \gtreqless Y_2/L_2w_2$. These two inequalities may move toward the same direction or conversely cancel out each other's effects. We can deal only with the textile industry due to the lack of available data for the machinery industry. However, it is not utterly impossible to make a realistic speculation for the machinery industry, assuming that the effect of the former inequality is much narrower and its changes less influential than those of the latter inequality. For postwar Japan and some other Asian countries where K data are available, the level of capital intensity (K/L) shows a minor difference between textiles and machinery on the average; the exception is transportation machinery (see Appendix 2 to Lecture 3).

The improvement process requires a tendency of narrowing the inequality $Y_1/L_1w_1 > Y_2/L_2w_2$. For the long-term approach, in our previous discussion of productivity performance, we found the growth rate of Y_2/L_2 is smaller than Y_1/L_1 (assuming that possible changes in the added value ratios were minor—an assumption that will be tested later). The problem pertains to the performance of real wages (w_1 and w_2).

The long-term pattern of Japan's output growth rate and price changes is as expected for almost all developing countries (compare the figures for output prices in Table 2.3 with those for output productivity in Table 2.2). Regarding relative changes, there are also swings between prices and growth rate of output. In the early periods (1902–16), the price ratio changed in favor of machinery, whose output growth rate is greater than that of textiles. This situation improved toward the last periods (1927–39): vigorous output growth of the machinery industry occurred in association with favorable prices. For the other years (1912–31), a reverse phenomenon occurred: relative prices remained unfavorable in the machinery industry, and its output growth performance worsened. The textile industry, in contrast, had much better performance in both areas.

Why did such drastic changes in relative prices take place? Are the relations between domestic investment swings and export variations relevant factors to be considered? The answers to these questions will be discussed together with nonmarket factors in the next section. First, however, let us focus our attention on the enterprisers' behavior in these circumstances.

As is found generally in less developed countries, the level of nominal wages differs greatly between the machinery and textile industries.

Table 2.3

The Textile and Machinery Industries in Japan: Output Prices and Wages, 1902–39 (in yen)

Period	Output Prices		Price Ratio	Nominal Wages		Nominal Wages Ratio
	Text. (1)	Mach. (2)	(2)/(1)	Text. (3)	Mach. (4)	(4)/(3)
1902–11	86.2	71.2	80.3	.23	.58	2.52
1907–16	89.6	78.0	87.1	.29	.79	2.72
1912–21	145.1	117.5	81.0	.50	1.30	2.06
1917–26	189.5	133.5	70.3	.84	2.04	2.43
1922–31	149.8	104.8	70.0	.92	2.46	2.67
1927–36	108.8	95.3	90.7	.78	2.38	3.05
1936–39	109.0	114.8	105.3	.73	2.26	3.09

Period	Real Wages		Real Wages Ratio	Rate of Change in Real Wages (%)	
	Text. (1)	Mach. (2)	(2)/(1)	Text.	Mach.
1902–11	.27	.81	3.00		
				3.7	4.5
1907–16	.32	1.01	3.16		
				1.2	1.7
1912–21	.34	1.10	3.23		
				5.3	6.7
1917–26	.44	1.52	3.68		
				1.7	9.1
1922–31	.48	2.35	4.90		
				8.5	1.2
1927–36	.72	2.49	3.46		
				−2.0	−6.1
1936–39	.67	1.97	2.91		

Source: Output prices are from the Shinohara data (implicit deflator by industry), *LTES*, Vol. 10, *Mining and Manufacturing*, Tables 1–11, p. 15. Nominal wages are from *LTES*, Vol. 8, *Prices*, Table 27 in Part III. Average wage earnings per day are by industrial manufacturing group (Series C), pp. 248–49.

Remarks: Real wages are calculated by deflating nominal wages by the output prices of each industry.

Although our data are "averages," the lower level for textiles represents wages of unskilled female workers, while the higher level for machinery is for semiskilled and skilled male workers. Real wages are deflated by output prices in each industry, not by the common procedure of deflating by general consumer prices. From the enterpriser's viewpoint, wage bills are paid from the value amount of proceeds, which depend on output prices.

Concerning long-term changes relative to real wages, two segments are clearly identified (Table 2.3): the earlier segment (1902–31) had a ratio increase, and the later segment (1922–39) had a sharp decline in the ratio. The ratio of nominal wages tends to increase from 1912 to 1939, reflecting changes in the supply and demand of skilled and unskilled labor. The machinery industry suffered a shortage of skilled labor. Therefore, output price performance is primarily responsible for changes in the real wages ratio during the later segment of prewar growth.

The term Y/Lw in our formula can be treated in growth terms as follows: $GY–GL–Gw$ (G represents the rate of growth). Let Q stand for gross output: namely, $GQ–GL–Gw$, in which $GQ–GL$ is the rate of productivity growth (see Table 2.2). Gw is the rate of change in real wages (see Table 2.3). The average percentages for Gw for textiles and machinery during different overlapping periods are as follows:

	Textiles	Machinery
1902–21	1.5	0.7
1917–31	−1.5	−11.3
1922–39	2.3	6.7

Until around the end of the phase of primary export substitution from 1902 to 1921, the productivity-wage relationship was favorable for textiles. Machinery made a favorable start and, around the time of World War I, rapidly expanded due to the import restraints. However, during the downswing, entrepreneurs in both industries faced an unfavorable productivity-wage situation and had severe difficulties: stagnated output productivity was combined with increasing pressure for a hike in real wages. From 1922 to 1939, during an upswing at the end of the 1930s, when military mobilization took place, the productivity-wage condition became favorable for machinery: its relative position had been reversed with that of textiles.

Conditions peculiar to Japan's history are certainly involved in such a process. Nevertheless, in general, the productivity-wage relation is a crucial factor for secondary import substitution, although it is influenced by changes in the macroeconomic growth pattern.

The second approach is a further clarification of the performance of Y/Lw for the crucial period of 1922 to 1939. By our formula, we would expect that the value of Y/Lw for machinery would be closer to that of textiles through either a relative increase in value productivity or a narrowing of the wage differential. To test this expectation, the percentage ratio of added value/gross output can be calculated for the years since 1929 (see Table 2.3a). For selected years it is as follows:

	Textiles	Machinery
1929	27.1 %	50.1 %
1930	27.0	60.7
1938	31.3	50.7

Changes in the prices of fuel and materials, as well as the structural changes in subsector composition, are mainly responsible for overtime changes. Actually, the ratio is not too changeable, and the use of gross output in our preliminary approach may not have created large distortions in overlapping decade averages. The annual data fluctuate, and for the years after 1938 they cannot be used accurately because of the effects of military mobilization. The average value of Y/Lw for two periods is shown in Table 2.3a.

From 1929 to 1933, the value of Y/Lw for machinery was still below that for textiles, but from 1934 to 1938 it became higher than textiles. As stated earlier, the value of Lw/K is estimated to be not smaller for machinery than for textiles. Therefore, the machinery industry must have become competitive in the domestic market by the latter part of the 1930s: the productivity lag still remaining was covered by output prices.

The arrival at this stage, however, seems to be supported by the decline of the wage differentials from 1934 to 1938. The records of

Table 2.3a
Average Value for Y/Lw, 1929–38

Period	Machinery	Textiles
1929–33	3.05	3.20
1934–38	3.58*	3.37*

Source: Ministry of International Trade and Industry (MITI), Kogyo tokei-hyo (KTH) [Manufacturing Survey].
* Excludes anomalous value for one year.

Table 2.3b
Average Wages per Hour (yen)

Years	Machinery	Textiles	Wage Ratio (mach./text.)
1931	2.25	.72	3.13
1938	2.31	.78	2.95
1939	2.31	.85	2.72

Source: MITI, KTH.

wage rates per hour are shown in MITI's KTH data. The ratio of wage rates of machinery to that of textiles was on average 2.68 for 1929 to 1933. This ratio decreased to 2.36 from 1934 to 1938. Using the same data as in Table 2.3a, the long-term tendency of widening wage differentials seems to change during the latter part of the 1930s (see Table 2.3b). During the upward-swing interval, the demand for unskilled labor increased greatly. Even agricultural wages increased due to a relative shortage caused by a faster migration of the labor force to the modern industrial sectors. The increase in textile wages is a reflection of the number of young female workers migrating from rural districts to form the majority of the labor in this industry. The moderate increase in machinery wages can perhaps be attributed to the increase of the potential stock of workers in this industry during the long downswing interval, which made possible a relatively flexible supply of labor for the upswing interval.

The final topic in this section is the negative effects of the increased machinery prices on domestic economic development. Certainly, if the price of a product is too high, the burden on other industries creates great pressure; thus, there must be protective price policies to offset high variable costs in new market-driven industries. In Japan's case, the domestic market was highly protected toward the latter part of the 1930s because of military mobilization. However, machinery prices increased at a pace slightly slower than prices of total manufactures. Since Japan's inflationary growth is like that in a number of contemporary developing countries the GNP deflator increased at a fast pace.[6] Thus, a machinery price increase may be allowed and acceptable if it is under the increasing pace of the general price of manufactured goods.

[6] Taking the average prices from 1902 to 1911 as 100, the 1930–1940 average is 147.2 for machinery and 154.1 for manufactured goods in general compared with 212.0 for the GNP deflator.

II. Heavy Industry Versus Engineering Industry

Metals and Chemicals
As discussed earlier, metals (iron-steel and nonferrous metals) and chemicals are the major subsector of heavy industry, which produce intermediate goods; the majority of machinery industry products are capital or investment goods. In dealing with the problems and policies

Table 2.4
Japan's Import Dependency Ratio: Metals, Chemicals, and Machinery for Selected Years, 1913 to 1936 (in current prices; unit: million yen)

Year	Domestic Production (Q)	Import (M)	Export (X)	Ratio (%) (M/Q)	(X/Q)
Machinery					
1913	233.5	81.0	10.5	34.6	4.5
1919	1,627.5	136.2	54.2	8.4	4.8
1931	694.3	83.0	61.5	12.1	8.8
1936	2,598.9	157.6	290.3	6.1	11.2
Metals					
1913	113.8	88.1	39.3	77.4	3.4
1919	839.5	360.9	124.2	42.9	1.4
1931	611.8	92.1	75.0	15.0	1.2
1936	2,245.0	376.4	249.4	16.7	11.0
Chemicals					
1913	309.6	115.1	49.3	37.1	15.9
1919	1,091.5	343.2	176.5	31.5	16.2
1931	997.1	192.2	115.0	19.3	11.6
1936	2,484.7	369.8	362.0	14.8	14.2

Source: Domestic production from Shinohara data in *LTES*, Vol. 10, *Mining and Manufacturing*, Appendix Table 1, pp. 142–43. Imports and exports from Yamazawa-Yamamoto data in *LTES*, Vol. 14, *Foreign Trade and Balance of Payments*, Appendix Tables 3 and 4, pp. 184–87.

Remarks: The B series of Shinohara data are used for domestic production, but use of the A series does not change the pattern.

Each year selected represents the swing pattern noted earlier in Tables 2.2 and 2.3.

Export ratios are added for reference. Net (import-export) percentages are not used. If the ratio of $M/(Q+M)$ is used, the pattern may not differ. If, however, domestic demand is at issue, the ratio may be better expressed as $M/(Q+M-X)$.

of secondary import substitution, certain criteria are necessary for selecting industries and defining their dimensions. To serve this purpose, analytical results are useful. Since we know the performance of machinery, we can compare it with that of metals and chemicals.

A simple indicator of import substitution is presented in Table 2.4. Regarding the decrease in the import-dependency ratio (M/Q), metals and chemicals appear behind machinery. Starting from the largest ratio, metals made a fast substitution, while a slower but steady process is seen for chemicals. During the downswing period, 1919–31, import substitution proceeded rapidly for metals, but machinery stagnated, and even seemed to decline. This decline may be related to the different performance during World War I. In 1936, the year immediately before the great influence of military mobilization, an excess of exports over imports (X > M) is seen for machinery but not for metals (excepting steel) and chemicals.

For reference, export ratios (X/Q) are added. Note that we do not use net ratios (import-export): the goods composition of X and M differs greatly, as exports were mostly for Asian neighboring countries.

Within the broad similarity in the long-term performance of import substitution activities, discussed in Lecture 1, there are notable differences among individual industries that pose a challenge for the analysis of their cases.

Applying the same formula for the two heavy industries, we first have to consider their greater capital intensity. If the wage level does not differ much—such as is the case in the machinery industry—the level of Lw/K must be lower for heavy industry in applying the formula $\pi = (Lw/K) \cdot ((Y/Lw) - 1)$.[7] To be competitive with machinery, the value of Y/Lw must be larger or nearly equivalent in value to π, the simple indicator for comparing the rate of capital return. Furthermore, if capital intensification proceeds at a faster pace in heavy industry— and this may be the case—the problem is more difficult to handle.[8]

Because of this technical handicap, reversing the previous order of

---

[7] No data are available for the prewar period. For reference, the 1957 value of Lw/K is as follows: chemicals 0.32, iron and steel 0.35, nonferrous metals 0.58, electric machinery 0.79, transportation machinery 1.01, and general machinery 1.31.

[8] The policy implications of the factor-proportion thesis, in general, recommend labor-intensive technology industries for developing countries with flexible supplies of labor and discourage capital-intensive technology industries. This thesis pertains essentially to the primary phase, but it also concerns Lw/K and the extent to which we stress labor quality. The reason that our formula is used is to find the value of Y/Lw in relation to Lw/K. A long-term concern with technological advance is needed, in our view, to use the factor-proportion thesis for making policy.

applying the formula, let us begin with the shorter period in nominal terms of Y/Lw. From the MITI data used earlier (*KTH*), the average value of Y/Lw is calculated as follows: for 1929–33, metals 3.84, chemicals 7.05; for 1934–38, metals 4.90, chemicals 8.09.

These figures are distinctly higher than the value of machinery mentioned earlier: on average for the whole decade 1929–38, chemicals were 2.15 and metals 1.28, taking machinery as 1.00. This is as expected, and we believe our formula can be applied in this case if qualification is adequately made. A substantive finding is that the value for machinery tends to increase distinctly from 1929–33 to 1934–38. This suggests the final spurt of these heavy industries in the 1930s, toward further substitution of imported goods by accelerating domestic production, but it actually was a stronger trend within the machinery industry: value productivity increased greatly over the wage level.

Regarding long-term performance, observed in real terms, see Tables 2.5a and b, arranged so correspond to Tables 2.2 and and 2.3, combined here for convenience.

Table 2.5a
Productivity and Wage Performance: Japan's Metals and Chemical Industries, 1902–40

(Average annual rate of growth, %)

Periods	Output (GQ)		Employment (GL)		Productivity (GQ−GL)		Real Wages (Gw)	
	Met.	Chem.	Met.	Chem.	Met.	Chem.	Met.	Chem.
1902–11/ 1907–16	17.3	5.8	10.8	8.6	6.5	−2.8	3.3	1.4
I								
1907–16/ 1912–21	18.1	6.7	14.8	13.9	3.4	−7.2*	1.9	3.9
1912–21/ 1917–26	9.0	5.5	4.8	9.3	4.2	−3.8	10.6	8.5
II								
1917–26/ 1922–31	7.3	7.8	2.7	4.4	4.5	3.4	14.9	10.0
1922–31/ 1927–36	12.1	11.6	8.9	7.3	3.2	4.3	1.0	4.1
III								
1927–36/ 1931–40	10.1	12.7	11.0	8.4	1.0	4.3	−8.4*	−1.7

Source: See Tables 2.2 and 2.3.
* Negative magnitude may be overstated.

64 PHASES OF DEVELOPMENT

The performance is almost self-evident, being essentially similar to the previous case: relatively favorable, somewhat depressed, and very favorable conditions are witnessed for both industries except at two points. During period I, the chemical industry was rather recessive, and during period II, both industries suffered much less than the machinery industry.

These features become more distinct when combined with real wage performance as shown by GQ − (GL + Gw). The figures are taken from Table 2.5a. The value of (GL + Gw) and its difference from GQ are rearranged in Table 2.5b. Machinery is added for comparison.

Japan's import substitution began with machinery and proceeded to metals and then to chemicals, although domestic production of these three industries expanded simultaneously. As will be discussed later, government policies played an important role in the time sequence, but the activities of private enterprisers were important as well. The formula applied is very simple, and yet something basic is revealed. During the early part of period I (1902–21), the relation between output and wage costs was worst for the chemical industry, which showed a big minus. Although allowance must be made for some exaggeration due to limited reliable data, the unfavorable situation is undeniable. During the World War I boom, the chemical industry's output and growth lagged behind those of other industries. On the other hand, as will be discussed in detail later, the early start of import substitution of machinery during World War I was notable. During the succeeding

Table 2.5b
Output/Wage Costs: Japan's Metals, Chemical, and Machinery Industries, 1902–40

		GL+Gw			GQ−(GL+Gw)		
		Met.	Chem.	Mach.	Met.	Chem.	Mach.
I	1902–11/1907–16	14.1	10.0	12.7	3.2	−4.2	0.2
	1907–16/1912–21	16.7	22.5	17.4	1.4	−15.8	1.2
II	1912–21/1917–26	15.4	17.8	14.3	−6.4	−12.3	−9.2
	1917–26/1922–31	17.4	8.5	14.9	−10.1	−0.7	−13.5
III	1922–31/1927–36	9.9	11.4	8.4	2.2	0.2	2.1
	1927–36/1921–40	2.6	6.2	9.1	7.3	6.4	8.3

Source: See Tables 2.2 and 2.3.

depressed period, this industry also suffered, although it later caught up with other industries.

The metals industry behaved very similarly to machinery throughout periods I, II, and III in the relation of output to wage costs, but, as noted earlier, it could sustain output growth at a relatively high level even in the downswing period II. The pressure of wage cost increases was relatively weak compared with machinery. The metals industry also was less sensitive to demand swings. We see no evidence for backwardness in this industry. However, because of greater capital intensity, its rate of capital intensification was faster than that of machinery. Parallel performance of the changes in $GQ - (GL + Gw)$ could not be enough to keep metals competitive with machinery. This is one of the reasons that metals showed some sluggishness during import substitution.

A steel mill was established by the government as early as 1901, implying that in Japan basic metals may have led the secondary import substitution process. If we follow the downstream notion, steel should come first and machinery should follow. However, in our view, there is no realistic reason for endorsing the validity of this notion. The machinery industry actually developed by depending on imported steel, and the proportion of iron and steel production by public sector to the total domestic production tended to decrease (from some 30% in the decade 1910–20 to 20% in the 1930s). The government adopted a policy of encouraging machinery industry in the early years, but its primary focus was on promoting steel shipbuilding. Production of machinery by the public sector in 1919 accounted for some 28% of total domestic production, but toward the 1930s it decreased to less than 20%. As will be discussed later (see the Appendix to this lecture), the role played by the government was influential, but it distorted development of this industry. Actually, private sector activity was dominant in the metal industry's development.

Scale Distribution of Enterprises
The next topic is distribution of enterprises or establishments by industrial scale. The conventional view states that changes in industrial organization create the industrial transformation necessary for import substitution. To transfer sophisticated technology requires large-scale enterprises that can finance technology transfer through high capital investment and hire a number of technicians and skilled workers. For transferring less sophisticated technology, the requirements are less rigorous and may be met by medium-scale enterprises. Is this view valid?

No doubt the domestic economic situation is relevant to the scale distribution of financial, technical, and managerial capability. As observed earlier, the import substitution process went through wide up-and-down swings of the economic growth rate. What were the differences in enterprisers' responses to these swings?

No direct data are available for applying our formula, so indirect data are used: relative value productivity by scale of establishment (see Table 2.6). The three group classifications small (S), medium (M), and large (L) for the number of employed workers are used for the sake of convenience. The relative value productivity is calculated by dividing the percentage proportion of value output (gross of intermediate goods) by the percentage proportion of labor employed. For example, the value 1.19 for L of machinery in 1940 is 53.6 (output proportion)/44.9 (labor proportion). In 1940, this indicator is higher for M than for L in machinery. The same holds true for chemicals, but the indicator is reversed for metals and textiles. The difference between M and L is much wider in metals (output proportion 68.3 compared with employment proportion 47.3).

The sharp contrast between machinery or chemicals and metals deserves attention. The emphasis here is on a high level of relative efficiency of M for machinery against a very low level in metals. This, of course, does not indicate the competitive power difference by scale because it is not combined with other terms such as capital productivity

Table 2.6
Relative Value Productivity by Establishment Scale, Selected Manufacturing, 1931, 1940

	S	M	L
1931			
Machinery	.58	.72	1.15
Metals	.74	1.17	1.28
Chemicals	.82	1.16	.92
Textiles	.91	.84	1.22
1940			
Machinery	.56	1.24	1.19
Metals	.54	.69	1.44
Chemicals	.82	1.29	.90
Textiles	.84	1.01	1.17

Source: MITI, KTH.
Notes: S = small-scale (fewer than 50 workers)
M = medium-scale (50 to 499 workers)
L = large-scale (more than 500 workers)

and wages. Nevertheless, it is useful for roughly indicating the different distribution of productivity. Considering the limited reliability of the data, it is safe to say that no substantive difference of efficiency exists between M and L in machinery, whereas there is a great difference of efficiency in the metals industry.

As compared with the situation of near-full employment in 1940, the picture appears quite different in 1931, when the economy was still under the influence of the Great Depression. Although the scale pattern is not essentially different for metals and chemicals, the inequality of the relative value of productivity is drastically reversed for machinery. One may be tempted to argue a productivity polarization, as it is almost equally low for M and S as against L. Why is there such a drastic difference between the two years? This is not accidental, but rather representative of the situation prevailing at that time.

Resistance to pressure brought forth by the depression was much weaker for medium-scale establishments than for large-scale establishments: the former had to cut output production much more than the latter. The percentage proportion of output in 1931 is 22.2 for medium-scale enterprises, against a high of 57.4 for large-scale enterprises. Under the lifetime employment system introduced around the time of World War I, enterprises kept a number of surplus workers and looked forward to a recovery of demand and expansion. Thus, the proportion of employment was much greater than that of output, resulting in an underutilization of capital stock. Actually, the import substitution process stagnated during the downswing interval for the machinery industry, but sustained its momentum for the basic metal industry.

Japan had no agency or policy to protect small and medium-sized enterprises against the influence of such pressures in the prewar period, although at present there are established institutions and policies for so doing.

Regarding the results of the simultaneous process seen as the changes in industrial organization by scale, data are available only for the number of workers. It is amazing to see little change over the entire period under review (Table 2.7). The scale organization of the textile industry is rather similar to that of heavy and engineering industries. Because of the effect of military mobilization, the average for 1931 to 1940 is added to Table 2.7. A shift from small to medium and from medium to large heavy and engineering industries is discernible only for the years 1931 to 1940. Engineering industries no doubt greatly contributed to form such a scale distribution pattern.[9] It should be noted

[9] The organizational aspects of scale distribution require separate treatment. The

Table 2.7
Employment Distribution by Establishment Scale, Selected Years, 1914–40

	S (%)	M (%)	L (%)
Textiles			
1914	30.4	38.3	31.3
1919	26.7	35.7	37.6
1931	25.5	41.2	33.3
1940	38.2	33.2	28.6
(average of 1931–40)	(31.9)	(37.2)	(30.9)
Heavy and Engineering			
1914	33.6	33.6	32.8
1919	27.8	32.4	39.8
1931	36.1	35.3	28.6
1940	24.5	25.7	49.8
(average of 1931–40)	(30.3)	(30.5)	(39.2)

Source: MITI, KTH.
Notes: S = small-scale (few than 50 workers)
   M = medium-scale (50 to 499 workers)
   L = large-scale (more than 500 workers)
Remarks: Heavy and engineering industries include rubber and rubber products in addition to metals, chemicals, and machinery.

that the scale distribution pattern of heavy and engineering enterprises in 1940 was created by resource mobilization for the war. Otherwise, a much less noticeable change would have occurred to conclude the long process of secondary import substitution, although it might have been delayed.

Despite limited available data the changes in industrial organization by scale can be summarized as follows. (1) The machinery industry has a relatively higher level of productivity for medium-scale establishments than does the metal industry. (2) Demand variations severely affect the competitive power of the machinery industry. (3) Employment distribution by scale among enterprises changed little during the phase under review except during the 1930s. Import substitution activity was carried out largely without a tendency toward polarization. The engineering industry contributed greatly to this tendency.

---

subcontract system was not as widely prevalent during the prewar period as in the postwar period when parts production in the automobile industry promoted its development. Nevertheless, organizational development of small and medium scale enterprises in the prewar machinery industry cannot be ignored. See Susumu Hondai, "Development of the Machine Industry and Standardization of Parts: Cases of Oil Engine and Sewing Machine Industries," IDCJ Working Paper Series No. 30 (March 1985).

III. The "By Use" Approach: Demand and the Government

Detailed discussion by industrial comparison in the preceding sections concerned production and supply. Now let us turn to demand. Competitive development of the industries under consideration involves the difficult problem of demand expansion for their products in the domestic market. It is a widely prevailing notion that the possibility of developing import-substitution industries is conditioned by restraint of domestic demand, and, because of this restraint, policies promoting import substitution can be recommended with qualifications.

The problem of developing import substitution industries is not limited to restraining domestic demand. The development of these industries also tends to enhance import demand for foreign goods. For example, to accelerate the growth rate of the economy, an increase in investment is required. In many contemporary developing countries, proportion of investment to GDP (gross domestic product) increased at a fast pace through the 1970s. Some developing countries have recorded investments of over 30%. Plans to increase the investment proportion further in the 1980s face difficulties—heavy import dependence on investment goods is one notable problem—particularly in the secondary phase of industrialization. A rise in domestic investment would create a foreign payments imbalance due to the import increase in investment goods. To combat this problem, one countermeasure is to promote import substitution by investment increases.

Another aspect of promoting import substitution pertains to both external and internal demand for intermediate goods. Further industrialization needs a greater proportion of intermediate goods to total manufacturing output through augmenting the input-output relationship. We share Shionoya's view that recognition of this long-term process of increasing the proportion of intermediate goods is indispensable for addressing the problem of secondary import substitution.[10]

Investment Goods, Intermediate Goods, and Import Dependency

Our approach thus far has been to classify enterprises or establishments by industry. Now we will concentrate on products or commodities. The problem of demand can only be handled from this direction. The products classification is thus emancipated from the category of

---

[10] Yuichi Shionoya, "Patterns of Industrial Development," in L. Klein and K. Ohkawa, eds., *Economic Growth: The Japanese Experience Since the Meiji Era* (New Haven: Yale University Press, 1968).

industry by adopting the category of use: investment, consumption, export, and intermediate use. For example, metals are of course used as mainly intermediate goods, but they are also used for consumption, for export, and for investment in construction materials.

Table 2.8 summarizes the data originally estimated by Shionoya, on the distribution by use of domestic manufacturing products (A) and the import dependency ratio (B) (import/domestic production). Consumption, exports, and investment are the conventional components of the final demand vs. expenditure for intermediate goods. Specifically, the investment goods category is broken down into producer durables and construction materials.

A long-term decline in consumption compared with a tendency toward an increase in intermediate goods gives a clear contrast: Exports appear mixed and tend to decline toward the end of the 1930s (see Table 2.8). Investment goods distribution seems to have a swing pattern and no long-term trend; they range from a low of 11% to a high of 18%. A sustained increase in intermediate goods is particularly significant, since some economists argue that this increase must be one of the basic characteristics of industrialization. Plans or programs for establishing heavy industries in many developing countries seems to depend on this rationale. Nobody can reject the significance of a sustained increase in intermediate goods, but using it as a basis for industrial policy is another matter.[11]

It is also important to note that because of the increasing proportion of intermediate goods, the percentage of other goods to the final demand for manufacturing has a tendency to decline: from 1905 to 1909 it was 80.3% (100.0 − 19.7), but it declined to 59.8% (100 − 40.2) from 1935 to 1939. The proportion of investment goods to total final demand shows a long-term increase with noticeable swings. For example, it went from 14.9% (1905-09) to 25.1% (1915-19), to 15.1% (1925-29), to 29.1% (1935-39). These percentages, conforming with an increasing overall investment proportion and swing pattern in Japan, illustrate well the role played by manufacturing in the macro expenditure performance of the developing economies.

As noted earlier, the fluctuations in producer durables proportions are in contrast with the steady performance of intermediate goods. The highest percentage in periods 1915 to 1919 and 1935 to 1939 coincides with what we call the "investment spurt" interval. The figures

[11] It is true that military mobilization encouraged this tendency in Japan, but the postwar data added in the remarks to Table 2.8 indicate that even without it the basic tendency is sustained.

in the remarks appended to Table 2.8 are the postwar version of this phenomenon. (For details, see Lecture 5.) Previously we noted that the import substitution of machines occurred at the fastest pace in this particular interval of investment spurts and stagnated in receding intervals. As is widely known, among the necessary conditions for realizing investment spurts—in particular for increasing their duration—import dependency on investment goods should decrease as far as possible. If this requirement is not met, an import boost of investment goods soon creates a serious international balance-of-payments deficit. In other words, the import dependency level of investment goods operates as a ceiling for domestic investment increases; this control often has been seen in contemporary developing economies. Yet how and why are Japan's investment spurts simultaneous with spirals in domestic production of investment goods?

The response to demand rises differed between the first (1915–19) and second (1935–39) investment spurts, as the former was the beginning and the latter close to the end of prewar import substitution of investment goods. However, we believe their common feature is a relatively rapid technology diffusion because of the available manpower resources. The number of workers, including skilled workers, employed by the machinery industry increased 4.6 times from 1909 to 1919 and 8.1 times from 1931 to 1940. For production of intermediate goods, a quick response to investment spurts is more difficult because of higher levels of technology and capital intensity.

Turning now to the import dependency ratio: because our focus is on production activity, a simple ratio of import–domestic output is used. First, look at the column for the manufacturing total, which shows very small percentages that have a tendency to slightly decrease over a long term. Consumption is the major cause for this tendency. A small import ratio of consumption is common to all developing countries, but for Japan it is perhaps extreme. The long-sustained pattern of a traditional way of life may be the cause.[12] A more relevant aspect is the slight decline in the import–export ratio (M/X) shown in the bottom half of Table 2.8. Because of Japan's poor endowment of natural resources, the M/X ratio for total manufacturing trade became stable in the primary phase of industrialization. This factor continued to operate strongly even during the phase of secondary import substitution. Because of the required increase in the imports of fuels,

---

[12] Henry Rosovsky and Kazushi Ohkawa, "The Indigenous Components in the Modern Japanese Economy," in *Economic Development and Cultural Change*, Vol. IX, no. 1, part II (October 1960).

Table 2.8
Percentage Distribution by Use and Import Dependency of Manufactured Goods, 1905–1939   (%)

Periods	Consumption Goods	Producer Durables	Construction Materials	(Investment Goods)*	Intermediate Goods	Exports	Total
A. Distribution by Use							
1905–09	47.0	5.8	6.1	(11.9)	19.7	19.4	100.0
1910–14	41.2	7.7	6.1	(13.8)	23.6	21.4	100.0
1915–19	31.2	12.2	5.4	(17.6)	29.9	21.3	100.0
1920–24	39.8	8.2	5.7	(13.9)	28.7	17.6	100.0
1925–29	36.4	5.4	5.3	(10.7)	31.0	21.6	100.0
1930–34	34.7	6.7	4.6	(11.3)	34.5	19.8	100.0
1935–39	24.5	12.8	4.7	(17.5)	40.2	17.6	100.0
B. Import Production Ratio						Import/Export	
1905–09	6.9	40.1	20.0	(30.0)	40.7	71.8	15.2
1910–14	5.2	25.4	19.4	(22.9)	35.6	48.5	10.4
1915–19	2.6	7.3	21.9	(19.6)	21.1	43.3	9.9
1920–24	4.5	21.0	27.8	(23.7)	27.8	73.3	13.2
1925–29	2.8	27.4	23.3	(25.7)	24.5	54.6	11.9
1930–34	3.7	16.3	13.9	(15.3)	17.8	44.6	9.1
1935–39	2.7	7.7	9.2	(8.6)	12.2	45.9	8.2

Source: Yuichi Shionoya, "Patterns of Industrial Development," in Klein and Ohkawa, eds., *Economic Growth: The Japanese Experience Since the Meiji Era* (New Haven: Yale University Press, 1968). The original annual data are taken from the Japanese version of his paper, in Kazushi Ohkawa and Ryoshin Minami eds., *Kandai Nihon no Keizai Hatten* [Economic Development of Modern Japan], Appendix Tables 13 and 14 (in current prices), pp. 592–611.

Remarks: For the postwar years, the data are arranged by Shionoya for four years which correspond to Distribution by Use. In two-year percentage averages, they are as follows:

	Consumption Goods	Producer Durables	Construction Materials	(Investment Goods)*	Intermediate Goods	Exports
1951, 1955	23.5	6.6	5.1	(11.7)	55.8	9.0
1959, 1965	22.7	8.7	7.7	(16.4)	52.1	8.8

* Investment goods include producer durables and construction materials.

minerals, and food, substitution of manufactured imports was as urgent as export promotion.

Investment and intermediate imports were replaced by expansion of domestic production at a fast pace toward the 1930s, as discussed earlier using the industry approach. This pattern, together with the effects of "early start," characterizes Japan's case in the phase under review. Several points deserve note. First, the two phenomena occurred simultaneously, as is shown by import–production ratio (lower half of Table 2.8), although the difference in swing variations mentioned above manifests itself: what is characteristic to the investment spurts previously mentioned is the notably small percentage ratio in the spurt intervals (7.3% from 1915 to 1919 and 7.7% from 1935 to 1939 for producer durables). Second, the simultaneous increase in the import/ production ratio does not imply that the relative share in total imports of manufactured goods remained unchanged between producer durables and intermediate goods. Instead, the share of intermediate goods imports in total imports of manufactures tended to increase, whereas that of producer goods remained unchanged due to the increasing proportion of intermediate goods for use in domestic production. During the interval of the rapid proportional increase of intermediate goods, the share of intermediate goods increased from 50.1% from 1925 to 1929 to 71.3% between 1935 and 1939: the majority of imports became intermediate goods.

Demand Enhancement: Market and Nonmarket Activities

The above-mentioned historical facts are important for our understanding of the behavior and mechanism of secondary import substitution in general. Supply-production, demand-use, and price performance (output, production factors, and materials) all interact in complex ways. If stable performance is expected for all these, an econometric model approach would be useful to gauge the policy implications. However, as may be supposed from what has been stated earlier, the applicability of such an approach may be limited:

Between 1914 and 1919 European and later American suppliers were diverted from normal international trade. Toward the end of the 1930's the Japanese Government encouraged a policy of self-sufficiency, and some of the supplier countries were less and less anxious to ship manufactures to a potential enemy. For these reasons one could perhaps argue that both phases of rapid import substitution were the result of largely *ad hoc* circumstances. We cannot deny that these international disturbances may have been contributory causes both to import substitution and to investment spurts. But the point is that the investment spurts are historical facts—no doubt the combined results of endogenous and exogenous causes—and import substitution was one necessary aspect of a prolonged period of rapid growth.[13]

By adopting a strategic approach with respect to the endogenous causes, we will emphasize the importance of demand pertaining to the market mechanism through prices and then to nonmarket forces. For import substitution, it is a commonly accepted view that the possibility of increasing domestic demand is crucial, subject to the specific condition that the goods at issue are produced by industries not yet competitive. Therefore, their relative prices are kept higher than at the competitive level and protected from international competition by various measures such as policies of exchange rates or tariffs and quota systems depending on the circumstances of each country. The problem of increasing domestic demand is at issue in such a situation. Surely there is a certain limit for the gap between domestic prices and internal competitive prices.[14] Prices that are too high hamper domestic demand, whereas too low prices discourage domestic production, although nobody can really tell its precise optimum level, as noted in the preceding section. The reason for discussing this problem again here is to explain the significance of the operation of the nonmarket forces. Other things being equal, demand that stems from the nonmarket requirement would augment domestic demand and encourage the industry at issue without raising the output price to too high a level. Hence, not only the price-gap performance but also evaluation of nonmarket forces are at issue.

Let us first take up the price performance. As a long-term trend, the gap between the domestic price and international price (import price) of the goods at issue should be narrowed. Otherwise, a genuine process

---

[13] Kazushi Ohkawa and Henry Rosovsky, *Japanese Economic Growth: Trend Acceleration in the Twentieth Century* (Stanford: Stanford University Press, 1973), pp. 189–190.

[14] Discriminative measures taken for strategic goods such as tariffs and subsidies illustrate the limit of this gap—for example, a special tariff exemption for steel imports for the shipbuilding industry.

Japan's import tariffs were rather moderate in percentage of value. For example, in 1913 steel (pipes and tubes) was 20.3%, machine tools 14.3%, dynamos and electric motors 20.8%; in 1938, they were, in the same order, 8.0%, 1.6%, and 13.0% (*LTES*, Vol. 14, Table 21 in Part III, pp. 250–51).

A low tariff rate is desirable for the imports of technological goods, whereas a high tariff rate is preferred for protecting the domestic market. We share the view that both perhaps were set at moderate rates by compromise.

Table 2.9

Comparison of Selected Goods Prices: Domestic and Imports, 1913–1940 (1934–36 = 100)

	Domestic Prices			Import Prices[a]	
	Machine	Steel	Nonferrous Metals	Machine	Metals
1913	76.0	96.0	76.6	25.9	64.9
1919	154.1	382.6	96.3	84.3	192.0
1931	71.5	69.9	50.6	75.9	60.0
1936	100.5	102.0	106.9	102.1	102.9
1939	148.7	186.7	125.7	125.1	–
1913–1936 (1913 = 100)	185	152	143	392	158

Source: Domestic prices are from the Shinohara data, LTES, Vol. 10, Table 3 in Part III, pp. 148–49. Import prices are from LTES, Vol. 14, Foreign Trade and Balance of Payment, by I. Yamazawa and Y. Yamamoto, Table 6, Part III, pp. 198–99.

[a]Import prices of metals are not fully comparable.

of import substitution would not be realized. Table 2.9 presents some data for testing this proposition.

A direct comparison between 1913 and 1936 shows that the rate of increase in domestic prices is smaller than that of prices of imported goods for both machinery and metals, although the degree of gap narrowing is much faster for machinery. The indexes of 1919 and 1939 are inserted to indicate abnormal price behavior in the domestic market. Despite the reverse tendency during World War I and the latter part of the 1930s, the import–production ratio dropped sharply (see Table 2.8), creating a special phenomenon brought forth by nonmarket forces.

The prices of imported goods are affected no doubt by the changes in the exchange rate. Taking 1913 as the base year, the exchange rate was rather stable during between 1913 and 1931, but during the 1930s the yen devaluation had an effect on increasing the import prices. The gap-narrowing tendency was no doubt supported by yen devaluation.[15] The tendency toward gap narrowing is much weaker in case of metals, mainly steel and iron, so that its influence must have been crucial. In case of machinery this was not the case.

Turning to the demand aspect, first, with respect to the intermediate

[15] In terms of the yen-dollar rate, in 1913, 100 yen = 49.5 dollars, and this rate was largely kept until 1930. It was followed by a yen devaluation (100 yen = 28.9 – 25.9 dollars between 1932 and 1939). The purpose of the policy was balancing foreign payments, but it resulted in increasing the prices of imported goods.

Table 2.10
Investment Demand for Steel, 1908-1937

	Steel, Domestic Demand (SD) (thousand ton)	Gross Domestic Investment (I) (¥10 million)	SD/I (ton/¥1,000	Proportion of Government in PDE Investment (%)
1908-17	422	117	3.60	31.5
1913-22	743	132	5.64	30.3
1918-27	1,263	236	5.35	39.3
1923-32	1,753	218	8.04	50.4
1928-37	2,331	236	10.65	52.1
(1933-37)	3,850	334	11.46	48.7

Sources: SD, from I. Yamazawa, Nihon no Keizai Hatten to Kokusai Bungyo [Japan's Economic Development and International Trade] (Tokyo: Toyo Keizai Shimposha, 1984), Appendix Table 3-2, p. 250. I and PDE, from Ohkawa et al. data in LTES, Vol. 1, National Income, Appendix Table 21, pp. 220-21.

Remarks: SD is the sum of domestic production and imports minus exports. I is in real terms using investment goods price indices (1934-36 is the base year) and does not include inventory changes. Both are in annual amounts.

PDE = producer durable equipment.

goods, let us examine the case of steel. The figures listed in Table 2.8 suggest that the demand for steel might be less sensitive to investment swings, as is true for investment in the private sector. As will be explained in Lecture 5, government investment played an important role during downswings. We see the operation of the nonmarket forces on the demand for steel in infrastructure and military investment (see Table 2.10).

The associated overtime performance of the physical amount of steel demand (SD) and gross domestic fixed investment (I) is revealed in the ratio SD/I with its clear trend to increase. Military investment specifically estimated is included in I. The proportion of this component varies. For example, it is only 5.1 % in 1918 but is much greater in the latter part of the 1930s (28.3 % in 1937).

The changing proportion of major components, producer durable equipment, structures, and buildings cannot be separately discussed in relation to the steel demand. However, partial data can supplement our knowledge (see Table 2.11).

Table 2.11

Percentage of Steel Use by Sector, 1926–36

Periods	Railways	Structural building, Construction	Machinery	Oil-gas, Elec- tricity	Mining	Military
1926–31	17.6	29.4	24.1	2.4	2.2	15.5
1932–36	8.7	28.1	31.2	2.7	2.7	14.8

Source: Takafusa Nakamura, Senzenki Nihon keizai seichō no bunseki [Analysis of Prewar Japanese Economic Growth] (Tokyo: Iwanami Shoten, 1971), table 5–9, p. 158.

Machinery is often taken as the best indicator of steel demand, but the data suggest the infrastructure investment is even more important in dealing with steel demand. The relative importance seems to change according to the shift in industrialization phases. In this regard, the increase in the ratio SD/I is important. The problem of changes in the linkage between investment and intermediate goods in general can only be dealt with as input-output analysis over time, but the picture of the general trend of investment expenditure shows a strong increase in the intermediate goods proportion, as seen earlier in our approach by use.

As an indicator of the operation of nonmarket forces in the demand for producer durables (the last column of Table 2.10), the percentage proportion of government investment to total PDE (producer durable equipment) investment is presented. It is about 30% in the earlier periods, but increases to about 50% in the later period. This percentage of course includes military investment. The proportional increase is mostly a reflection of a decrease in PDE investment in the private sector. As will be discussed in detail in Lecture 5, investment activity by the government was particularly active in the downswing intervals, operating as a substantial influence on the demand in the stagnated market of producer durables and the machinery industry. Government investment has often been illustrated by the navy's support of the ship-building industry. Certainly in the latter part of the 1930s, movement toward military mobilization did have a great impact on the demand for machinery. Beyond these partial aspects, we want to point out that demand from public expenditures continued to be substantial in promoting the process of PDE import substitution.

We are not saying that the public investment expenditure was not price-conscious. Instead, the government was rather particularly concerned with prices as well as the quality of the goods to be purchased from the private sector. As noted earlier, domestic prices had a tendency to narrow the gap with import prices. The government function at least was not against this tendency in our rather conservative judgment.

Early Start: The Government's Function

We have concentrated on *ad hoc* factors, such as nonmarket forces, but now we wish to identify their sustained operation in general through the entire phase of secondary import substitution. In the context of the simultaneous process, this is a sharp contrast to the case of textile manufacture, which depended almost entirely on private-sector demand in the domestic market as well as in exports.

With respect to the role played by the public sector in Japan's process of secondary import substitution, evaluation differs among economists. We believe the differences may be much less for the demand aspect than for the supply-production aspect. Detailed discussion of the government's policy on industrial technology requires separate treatment, and our views will be presented in Lecture 7. As far as the present topic is concerned, the discussion briefly presented below is preliminary.

The government's Yawata steel mill was established with the help of foreign technicians at the turn of the century. This marked the real inauguration of modern steel production in Japan. However, since public business was limited, it took nine to ten years for the mill to reach the point of making a profit. We believe that Japan's capability of absorbing high-level foreign technology was lacking at that time. Through spending money from the government's general budget over a decade, how did it eventually become economically stable? The answer is essentially through attainment of two factors: one is technological, "learning by doing" through practical experience, and the other is economic, realization of economies of scale.[16]

This experience of both failure and success eloquently suggests the nature of the real problem in catching up in the production of intermediate goods, which requires high capital intensity. Let us discuss several major points.

First, the initial lead was taken by the government, because the lump sum capital investment required and the risk-bearing burden involved prevented the private sector from getting a head start. In the

---

[16] Akira Ono, "Borrowed Technology in Iron and Steel: Brazil, India and Japan," in Ohkawa and Ranis, eds., *Japan and the Developing Countries* (Oxford: Basil Blackwell, 1985).

early years of the primary phase, as we saw in Lecture 1, the Ministry of Industry inaugurated modern factories. The initial lead taken by the government was later transferred to the private sector. The government sustained the Yawata steel mill and even enlarged it twice (first from 1907 to 1909, and second between 1911 and 1916). Thus, the government took the lead in developing modern steel production, private enterprises followed, and total steel production started to increase even before World War I.

Second, regarding leadership and guidance in making technological advances, the government's lead also pertains to industrial policy and actually includes an aspect of technological advance. As a matter of fact, in the machinery industry, the ministries of railways and government factories for military production often were the leading users of imported modern technology. Through its inspection system, the government contributed to increasing quality levels, although its function was not all-encompassing. For example, in the case of the machine-tool industry, the real technological advances based on systematic standardization were realized as late as the end of the 1930s, although they started even before World War I.[17]

Let us discuss the points raised by the Yawata experience. First, there were difficulties the private sector encountered in transferring modern technology in the phase of secondary import substitution. The early start of heavy industry was directly led or indirectly encouraged by the government, as in the case of shipbuilding,[18] which of course had a strategic purpose. But viewed from the standpoint of technological advance, it implies that the problem was beyond the capability of the private sector. Today the government function is often called intervention in the market mechanism. Conceptually this term is usually used under the assumption that intervention is indispensable when there are certain "failures" in the operation of the market mechanism. The case at issue might be said to contain failures, if

[17] Yukihiko Kiyokawa and Shigeru Ishikawa, "The Significance of Standardization in the Development of the Machine-Tool Industry: The Cases of Japan and China," Discussion Paper Series No. 123, The Institute of Economic Research, Hitotsubashi University (April 1985). Also see discussion in the Appendix.

[18] The Shipbuilding Promotion Law enacted in 1896 was a strong decision by the government. The amount of subsidy was set to compensate for the difference in steel prices between Japan and the U. K. Even before 1896, modern shipbuilding was inaugurated by private enterprisers, and their initial efforts faced great difficulties. Therefore, "beyond the capability of the private sector" does not imply that initiative was entirely in the hand of the government. See Katsuo Otsuka, "Zosen-gyo no Gijutsu Sentaku" [Technology Choice in Shipbuilding], chapter 8 in Minami and Kiyokawa, eds., Nihon no Kogyo-ka to Gijutsu Hatten.

we define the market mechanism in the innovative sense of development (see also Lecture 7). Irrespective of definition, however, the point is that although actual government activities may differ according to the industry and technology concerned, it is inevitable if import substitution is to be completed within a certain time.

Two related points draw our attention. First, the learning-by-doing process needs a long time to be really effective in assimilating technologies of foreign origin for local production. Its effects cannot be expected merely as a function of time duration. This is especially so when we think about the necessity of making various devices to meet local requirements, as discussed previously for the textile industries. Second, for the phase of secondary import substitution in particular, the problem is beyond individual technologies and involves their accumulated process as a whole. This means a different aspect of the time dimension. In Japan's case, the early start eventually culminated around 1933 by reaching the point of crossing of two curves ($M = X$, the import-decreasing curve and export-increasing curve) with respect to steel and general machinery. However, its real shift to the next phase of secondary export substitution eventually began by the mid-1950s, when the exports of textiles were surpassed by those of the sum of machinery, metals, and chemicals. Such a long time can be shortened in the contemporary developing countries by what we call the "telescoping" process, yet tremendous efforts for technological advance are involved in this long process. The government function must be sustained and requires long-term decision-making. Japanese government policy actually was not necessarily systematic in this regard but rather was often affected by *ad hoc* causes and trial and error.

The final topic concerns the fast pace of decreasing Japan's import dependency. The import–production ratio of any product is determined by such factors as the initial conditions, typology, and country size. Therefore, a country's high or low ratio of producer durables cannot be evaluated simply as good or bad. The ratio of producer durables is a broad, long-term pattern. The ratio tends to increase during the primary phase and is followed by an almost unchanged level (say, 25% to 35% for contemporary developing economies). At a certain time it tends to decrease (import substitution), but the shape of this tendency is at issue. For Japan the turning point came early and was followed by a fast decline (see Table 2.8, import–production ratio).

To understand such performance, the function of the private sector is important. First, in relation to technological advance, such performance might retard the pace of transferring foreign advanced technologies. This is a legitimate question because producer durable equipment

(PDE) is a carrier of technological knowledge. With a low level of technological development, if a nationalistic policy or the like enforces import restrictions on PDE to promote local production, it would certainly retard technology transfer. For example, in the 1930s, prohibitive measures for automobile imports were taken by the government in Japan. However, in general, selective import activities of the private sector are often supported by a government's discriminative tariffs or other trade restrictions. High-quality PDE—an indispensable carrier of advanced technological knowledge—was selectively imported. For example, the import ratio of electric machinery is estimated to have been over 50% from 1910 to 1914 (see Table 2.8), and large, heavy dynamos were all imported (see Appendix).

Second, the use and selection of machinery seem to have been adapted to the local industrial organization. As discussed earlier, the manufacturing industry is organized into a large number of medium-sized and small establishments together with a few large, modern ones. The PDE used by the former firms was not necessarily of high quality. Low prices were their particular concern, and widespread use of second-hand machinery is a good illustration of their cost-cutting measures. Domestically produced machines are preferred by them because of their cheaper price even if the quality and standardization are inferior.

Third, unlike contemporary developing countries, consumer durables were not widespread in prewar Japan, although government policy was partly responsible, as in the case of automobiles mentioned earlier. Import substitution concentrated on PDE and made it easier to reduce the import ratio quickly. Today, a major part of production in many developing countries is consumer durables. This raises a problem beyond historical circumstances: what is the resource allocation between PDE and consumer durables? What is most relevant is the evaluation of increasing technological potential over the long run. In many developing countries the importance of PDE tends to be underestimated and high priority given to pursuing technological progress. Perhaps the performance of foreign direct investment is related, but a longer-term perspective on technological advance deserves more attention for local development strategies.

Concluding Remarks: The Telescoping Process
When the entire development process is considered in historical perspective, the relevance of the phenomenon of telescoping, which we discussed in Lecture 1, is particularly intensive for the phase of secondary import substitution. South Korea and Taiwan required a much shorter time than Japan to achieve the same phase of development; in other

words, Japan's long process was telescoped by Taiwan and South Korea.[19] This time dimension is essential to our phase approach.

If we consider that development began in 1885, Japan's primary phase took 34 years (1885–1919) to arrive at the first turning point: the 34 years can be divided into a first subphase of 15 years (1885–1900) and a second subphase of 19 years (1900–19). If we begin counting for Taiwan and South Korea in 1950, the primary phase is just 20 years (1950–70) for Taiwan and 19 years (1953–72) for South Korea. For Taiwan the first subphase covers 11 years (1951–62) and the second subphase 8 years (1962–70); the corresponding figures were 11 years (1953–64) and 8 years (1964–72) for South Korea. With respect to the particular phase of secondary import substitution, after passing through the turning point at the beginning of the 1970s, both South Korea and Taiwan sustained vigorous growth and now, some 15 years later, are at the threshold of the next phase of secondary export substitution, although it is still too early to say anything definitely on the duration of this phase. Nevertheless, it is absolutely clear that their time frames are much shorter than Japan's. As noted earlier, the phase of secondary import substitution covers some 40 years (1919–60) for Japan. This phase is being telescoped greatly, by at least one-half or even one-third, for South Korea and Taiwan.

Other data on such a telescoping process are available. As was noted in Lecture 1, section I, the rates of growth of industrial output and labor employment in Korea were much higher than for Japan. A similar performance is seen in agriculture; for example, the rate of increase in the rice yield is notable in recent years, and even tends to surpass Japan's level of yield, since a much longer time originally was required for Japan to create high-yielding varieties of rice. Recalling our comments about the simultaneous process, the effects of country size as well as of the different international environments on the pattern of international trade require careful qualification in estimating telescoping effects. The favorable postwar climate was a significant advantage for Taiwan and South Korea compared with Japan's situation in the interwar period. The function of the inflow of foreign resources though both public and private routes makes another important difference between the two cases.

Our concluding remarks are focused on two aspects: the qualification that must be made in order to interpret the cases of Taiwan and

---

[19] In Ohkawa's earlier papers, the process was called "compressed"; "telescoping" was first used in a joint paper with Fei and Ranis, "Economic Development in Historical Perspective," in Ohkawa and Ranis, eds., *Japan and the Developing Countries*.

South Korea and the essential property of the telescoping process in general. First, the performance of Taiwan and South Korea cannot be treated as representative of all developing economies in historical perspective. For these two cases, the given conditions as well as the policies selected were most favorable for accelerating the telescoping process. For industrializing Latin American countries such as Brazil, Mexico, and Argentina, which are postwar latecomers to development even though their industrialization began much earlier than that of the East Asian newly industrializing economies (NIEs), a prolonged phase of secondary import substitution—often with export promotion of producer durables—is a problem. The telescoping process has been realized widely by many contemporary developing countries, but the most important factor that prolongs the process is a greater rate of increase in the total population and labor force than that of industrialized countries (see Lecture 1, section I). The problem of individual countries must also take into account another important factor: the dissimilarity of typology and country size as well as policies. What we can say generally is that the telescoping process will be realized at different speeds.

Second, the essential element for such variance is found in the operation of each nation's capability for absorbing advanced technological knowledge from forerunners in industrialization. As we have discussed in some detail in this lecture, during Japan's prolonged phase of secondary import substitution we found no easy absorption of technological progress for catching up with advanced countries. Innovational process is always a struggle, but particularly for developing industries of producer durables and intermediate goods of higher quality. The struggle both in private and public activities appears greater in comparison with the development of light industries in the phase of primary export substitution. Generally speaking, borrowed technology can provide the basic incentive to the possibility of telescoping activity, because borrowing is more economical and quicker than original efforts to create new technologies. However, the process of assimilation is not automatic. In light of Japan's experience, the difficulties to be surmounted seem to be particularly great for completing the phase of secondary import substitution to shift the economy to the next phase of secondary export substitution. A wide range of variation could thus take place in realization of the possibility of telescoping among the developing economies, according to the different performance of upgrading social capability. This process will be further discussed in Lecture 6.

Appendix: Changes in the Composition of the Machinery Industry, 1909–40

This appendix attempts to briefly describe over-time changes in the composition of the machinery industry during the period covered in the text. This industry, treated as a sector-aggregate, is actually composed of a great number of subsectors (30 in the usual Manufacturing Survey). First, the performance of representative subsectors will be observed. Second, the conditions responsible for different performances over time, focusing on technological properties and government policy, will be examined.

The MITI data[20] are used to show the changes over time in the composition of the machinery industry by examining four years: 1909, 1919, 1930, and 1940 (see Table 2A. 1). The year 1909 is the start of the Manufacturing Survey (*KTH*). The year 1919 in essence demarcates the start of secondary import substitution. The interval (1909–19) shows the performance of the early start mentioned in the main text. The year 1930 is near the start of the second investment spurt, and 1940 is near its end. The changes in this period (1930–40) reveal the effects of military mobilization, while the preceding period presents the effects of a downswing in the economy.

Concentration in steel shipbuilding and in mining machinery and equipment is a feature of the period 1909 to 1919. The sum of the shares of the two is roughly 60% (58.7% in 1909 and 60.8% in 1919). The minor share of electric machinery and machine tools, along with railway equipment, increased slightly during World War I, but the basic compositional pattern was almost unchanged despite extraordinary progress in the import substitution of machineries. In evaluating the significance of the development of the machinery industry before 1919, the distorted composition maily by government policy is to be noted: "early start" implies this recognition.

The subsequent period (1919–30), representing an unfavorable downswing of the economy, is particularly important in three respects: the high rate of increase in the share of electric machinery, the appearance of textile machinery, and the disappearance of machine tools in the statistics. Because of the so-called electric revolution which took place in this period, the electric machinery subsector rapidly expanded to 10% of the output share of this sector, though the shipbuilding sub-

---

[20] *Kogyo Tokei Gojunen-shi* [Fifty-Year History of the Manufacturing Survey, 1909–1958], Ministry of International Trade and Industry, 1961.

Table 2A.1

Percentage Changes in the Prewar Composition of the Machinery Industry: Output Shares

	1909	1919	1930	1940
Miscellaneous machinery	4 (8.4)	6 (5.0)	7 (4.8)	1 (22.0)
Machine tools	7 (2.8)	4 (6.5)	–	2 (11.9)
Weapons[a]	–	–	–	3 (9.3)
Electric machinery equipment	8 (2.8)	7 (3.2)	2 (10.2)	4 (8.4)
Steel shipbuilding	1 (39.9)	1 (46.9)	1 (26.0)	5 (8.0)
Motor vehicles	–	8 (2.4)	3 (7.3)	6 (6.8)
Communications equipment[b]	–	–	6 (5.5)	7 (4.7)
Railway equipment	–	5 (5.0)	5 (5.6)	8 (4.6)
Prime movers	3 (13.9)	3 (6.5)	4 (6.2)	9 (3.7)
[Aircraft]	–	–	8 (3.5)	–
[Textile machinery]	–	–	9 (3.5)	–
[Mining machinery and equipment]	2 (19.8)	2 (13.9)	–	–
[Testing machines[c]]	5 (4.8)	9 (1.6)	–	–
[Weighing and measuring instruments]	6 (2.8)	–	–	–
Miscellaneous rolling stock	9 (2.6)	–	–	–
Subtotal	98.0	96.6	72.6	79.4
Total (incl. all others)	100.0	100.0	100.0	100.0

Source: MITI, KTH (1909–1958).

Remarks: The percentage share of gross output is in current prices; the number indicates the order of shares of each subsector (percentage share in parentheses). Until the ninth rank, a subsector is registered in each year; the order of subsector in the last column is that of 1940 and includes the addition of the bracketed subsectors, which do not appear in 1940. A blank (–) means the rank is under nine.

Notes: [a]Small arms, artilleries, and miscellaneous weapons.
     [b]Batteries and communications equipment.
     [c]Testing machines and physical and chemical instruments.

sector was still much larger (26%). This was a sign of a general trend of ameliorating the initial distortion by government policy. As discussed in Lecture 1, the textile industry was the major subsector carrying out primary export substitution by labor-intensive technology, but later the focus shifted to capital-intensive technology. The two coincide with the development of textile machinery, based on Toyota's technological invention among others. The machine tools sector disappeared in 1930. This may be surprising, as it ranked number four in 1919, but is symbolic of the performance of the machinery industry, whose import substitution activity was not entirely encouraged by government policy.

The compositional change in the final interval (1930–40) represents the strong effects of artificial reallocation of resources toward military mobilization not only for weapons also but for other resources that were encouraged by government policy. (Aircraft manufacture disappeared because of its shift to the state factory.) To enhance the technical capability of developing various subsectors of the machinery industry, military mobilization contributed a great deal. Its spillover effects on the postwar performance will be discussed in Lecture 4. The top-ranked subsector of miscellaneous machinery and second-ranked machine tools contributed to ameliorating the initial distortion of composition that was prolonged in this sector. For example, the subsector of machine tools made a fast recovery, actively responding to the Special Act (1938) that encouraged this subsector by tariffs and tax exemptions, special treatment of capital depreciation allowances, and other measures.

The second major aspect of our focus is technological properties of subsectors, relative to the role played by the government policy. The technological property of the machinery industry differs from the textile industry not in its higher capital intensity but in its higher quality of workers in general. Some economists as well as scholars of technology in Japan[21] have characterized this industry as a backward sector in technological advance. Latecomers to technology are of course economically and technologically backward; in this sense, this view is a tautology. Such an argument can only make sense in recognizing that relative backwardness is within a time frame, or development phase, as compared to a specific industry—say, the textile industry. The technological gap between Japan and more advanced countries was much wider, and there was less possibility and flexibility of modifying borrowed technology, in the machinery industry than in the textile industry. We believe this must be the basic viewpoint of examining technological properties of the subsectors composing the machinery industry.

---

[21] For example, Yoshiro Hoshino, *Nihon no Gijutsu Kakushin* [Technological Innovations in Japan] (Tokyo: Keiso Shobo, 1966).

If there were no government participation at all, the time sequence of development would follow inversely the magnitude of the gap of technological level. Such a highly simplified assumption of course would need a number of qualifications. The most important is the possibility of scale economies at the industrial base. Nevertheless, such an assumption could indicate the path of technology transfer through the market mechanism. In Japan, though, the role played by government intervention modified and even changed this natural order of time sequence.

A long-term pattern which can be seen in Table 2A.1 was a tendency from a distorted toward an evenly distributed composition. We cannot simply say that steel shipbuilding was most accessible in terms of its technological gap. However, the level of indigenous technology of wooden shipbuilding developed considerably, depending upon the manual skill of craftsmen. In the case of mining machinery, instead of technology being the driving force for mechanization, supplementary instruments and tools were the major technological products. Indigenous technological capability is supposed to be of significance, but in both cases early start was pushed by the government policy.

Toward ameliorating the original distortion, the later development of electric machinery may be representative of private activity, even though indirectly backed by the government. The leading local companies mostly adopted means of cooperation in obtaining capital and technology with foreign companies (joint ventures) with the particular aim of transferring foreign advanced technology efficiently. In general, almost all subsectors of the machinery industry depended upon the guidance of foreign experts directly or indirectly. But electric machinery illustrates a path of normal development based on realizing scale economies at the industry base (mass production). In the case of miscellaneous machinery, private activities were not directly supported and encouraged by government policy. Even so, this sector did proceed toward mass production.

The case of machine tools draws our final attention. Because of its greater technological gap, this subsector was backward despite the efforts of foreign experts. The government adopted a policy of importing machine tools of a higher technological quality by tariff discrimination rather than encouraging domestic production. This selective import policy can be found in other subsectors as well. As stated earlier, government policy is another important aspect of borrowing technology. Toward the 1940s this policy was changed because of military mobilization. The standardization system made speedy progress in implementing its upgraded technological level in domestic production.[22]

---

[22] For a history of the machine tools subsector, Toshiaki Chokki, *Nihon no Kosaku Kikai Kogyo no Hatten Katei no Bunseki* [Analysis of the Development of the Machine Tools Industry in Japan] (Tokyo, 1963). For a history of the machinery industry in general and selected subsectors, in Hiromi Arisawa, ed., *Gendai Nihon Sangyo Koza* [Modern Japan: Lectures on Industry] (Tokyo: Iwanami Shoten, 1960, 1961), Vol. IV [*Machinery Industry* I] and Vol. V [*Machinery Industry* II].

3

Technology, Productivity, and Employment:
From Secondary Import to Secondary Export Substitution

I. Economic Assessment of Technological Property

Secondary import substitution in Japan was not completed in the prewar period. The shift to this phase was postponed by World War II to the 1960s. Covering over 40 years, this prolonged phase was affected by the war in both acceleration and deceleration: acceleration by artificial mobilization of the economy toward drastic progress in industrialization, and deceleration by enormous war damages to the economy. Japan's example may be evaluated as distorted, and deriving a normal long-term perspective from it regarding industrial transformation and compositional changes in international trade throughout the secondary phase is difficult. Nevertheless, enhancement of the competitive power of industries is confirmed, particularly in the machinery sector, first domestically and then internationally, and is essential for any industry completing the secondary import substitution phase in a developing economy.

We believe that toward the latter part of the 1930s the domestic competitive power of such industries was established, though some differences remained among them. Lecture 3 will evaluate these industries at their postwar starting point, noting the signs or evidence for the shift to the next phase of secondary export substitution in subsequent years, and provide the historical background for Lecture 4, which will deal mainly with the phase of secondary export substitution.

Another reason for Lecture 3 is conceptual and methodological. In the preceding lecture, the importance of competition was stressed, but the approach was rudimentary, and coverage was limited to a few industries. Limited data did not allow us to directly apply our conceptual framework. In this lecture, competitive development of manufacturing subsectors at the two-digit level will be explored more thoroughly using simple but specific analytical measures. The central measure is what we call the factor-input ratio.

Although Japanese data are used, their potential contribution to providing useful facts is our aim. Our method is intended to be applied to the usual data of manufacturing surveys conducted in contemporary developing countries. Such an analysis can be used for upgrading subsector analysis to bridge macro sectoral and micro project approaches to development planning in developing countries. Analytical use of our data is subject to several qualifications. We should not expect perfect results; yet our approach will reveal a number of beneficial findings for policy-making and planning. Given the present lack of a systematic approach to sectoral and subsectoral allocation of resources, technological and scale-organizational properties of subsectors will be empirically clarified in detail for economists. Readers interested in the conceptual framework of our approach should concentrate on our criteria for selecting the industries and scale organization analyzed.

The results of our observations will reveal that in the early postwar years competition within the manufacturing industry developed largely in the private sector, with the monopolistic or oligopolistic market structures involved. This broad finding is an important confirmation that the subsectors at issue for the particular phase under review began with a competitive power gained in the prewar phase and used in the early postwar years. Particularly for the machinery industry, its superior competitive power compared with that of the textile industry appears to confirm a phase shift.

The Factor-Input Ratio

Technical examination of what is above outlined requires elaborate procedures using both technology and organization as factors. Industrial technology is not as flexible for factor substitution as is often assumed by theoretical models. Iron and steel manufacturing differs distinctly from textile production. Each industry has its own technological requirements that have an impact on the factor-input ratio—the ratio of wage bills to reproducible capital stock, hereafter referred to as FIR. Why competition is possible despite differences in technological requirements among subsectors is the first topic raised by FIR.

FIR is not entirely rigid. It is actually possible to change it in each subsector. In this regard, we will pay more attention than usual to the function of organizational change and selection by scale. Co-development of large- and small-scale enterprises by competitive choice of scale and technology will also be analyzed in the same framework.

Our focus will be on the relationship between productivity and employment and the resultant performance.

Two aspects make Lecture 3 a bridge between the prewar and postwar periods: first, the period covered resembles prewar economic performance; second, the years nearly coincide with postwar industrial performance at the beginning of the phase of secondary export substitution. Two years, 1957 and 1966, have been selected based on data from a Japanese governmental special manufacturing survey. As described earlier, between these two years a third investment spurt occurred, demarcating the second turning point. The level of real wages of unskilled labor went up, and the wage differentials between unskilled and skilled labor narrowed distinctly. These changes are reflected in the data for these two years.[1]

In discussions of industrial development, simple dichotomies such as light versus heavy, or capital-intensive compared with labor-intensive, are often used. Because of their broad applications and imprecise definitions, discussion based on these criteria often turns out not to be useful and is even misleading. For example, machinery manufacturing is often treated as a heavy industry together with petrochemicals, chemicals, and iron and steel. As we stated in Lecture 2, if we follow the usual definition of heavy industry as capital-intensive, it is a mistake to classify the machinery industry as heavy because its capital intensity is rather low and is similar to that of the textile industry. Yet the machinery industry is not a light industry either, since the level of labor quality expressed by wages is quite different: it is low in textiles and high in machinery. The latter might better be called an engineering industry to distinguish it from the so-called light industries.

The above example illustrates the problem and need for an appropriate industrial classification. To meet this requirement, we will use the term Lw/K (L: labor, w: wages, K: capital). Lw/K is an input ratio and can be used to represent the factor combination of production. Depending upon the purpose, the technological property of an industry can be indicated in such ways as knowledge-intensive rather than -extensive or in terms of raw materials used. Actually, technical specialists assess the technological properties of industries by technical coefficients, often called standard unit requirements, that cover not only capital and labor (skilled and unskilled) but also the raw materials and energy resources required. Therefore, a financial or economic evaluation of input combinations and technological properties can be

---

[1] The performance of FIR, in particular the comparison between the machinery and textile industries, will be tested by examining similar cases in India and Malaysia. Their performance is discussed in Appendix 2 to this lecture.

expressed in several ways, depending upon the purpose. The term Lw/K is one indicator that is convenient to use with data on capital intensity and wage rates.[2]

Before moving to the technical application of Lw/K, we should briefly explain its implications. It is often believed that capital intensification through industrial transformation (say, a shift from light to heavy industry) is an influential element of economic modernization. Technological progress is assumed to be almost synonymous with capital intensification (an increase of K/L). We think this assumption requires an important qualification. As a long-term trend, an increase of K/L is necessary, but at the same time, much more attention must be paid to the role played by labor. In any industry without an increase in the contribution of labor, sound technological progress cannot be made. The term Lw/K is a reflection of this basic fact to assess technological characteristics of industries. Although wages alone do not fully represent labor skills, they do indicate the quality differences in combination with capital among industries.

Subsector Classification

A manufacturing census or survey helps to classify subsectors, when capital stock data (physical assets) are fully available.

In 1957 the K/L of nonelectric industrial machinery was even lower than that of textiles, but in 1966 their levels were almost equal; however, the value of Lw/K shows a distinct difference: 1.31 vs. 0.56 in 1957 and 0.81 vs. 0.52 in 1966 (see Table 3.1). Such a different pattern is not exceptional, but rather common for the subsectors located in intermediate K/L level, since high capital intensity requires highly skilled technological labor. Therefore the high level of K/L for heavy industries in subsector group A is associated with the highest wage levels. The value of Lw/K is extremely low for this group.

Another extreme is found for traditional industries in subsector

---

[2] In the neoclassical approach, the quality of labor is indicated by labor augmentation, while the relation between K/L and w is treated by factor substitution. We do not deny factor substitution, but our approach is different. Substitution measures the degree of the K/L proportion responding to the changes in the relative prices of input factors. When wages become higher, K/L will be higher. However, this change takes place within the restraint of the technological property of each industry. K/L as measured by "wage unit" (cf. Joan Robinson) is K/Lw and seems the same as our notion, but our Lw/K is not for the analytical purpose of fixing the category of capital.

In the classical thought, Marx's category of the "organic composition of capital" can also be expressed by K/Lw. An ever-increasing tendency of K/Lw in capitalistic development was the core of his doctrine, but it ignores the differences of technological properties among industries.

Table 3.1

The Factor-Input Ratio in Manufacturing Subsectors: 1957 and 1966
(¥ 10,000 Average a Year)

Subsectors	1957			1966		
	K/L	w	Lw/K[a]	K/L	w	Lw/K[a]
A						
1. Petroleum	121	32	.26	882	76	.09
2. Chemicals	84	27	.32	230	65	.28
3. Steel	63	33	.35	272	62	.22
4. Pulp and Paper	56	22	.36	122	47	.38
5. Nonferrous Metals	48	28	.58	161	63	.39
B						
6. Transportation Machinery	30	28	1.01	110	58	.50
7. Electric Machinery	27	23	.79	69	48	.69
8. Food	24	15	.53	77	38	.49
9. Ceramics	23	18	.72	96	47	.49
10. Textiles	22	13	.56	61	32	.52
11. Printing	22	22	.99	54	53	.98
12. Rubber	21	17	.81	68	45	.66
13. Nonelectric Industrial Machinery	16	21	1.31	62	51	.81
14. Precision Machinery	15	21	1.37	47	45	.96
C						
15. Leathers	13	17	1.31	39	44	1.13
16. Metals	12	18	1.55	56	46	.82
17. Wood	9	13	1.29	50	35	.70
18. Furniture	7	14	1.72	44	38	.86
19. Clothes	5	11	1.79	25	27	1.04
Total Manufacturing	28.9	19	.62	91	46	.51

Source: See Appendix 1.

[a]The values of Lw/K do not necessarily correspond to those of w/(K/L) since K/L and w are rounded to nearest whole numbers.

group C. A combination of the lowest capital intensity and lowest wage level is indicated by the highest values of Lw/K in 1957.

Subsector group B is for intermediate industries. Both K/L and w are at an intermediate level, but the combination of the two terms varies greatly. Therefore, the level of Lw/K is not uniform but rather has a fairly wide range due to the strong influence of wages compared with heavy industry group A. Lw/K in subsector group B is high for machinery and printing but low for food, ceramics, textiles, and rubber in 1957. (The difference between the two subgroups becomes less clearcut in 1966, as will be discussed later.)

The significance of the intermediate range cannot be evaluated by the number of subsectors. It is dominant in labor employment, as illustrated by comparison of 1957 and 1966 data. The total labor force employed in manufacturing in 1966, according to the survey, is 10,840,000. The employment in the subsectors of the intermediate range is 6,700,000 or 62% of the total—a dominant proportion, of which the subgroup with the higher Lw/K (mainly the machinery industry) is 31.1% and the other subgroup (textiles, food, and others) is 30.9%. We believe that without comparing Lw/K, it is very difficult to grasp the process of structural transformation in the two subgroups.

Over-time changes can be observed only in a relative sense among groups. Between 1957 and 1966 a drastic change had taken place in the labor market: a shortage of unskilled labor supply created a faster increase in these workers' wages as compared with skilled labor wages. The survey wage data are averages for each subsector and do not precisely represent this phenomenon. Yet, looking at the figures in Table 3.1, in the nine years between 1957 and 1966, total manufacturing wages, taking 1957 as 100, increased to 227. On average it is 200 for heavy industry in subsector group A, 222 for high FIR and 244 for low FIR intermediate industries in group B, and 265 for traditional light industries in group C. As expected, the impact of wage increases was strongest for C, most moderate for A, and in between (depending on FIR) for B. In the same interval, K/L increased to 307 in 1966 for total manufacturing. On average, it is 386 for A (315 if an exceptional high of 729 for petrochemicals is excluded), 316 for high FIR industries and 334 for low FIR industries in B, and 491 for C.

The response of capital intensification by substitution is particularly noticeable for group C, while within groups of B it is hard to tell the difference. The pattern of FIR variance appears to be essentially unchanged.

With respect to the possible relevance of Japan's experience to contemporary developing countries during the development phase of flexible supplies of unskilled labor, the pattern of FIR variance among subsectors of manufacturing may be close to that of 1957, the data of which is used because of the lack of available data for the prewar period. The value of FIR is very high for traditional light industries. An important qualification is the machinery industry. In Japan's case, this industry started rather early and developed to a considerable extent in the late prewar period. Except for the electric machinery subsector, machinery industries in Japan were subsectors of relatively high FIR value in 1957. A similar or dissimilar pattern may be found for developing economies depending upon economic performance and industrial policies (see Appendix 2).

The average wage by subsector is an index of labor quality differences due to education, age, sex, and other factors. It is assumed that labor quality differences can be evaluated by the wages determined in the labor market. When a dualistic employment structure exists, however, workers of the same quality are paid lower wages in the traditional sector than in the modern sector. To that extent, the index is distorted, making the value of FIR lower than normal. The wage differentials by enterprise scale, not by industry, have been analyzed with special emphasis on trade unions to elucidate differences of labor quality due to education, age, and sex.[3] What follows is relevant to our present discussion. First, two kinds of wage differentials can be distinguished: one attached to the labor force and the other unattached. Second, for a case of surplus labor the attached wage differentials influence tends to be less than the unattached differentials. Between 1964 and 1967 the labor supply became much less flexible, and the wage differential among enterprises by scale appears to be more closely associated with differences in labor quality—that is, the attached property (subject to attributing part of the wage differential by age to the effects of trade union). Third, with respect to the labor quality index, the rate of increase is moderate to the effect of confirming the conventional view. Fourth, even for small-scale enterprises, the labor quality index tends to increase. For male workers, the rate of its increase is greater for small-scale than for large-scale enterprises.

These four points endorse the validity of our procedure of using average wage differentials to indicate the quality of labor, although with the noted qualifications. The last point seems particularly relevant to the performance of the machinery industry.

II. Productivity Assessment

Economic development implies a productivity increase, and a development plan aims at its realization on both the macro and sectoral levels. The problem is how to specify productivity. In most cases, we suppose, what is actually meant is labor productivity. In compiling development plans, for instance, based on this criterion, heavy industry is promoted

[3] See Akira Ono, "Rodo no Shitsu to Chingin Kakusa" [Quality of Labor and the Wage Differentials], chapter 11 in *Sengo Nihon no Chingin Kettei* [Wage Determination in Postwar Japan] (Tokyo: Toyo Keizai Shimposha, 1973).

for its high values in labor productivity. Enhancement of labor productivity is of course a basic objective of development, but another important and indispensable criterion, capital productivity, is not necessarily high for heavy industry.

Let Y stand for output, Y/L for labor productivity, and Y/K for capital productivity.[4] Modern industries of higher labor productivity (Y/L) are generally supposed to have also higher capital productivity (Y/K), but this is erroneous. As will be seen by industry comparison, there is a "trade-off" between Y/L and Y/K; industries with high Y/L tend to have low Y/K, while industries of high Y/K tend to have low Y/L. The objective of labor productivity enhancement should be to use more investment capital, the scarcest source in the development process, so that Y/K should not be lower in order to meet the efficiency criterion. Under this condition, the basic problem for planning is how to select appropriate industries to develop further. Productivity assessment based on past experience provides useful background knowledge for addressing this problem.

The output Y should be added value—the output net of intermediate inputs—because of the required consistency to be held between the sectoral and macro approach. Industrial economists often deal with the output gross of intermediate goods inputs, and this is also the conventional procedure adopted by project appraisal methods. Technical coefficients should be assessed in gross output. On the other hand, sector information should be coordinated with a macro approach. As a bridge between the two, we need an added-value ratio.[5]

Our primary concern here is capital productivity, Y/K, and its relation to the FIR, Lw/K. The reciprocal, K/Y, is the capital-output ratio. It is usually treated in its incremental form $\Delta K/\Delta Y$, which can be equivalent to $I/\Delta Y$ (I: investment), if capital replacement investment is duly taken into consideration.[6] Both Y/K and Lw/K are in relation to capital. The difference between them, that is, $\pi = Y/K - Lw/K$, is an indicator of the rate of return on physical fixed capital: added value or revenue (Y) minus labor costs (Lw). This is a simple approach, but it is convenient to use for subsector industrial comparison.

Another important term, Lw/Y, is labor's share: the share of com-

---

[4] Analytically, these values are partial productivity and, for agriculture, include land productivity. Total productivity is a weighted average of these values (see Lecture 1, section II).

[5] The ratio of added value to gross output is often called the income ratio because added value is equivalent to income in national income accounts. Manufacturing surveys in developing countries often lack added-value information, making it difficult to link a sector with a macro approach.

[6] The incremental capital-output ratio, $I/\Delta Y$, is discussed in detail in Lecture 5.

Table 3.2a
Productivity in Manufacturing Subsectors: 1957 and 1966

	1957				1966			
Subsectors	Y/L^a	Y/K	Lw/Y^b	π	Y/L^a	Y/K	Lw/Y^b	π
A								
1. Petroleum	154	1.27	20.8	1.01	415	.46	19.3	.37
2. Chemicals	97	1.15	27.9	.83	243	1.16	26.7	.88
3. Steel	90	1.44	37.1	.91	136	.50	50.0	.28
4. Pulp and Paper	66	1.18	31.1	.82	129	1.05	36.4	.67
5. Nonferrous Metals	96	1.99	28.8	1.14	191	1.20	36.0	.81
B								
6. Transportation Machinery	55	1.84	55.1	.83	157	1.43	36.7	.93
7. Electric Machinery	68	2.36	33.6	1.57	127	1.84	37.2	1.15
8. Food	48	1.97	26.4	1.44	113	1.47	33.6	.98
9. Ceramics	52	2.26	31.4	1.54	127	1.32	37.0	.83
10. Textiles	32	1.47	36.8	.91	72	1.18	44.1	.66
11. Printing	56	2.57	38.3	1.58	118	2.18	44.9	1.20
12. Rubber	58	2.74	29.4	1.93	116	1.71	38.9	1.05
13. Nonelectric Industrial Machinery	50	3.19	41.3	1.88	113	1.82	45.1	1.01
14. Precision Machinery	41	2.74	49.8	1.37	95	2.02	50.5	1.06
C								
15. Leathers	37	2.93	37.8	1.62	83	2.13	53.0	1.00
16. Metals	47	4.02	38.7	2.47	95	1.70	48.4	.88
17. Wood	30	3.33	38.9	2.04	79	1.58	44.3	.88
18. Furniture	25	3.71	46.5	1.99	71	1.61	53.5	.75
19. Clothes	25	5.04	35.7	3.25	59	2.36	49.2	1.32
Total Manufacturing	52	1.79	34.4	1.17	117	1.28	39.3	.77

Source: See Appendix 1.

ₐTen thousand yen per unit labor. Values of Y/L are rounded and do not exactly correspond to related terms.

^{b}Lw/Y is a percentage ($\alpha + \beta = 100$).

pensation for workers in the total added value produced. For simplicity, if we assume all output is distributed as income, Lw/Y is labor's income share. It is expressed as β as against α, the share of capital. It is easy to see $\pi = Y/K$ $(1-\beta)$ or $\alpha \cdot (Y/K)$ as $\alpha + \beta = 1$. In defining the rate of capital return, it is possible to replace Lw/K by Lw/Y, that is, β, in a conventional formula.[7] The pattern of β variance through industries in our formula is that when competition prevails between various industries, the rate of capital return, indicated by π, is expected to be near equal. If an industry's value of π is large, it will be more productive than the competitive level; if its π value is small, the industry will be less productive than the competitive level.

Sector Observations

Let us illustrate actual performance by comparing subsectors at the two-digit level (see Table 3.2a).

Y/L and Y/K in Table 3.2a appear to have an inverse association when subjected to simple average comparison (see Table 3.2b).

The inverse association in such a broad cross-sectoral observation implies historical trends: industrial transformation either from traditional to intermediate industries or from intermediate to heavy industries. A possible increase in the labor productivity can be realized with an accompanying decrease in capital productivity. If labor productivity increases sharply, there is a great restraint on further development, and technological progress can weaken this restraint (see Lecture 6). Regarding comparison between industries, the inverse associa-

Table 3.2b
Y/L and Y/K in Manufacturing Subsector Groups
(¥ 10,000 per unit labor)

Subsector	1957		1966	
	Y/L	Y/K	Y/L	Y/K
A	101	1.41	223	.88
B	51	2.35	120	1.66
C	33	3.81	78	1.88

[7] In neoclassical analysis, β (and α) is used as the basic term of defining the technological property of an industry: a larger β is labor-intensive and a smaller β is capital intensive. In Hicksi's definition, β is the ratio of marginal value product of labor to the average productivity of labor, Y/L. When β is used, it implies that the marginal value of labor is near equal to the prevailing wage rates in a competitive market.

FIR defines the technological property of industry solely by the input level, while the use of β defines it as an output-input ratio.

Table 3.2c
FIR in Subsector Group B

| | 1957 | | 1966 | |
| | | | (¥ 10,000 per unit labor) | |
Subsector	Y/L	Y/K	Y/L	Y/K
B_1	54	2.45	130	1.85
B_2	47	2.11	107	1.42

tion is a broad tendency, and a positive association between Y/L and Y/K is possible in a specific setting. By breaking down intermediate subsector group B into B_1 (greater FIR) and B_2 (smaller FIR), positive association is distinctly identified (Table 3.2c). Group B_1 shows higher values than Group B_2 for both labor and capital productivity.

There is a distinct relationship between the actual performance of Y/K and Lw/K in 1966 and in 1957 (see Figure 3.1), implying that the capital productivity or capital-output ratio is largely related to the technological properties of sectors. However, this is a broad tendency, and closer observation would clarify specific deviations: for example, in Figure 3.1 steel (3) and furniture (18) are distorted to the right, while electric machinery (7) and clothes (19) are distorted to the left. A specific analysis of each industry would clarify the reasons for these deviations.

Looking at the performance of Lw/Y (β) before moving to an explanation of the rate of capital return, π, let us assume that a perfect relationship between Y/K and Lw/K is a straight linear line. In this hypothetical case the ratio of the two terms Y/Lw (Y/K / Lw/K) would be constant for all manufacturing subsectors. Y/Lw would be reciprocal of Lw/Y or β (labor's income share) in this hypothetical world of constant β. The actual real deviation from this hypothetical case is not accidental but seems to have a broad regularity through subsectors. The value of β appears small for heavy industries (A), large for traditional industries (C), and in between for intermediate industries (B). It is 28.3 (A), 38.1 (B), and 39.5 (C) in 1957 and 33.7 (A), 41.5 (B), and 49.7 (C) in 1966. The significance of these deviations will be discussed in the section that follows.

The range of sector variance of π appears to be rather wide, ranging from 0.82 (pulp and paper) to 3.25 (clothes) in 1957 and from 0.28 (steel) to 1.32 (clothes) in 1966. However, a closer look reveals a broad tendency that π is small for A, great for C, and intermediate for B in both years.[8] These differences do not flatly indicate competitiveness

[8] Simple averages of π for these groups are A, 1.00; B_1, 1.45; B_2, 1.45; and C,

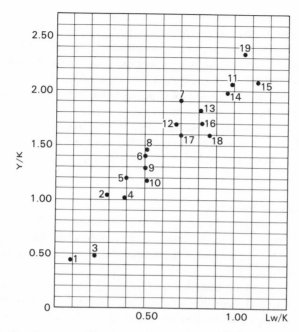

Figure 3.1
The Factor-Input Ratio (Lw/K) and Output-Capital Ratio (Y/K): 1966
Source: The numbers of the industries and the figures are from Tables 3.1 and 3.2.

and need cautious interpretation.

The numerical value of the rate of return on capital in our formula measures productivity with regard to fixed *reproducible* physical capital, excluding all other capital such as inventories, financial assets, and land. Often the evaluation of fixed physical assets (such as book value or assessment for taxation) is a considerable underestimation from the viewpoint of productivity. In our formula, fixed capital is evaluated by its reproducible value, which is not equivalent to capital's contribution to production.[9]

2.27 in 1957 compared with A, 68 (steel excluded); B_1, 107; B_2, 88; and C, 97 in 1966. Taking the average value of π for the total manufacturing (1.17 in 1957 and 0.77 in 1966) as 100, the group averages are A, 86; B_1, 124; B_2, 124; and C, 194 in 1957, compared with A, 89; B_1, 144; B_2, 115; and C, 126 in 1966.

[9] Whether to use gross or net value for capital depreciation, or consumption, is a controversial issue in any productivity approach. In applying such a subsector approach to the development process, we prefer a gross value because depreciation allowance estimates cannot be precise.

Another important difference is treatment of the depreciation of physical assets—especially equipment and structures. In our productivity approach, fixed reproducible physical capital is treated as as undepreciable. In an industrial comparison, however, when K is related to output (Y/K), depreciation is a problem. Surely a long time span decreases the value of Y/K; its value actually becomes lower in our data. Because of this decrease, a capital-output ratio is often criticized as misleading. Admittedly, this is a weak aspect of our approach, but, in our view, the use of the ratio can be justified if qualification is made not only for K but also for Y in combining Y/K with Lw/K.

Competition by Subsector

How do we interpret the actual measured values of π? The figures in the table appear to be distorted to a considerable extent: generally underestimated for subsector A and overestimated for subsector group C, especially for 1957.

If the data can be qualified and adjusted, the range of dispersion can be narrowed considerably, leaving only the adjustment for Y. Here we will examine the data to determine the degree of underestimation of Lw (overestimates of π) due to the mixed income sector. The degree of overestimation of capital will be discussed separately in Appendix 1.

Regarding our approach, a simple yet useful and realistic assumption is that mixed income earners compete with workers hired in the modern sectors. Their average income, Y/L, should be at least equal to the wage earners of a comparative qualification, although in a favorable or unfavorable situation it will be over or under the income of wage earners.

Such a procedure of dividing mixed income into wage compensation and return on capital requires an imputation to evaluate labor income or wage earnings for proprietors and unpaid family workers. If our imputation is successful, underestimates of Lw for subsector group C can be considerably reduced. The percentage of self-employed labor (proprietors and family workers) is actually large; in group C, it was 11.0 (leathers), 8.7 (metals), 11.6 (wood), 15.0 (furniture), and 12.9 (clothes) in 1966.[10]

---

[10] The imputation of average wages of family workers in the 1966 data for small-scale enterprises (one to nine workers) is applied by each subsector. This is one reason for the much narrower difference of the π index between group C and subsectors B$_1$ and B$_2$ in 1966 than in 1957.

We will assume that the rate of return on capital is equal between the corporate and unincorporated sector: an institutional classification in which the latter largely represents the mixed-income sector. The assumption implies that competition between the two sectors is possible only for total manufacturing with no subsector breakdown. Proprietors' average wage earnings for 1952, 1955, 1958, and 1961, when estimated as a residual, are around 10% higher than the average wages of workers hired in the corporate sector. (Family workers' wages are approximated by wages of hired workers in the unincorporated sector.) This percentage may shed some light on the actual competitive conditions prevailing in 1957 and 1966, when a relatively favorable economic situation kept proprietors' wages higher than those of regular workers, and indicates that the mixed-income sector in manufacturing was very competitive, and that overestimates of the rate of return on capital—specifically for subsector group C traditional light industries—can be adjusted considerably for underestimates of Lw.[11]

Thus far we have been concerned with identifying the competition prevailing among manufacturing subsectors. We believe competition is essential for the active operation of enterprises in a market economy. The value of π tends to be balanced through competition but un-

---

[11] Our estimates depend on the special data compiled by the Economic Research Institute of the Economic Planning Agency. For details see "Measurement and Decomposition of Relative Income Shares," in Kazushi Ohkawa and Henry Rosovsky, *Japanese Economic Growth: Trend Acceleration in the Twentieth Century* (Stanford: Stanford University Press, 1973).

An extreme case where Y/L=w in the mixed income sector is illustrated by our 1966 data. For small-scale enterprises (one to three workers) in group C industries on average, the output by worker (Y/L) is 42 (× 10,000 yen), and average wage of hired workers employed in the same subsectors (w) is 39. Thus Y/L is very close to w.

From the imputation, assuming competitive π for the unincorporated sector, we can estimate the following values of Lw for total manufacturing:

	Corporate Sector	Unincorporated Sector
1955 :	25.4 (100.0)	37.4 (147.3)
1961 :	24.8 (100.0)	58(2 (234.7)

The variance between the two years may appear large, but it is acceptable because of the drastic change in economic conditions during this interval. These values are estimated to have changed corresponding to big changes in the value of Y/K. An average of 190 in the unincorporated sector, taking the Lw corporate value as 100, can be used for 1957 with group C. If 15% of employment is assumed to be the mixed income sector, Lw underestimates may be around 29%. The π index of C, previously calculated as 227, would be corrected to be 161, which is much closer to 145, the π index of groups B_1 and B_2. If similar adjustment is made for 1966 (adjustment for family labor already having been made), the π index of 97 for C would be corrected to 87, a value close to that of B.

balanced by differentials of competitive power. Is it possible to identify the differentials of competitive power in the subsectors of manufacturing? Our data are limited for an answer to this question, but let us look at change over time, particularly for subsector group B_1. The π index was almost equal on the average for this subsector and B_2 in 1957, but B_1 became distinctly greater than B_2 in 1966. We surmise that B_1 (mostly the machinery industries) became relatively stronger in their competitive power among manufacturing industries. (The total factor productivity measurements to support this conjecture will be given in Lecture 4.)

The records in 1957 and 1966 for simple averages of B_1 and B_2 indicate that labor productivity changed from 100 to 241 for B_1 as against 228 for B_2, while capital productivity went from 100 to 75 for B_1 as against 69 for B_2. Changes in wages, as previously noted, were from 100 to 222 in B_1 and to 244 in B_2, a change also in favor of B_1. Evaluation of this data changes over time with the competitive power among subsectors in the domestic market. Between 1957 and 1966, output prices were relatively stable, but the range of changes among commodities varied. Generally, prices for A and B_1 industry products declined, product prices for C industries increased, and B_2 industry product prices rose and fell.[12] It is possible to compare the values of Y/K, π, and Y/L in Table 3.1 by deflating them with these indices. For example, the Y/K of petroleum would be 0.58 (instead of 0.46) in 1966, compared with 1.27 in 1957, and the Y/K of wood would be 1.09 (instead of 1.58) in 1966, compared with 3.33 in 1957. These deflated values are useful for interpreting the changes in the subsector distribution of π in Table 3.1 in two respects. First, the relatively small values of π for A subsector industries in 1966 are partially due to the decrease of output prices, reflected in a productivity increase on the supply side. Second, a similar situation exists for subsector group B_1 industries, but with a different implication. Their values of π are high, despite a low output price level, because B_1 industries had the most innovative process of advancing their efficiency and cutting production costs during this period. During the prewar phase of secondary import substitution, as

---

[12] Taking 1957 as 100, the wholesale price indices approximated for 1966 are as follows. Group A: 79 (petroleum), 84 (chemicals), 73 (steel), 99 (pulp and paper), 131 (nonferrous metals); B_1: 91 (transportation machinery, electric machinery, nonelectric industrial machinery, precision machinery); B_2: 101 (food), 109 (ceramics), 98 (textiles); C: 145 (wood). The total is 101. The data are from the wholesale price indices compiled by the Bank of Japan. The indices based on 1960 to 1966 are linked with the preceding indices. The price data are not available for the goods produced by these industries.

discussed in Lecture 2, development of the machinery industries was supported by high output prices. A shift from secondary import substitution to secondary export substitution requires the fulfillment of this important basic condition.

III. The Scale of Enterprises Approach

According to the classic doctrine of polarization, modern industrial enterprises will grow larger and larger in scale, in either their amount of capital or number of workers, leaving remaining labor unemployed or underemployed in the premodern enterprises small or tiny in scale; there will be no possibility of developing middle-scale enterprises. In light of the increasing employment problems in postwar developing economies, the importance of developing middle-scale enterprises along with further development of modern, large-scale technological enterprises has recently been recognized.

Japan's experience has often been referred to as a case study of success. It is true that Japan's manufacturing sector did not polarize: until the mid-1960s, the proportion of enterprises that were large, medium, and small in scale was almost unchanged.[13] How was this possible? Let us examine the actual performance.

Competition by Scale

Subsector assessment and enterprises of scale are related to a nation's industrial organization. Generally, subsector group A enterprises are large scale, group C enterprises are small scale, and group B_1 and B_2 enterprises are medium scale. However, let us observe the actual situation using 1966 data classified into four enterprise categories: large, medium, small, and very small (Table 3.3).

In group A, large-scale enterprises predominate, with the exception of paper and pulp, which is a mixed subsector, and decrease in scale from medium, to small, to very small. Among group B_1 industries, the distribution pattern appears to be similar to group A for rubber, transportation, and electric machineries, while others show a relatively even distribution pattern. For machinery the pattern is medium, small, very small, and large scale; the differences in scale are rather small. For Group B_2 industries there is a similar distribution pattern, although the proportion of large-scale enterprises differs among textiles, ceramics, and food. Group C industries show a distinct

---

[13] Kazushi Ohkawa and Mutsuo Tajima, "Small-Medium Scale Manufacturing Industry: A Comparative Study of Japan and Developing Nations," IDCJ Working Paper Series No. A-02 (1976).

Table 3.3
Scale Distribution in Manufacturing Subsectors: 1966

Scale	Very Small (1–19)	Small (20–99)	Medium (100–999)	Large (over 1,000)
Total Manufacturing (%)	25.2	23.4	23.5	27.9
Subsectors (%)				
A				
1. Petroleum	4.8	10.5	22.3	62.4
2. Chemicals	4.5	9.5	25.4	60.6
3. Steel	6.6	15.5	18.6	59.3
4. Pulp and Paper*	26.7	30.2	26.7	16.3
5. Nonferrous Metals	9.7	13.7	26.5	50.9
B				
6. Transportation Machinery	8.5	13.5	21.1	56.9
7. Electric Machinery	7.3	16.1	25.2	51.4
8. Food	40.2	23.6	24.2	12.0
9. Ceramics	26.6	25.8	29.0	18.6
10. Textiles	28.0	21.6	20.5	30.2
11. Printing	26.3	19.3	21.2	23.2
12. Rubber	9.6	16.5	19.0	54.9**
13. Nonelectric Industrial Machinery	20.4	27.4	32.6	19.6
14. Precision Machinery	21.1	26.4	31.7	20.8
C				
15. Leathers	49.4	29.7	13.8	7.1**
16. Metals	34.8	32.6	24.6	8.0
17. Wood	47.4	36.5	13.5	2.6
18. Furniture	48.4	30.2	16.1	5.3
19. Clothes	39.9	35.6	22.3	2.2

Source: See Appendix 1.
Notes: * Mixed sector values do not follow a normal scale distribution.
   ** Medium-scale enterprises of 500 to 999 workers are included.

pattern (from very small to large scale) in sharp contrast to that of group A. The sector distribution of workers in total manufacturing has a surprisingly uniform pattern among the four categories.[14] Let

[14] Output per worker (Y/L) increases with the scale of the enterprise. The same is true for capital output (K/L), though the difference is less distinct for K/L than for Y/L.

us now examine the performance of our key terms (Table 3.4).

For enterprises of small, medium, and large scale, K/L, Y/L, and Y/K show a close association with w and Lw/K, as expected from our previous analysis. A notable exception is the very small-scale range: as scale becomes larger, Y/L increases despite a decrease in K/L; Y/K also rises, against the normal tendency for enterprises in the small- to large-scale range.

Y/Lw, the reciprocal of β, tends to increase by scale (with the exception of enterprises with 555 to 999 workers), implying that the decrease FIR, of Lw/K, toward large-scale enterprises does not accompany a parallel decrease in the value of Y/K, but rather accompanies higher capital productivity.[15]

Table 3.4
Productivity of Manufacturing by Scale: 1966

Scale (workers)	K/L*	Y/L*	Y/K	w*	Lw/K	π	β(Lw/Y)	Y/Lw
Very Small								
(1–3)	48	39	.77	44	.90	.11	1.13	0.88
(4–9)	43	58	1.35	35	.81	.54	.60	1.66
(10–19)	42	74	1.76	37	.88	.88	.50	2.00
Small								
(20–29)	43	85	1.97	39	.91	1.05	.46	2.15
(30–49)	44	88	2.00	39	.88	1.12	.43	2.27
(50–99)	52	94	1.81	41	.79	1.02	.43	2.29
Medium								
(100–199)	62	105	1.69	43	.69	1.00	.41	2.49
(200–299)	72	119	1.65	45	.63	1.02	.38	2.62
(300–499)	90	130	1.44	48	.53	.91	.37	2.72
(500–999)	115	148	1.29	60	.52	.77	.41	2.46
Large (1,000 or more)	177	183	1.00	56	.32	.68	.31	3.12
Total Manufacturing	91	117	1.28	46	.51	.77	.39	2.50

Source: See Appendix 1.
* In units of ¥10,000.

[15] In Lecture 2 we used the equation $Y/K - Lw/K = \pi$, expressed also as (1) Y/K $(1 - Lw/Y) = \pi$ or (2) Lw/K $(Y/Lw - 1) = \pi$. Capital productivity, Y/K, is measured in (1) with Lw/Y (β)—labor's relative income share—while labor productivity, Y/Lw, is measured in (2) with the FIR value of Lw/K.

Now let us assess five manufacturing subsectors by scale (Table 3.5). The simple averages for enterprises of small, medium, and large scale show an increase in Y/Lw toward large-scale entereprises. Irregularity within the small and medium-scale enterprises appears to vary from one industry to another: the averages show that the decrease of FIR, Lw/K, toward large scale enterprises is largest in chemicals and smallest in machinery.[16]

Comparing these five subsector industries, the most notable feature is that π is almost unchanged for electric and nonelectric machinery enterprises (small, medium, and large scale) but decreases from small-scale to large-scale chemical and textile enterprises. The contrast in π between textiles and nonelectric industrial machinery subsectors stems not from lesser Lw/K but from greater Y/Lw, illustrating the scale characteristics of these industries. The dynamic performance of machinery industries pointed out earlier is also supported by scale values.

It is generally assumed that technological innovation is realized first in large-scale enterprises and then spreads to medium- and small-scale enterprises. Innovation stems from different levels of entrepreneurial capability such as long-term planning, technical and managerial personnel skills, financial power, and risk management. However, as technological innovation spreads to medium- and small-scale enterprises, scale distribution often will be changed as a result of by new or improved technology.

Two subcategories of manufacturing will emerge: one progressive and the other recessive in innovation. The scale performance for the rate of capital return, π, will either increase (such as for machinery, which represents a progressive category) or decrease (such as for textiles, a recessive category). The importance of competition is thus both by industry and by scale. We believe these assumptions are acceptable and of great significance; their validity can be tested by linking a scale analysis with the innovative process of developing economies at any phase (see Lecture 4).

Very Small-scale Enterprises and Employment Distribution
The first topic is very small-scale enterprises, the majority of which are in manufacturing subsector group C. Very small-scale enterprises are not the same as cottage industries. They include unincorporated (mixed-income) enterprises and very small-scale corporate enterprises. The criteria for distinguishing very small-scale enterprises from small-

---

[16] Y/Lw, unlike Lw/K and hence π, does not need qualification for capital value distortion when assessing scale performance of FIR.

Table 3.5
Economic Performance and Enterprise Scale: Five Manufacturing
Subsectors, 1966

Scale (workers)	Y/K	Lw/K	π	Y/Lw	Y/K	Lw/K	π	Y/Lw
Small	Chemical				Electric Machinery			
(20–29)	2.06	.83	1.23	2.48	2.51	1.34	1.14	1.88
(30–49)	2.45	.83	1.62	2.96	2.33	1.18	1.15	1.99
(50–99)	1.80	.60	1.20	3.00	2.50	1.12	1.38	2.23
Average	2.10	.75	1.35	2.81	2.45	1.21	1.23	2.03
Medium								
(100–199)	1.59	.49	1.10	3.25	2.22	1.22	1.00	1.91
(200–299)	1.92	.50	1.42	3.84	2.08	1.08	1.00	1.93
(300–499)	1.21	.32	.89	3.78	2.02	1.00	1.02	2.06
(500–999)	1.34	.33	1.01	4.06	1.94	.97	.97	2.49
Average	1.51	.41	1.10	3.73	2.07	1.07	1.00	2.09
Large								
(1,000 or more)	.93	.23	.70	4.04	1.75	.55	1.20	3.18
Small	Nonelectric Industrial Machinery				Textiles			
(20–29)	1.80	.92	.91	1.99	1.71	.76	.96	2.25
(30–49)	1.87	.94	.93	1.99	1.83	.78	1.05	2.34
(50–99)	1.78	.84	.94	2.12	1.56	.68	.88	2.29
Average	1.83	.90	.93	2.03	1.70	.74	.96	2.29
Medium								
(100–199)	1.80	.85	.95	2.12	1.36	.61	.75	2.23
(200–299)	1.56	.74	.81	2.10	1.48	.58	.90	2.55
(300–499)	1.84	.77	1.07	2.39	1.x2	.49	.63	2.29
(500–999)	1.73	.70	1.03	2.47	1.06	.48	.58	2.21
Average	1.73	.77	.97	2.27	1.25	.54	.72	2.32
Large								
(1,000 or more)	1.55	.53	1.02	2.97	1.04	.41	.63	2.53
Small	Wood							
(20–29)	1.74	.48	.90	2.07				
(30–49)	2.02	.80	1.12	2.52				
(50–99)	1.85	.81	1.04	2.28				
Average	1.87	.82	1.05	2.29				
Medium								
(100–199)	1.72	.62	1.10	2.77				
(200–299)	1.34	.53	.81	2.53				
(300–499)	3.42	1.12	2.30	3.05				
(500–999)	1.60	.58	1.02	2.76				
Average	2.02	.71	1.31	2.29				
Large								
(1,000 or more)	1.59	.41	1.18	3.88				

Source: See Appendix 1.

scale enterprises are the performance differences of our key terms (Table 3.4).

Statistically, in the very small-scale range, greater adjustment for possible overestimates of capital (for instance, joint use of physical assets with household consumption) is needed as the number of workers decreases. Y/K decreases and Lw/K increases. The decline of Y/Lw is reversed: for the very small-scale range, diseconomies prevail toward the smallest scale.[17]

The contribution to enlarging employment is of course recognized for the very small-scale range, as a residue of underemployment is unavoidable. But regarding productivity, the policy implication is obvious. Industrial policy in developing nations should take into consideration an optimum scale toward the small-scale range. For that purpose, finding the kink point in the Y/K curve by subsector is important and useful.[18]

The second topic is the performance of labor employment distribution by subsector and its relation to the differential level of FIR. The scale distribution of labor employment in manufacturing is fairly even. However, regarding employment distribution by scale, there are distinct variances by subsector. Since their patterns are regular, they can be classified into four groups (Table 3.6).

The patterns in scale distribution of employment shares are as follows: group A, a straight decline from large scale to very small scale without exception; group B, a straight decline from medium scale to very small scale with the smallest share of large scale (with the exception of ceramics); group C, a straight increase from large scale to very small scale (with the exception of food); group D, a mixed pattern.

It is worthwhile noting that the groups appear to broadly coincide with the manufacturing subsectors classified earlier by Lw/K (A, B_1, B_2, C), but deviations are noteworthy. (For instance, comparing the values of Lw/K, transportation machinery (0.50) and electric machinery (0.69) are included in subsector group A, machinery (0.81) and precision machinery (0.96) in group B, and food (0.49) and wood (0.70) in group C.)

We believe that the FIR value is a primary determinant for group

---

[17] The imputation for the self-employed may be overestimated, resulting in a greater value of β over unity and a negative value of π.

[18] The kink point of the Y/K scale curve in the 1957 data is 30 to 49 workers for total manufacturing; the subsector distribution is (1) 50 to 90 workers: wood and nonferrous; (2) 30 to 49 workers: food, textiles, clothes, furniture, metals, nonelectric industrial machinery, and precision machinery; (3) 10 to 29 workers: petroleum, chemicals, pulp and paper, steel, printing, rubber, ceramics, transportation machinery, electric machinery, and leathers.

Table 3.6
Proportion of Scale Distribution of Employment in Manufacturing Groups: 1966

Scale (no. of workers)	Group A (3.2 million workers)						
	Petro-leum	Chemi-cals	Steel	Trans-porta-tion Ma-chinery	Elec-tric Ma-chinery	Rubber	Non-ferrous Metals
S' (1–19)	4.8	4.5	6.6	8.5	7.3	9.6	8.9
S (20–99)	10.5	9.5	15.5	13.5	16.1	16.5	13.7
M (100–999)	22.3	25.4	18.6	21.1	25.2	19.0	26.5
L (1,000+)	62.4	60.6	59.3	56.9	51.4	54.9	50.9
Total	100.0	100.0	100.0	100.0	100.0	100.0	100.0

Scale (no. of workers)	Group B (2.3 million workers)			
	Nonelectric Industrial Machinery	Precision Machinery	Metals	Ceramics
S' (1–19)	20.4	21.1	24.8	26.6
S (20–99)	26.4	26.4	32.6	25.8
M (100–199)	33.6	31.6	34.6	29.0
L (1,000+)	19.6	20.8	8.0	18.6
Total	100.0	100.0	100.0	100.0

Scale (no. of workers)	Group C (2.4 million workers)				
	Food	Wood	Leather	Furniture	Clothes
S' (1–19)	40.2	48.4	49.4	48.4	39.9
S (20–99)	23.6	30.2	29.7	30.2	35.6
M (100–999)	24.2	16.1	13.8*	16.1	22.3
L (1,000+)	12.0	5.3	7.1*	5.3	2.2
Total	100.0	100.0	100.0	100.0	100.0

Scale (no. of workers)	Group D (2.4 million workers)			
	Pulp and Paper	Printing	Textiles	Total Manufacturing
S' (1–19)	26.8	26.3	28.0	25.2
S (20–99)	30.2	29.3	21.3	23.4
M (100–999)	26.7	21.2	20.2	23.5
L (1,000+)	16.3	23.2	30.2	27.9
Total	100.0	100.0	100.0	100.0

Source: Motai and Ohkawa, "Small-scale Industries," IDCJ Working Paper Series No. 11 (1978, Appendix Table 3. (For original data, see Appendix 1.)

Remarks: Scale (S', S, M, L) is the same as for Table 3.3. S' stands for "very small."

* Scale X (500–999) in the original data is included in L, not in M.

or subsector classification, but a secondary determinant may be modern innovative technology compared with traditional production processes. Transportation and electric machinery, as technologically progressive industries, have a larger share of employment for large-scale enterprises, although their FIR is relatively small. Nonelectric industrial machinery and precision machinery show a similar phenomenon in the medium- and small-scale range. Group C is characterized by the largest share of very small-scale and small-scale enterprises that use traditional production processes. Thus the scale distribution patterns of subsectors conform with the characterization by the innovative process discussed earlier.

Concluding Remarks

First, our analysis indirectly revealed the characteristics of the postwar investment spurt: the import dependency of PDE (producer durable equipment) decreased to a minimum (less than 10%) by a speedy expansion of domestic machinery industry and contributed to realizing the second turning point in the basic structure of the labor market.

For the first investment spurt, two roles were played by different industries: PDE import substitution was carried out by the machinery industry, but the major role of enhancing demand for labor was played not by machinery but by other sectors (primarily textiles). Increased demand for labor by the machinery industry became possible by enhancement for PDE through investment spurts, and the investment climb was sustained by lowering the level of the resource gap. Such an analysis, extended technically, clarifies the background for a final phase shift in Japan.

Regarding the possible performance of subsectors manufacturing in contemporary developing economies, research[19] indicates that the framework and method used in this lecture can usefully be applied. Some developing nations show economic patterns similar to Japan's; however, with regard to observation by scale, irregularity often interrupts identification of patterns of key terms such as Y/K and π. Regarding the subsector approach, available data are very limited at present, and further surveys and analyses are needed. We do not

---

[19] For example, for Asia (nine countries), see Mutsuo Tajima, "Small-Medium Scale Manufacturing Industry: A Comparative Study of Japan and Developing Nations," IDCJ Working Paper Series No. A-08 (1978); and for Latin America (six countries), see ECLA and IDCJ, *Towards New Forms of Economic Cooperation between Latin America and Japan* (Tokyo: IDCJ, 1980).

expect a similar performance of key terms as found for Japan. The effects of telescoping, for instance, may change the pattern.

Because of the importance of increasing employment through the development of manufacturing, the growth of medium- and small-scale industries should be encouraged. A subsector approach for very small-scale enterprises is indispensable to provide useful data for employment policies. Japan's success in developing medium- and small-scale industries by appropriate policies had two effects.

First, industrial policies—especially with government support—helped them survive and develop in market competition.[20] The essential element was the diffusion of technology appropriate for these industries. Second, technological innovation enhanced labor employment, as illustrated by the machinery industry, although very small-scale enterprises continued to sustain a quarter of total manufacturing employment at the bottom.

Appendix 1:   The Basic Data

The basic data for both 1957 and 1966 are from the Ministry of International Trade and Industry's *Chusho Kigyo Sogo Kihon Chosa* [Basic Survey of Medium- and Small-scale Enterprises]. In using these data for Tables 3.1 to 3.5, we depended heavily on the book *Shihon Kozo to Kigyo Kakusa* [Capital Structure and Enterprise Differentials], Study Series No. 6, Economic Research Institute Economic Planning Agency (1960) and on Kazushi Ohkawa and Shokichi Motai, "Small-scale Industries: A Study on Japan's 1966 Manufacturing Census," IDCJ Working Paper Series No. 11 (1978)—particularly the appendix statistical tables for 1966.

The survey cited above contains the best data for our analysis because of its wide coverage, detailed information for measuring analytical terms, and comparison over an interval of nearly ten years. Our focus was on medium- and small-scale enterprises, but the survey includes information on all enterprises of smaller scale: a census on enterprises employing more than 100 workers and a survey for other smaller enterprises based on a random sampling by industry and scale classification. The largest-scale industries included are those employing more than 1,000 workers. The survey gives data on the following factors:

[20] Kazushi Ohkawa and Mutsuo Tajima, "Small-Medium Scale Manufacturing Industry: A Comparative Study of Japan and Developing Nations."

Scope of capital:
Tangible, fixed assets (machinery, equipment), including structures and buildings. Inventories are not included.

Valuation of capital:
The standard assessment value for taxation. A special method of reproduction pricing is applied for buildings.

Wages:
Salaries of executives are included, excluding bonuses, in total average. Welfare expenditures are excluded.

Workers employed:
Total regular workers and family workers as well as executives and proprietors are included. Employment is the average for 12 months at the end of each year.

Unit of survey:
For enterprises with more than two establishments, special arrangements are made in sampling.

Added value:
The usual definition of gross of capital depreciation is used. For actual estimates, the added value equals the value proceed minus expenditures for raw materials and energy resources; the value proceed equals the value of sold manufactured goods plus wage revenue for processing plus revenue for maintenance.

Note that general administrative expenses and a part of selling expenses are included in these factors.

Remarks on Distortions of Capital Value Estimates
In statistical analysis, possible overevaluation of capital for large-scale enterprises may be caused by either capital evaluation distortion or the scope of capital. To redress the former, inasmuch as direct reevaluation is impossible, indirect judgment is made by a comparison of two surveys: the 1955 National Wealth Survey and the 1957 Corporate Enterprise Survey.[21] The method of capital evaluation is acceptable in the 1955 survey, but is not duly evaluated in the 1957 survey, nor is it in our data. The distortion is judged to be relatively larger for bigger-scale enterprises: roughly 5 to 10% for 300-to-499-worker enterprises and

---

[21] Capital valuation of the surveys in 1955 and 1957 is as follows: in 1955 it is based on the acquisition price registered by enterprises at the time of the survey, and the repurchasable price in 1955 is uniformly estimated by price series; the 1957 data are less reliable for uniformity among enterprises, but appear closer to the *Chosho Kigyo* than do the 1955 survey data. Reevaluation for price changes is unsatisfactory for both the *Chosho Kigo* survey and the 1957 survey.

Table 3A.1
Economic Performance and Scale: Chemical Industry, 1966

Scale	Y/K	$-(Lw/K)$	π
Medium	1.51	$-.41$	1.10
Large	.93	$-.23$	.70
Difference	$-.58$	$+.18$	$-.40$

Source: The same as for Table 3.5.

10 to 15% for enterprises of 500 to 999 workers and those with 1,000 or more workers. With respect to scope coverage, the ratio of fixed capital to the total physical capital, including inventories, provided by the 1955 survey presents fairly constant figures for a wide range, covering the entire medium-scale range in our scale classification: the average total/fixed capital ratio seems to be around 1.70 for the medium scale and 1.60 for the large-scale range. Since the value of π represents fixed capital, there is a 10% difference between our approach and the total capital approach.[22]

The problems stemming from a conceptual difference cannot be answered by numerical estimates, but we know its effects are most serious for group A industries in which equipment of long service life is dominant, particularly in large-scale enterprises. Actually, the small value of Y/K and π of the largest scale (1,000 or more workers) is most prevalent in petroleum, chemical, and steel industries. If their output, Y, is adjusted to be comparable to other cases by the equivalent production time, instead of an annual approach, Y/K would be considerably larger, as illustrated in Table 3A.1.

To make π equivalent, Y/K would need to be raised by 0.40, to 1.33. In other words, if its capital is usable 43 percent longer than medium scale π would be the same for the two. This increase seems to be not unrealistic. Note that the adjustment should be just for Y/K, but the effect of the FIR should also be counted.

We assume that if these qualifications are made for the data on individual industries, the competitive power of large-scale, heavy industries will be evaluated appropriately. If the general suggestion for adjusting capital evaluation and scope can be applied for subsectors by scale as well, the situation of these enterprises may even be beyond merely competitive.

---

[22] It is possible (or maybe better) to include inventories in our formula without making exceptions for a productivity approach, if the data are available.

Appendix 2: Factor Input Ratio of Manufacturing: India and Malaysia

The technological property of the machinery industry in comparison with the textile industry in Japan exists for other contemporary developing economies. Because of limited availability of capital stock data, a test is possible only for a small number of countries. K/L, w, and Lw/K data for 1981 will be examined for India and Malaysia.[23]

Table 3A.2
Factor-Input Ratio of Manufacturing: India and Malaysia, 1981

Subsectors	India			Malaysia		
	K/L	w	Lw/K	K/L	w	Lw/K
A						
1. Petroleum	144	13	0.09	180	18	0.10
2. Chemicals	83	13	0.16	28	7	0.25
3. Steel	88	12	0.14	41	9	0.23
4. Pulp and Paper	61	10	0.16	17	4	0.25
5. Nonferrous Metals	90	13	0.15	30	8	0.25
B						
6. Transportation Machinery	30	13	0.43	22	7	0.32
7. Electric Machinery	25	13	0.50	11	5	0.42
8. Food	10	3	0.33	31	5	0.15
9. Ceramics	25	6	0.26	31	5	0.15
10. Textiles	13	8	0.64	17	5	0.27
11. Printing	14	3	0.25	13	6	0.43
12. Rubber	28	9	0.34	20	4	0.22
13. Nonelectric Industrial Machinery	23	12	0.50	11	5	0.48
14. Precision Machinery	24	10	0.40	12	6	0.49
C						
15. Leathers	13	7	0.55	8	3	0.39
16. Metals	15	9	0.60	12	5	0.37
17. Wood	8	4	0.50	14	5	0.36
18. Furniture	12	6	0.54	5	3	0.67
19. Clothes	11	7	0.62	4	3	0.74
Total Manufacturing	45	9	0.20	18	5	0.27

Remarks: K/L, physical fixed capital stock per worker in Rs (thousand) for India and in M$ (thousand) for Malaysia.

[23] India, Central Statistical Department, Annual Industrial Survey (1981–82), Factory Sector; Malaysia, Department of Statistics, Industrial Survey (1981).

Despite such differences as the phase of industrialization, the enterprise distribution between public and private sectors, and the coverage by scale, our approach appears valid though with some dissimilarities (Table 3A.2).

First, in the broadest comparison, the four sectors of machinery industry all rank in group B. The level of capital-intensity, K/L, of the machinery industry is intermediate: higher than the traditional industries (mostly group C), but lower than the heavy industries (group A). The wage differentials among subsectors in India and Malaysia are broadly similar to Japan: the wage level of machinery subsectors is also intermediate, though in the case of India it is closer to that of group A. The value of FIR, Lw/K, in the machinery industry is intermediate.

Second, a direct comparison of nonelectric industrial machinery with textiles shows a pattern similar to that of Japan: Lw/K of nonelectric industrial machinery is higher than textiles in Malaysia (0.48 versus 0.27), but is reversed in India (0.50 versus 0.64). We believe that the especially low value of K/L for textiles in India may be the major factor for reversing what we think is a normal pattern represented by Malaysia and Japan. Among group B industries in India, the K/L of textiles and food processing is exceptionally small (close to the level of group C), perhaps owing to the delay in the modernization of these industries.

Third, Malaysia, though broadly interpreted as having a normal pattern of development, would require further examination of wages. Wage levels of machinery subsectors—in particular electric machinery—appear lower than expected. If female workers are employed for simple parts production, lower wages are understandable. Partial information suggests that this is the reason, but no data are available to confirm it.

Lecture 4

Completing Development:
The Phase of Secondary Export Substitution

I. The Problem and a Framework for Approaching It

If the phase of secondary import substitution is successful, it will lead to the final phase, which we label secondary export substitution. Domestic production of capital goods, intermediate goods, and consumer durables will eventually become internationally competitive, and the production of nondurable consumer goods, such as textiles, will become less competitive. Export substitution will eventually occur through shifting the comparative advantages of the two categories of industries. The conditions involved in this process are determined not only by a country's local situation but also by its place in the international environment. Examination of Japan's secondary export substitution phase is useful to identify the basic factors responsible for its performance from the beginning of the 1960s to the mid-1970s.[1]

Technological-Organizational Progress and Factor Prices

The phase of secondary import substitution in Japan appeared completed toward the end of the prewar period, and export substitution began after postwar reconstruction in the 1950s. A closer look, however, reveals that during the 1950s textiles still were the major export: machinery exports would surpass those of textiles in 1961. A decade later, in 1971, machinery exports were 50% of the total exports of manufactured goods, while textiles were only 11%. During the 1970s, the substitution process continued; in 1980 the export proportions were

---

[1] This phase in its full range is found only for postwar Japan. A rapid increase in exports of machineries (automobiles in particular) and steel from the newly industrializing countries has been noteworthy in recent years, but these countries are still either at the threshold of development or else partway along the road to fuller industrialization. A detailed explanation for the dating is in Appendix 2 to this lecture.

118

63 % for machinery and 19 % for metals and chemicals: together they composed 82 % of total merchandise exports (textiles were only 4 %).

The 1970s were an important interval in Japan's development and marked a basic change in the structure of an economy moving toward completion of the process of development, although the importance of manufacturing to macroeconomic growth did not decrease as expected for developed economies. The rate of GDP growth decreased (from 10.5 % in the 1960s to 5.8 % in the 1970s); proportion of fixed investment to GNP decreased (from 35.1 % in 1971 to 30.6 % in 1981); and proportion of exports of GNP increased (from 11.5 % in 1971 to 15.4 % in 1981). The preceding decade of the 1960s featured the postwar investment spurt and its aftermath, particularly inflationary growth caused by the government's expansion policy. During the 1970s Japan's economy faced difficult problems in adjusting to two oil-price increases, in 1973 and 1978.

During this complicated series of events secondary export substitution was completed. The basic factors that can be relevant to contemporary developing economies at present and in the future, in our view, are essentially two: one is the possibility of technological-organizational progress; the other, an increase in wage levels due to basic changes in the structure of the labor market. The two were closely related. Let us discuss them one by one in some detail.

The massive inflow from abroad of technological knowledge led prewar Japan to proceed with secondary import substitution supported by government policy. Dependence on this advantage of borrowed technology, however, did not end in the prewar period; it was sustained in an even more vital way during the early postwar years of the 1950s and 1960s. Inflows of foreign technological knowledge permitted the modernization of old industries built during the 1930s and the war years and the creation of new industries—a process we will refer to as simultaneous infusion. Japanese enterprises adopted foreign methods through a process of what has been called "improvement engineering."[2]

Since the 1970s, however, the situation has begun to change. The technological gap, the crucial factor for the phase of secondary import substitution, has been rapidly growing narrower. Private enterprises began to make efforts through increased investment expenditures for R & D to develop their own advanced technology, and the government supported and encouraged these activities (see Lecture 7). When

---

[2] Kazushi Ohkawa and Henry Rosovsky, *Japanese Economic Growth: Trend Acceleration in the Twentieth Century* (Stanford: Stanford University, 1973), chapter 9, particularly p. 226, pp. 234–38.

a sign of this basic change was observed, we thought its long-run implications were crucial:

There are many reasons for believing that in the coming decades Japan will create numerous significant and profitable technological advances. No doubt Japan will also continue to avail itself of progress made elsewhere. There is, however, a fundamental difference between closing a gap (or eliminating a lag) and depending on the extension of a domestic or foreign technological frontier. In the former case, if the other conditions are right, one can proceed at great speed. Gains can accrue in a relatively short time. In the latter case, one may face lengthy bottlenecks. The technological frontier is inevitably surrounded by uncertainties, hesitations, and false starts—soon an element of easy success in Japanese development may disappear.[3]

These long-run implications elucidate the essential problem for secondary export substitution. The situation has frequently been misunderstood, the assumption being made that success in the earlier import substitution will almost automatically lead to later success at export substitution and that government support (export subsidies, for example) will be effective in enhancing the phase shift. Japan's experience suggests that this is not the actual case.

Structural changes in wage-labor relations are crucial for pursuing secondary export substitution. After the second turning point, a characteristic of further industrialization is an increase in wages relative to capital prices. Wage differentials between unskilled and skilled workers, and between small-scale and large-scale firms, are now normalized. To become internationally competitive, enterprises have to respond to this new situation of factor prices through industrial and technological organizations of greater efficiency.

The dynamic role played by manufacturing in macroeconomic growth has not become weaker in the 1980s. However, a change in the sectoral distribution of labor employment has been taking place. In the 1970s the absolute number of workers employed in manufacturing remained almost stationary, and its share in total employment decreased from 26.8% in 1970 to 23.9% in 1980–81. In this respect, Japan appears to be following the regular pattern of its Western predecessors. However, in Japan's industries for expanding

---

[3] Ohkawa and Rosovsky, *Japanese Economic Growth*, chapter 9, p. 235.

exports, such as machinery manufacturing, the restraint on labor supply has become a matter for serious concern, along with wage hikes.
The problem now is efficient use of limited labor resources, instead of
fuller utilization of cheap labor based on flexible supplies, as was the
problem in the phase of secondary import substitution.[4]

A related serious concern is the supply price of industrial output.
Export goods should be cheaper than other goods, at least at the local
market. This is a necessary condition, although the sufficient condition
that the producer have a comparative advantage will be met in the
environment of international competition. (Basically, it depends on
a supply curve shift due to cost reductions.) What we are specifically
concerned with here is the effect of the supplies on the level and trend
of real wages viewed from the entrepreneur's standpoint. The pressure
of higher wage levels is actually stronger for machinery manufacturing,
even though the nominal wage level for workers of similar quality is
almost the same as for other industries: production cost is higher
simply because output price is required to be lower. In Lecture 2, an
analogous question was discussed in the context of domestic competition between textiles and machinery. The nature of the issue is the
same, but with an important difference in the labor-wage structure:
machinery manufacture cannot depend upon a cheap and flexible
supply of labor, unlike textile manufacture.

With these conditions and restraints, what will be the pattern and
mechanism of technological-organizational progress for export-ex-
panding industries? To answer this question is our central problem
in this lecture.

First, it appears to be possible to follow the conventional method
of economic analysis by using the concept of factor substitution. Because of a distinct upgrading of wages relative to capital prices, entrepreneurs will naturally substitute increased capital investment for
labor. The process of capital intensification would thus be expected
to have begun in the 1970s; and in fact a tremendous amount of capital was invested in machinery as well as metal industries during the
decade, as will be discussed later in detail.

Second, however, we want to know more about what form this
process actually took in Japan, particularly with respect to the ad-

---

[4] Interpreting the coincidental occurrence of structural change in the labor market
and the shift toward the phase of secondary export substitution is difficult. For
East Asia, the coincidence seems highly probable. However, in Latin America, Brazil appears to have structural changes in the labor market that lag behind the exports of advanced manufactured goods.

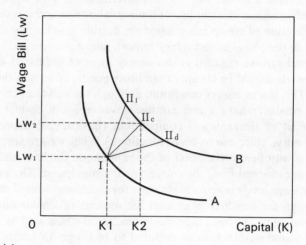

Figure 4.1
Hypothetical Illustration of the Changes in Lw/K and Shifts of the Isoquant Curve

vancement of technology-organization. For this purpose, the framework developed in Lecture 3 will be used again here, the factor-intensity ratio (FIR) being the central term. Because of the richer data available, the method will be applied in a refined way. Figure 4.1 is intended to illustrate hypothetically what we have in mind.

The possibility of varying combinations of capital (K) and labor costs (Lw) to produce the same amount of output is illustrated by the A and B curves, borrowing the conventional concept of "isoquant curves." This graph shows the substitution of K for Lw to produce the same output as we go down along each isoquant curve and the substitution of Lw for K as we go up. Let us assume I as the starting point, which is chosen by an entrepreneur for a certain industry at a certain given time. FIR is, say, 0.65, which can be measured by the ratio of the distance $0 - Lw_1$ on the vertical axis to the distance $0 - K_1$ on the horizontal line.

The innovational process of technological-organizational change is illustrated by a shift of the isoquant curve from A to B. We emphasize the significance of this shift rather than the behavior of factor substitution. (It may be more realistic to draw these curves shorter because the range of substitution actually possible is limited.) Entrepreneurs' options lie in two dimensions: one is expansion from point I to points

IIc, IIi, IId, etc.; the other, a parallel shift to a sharper slope or a moderate slope. Let us take the simplest path: an unchanged ratio of Lw/K from point I to point IIc with a parallel shift from A to B. At the latter point a greater output Y can be produced by keeping the FIR unchanged. The path I→IIi illustrates a case of increased value of Lw/K (say, 0.75); the path I→IId, a case of decreased value of Lw/K (say, 0.55). In the former a greater amount of Y will be produced by a larger payment of wages per capital, whereas in the latter a smaller amount is paid. For the sake of avoiding complexity, non-parallel shifts are not discussed here, and we focus on the comparison of I with IIc, IIi, and IId.

The data recording past performances provide us with the points which can be interpreted to correspond to these points hypothetically described in the figure. For example, for electric machinery, the performance data for 1970 and 1979 (the first and the last years of the 1970s) will be compared in the section that follow. The important point is that the change illustrated by comparing I with IIc, IIi, and IId cannot be treated adequately by a direct application of factor substitution (usually by measuring its rate of elasticity). It is our view that without considering the effects of changes in technology-organization, the changed or unchanged magnitude of Lw/K cannot be interpreted realistically. In short, the process of increased capital investment in the 1970s should be understood primarily by looking along the expansion path rather than along the isoquant curves.

II. Performance of Representative Industries

The activity of "export substitution" has been carried out primarily by the machinery manufacture industries, although steel and chemicals also played an important role. These are often called "export industries," but this name is misleading because they do not confine their activities to exports; domestic demand plays an important role as well. Details will be given in Appendices 1 and 2 to this lecture; for instance, the share of machinery in total manufacturing production increased from 8.5% in 1961 to 18.2% in 1971 and to 29.7% in 1981: machinery exports' share of total exports of manufacturing products increased from 30.9% in 1961 to 48.5% in 1971 and to 65.9% in 1981.

The shift of the supply curve to the right direction was achieved by the effects of scale economies as well as technological advance. As we analyze this process, it is important to recognize the fact that the expansion of demand for machineries was stimulated primarily by the local market; export expansion, while important, played an incremental role. At the outset of the preceding section, it was pointed out that the 1970s were characterized by the decline of manufacturing's contribution to GDP growth. Actually the output growth rate of manufacturing decreased from 14.1% in the 1960s to 6.7% in the 1970s, and its weighted growth rate (weight : output proportion of manufacturing to GDP) decreased from 4.7% in the former decade to 2.4% in the latter. This does not imply, however, that domestic demand had stagnated.

Differentials in Innovative Process: Measurements
So the 1970s will be the focus for our observations, for several reasons. i) The 1960s were covered to a considerable extent by Lecture 3. The 1966 data cited there will be used below, when possible. ii) Although the end of the phase under review is demarcated at the mid-1970s, as explained in Appendix 2, the latter part of the 1970s cannot be excluded from our observation. The innovative process continued despite the economic shock caused by the second oil-price increase, and a new phenomenon that attracts our particular attention began to emerge. The exports of metals and chemicals tended to decrease, while exports of machinery continued to increase. The phenomenon is confirmed in terms of the share to the total exports of manufactured goods in Appendix 2 to this lecture. This may be a sign of movement toward the fully industrialized phase to be discussed in Lecture 8. The possibility of interpreting it as the "tertiary" export substitution of machinery for metals and chemicals is a challenge for us. The actual process of launching this phenomenon can effectively be investigated by observing the 1970s as a set, as is suggested in Appendix 2.

The framework explained in the preceding section can be tested by use of the Manufacturing Survey (*Kogyo Tokei-hyo* [hereinafter *KTH*], compiled annually by the Ministry of International Trade and Industry).[5] A comparison of 1971 and 1981 mey be tried to examine the performance during the 1970s by use of industrial classification at the two-digit level. Details of the nature of the data and procedures for arranging them are explained in the Technical Notes appended to this section.

In Table 4.1 all the data arranged and processed for our purpose are listed in terms of the total or average for each subsector. The subsectors selected are steel, chemicals, food processing, textiles, and the four subsectors of machinery manufacturing: general, electric, transportation, and precision. We believe these are representative for

---

[5] The same data series as that used in Lecture 2, but much revised.

our purpose,[6] which is to identify the differences in the process of innovation performance by industry. The results of measurements are presented in two groups. The first group contains the terms related to Lw/K, the basic concept. The second group covers the terms of output-input relationships. Finally, we attempt to integrate these in order to quantify the innovative process by industry. Table 4.1 appears quite complex, but in fact it is simply constructed of five horizontal panels. Panel A shows conventional terms of prices of labor, L (w, wages), and capital-labor ratio (K/L) (capital intensity). In Panel B, the term specifically defined as FIR in the preceding section is derived from Panel A with the deflated values for K(b). Panel C gives capital-output ratio, the reciprocal of output-capital ratio Y/K, again with its deflated values of K(b) and Y/L; Panel D, output-wage bill ratio Y/Lw, the reciprocal of Lw/Y (labor's relative share of income); Panel E, output prices, P, for manufacturing subsectors. Deflators for fixed physical assets are explained in the Technical Notes.

Let us begin with Panel A. It echoes what we discussed in Lecture 3 when we compared machinery with textiles, pointing out that the equality of K/L between the two sectors in 1966 is of great significance: the superior productivity of the former depends on the availability of high-quality workers to deal with the more advanced technology. During the 1970s, K/L in the machinery industries as a whole increased more rapidly than that of textiles, but K/L values for electric machinery are still lower than those for textiles. The importance of technology in machinery production has surely been underlined. In other subsectors, the number of workers employed decreased, as is seen from the figures in Panel B, whereas in the machinery industries as a whole it remained almost unchanged. (In the electric and precision machinery subsectors it even increased.) Thus it was not only in export industries that machinery substituted for workers, even female workers. For example, in 1981 total employment in electric machinery (in establishments employing over 30 workers) was 1,201,000 (females, 529,000); in textiles, 376,000 workers (223,000 females) were employed.

What we are concerned with here is wage performance. As is shown by the average annual rate of change (Gw, a), the rate of increase in nominal wages is remarkably uniform across subsectors; wage differentials among subsectors are almost unchanged. What is more important is the fairly wide differential of Gw*—the rate of change in

[6] As is shown in Appendix 1, in the machinery industry, the overtime compositional changes within each subsector are notable. It is assumed that our formula can usefully be applied despite these changes.

Table 4.1
Performance of the Representative Subsectors of Manufacturing During the 1970s: Industry Approach

	Machinery				Steel	Chemicals	Textiles	Food
	General	Electric	Transportation	Precision				
	(1)	(2)	(3)	(4)	(5)	(6)	(7)	(8)
(A) w: (average annual earnings; unit: 10 thousand yen)								
1971	111	89	112	92	113	131	71	76
1981	353	237	356	279	422	382	219	246
Rates of change (%)								
Gw	12.3	10.8	12.3	11.7	13.8	11.3	11.9	12.5
Gw^*	7.8	7.2	7.4	9.2	7.3	3.7	6.7	5.3
K/L: (per person; annual amount: 10 thousand yen)								
1971	164	108	222	94	345	631	194	137
1871	389	234	543	266	6,274	1,148	266	485
(B) Lw/K (%)								
1971	67.3	81.8	50.4	98.5	17.8	20.7	36.6	54.0
1981 (a)	69.2	76.7	49.9	104.9	20.4	21.8	82.8	38.5
(b)	59.1	65.5	42.7	89.6	17.4	18.9	70.8	32.9
Growth rate (%)								
GK^*	5.2	8.9	8.0	10.6	4.4	4.8	0.6	8.5
GL	-2.4	2.3	0.3	1.3	-5.0	-1.1	-8.3	-3.0
GK^*-GL	7.6	6.6	7.7	9.3	9.4	3.7	14.3	11.5
$Gw^*+GL-GK^*$	0.2	0.6	0.3	-0.1	2.1	0	-7.6	-6.2

(C) Y/K							
1971	1.90	2.21	1.34	2.09	0.42	1.16	1.68
1981 (a)	2.21	2.66	1.61	2.16	0.68	1.71	1.56
(b)	1.89	2.28	1.38	1.84	0.59	1.46	1.33
Growth rate (%)							
GY*	5.1	10.1	6.9	9.9	4.9	-1.4	3.5
GY*-GK*	-0.1	1.2	-1.1	-0.7	0.5	-2.0	-5.0
GY*-GL	7.5	7.8	6.6	8.6	9.9	9.7	9.5
(D) Y/Lw							
1971	2.56	2.70	2.63	2.00	3.03	2.08	2.94
1981	2.58	2.63	2.44	2.06	2.86	2.08	3.12
Growth rate (%)							
GLw	10.1	13.1	12.6	13.1	8.8	3.6	9.5
GY	9.6	13.7	11.6	12.4	11.4	3.6	10.7
GY-GLw	-0.5	0.6	-1.0	-0.6	2.6	0	1.2
(E) Output prices (P): (1975=100)							
1971	69.0	62.8	70.2	74.3	64.2	74.8	64.5
1981	107.6	90.2	113.3	96.2	120.8	123.9	108.6
Rates of change (%)	4.5	3.6	4.9	2.5	6.5	5.2	7.2

Source: KTH for all items other than output prices, which are from Economic Planning Agency, Annual Reports of National Accounts, 1983. For details, see the Technical Notes at the end of this section.

Remarks: Growth rates are annual averages, obtained by simply bridging the two years by series. Those marked with an asterisk (*) are deflated values.

(a) 1981 data using the original value of K, capital, and (b) using its adjusted value (see Technical Notes).

real wages, which is deflated by output prices of subsectors (Panel E). Broadly, two groups of industries can be distinguished: one consists of machinery and steel; the other, of chemicals and food processing, with textiles in between. For the former group rapid increases in real wages acted as a major source of pressure, while they were a much weaker source for the latter group. We know that machinery and steel played the major role in pursuing secondary export substitution; as was pointed out in Lecture 3, a relative decline in the price of the goods they produce is a necessary condition for enhancing comparative advantage. This was actually realized (Panel E). The only way of combating wage hike pressure in these subsectors is faster technological-organizational progress, together with a realization of the effects of scale economies.

Interpretation of the change in magnitude of our basic term, Lw/K, shown in Panel B, requires comment and qualification. Its rank among industries in 1971 was largely the same as in 1966 (Lecture 3). During the 1970s, despite the rapid increase in the capital-labor ratio (K/L) noted earlier, the rank appears to have changed little except for textiles and food. Two figures, (a) and (b), are presented for 1981 in Table 4.1: (a) is the ratio calculated from the original data, and (b) is the ratio calculated using the adjusted value of capital K. The original data are book-values, and a direct comparison of 1981 with 1971 is not adequate for our purposes. A crude adjustment is made for (b) by multiplying a flat coefficient to the figures of all industries in (a). To revalue roughly the asset items bought during 1971–80, averaged price indices are estimated as 117 (with 1975 as base). For details, see the Technical Notes. The values of Lw/K for 1981 (b) appear to be somehow smaller than those for 1971, except in textiles.

In Panel B average annual rates of change (annotated with G hereinafter) are shown in addition for the terms at issue. As has been touched upon earlier, GL is negative for all industries other than machinery (with the minor exception of general machinery). In terms of adjusted value of K, GK* is very high for precision, electric, and transportation machinery, whereas it is moderate for steel and chemicals. What we are concerned with particularly is the performance of the rate of change in Lw/K. In the table, it is measured by use of K* (w* listed in Panel A), and expressed by Gw* + GL − GK*. The characteristics of the industries seem to be distinct. Broadly, two groups can be identified: one is almost unchanged, and the other shows a distinct decline. Textiles and food industries are in the latter group; machineries and chemicals, the former. (Steel may be in between, though its rate of increase is very modest.)

COMPLETING DEVELOPMENT 129

The term estimated by use of deflated wages and adjusted capital is interpreted as follows on the basis of entrepreneurs' behavior. The labor costs calculated by output value are compared with the capital used. The capital amount should be evaluated in the same way each year, regardless of the methods used. Our crude adjustment is one such method, and we cannot claim its absolute validity. Nevertheless, we believe the performance thus obtained is characteristic of industries with respect to FIR and is of great significance. It echoes the direction and pattern of the expansion path in Figure 4.1.

The output effects of the inputs presented by FIR are measured in two ways: one is the ratio to capital, Y/K; the other, the ratio to labor, Y/L, and to wage costs, Y/Lw. In Panel C the performance of Y/K is shown. Again, due to differences in capital evaluation of the same type as in Panel B, two figures, (a) and (b), are presented. The rank of output level in 1971 is not much different from that in 1966. Let us look at the pattern of change by 1981 (b): almost unchanged for machinery and chemicals; noticeable increases for steel and textiles; and a decrease in food. Growth rates for the two terms are added, using the deflated values. As expected, GY* is highest for machinery, in particular electric, precision, and transportation machinery, whereas it is slightly negative for textiles. The pace of "substitution" in domestic production is extremely fast for the 1970s. Particular attention is drawn to the performance of GY* - GK* for electric and transportation machinery: the output-capital ratio is increasing, while it is decreasing for the chemicals, textiles, and food subsectors; in between it appears almost unchanged for general and precision machinery and steel.

The other output effect, Y/L, is a conventional term, labor productivity. Its rate of growth (GY* - GL in Panel C) appears uniformly fairly rapid for all industries except chemicals. However, a closer look reveals that growth rates in the machinery industry without exception are slower than those in steel, textiles, and food. This may be contrary to expectation, but actually it is natural: the much higher rate of output (GY*) for the machinery industry is a result of lack of reduction in labor employment while other industries reduced their labor forces considerably.

In Panel D the figures for Y/Lw are listed. Here we have no problem of adjusting price changes, as both nominal and real terms have the same ratio, except in steel and (to a minor degree) in chemicals. Its reciprocal is Lw/Y, the term for labor's relative income share. The near-constancy of this ratio in the machinery industries, in contrast to its decline in the steel industry, draws our attention.

Differentials in Innovative Process: Integration

With the preceding lengthy explanation of Table 4.1 in mind, we now intend to integrate these partial performances of individual terms and their ratios into an aggregate observation, focusing our concern on the shift of isoquant curves shown in Figure 4.1. Among varied ways of doing so, we choose the simplest one, that is, the conventional way of measuring "total factor productivity" change (GT), as we did in Lecture 1.[7]

This is not a precise measurement of technological progress, but an attempt at crude quantification of the process of innovation, in which of course technological-organizational progress is the major element. A measurement of this kind requires relevant terms; except for Lw/Y, we will select them out of the preceding partial observations. For capital, K, the adjusted value is used together with deflated output Y*. The differential performance of industries found above is worth noting in itself, in particular the behavior of Lw/K and the partial productivities of capital and labor. Nevertheless, such an integration by total factor productivity is indispensable.

The results are shown in Panel A of Table 4.2. The annual growth rate of total factor productivity is greatest for steel and precision and electric machinery, high for general machinery and transportation machinery, and negative for the other two sectors. As a whole, with the possible exception of chemicals (for which input growth may have been overestimated), during the 1970s a considerably fast-paced shift in isoquant curves is indicated. It is important to recognize the practical significance of the measured results in that the magnitude of GT is far greater than the rate of change in Lw*/K* for machineries and steel, whereas the relation is reversed for chemicals, textiles, and food. In particular, machineries recorded fast increases in total factor productivity with almost unchanged magnitude of Lw*/K*.

In Panel B, the result of total factor productivity measurement is converted to magnitude per unit investment, I. Since it gives the incremental increase of the "residuals," ΔR, as GT = $\Delta R/Y$ (for details, see section III, Lecture 5), $\Delta R/I$ is given by GT/(I/Y). Its rank of magnitude differs a great deal from that of GT: for electric, precision, and general machineries $\Delta R/I$ is highest, whereas it is rather modest for steel and transportation machineries. The difference is, in our view, extremely

---

[7] Using the notations and terms presented in Panel B of Table 4.1 and as explained earlier, we derive GT = $\alpha(GY^* - GK^*) + \beta(GY^* - GL)$, where the weights are assumed $\beta = Lw/Y$ and $\alpha = 1 - \beta$. The value of β is given by the average of reciprocals of Y/Lw in the two years in Panel D of Table 4.1. Note that for most subsectors the value of GT is stable.

Table 4.2
Rates of Total Factor Productivity Increases in Selected Industries in the 1970s

(annual average rate, %)

| | General | Machineries | | Precision | Steel | Chemicals | Textiles | Food |
| | | Electric | Trans-portation | | | | | |
	(1)	(2)	(3)	(4)	(5)	(6)	(7)	(8)
(A):								
$\alpha(GY^*-GK^*)$	-0.1	0.8	-0.7	-0.4	0.3	-2.5	-1.2	-3.3
$\beta(GY^*-GL)$	3.1	2.8	2.5	4.1	3.4	0.6	3.1	3.2
GT	3.0	3.6	1.8	3.7	3.7	-1.8	1.9	-0.1
(B):								
I/Y	14.3	13.8	21.8	16.3	44.9	16.4	13.3	18.4
$\Delta R/I$	21.0	26.1	8.3	22.6	8.2	-1.1	14.3	0

Source: Investment, I, is from KTH, the same editions.
Remarks: I/Y is an average of the figures of 1971 and 1981. No remarkable change is witnessed except for the steel industries, in which I/Y is very high in 1971.

important. It implies that specifically viewed from the standpoint of capital investment, instead of from that of output growth, efficiency in terms of residual creation is greater for the subsectors with higher magnitude of FIR, Lw/K. Note, in Panel B of Table 4.1, the difference between 65.5 for electric machinery and 17.4 for steel in 1981(b) and between 81.1 for the former and 17.8 for the latter in 1971. A higher level of FIR is witnessed for textiles in 1981(b). However, the value of $\Delta R/I$ for textiles is modest. It is our view that particular attention should be paid to these machinery subsectors with their innovative domestic production processes, which brought about a faster pace of export expansion and internal innovation. The significance of techno-logical property assessed by the term Lw/K is thus fully identified.[8]

Our analysis is confined to domestic production, and we cannot talk directly about the changes in comparative advantage among in-dustries. Even so, the findings may help us a great deal in interpreting the differential performance of export substitution in machinery vs. metals and chemicals. The differential quantified by the residual per unit of investment broadly between the two groups is particularly note-worthy in this regard. This must be the major factor responsible for bringing forth the new phenomenon described earlier for the 1980s.

Before ending our discussion in this section, we want to look back at technological advance during the postwar period up to the 1970s. Some of the useful data compiled by Japanese economists can be used for this purpose.

According to Watanabe and Egaitsu, for 1952–1961, the residuals (equivalent to GT) of representative industries are measured as follows (average annual rate of increase) by essentially the same formula as ours: (a) chemicals 18.8%, paper pulp 11.7%, transporta-tion machinery 11.8%; (b) general and electric machinery 8.7%, metal

---

[8] A few words on the relation between total and partial productivity. The meas-ured results show that the rate of increase in the partial productivity of labor is dominant, while that of capital is minor. This is a naturally expected pattern judging from the formula used for a case of near constancy of capital-output ratio (the so-called "Harrod-neutral" type of technological change). It is to be noted, however, that this does not necessarily mean the real process is actually "labor-augmenting": labor's contribution is dominant. The formula contains the assumption that GY will be divided into αGY and βGY so as to be equivalent to the residual measure-ment GY = GT + αGK + βGL. Such a simple formula cannot specity the fac-tors' contribution to technological change. But even more sophisticated ones cannot solve this important but most difficult problem satisfactorily.

This simple approach leaves the measurement of scale-economies and "biases" of technological change unsolved. However, it is our view that for practical pur-poses the primary task is to know the pace of the shift, faster or slower, and that ignorance of these effects may not be so serious from this standpoint.

and metal products 5.1%; (c) textiles 4.4%, food 1.4%.[9] In Lecture 3, relevant terms are estimated for 1957 and 1966. A broad comparison of the residual magnitude and the level of FIR, Lw/K, lead to the following suggestion. The high rate of residual increase in group (a) corresponds to the low level of FIR (note that transportation at that time was at a low value, unlike at present); the low rate of residual increase in group (c) corresponds to moderate values of FIR; finally, intermediate magnitude of residual increase in group (b) corresponds to the high level of FIR, typically for machineries (we guess metal and metal products would be a mixture of (a) and (b)).

The suggested picture of the latter part of the 1950s appears to be partially similar to and partially different from that of the 1970s. The similarity is that the residual growth of machineries was already greater than that of the traditional subsectors, such as textiles. The difference is that a high rate of residual growth was attained by subsectors of low FIR at that time, whereas in the 1970s machineries of high FIR realized higher rates of residual growth.

As has been touched upon earlier, "simultaneous" infusion of borrowed technologies was a characteristic of domestic technological advance by industries at that time. The war-caused backwardness due to international isolation required a fast catch-up for both "old" and "new" technologies of groups (a) and (b). What is suggested is that the "new" was just at its beginning in the 1950s.

Matsukawa's work for the period, 1954–1968, can also be cited usefully.[10] Among his various interesting findings, we draw attention to two points: technological progress and import substitution. Manufacturing development is analyzed by dividing the sector into three groups, A, B and C, by the share distribution of establishment scale. Group A has the largest share of small-scale enterprises (1–49 workers); C has the smallest share, and B is intermediate. (These different distributions will be discussed in the sections that follow.) Rate of technological progress, measured as the shift of production function of the Cobb-Douglas type,[11] is 2.8% for group A, and for groups B and C combined it is 6.5%. Group A largely consists of enterprises in the food and other

[9] T. Watanabe and N. Egaitsu, "Gijutsu Shimpo to Keizai Seicho" [Technological Progress and Economic Growth], in M. Kaji, ed., *Keizai Seicho to Shigen Haibun* [Economic Growth and Resource Allocation] (Tokyo: Iwanami, 1967). This is a pioneering work in this field.

[10] Shigeru Matsukawa, "Dualistic Economic Development: An Econometric Model of Japan," IDCJ Working Paper Series No. 17, March 1981.

[11] Between this type of production function approach and the simple formula we previously used, there is essentially no difference in nature and assumptions.

traditional industries, and B and C consist of all other industries of both old and new types. Although it is not possible to quantify the difference between B and C, we can learn that during the 1960s modern manufacturing sectors recorded a much faster rate of technological progress than during the 1970s, in sharp distinction to the slower technological progress in the traditional sectors.

The larger-scale group, in Matsukawa's view, contributes most to promoting import substitution. The estimated percentage change of imports associated with one percentage change in domestic demand is smaller than unity for large-scale manufacturing products. As has been pointed out, the period 1954–68 was an interval of mixed performances both for completion of secondary import substitution (especially in the former part) and for beginning secondary export substitution (especially in the latter part). In this context, Matsukawa's econometric confirmation of import substitution endorses our view. Let us repeat our statement that without effective import substitution, the postwar investment spurt could not have taken place. In comparison, the 1970s' investment performance is much more moderate in pursuit of export substitution.

Technical Notes

The *KTH* (*Kogyo Tokei-hyo*) is published annually in two volumes: "Industry version" and "Enterprise version." This section uses the former. Essentially, the design and contents are similar to the "Manufacturing Surveys" used today internationally, including in many developing countries. The concepts and terms tabulated are largely consistent with those of economic analysis. The following are noted with regard to the use of the *KTH* data.

For the data tabulated by establishment (not enterprise) unit, four basic terms are available for analytical purposes: Y (added values in current prices), L (number of employees), K (fixed capital stock in book-values), and Lw (payments of wages and salaries). The average wage, w, is obtained by dividing Lw by L. The deflators required to compare the data (Y, w, and K) of the two years in 1975 prices are from other sources.

Data classified by establishment scale in terms of number of employees are used for the coverage of firms with 30–40 employees and larger, with smaller-scale firms excluded. We intend to focus our present observation on these establishments (see Section III); the analysis of small-scale establishments was discussed in Lecture 3. An additional reason is that data on K are available only for the scale over 30–40 employees. Therefore, the figures for these basic terms are the sums of those for the establishments thus specified and differ from the total amounts for each subsector, which include a wide range down to the scale of 4–10 employees. However, except for the case of textiles, our selected coverage can largely represent the performance of each subsector as a whole.

Output, Y, is added value net of depreciation allowances. Gross added value is shown, but the coverage is not entirely consistent with the data for labor, L, in terms of the total number of persons engaged. The alternative would be to use "regular workers." Wage bills, Lw, are given as "total annual cash payments of wages and salaries." "Wages," w, are "averages" calculated by dividing Lw by L. The amount of assets is used as fixed capital, K, although small amounts of land in it cannot be excluded. The same is true for investment, I. The assets amount at the year's end, instead of at the beginning, is used for K, but it is registered in "book values," and this needs adjustment for the use of overtime comparisons. Since the data for revaluation are not available, a simple adjustment is made as follows by use of the price indices of assets available from the *Annual Reports of National Income Accounts*, Economic Planning Agency, Japanese Government (1983 issue, pp. 152–153).

Assuming simply an even distribution of the asset items bought in the past ten years, averages of price indices are applied to adjust the total amount at 1981 book values. An average of 117 is found fairly appropriate to be flatly applied to all subsectors, making allowances of three years for the shorter service life of machinery and equipment. Actual indices (1975 = 100) are as follows at the beginning and the end years:

	Machineries (1)	Transport Equipment (2)	Structures (3)	Non-residential Buildings (4)
1971	70.4	73.9	58.6	60.6
1981	105.7	108.4	149.5	140.7
(1971 = 100)	150.1	146.7	255.1	230.5

According to the data available for 1966, the share of asset distribution of total manufacturing is 40% for (3)+(4) and 60% for (1)+(2). Ratios of 7:3 for steel and chemicals and 3:7 for other subsectors are used.

Note that this is not deflating in the usual sense. The purpose of adjustment is to obtain a comparable basis of approximation for evaluating capital stock in 1981 and 1971.

III. Performance by Establishment Scale

Japanese manufacturing is widely known for its salient feature of developing concurrently both large- and small-scale enterprises. The relevance of this characteristic is great for contemporary developing economies. In Lecture 3 we discussed this scale aspect for the 1960s, paying special attention even to very small-scale enterprises.

During the shift of secondary phase from import substitution to export substitution, what change occurred in the scale distribution of representative industries? Did the innovation process discussed in the preceding section concentrate on large-scale enterprises? If not, how about the role played by medium and small-scale enterprises? In trying to answer these questions, the same conceptual framework used in Lecture 3 will be extended to this section by use of the *KTH* data on firm size, which are adequate to observe the economic aspect of technological differences and changes. The scale classifies establishments on the basis of size in terms of number of workers. As noted earlier, very small establishments (fewer than 30 workers) are dropped, and the average performances of three groups are observed: S, small scale (30–199 employees); M, medium scale (200–999); and L, large scale (1,000 and over). This scale is used for the sake of analytical convenience, but no rigid standard can actually suffice, as circumstances and policy aims (including legal provisions) vary from one country to another.

Scale Organization by Industry

Since 1909, the first year for which the data became available, the scale distribution among S, M, and L has been largely unchanged until recent years: neither a trend of change toward L nor one toward S is discernible, although it shows swingwise variations. This is an amazing fact in view of the drastic structural changes that took place during this long-term interval. Postwar performance, too, shows minor changes in distribution: for 1953, the percentages are S 43.4, M 30.8, and L 25.8; for 1961, S 37.6, M 35.2, and L 27.1; and for 1971, S 41.4, M 33.0, and L 27.2.[12] This pattern is sustained despite basic changes in the labor market which narrowed wage differentials.

To understand the scale distribution pattern, labor employment alone is not enough. For the 1970s, capital and output distribution is looked at in terms of the *KTH* data, and a three-step scale is used:

---

[12] The source is *KTH*. The scale classification is fewer than 50 for S, 50–499 for M, and 500 and over for L.

S = 30–199 employees, M = 200–999, and L = 1,000 and more (Table 4.3).

Contrary to expectation, the share of L decreases and the share of S increases, with the share of M increasing slightly or remaining almost unchanged. This pattern is seen for capital, output, and labor without exception. However, the ratio terms in the lower panel (B) of Table 4.3 reveal another aspect. Despite the relative decline in the capital-labor ratio, K/L for large-scale establishments, both capital, Y/K, and labor, Y/L, increased in efficiency for the large-firm sector; in contrast, despite their relative increase in K/L, small-scale establish-

Table 4.3
Share of Capital, Output, and Labor by Scale: Manufacturing, 1971 and 1981

(%)

	L	M	S	Total
(A): (%)				
Capital (K)				
1971	41.0	36.0	22.0	100.0
1981	31.0	36.3	30.7	100.0
Output (Y)				
1971	34.4	33.0	32.6	100.0
1981	31.3	35.3	33.4	100.0
Labor (L)				
1971	27.3	30.0	42.7	100.0
1981	21.9	30.0	48.1	100.0

	L	M	S	S′	Total
Including establishments employing fewer than 30 workers (S′)					
1971	17.0	20.6	29.5	30.9	100.0
1981	14.2	19.4	31.3	35.1	100.0

	L	M	S	Total
(B): (ratio)				
K/L				
1971	1.50	1.20	.51	
1981	1.41	1.28	.62	
Y/K				
1971	.84	.92	1.48	
1981	1.00	1.00	1.08	
Y/L				
1971	1.26	1.10	.76	
1981	1.43	1.17	.69	

Source: MITI, KTH.

Remarks: The ratio in (B) is calculated from the shares in (A).

ments lost efficiency of both capital and labor. In between, for the case of medium scale, a moderate increase in K/L brought forth a slight increase in relative efficiency.

The implication drawn from these facts is suggestive for observing changes in the industrial subsectors. Since the rapid development of the machinery industry formed the core of manufacturing performance, the scenario described here may be particularly applicable to it. Second, the scale differential of relative change in factor efficiency may be relevant to the varying pace of technological advance with scale. The fast pace confirmed in the preceding section may have scale differentials: faster for L, slower for S, and M in between. To test this expectation, let us begin by looking at distribution of capital by establishment.

Capital distribution for the representative subsectors is presented in Table 4.4. Two patterns of scale distribution of capital are found in the 1970s: one tends toward even distribution, represented by machineries and chemicals, and the other shows almost no variation, as typified by the steel industry. Food and textiles appear to be mixed. Because the data for 1966 are not precisely comparable, as noted in the table, we cannot be precise about the change between 1966 and 1971. Yet the data for 1966 may be a good reference-point by which to evaluate the pattern witnessed for 1971. The aggregate performance found earlier is thus decomposed.

The even distribution type draws our particular attention. In the machinery sector, general machinery was characterized by even distribution even before the adoption of new tendencies, but the characteristic was further strengthened: in 1981 distribution was almost even among S, M, and L. Capital distribution in transportation machinery was of a much more uneven type in the 1960s, and yet a shift from L to M is witnessed during the 1970s. A similar pattern of change is seen for electric machinery. Capital investment went on at a faster pace for medium-scale than for large-scale establishments in all these machinery subsectors including precision machinery. Thus the differential of capital intensity, K/L, became narrower. For example, taking $M = 100$, K/L of L (large-scale establishments) decreased from 1.31 in 1971 to 1.19 in 1981 for general machinery, and from 1.55 in 1971 to 1.29 in 1981 for transport machinery, though for electric machinery it was almost unchanged (1.21). These make a sharp contrast to the case of steel, for which K/L of L increased from 2.71 in 1971 to 3.60 in 1981. The industrial organization in terms of establishment scale distribution thus changes distinctly when viewed in terms of input intensity. This is an important problem that must be examined further.

Table 4.4
Scale Distribution of Capital in Representative Industries in Selected Years

(unit: million yen in current prices, %)

| | Machineries | | | | Steel | Chemicals | Textiles | Food |
| | General | Electric | Transportation | Precision | | | | |
	(1)	(2)	(3)	(4)	(5)	(6)	(7)	(8)
1981:								
S	35.6	22.1	12.9	27.6	10.6	28.1	68.3	57.8
M	31.6	33.2	34.4	43.4	13.2	47.2	36.7	32.8
L	32.8	44.7	62.7	29.0	76.2	24.7	–	9.4
Total	100.0	100.0	100.0	100.0	100.0	100.0	100.0	100.0
Amount	(2,840)	(3,274)	(4,190)	(553)	(6,279)	(4,226)	(877)	(3,214)
1971:								
S	33.5	19.1	11.1	29.2	11.5	22.5	42.2	49.3
M	30.0	30.0	18.4	38.1	12.1	42.2	46.6	44.8
L	36.5	50.9	70.5	32.7	76.4	35.3	11.2	5.9
Total	100.0	100.0	100.0	100.0	100.0	100.0	100.0	100.0
Amount	(1,446)	(1,125)	(1,712)	(172)	(2,451)	(2,588)	(906)	(1,205)
1966:								
S	33.9	9.9	9.6	34.2	5.8	9.4	24.8	28.6
M	30.5	18.6	10.3	29.9	7.9	13.9	21.4	29.2
L	35.6	71.5	80.1	35.9	86.3	76.7	53.8	42.2
Total	100.0	100.0	100.0	100.0	100.0	100.0	100.0	100.0
Amount	(499)	(713)	(767)	(88)	(1,052)	(1,367)	(727)	(588)

Source: 1971, 1981 from KTH; 1966 from Basic Survey of Medium-Small Enterprises (see Lecture 3, Appendix 1).
Remarks: Unit of survey is establishments for 1971 and 1981, enterprises with some adjustments for 1966.

Innovation by Organizational Change

The concept of "technological-organizational" progress or change has repeatedly been used hitherto in a basic recognition that technology and organization are both involved in the process of innovation. What emerged during the phase under review, however, posed a challenge for us: the possibility of discussing "innovation by organizational change."[13] In response to this challenge, we will discuss the relation of organization to technological change with our focus on the process of diffusion of new or improved technology. It is our hypothesis that a leader-follower relationship in diffusing technology operates differently in organizations of different scale.

Three major terms will be used for our scrutiny: Lw/K, Lw/Y, and Y/K. All these are presented in Table 4.5, Panel A, as ratios in current prices. In this section, no attempt is made to observe over-time change.

These data remind us of the finding, in the final part of Lecture 3, that the level of Lw/K in 1966 had a predictable tendency to decline as the scale became larger. A noticeable change manifests itself in the 1970s. A typical case is that of general machinery. In 1971, it still kept the same pattern as in 1966, but it turned out to be almost flat through the three scale groups, showing neither an increasing nor a decreasing tendency. The ratio decreased in S firms and increased in M and L firms. Since the wage differentials due to the so-called "dualistic structure" of small and large firms mostly disappeared in the 1970s and very small-scale establishments are excluded from the data, this is primarily due to the increase in labor quality relative to capital intensity in M and L firms.

This phenomenon appears to take place also in other subsectors, although less predictably. For example, in the case of electric machinery the flat pattern appeared in 1971 for M and L and continued to 1981; for S, however, the performance differs, though the reason is not clear. The flat pattern seems also to be witnessed for steel and chemicals from 1971 on. In comparison with the pattern for 1966, a similar change may have taken place in chemicals, although for steel, K and Lw concentrate much more at the end of the larger scale, L. The mixed pattern seen for textiles and chemicals suggests bi-modal composition of these industries and requires further examination. Finally, the performance of transport machinery draws attention, as it sustains the "conventional" past pattern of decline even in 1981, in

---

[13] The term "organization" is used here narrowly, in the sense of the distribution of enterprises by industry. It differs from the term "industrial organization," defined broadly.

sharp contrast to other machinery subsectors. This pattern is also seen in sections of other industries such as textiles and food processing. The performance of Y/Lw is clear-cut. In almost all subsectors the ratio shows a tendency to increase with firm scale, an exceptional mixed pattern being seen only for chemicals and food processing. This same phenomenon was witnessed earlier for 1957 and 1966 data. It can be said that the pattern is a well-established one in Japan's historical experience.[14] Past interpretations tended to adopt one of two views: one emphasizes a tendency toward increase in the wage-productivity gap (the reciprocal of Y/Lw is w / Y/L) as scale becomes larger, and the other emphasizes the difference in technology with scale, taking Lw/Y (β, earlier) as elasticity of output with respect to labor in an equilibrium situation: labor-intensity for small firms vs. capital-intensity in technology for large enterprises. Since surplus labor disappeared in the 1970s, the latter view is closer to reality, even though our interpretation differs somewhat, as will be explained later.

The performance of Y/K shown in the table may be shocking to many economists who have long been familiar with its conventional pattern—that is, a distinct tendency toward decline in larger-scale establishments. During the 1970s, a sign of new behavior appears to emerge: absence of the conventional pattern. The typical case is again presented by general machinery. Starting in 1971, an inverted pattern is apparent, and electric and precision machinery seem to follow it, though M still lags behind. The same movement is seen for transportation machinery in 1981, starting from the conventional pattern in 1971. A similar pattern change is found for other industries such as food processing. A two-year comparison may not be enough to confirm a tendency to inversion, but a conservative view at least holds that the conventional pattern began to disappear in machinery and some other subsectors. However, it is also important to recognize that the conventional pattern of Y/K decline at larger scale is still distinctly evident for the steel and chemical industries in 1981, though its performance is mixed in 1971. In sum, with respect to Lw/K and Y/K, noticeable changes are identified, and these are important.

Panel B of the table shows scale comparison of rate of return on capital, π. Since $\pi = Y/K - Lw/K$, it is a combined expression of the two terms discussed above. Here again two patterns are identified: the conventional pattern is the tendency of decline from S to L (steel), recognized for 1966 in Lecture 3; the other, a new one (for machinery

---

[14] See, for example, S. Motai and K. Ohkawa, "Small-Scale Industries," IDCJ Working Paper Series No. 11, December 1978.

Table 4.5
Performance of the Representative Subsectors of Manufacturing During the 1970s: Scale Approach

| | Machineries | | | | Steel | Chemicals | Textiles | Food |
	General (1)	Electric (2)	Trans-portation (3)	Precision (4)	(5)	(6)	(7)	(8)
(A) Lw/K:								
1971								
S	.95	1.07	1.19	1.08	.21	.21	.59	.44
M	.69	.76	.59	.98	.19	.19	.48	.35
L	.59	.77	.45	.91	.22	.22	.60	.35
1981								
S	.86	1.23	.75	1.96	.34	.34	.85	.52
M	.85	.94	.69	2.23	.33	.33	.75	.47
L	.86	.95	.44	1.61	.35	.35	-	.55
Y/Lw:								
1971								
S	2.23	2.08	2.26	2.32	2.25	3.90	2.21	2.15
M	2.52	2.48	2.41	1.92	2.30	5.12	2.05	3.85
L	2.89	3.16	2.85	2.32	2.23	4.68	1.76	3.20
1981								
S	2.33	2.02	2.18	2.07	2.39	3.86	2.09	3.20
M	2.41	2.54	2.19	2.21	2.33	4.75	2.06	3.02
L	2.66	3.10	2.68	1.79	3.23	3.27	-	3.15
Y/K:								
1971								
S	1.65	2.18	1.57	2.48	.73	.82	1.24	.93
M	1.74	1.91	1.37	1.90	.77	.99	1.74	1.37
L	1.72	2.43	1.29	2.11	.32	1.04	1.07	1.12

	1	2	3	4	5	6	7	8
1981								
S	2.00	2.48	1.60	2.71	1.14	1.38	1.77	1.18
M	2.10	2.40	1.47	2.48	.93	1.49	1.56	1.44
L	2.29	2.95	1.67	1.72	.58	1.33	–	1.73
(B)π:								
1971								
S	.70	1.13	.38	1.40	.52	.61	.65	.49
M	1.05	1.15	.78	.92	.58	.80	.96	1.02
L	1.13	1.67	.84	1.20	.10	.82	.47	.77
1981								
S	1.14	1.25	.85	1.43	.80	1.04	.92	.66
M	1.15	1.46	.78	1.55	.60	1.16	.81	.97
L	1.33	2.00	1.25	.72	.23	.98	–	1.18
w (average annual earnings, 10,000 yen):								
1971								
S	100	70	87	77	109	111	65	69
M	113	87	101	94	128	115	76	84
L	128	105	125	112	148	131	74	124
1981								
S	275	198	272	225	342	344	215	226
M	359	276	332	290	402	390	326	231
L	419	362	404	366	472	431	–	352

Source: KTH, Industry version, 1971, 1981. The data for textiles for L are lacking in 1981.
Remarks: For the definitions of terms, see Technical Notes appended to section II of this lecture.

and some other subsectors), is an absence of the conventional pattern. Thus the new and the old elements concurrently operate among industries in the 1970s. We believe this is of great significance in interpreting the changes in scale organization. It is our conjecture that these phenomena essentially indicate the achievement of wider diffusion of technological-organizational progress observed in the preceding section. Progress was led by large-scale enterprises, which made innovational progress; medium- and small-scale enterprises followed. The machinery subsectors are a special case: their capital intensification could bring rapid technological progress. A relevant hypothesis was presented in Lecture 3. By use of the pattern of key terms identified earlier, a simple speculative observation will be used as we attempt to explain these phenomena further schematically.

A simple production function of the Cobb-Douglas type is hypothetically set as $Y/L = A(K/L)^\alpha$, where A is "constant." This is converted to $Y/K = A(L/K)^\beta$. Let us assume that this function can be applied variously to S, M, and L. In comparing these functions, the typical new pattern of equal value of Y/K can be explained as follows. On the right side of the equation, we know that both L/K and β decrease at larger firm scale ($\beta = Lw/Y$, and its reciprocal is Y/Lw). To keep Y/K equal, say, for M and L, the constant, A, should be greater at M than at L. For the conventional pattern of a decreasing tendency of Y/K, this is not required. Assuming an equal magnitude of A for M and L, Y/K would be smaller for L than for M to the extent that L/K and β are smaller for L.

The "constant," A, is actually the sum of unknown factors other than L/K which affect Y/K. In the cross-section comparison of establishments of different scales, we speculate that this can essentially be the indicator of technological-organizational factors. Therefore, a set of S, M, and L cannot be assumed to form a single production function as both β and A should be different for S, M, and L.[15] What is appropriately proposed is an application of the "envelope-curve": a conventional concept which links the observed points (S, M, and L in this case) assuming they are at near-equilibrium states. The newly emerged pattern can be interpreted by a shift of the envelope-curve, as illustrated by Figure 4.2.

Small curves f_1 and f_2 are the production functions for S and L (with M in between). At time 1, envelope-curve e_1 is drawn linking E_1 and

---

[15] Sometimes economists do assume a single production function in treating the data classified by scale. This can be acceptable as an approximation insofar as the difference in β and A at different enterprise scales is limited to a narrow range.

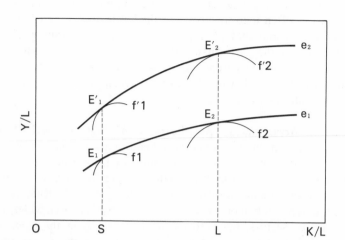

Figure 4.2
Hypothetical Illustration of Changes in the Scale Organization by the Envelope Curve

E_2, the observed points. e_1 is thought to make a shift to e_2 at time 2, corresponding to the supposed shift of production functions from f_1 to f_1' and from f_2 to f_2'. As $Y/K = Y/L \, / \, K/L$, the two points E_1' and E_2' illustrate an increase of Y/K, not in parallel, but in a relatively greater degree for the latter. The wage rate, w, is given at equilibrium on the vertical axis at the point of intersections with the extrapolated line tangent to f_1, f_2 at points E_1, E_2 along e_1, and likewise for e_2. Thus the level of Lw/K is determined for these points on the vertical line: SE_1E_1', LE_2E_2'. Corresponding to e_1 and e_2, the line passing through these points can be drawn. This is the line FIR, the slope of which was discussed earlier in connection with Figure 4.1.

The real world cannot always be assumed to be in a near-equilibrium state as it is presented in this exercise. But the assumption may be helpful for understanding the nature of the technological changes in scale organization of industries. Its economic character, in our view, can be indicated by the shape of the envelope-curve for input-output ratio and the FIR curve for input combination. This model may aid in understanding the basic mechanism of factors operating in firms of different scales. To the extent that the restraint on forming a competitive market is stronger, the model's power of interpretation would be weaker. For example, in some developing economies, the large-scale firms are either directly run by public enterprises or indirectly supported strongly by the government. The Manufacturing Survey data in such cases often tend to show that the levels of K/L and K/Lw are extremely high and that of Y/K is extremely low, forming a sharp discontinuity of the performance difference for relevant terms. Even in such cases, the conceptual framework and measurements may not be utterly irrelevant: they can be used for testing the degree of operation of the market mechanism.

Subcontract Arrangements: An Illustration of Organizational Changes
Our final topic in this lecture is the subcontract arrangement. We will not discuss subcontracting in depth, but only insofar as it is relevant to the major points of discussion. What we are specifically concerned with is the role of subcontracting in promoting technological advance. The subcontract system of manufacturing in Japan has been widely used in various subsectors, but with particular intensity in the machinery industry. It is a common view that the modern enterpriser's systematic use of cheap labor in the dualistic labor market was the original cause behind the development of subcontract arrangements. However, flexible supplies of cheap labor were used in all traditional industries. What is characteristic of machinery is its property of technology. This can be called the "divisibility" of production process: dividing the processes of production of parts and components in preparation for the final assembly stage, so as to dispense with diseconomies of scale. Hondai's analysis draws our attention in this respect.[16] Organizing for profitable use of this technological advantage is the essence of subcontracting. This is the reason why this system did not fade away as the dualistic structure of the labor market disappeared. Instead, it appears to have actually strengthened and widened its scope of application during the 1970s.

There is no direct indicator for subcontracting, but indirect ones are

[16] Susumu Hondai, "Organizational Innovation and Development of Japan's Sewing Machine Industry," Daito Bunka University, Tokyo (mimeographed), 1986. The basis of Hondai's analysis stems from the observation that a machine consists of many parts, not all of which must necessarily be produced by a large-scale firm which can assemble final products. The divisibility of the production process is its basic property. In his paper, Hondai emphasizes the importance of standardization of parts and explores historically the long and difficult process of establishing a standardization system for the sewing machine in Japan. The significance of complementary benefits for large and small firms are stressed in particular. The relationship of activities of small, medium, and large enterprises in terms of technology-organization is complex and may not be exactly of the same nature within machinery industries. Nevertheless, we share his view in its essence.

Table 4.6
C/Y Ratio for Machinery Industries

	General Machinery	Electric Machinery	Transportation Machinery	Precision Machinery
1971	28.9	16.4	22.1	27.7
1981	32.2	34.2	21.6	37.6

Source: *K T H*.
Note: 1971 data are for establishments with 20 or more workers, and 1981 data are for those with 30 or more; so the data are not strictly comparable.

available. One may be the ratio (C/Y) of the cost of the consignment of production or processing to other enterprises (C) to the net added value of products (Y). The percentage value of C/Y for key machinery industries is shown in Table 4.6.

For other industries, the percentage is minor, with the exception of textiles (25.9 in 1971 and 24.9 in 1981). Another rough indicator may be the ratio of the revenue from processing or production that is classified as added value. The percentage for small-scaleest (S') establishments is shown in Table 4.7.

Odaka, after presenting a detailed analysis of the performance of ancillary firms in subcontracting arrangements, discussed a switching point in technological upgrading of these firms[17]:

A transform came in 1960 or its neighborhood. Parts manufactures were actively engaged in the installment of newly-developed machinery, increasing the number of Japanese-made [parts]. . . . Not

Table 4.7
Percentage of Small-scale Establishment Revenue in Added Value

	Gen. Mach.	Elec. Mach.	Trans. Mach.	Precision Mach.	Textiles	Steel
1971 (under 20)	45.0	44.0	64.9	41.4	24.9	12.1
1981 (4–29)	35.4	47.1	61.0	40.8	70.0	24.1

Source: *KTH*.

[17] Konosuke Odaka, "The Place of Medium- and Small Scale Firms in the Development of the Automobile Industry—A Study on Japan's Experience, in *Papers and Proceedings of the Conference on Japan's Historical Development Experience and the Contemporary Developing Countries: Issues for Comparative Analysis* (Feb. 13–16, 1978; IDCJ), October 1978.

only did the medium-and-small firms increase the capital intensity of their production facilities, but they pushed it much further than the larger corporations.

As statistical evidence, Odaka shows over-time change in the number of existing machine tools per employee for automobile and automobile parts manufacturers from 1960 to 1973, by scale of establishment. The number of machine tools, secondary metal forming and cutting machines, and other types of equipment increased at least from 1963 to 1973 for S and M, while it tended to decrease slightly for L. Of course the number cannot precisely represent K/L; yet Okada's view is suggestive in light of the findings of our analysis, described earlier. The switch appears to be the outset of a long-sustained development in later years. Our earlier description of the course of technological progress seems to be consistent with his view, though ours deals with the machinery industries in general. Figure 4.3 may aid in understanding the point. The performances of K/L, w, and K/Lw (here the reciprocal of Lw/K, for convenience) are shown for 1966 and 1981, for purposes of comparison; transportation machinery is examined by the use of indices, taking the largest scale, L, as 100.

The picture is self-evident, but several points are worthy of note. As expected, the difference in level of K/L had clearly been narrowed almost uniformly over the total range of M and S, except for the smallest-scale firms (S′). In other words, in 1966 the largest firms (L) had extremely high levels of capital intensity, while the difference in level among M and S firms was relatively small. Thus the level of K/L took a bi-modal position between L and all other ranges of scale. In 1981 the shape of the scale distribution curve became quite different: it is almost a straight line, showing no kink; the bi-modal structure has disappeared. The change in K/Lw is also remarkable but is not uniform for all scale ranges: for the M range it narrows (the upper scale of M moves closer to L), and for the S range it widens. This is the result of a distinct narrowing of the difference in Lw/K: its level of L increased greatly relative to those of M and S.

The difference in the shapes of K/L and K/Lw is of course caused by wages. The movement of scale difference in the average wage level draws our attention: the relative level of M is raised distinctly while that of S remains almost unchanged. With respect to FIR, we find that the pattern of change in the 15 years under review differs between medium and small-scale establishments, although both narrowed the gap with large firms.

Let us consider the implication of these findings. First, a gradual

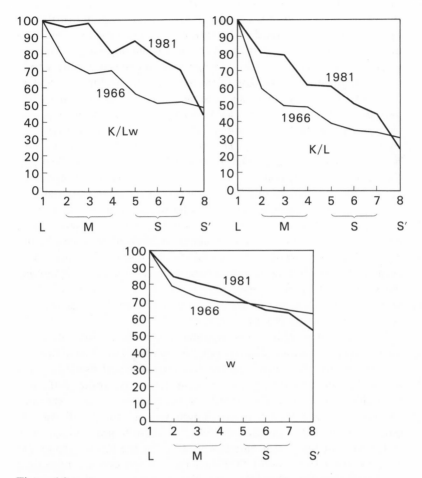

Figure 4.3
Scale Performance of Capital-intensity (K/L), Wages (w), and Factor-Input
Ratio (Lw/K) of Transportation Machinery: 1966 and 1981 in Comparison.
Source: MITI, *Basic Survey of Medium–Small Scale Enterprises*, 1966.

Remarks: i) K=capital, L=number of workers, w=wage, average annual
earnings.
ii) Indices, taking the largest scale (1)=100.
iii) Scale by the number of workers:
1 (1,000 and over); 2 (500–999); 3 (300–499);
4 (200–299); 5 (100–199); 6 (50–99);
7 (30–49); 8 (4–29)

phasing out of the bimodal organization is expected on the basis of our earlier discussion of the tendency toward even capital distribution by scale. As was discussed in Lecture 3, the subcontract arrangement at its outset had the serious problem of a technological gap between assemblers and ancillary firms. The gap was narrowed by direct technological guidance in the case of the assemblers. But for the ancillary firms, two factors in particular were necessary in order to narrow the gap: one is human technical capability and the other is superior machinery, equipment, and structures. Thus capital financing is inseparable from technological progress. The picture presented here is of transportation machinery manufacture as a whole and not specifically of the firms with a subcontract system. Yet the broad pattern can be applied to the latter. In our view, the level of capital intensity required by the assemblers (represented by L) had not yet been reached in the bi-modal organization in 1966. The capital-embodied concept may not be acceptable, but at least capital in its physical sense can be understood as the "carrier" of technology. As discussed earlier, more even capital distribution by scale is most distinct for machineries among the various subsectors. Financing is also one of the activities of assemblers, but this aspect requires separate treatment together with the government function (see Lecture 7).

The fading away of bi-modal organization, however, does not necessarily promise an even distribution of enterprises by scale. Instead, assemblers are of course among the largest enterprises. In 1974 automobile manufacturing, for example, ten corporations with over ten billion yen in capital and with 52 establishments are at the top; 34 corporations with one to ten billion yen in capital and with 94 establishments are in the second rank. The share of gross added value to the total of this sector amounts to 48% for the former group and 19% for the latter group (*KTH* data for enterprises with more than one establishment). These firms are the leaders in carrying out technological innovations; others are followers, though their own contributions to new devices cannot be ignored. We thus emphasize the importance of organizational activity in diffusing new and/or improved technological knowledge: subcontract arrangements do it more directly and at a faster pace than would be the case otherwise.

The pattern of wage change was discussed in relation to human capability—the level of worker quality. The subcontract system has long been characterized by a number of economists as merely a means to use cheap labor. However, by 1966 the dualistic pattern of wage differentials had already faded away. Since then, during the interval under review, as is suggested in Panel A of Table 4.1, the narrowed wage differential has essentially remained unchanged. The basic indicator, Lw/K, of M is now closer to that of L, which implies that the gap in wages becomes narrower than that in capital intensity. If the market evaluation of the quality of workers is essentially reflected by wages, the level of human technical capability of M must have become closer to that of L. This can actually be the case in the development of the subcontract system. In a comparable sense, S firms have not yet undergone this process. The diffusion of technology implies the narrowing of the gap in K/L and also of that in the level of human capability. This factor may be improved by "learning by doing" through the subcontract system itself with the guidance of the assemblers. However, basically, improvement is achieved by education and other social activities beyond the enterpriser's reach. For private enterprisers, the problem is how to utilize efficiently the labor force of improved quality.

We do recognize the "conventional" aspect of profitability of utilizing labor-intensive production of ancillary firms for assemblers, but, in our view, the new phenomenon thus found deserves particular attention.

Concluding Remarks

By way of conclusion, the major findings are summarized from a broad standpoint, including suggestions for further scrutiny on some of the points. In a historical perspective set in the long-term framework of over a century, Japan was successful in completing the final subphase of secondary export substitution, covering the entire secondary major phase. The characteristics of this final subphase can be summarized as follows, in three points.

First of all, an important switch was made as Japan evolved from a long-term latecomer depending upon borrowed technology to an economy that created its own technology. Our measurements of the innovative process in key industries provide empirical evidence for this transition, though not directly. Its amplification of technology transfer and other related aspects of the process will be further discussed in Lecture 7. However, it is our view that the tenacious technology gap was eventually eliminated with the completion of the phase under review. This pertains to the industries concerned with export substitution but not to industry in general. The machinery industry should be noted in particular in this regard. Within this industry, the technology-intensive areas, such as electronics, are highlighted. The conventional notion of durable goods in defining secondary export substitution may need reconsideration. At minimum, a breakdown into two categories would be required to grasp the reality: one category comprises industries with low factor input ratios (FIR); the other, those with high FIR. Steel is an example of the former category; machinery, of the latter.

Second, the organizational aspect of innovation seems to require much more attention. Our observation suggests that a sort of mechanism operant in the interaction between advances in technology and changes in scale-organization should be investigated further. For instance, with respect to the policy of promoting the development of medium- and small-scale enterprises, adoption of "appropriate" technology on the one hand and enhancement of labor employment on the other are emphasized often, though not in ways closely interrelated. In the diffusion of borrowed technology, the leader-follower relationship is recognized domestically in Japan's case. This suggests that if scale-organization can be arranged to operate the leader-follower relationship more efficiently, it would surely contribute to accelerating the process of diffusing advanced technology over a wide area in developing economies. This is a more general suggestion beyond the particular phase under review.

Third, we must say a few words on the time dimension of shifting phases. The phase of secondary export substitution in Japan was completed in fifteen years according to the dating system we used (Appendix 2). It would be a little longer or shorter under a different dating system. At any rate, it is much shorter than the long phase of secondary import substitution. Of course one cannot evaluate the length of the phase of secondary export substitution phase as such, because it has actually been experienced fully only by Japan. Nevertheless, it may be worthwhile noting the factors that influenced its duration. i) Externally, the international environment continued to be favorable, despite the occurrence of the first oil crisis toward the end of the secondary export substitution phase. This is in contrast to the phase of secondary import substitituion. ii) Internally, domestic demand for the export substituting industries expanded at a fairly fast rate, augmenting the effects on them of economies of scale. Not only high-income elasticities of consumer durables, but also a sustained high proportion of domestic investment to GDP (over 30%) is noted as resulting in a high level of demand for machinery and other investment goods. iii) Finally, the government policy had been kept "protective" against international competition. The liberalization policy proceeded rather reluctantly, actually covering the major part of the phase under review. Its evaluation differs from one observer to another and poses a controversial problem. In our view, at least, what is clear is that the time dimension was a crucial element in the government's protection policy, with its aim of strengthening the competitiveness of domestic industry without delay. The selective reaction of the private sector eventually succeeded in making this phase shorter than otherwise. The details will be discussed in Lecture 7.

Appendix 1   Postwar Changes in the Composition of the Machinery Industry, 1951–81

This Appendix attempts to arrange the data to observe over-time changes in the composition of the machinery industry during the postwar period, simply by selecting four years, 1951, 1961, 1971, and 1981. The resultant *KTH* data are used in Table 4A.1. The procedure of data arrangement is the same as for Table 2A.1.

Several points should be noted. i) The composition immediately after the war, represented by 1951, is close to that of 1930–40, as seen in Table 2A.1, with a transformation back to a peacetime pattern. ii) The period 1951–61 is the interval during which secondary import substitution was completed. Changes in the form of greater shares for categories (1), (2), and (4) and smaller shares for (8), (13), and (14) are particularly noteworthy. A shift from the old to a new type of industrial composition took place. iii) During the period 1961–81 secondary export substitution continued. Both an extension of the new composition established in the 1950s and a new movement were noticeable. The former was evident in the continued tendency toward an increasing share for category (1); the latter, in the emergence of category (3).

The products of category (1), motor vehicles and motor vehicle equipment, compose the major part of "the products of" transportation machinery, since shipbuilding (7), the pioneer sector of the machinery industry, now plays a minor role. Category (3), parts for electronic appliances, together with applied electronic equipment (a) and electric measuring instruments (b), composes the major part of the high-technology subsector (including semiconductors). The percentage share of the sum, (3)+(a)+(b), did increase tremendously: from 1.1% in 1951, it increased to 2.3% in 1961, 8.2% in 1971, and 12.4% in 1981.

These subsectors belong to the "electric machinery" sector, whose percentage share of the manufacturing total has increased only a little during the period, from 32.2% in 1961 to 33.4% in 1981. Therefore, within "electric machinery," there was a dramatic drastic change in the composition of new and old subsectors. Surely this is a remarkable process of innovation. Could our measurement with no disaggregation

Table 4A.1
Changes in the Composition of the Machinery Industry in Terms of Output
Share: Selected Postwar Years

(%)

	1951	1961	1971	1981
(1) Motor vehicles and motor vehicle equipment	2 (13.6)	1 (21.9)	1 (25.7)	1 (30.9)
(2) Communications machinery and related products	5 (5.9)	2 (12.2)	2 (11.0)	2 (9.3)
(3) Parts for electronic appliances and communications equipment	–	–	6 (5.1)	3 (6.6)
(4) Electrical generating, transmission, distribution, and industrial apparatus	3 (11.9)	3 (12.0)	4 (7.6)	4 (6.5)
(5) General industry machinery and equipment	6 (5.2)	4 (7.5)	3 (7.6)	5 (6.4)
(6) Applied electronic equipment	–	–	–	6 (5.1)
(7) Shipbuilding and repairing, and marine engines	1 (15.3)	5 (6.9)	5 (6.9)	7 (3.7)
(8) Metal working machinery	–	6 (5.1)	7 (3.9)	8 (3.6)
(9) Office service industry and household machines	7 (4.1)	–	8 (3.7)	9 (3.5)
(10) Miscellaneous machinery and parts	–	9 (3.0)	9 (3.5)	–
(11) Household electric appliances	–	7 (4.3)	–	–
(12) Boiler engines and turbines	8 (4.0)	8 (3.4)	–	–
(13) Textile machinery	4 (10.1)	–	–	–
(14) Railroad equipment and parts	9 (3.9)	–	–	–
Subtotal	73.9	76.3	74.8	75.7
Grand Total	100.0	100.0	100.0	100.0

Remarks: i) Percentage share of gross output in current prices. ii) The number indicates the order of shares of each subsector (percentage share in parentheses). iii) Subsectors 1 through 9 are registered for each year. Blank (−) means the rank is below 9th. iv) The composition in terms of shipments will be given in Table 8.3.

have grasped it or not? Further scrutiny will be required in order to know.

Appendix 2   Dating the Secondary Export Substitution Phase: Changes in the Export Composition of Manufactured Goods

This appendix provides the basic data for analyzing over-time change in the export composition of manufactured exports during the postwar period. Table 4A.2 gives the data for observing sectoral shift to secondary export substitution, and Table 4A.3 shows the relation between exports and domestic production in the machinery industries.

In Lecture 2, two approaches (one by commodity, the other by use) were presented for the discussion of secondary import substitution. Our view is that both approaches can be adopted, complementarily.

Table 4A.2
Changes in the Export Composition of Manufactured Goods, 1951–84: Selected Years

(%)

	Machinery	Metals	Chemicals	Subtotal	Textiles	Other	Subtotal	Total
	(1)	(2)	(3)	(4) (1)+(2) +(3)	(5)	(6)	(7) (5)+(6)	
1951	9.5	24.1	5.7	39.3	48.0	12.7	60.7	100.0
1955	14.6	21.6	6.7	42.9	39.5	17.5	57.0	100.0
1960	26.8	16.1	6.6	49.5	31.4	19.1	50.5	100.0
1961	30.9	15.7	7.6	54.2	28.2	17.6	45.8	100.0
1968	43.2	18.5	9.9	71.6	14.4	13.9	28.3	100.0
1969	47.4	18.8	9.9	76.1	13.4	11.5	24.9	100.0
1975	54.1	23.0	10.6	87.7	6.0	6.3	12.3	100.0
1976	58.7	20.0	8.7	87.4	5.6	7.0	12.6	100.0
1983	68.0	12.8	7.6	88.4	4.2	7.4	11.6	100.0
1984	70.8	11.5	7.2	89.5	3.7	7.8	11.5	100.0

Sources: 1951–70, LTES, Vol. 14, Table 1 in Part III. 1970–84, United Nations Statistical Office, Yearbook of International Trade Statistics.
Remarks: (i) "Other" is the sum of processed food, wood products, ceramics, and miscellaneous.
(ii) The percentages are based on the export value in current prices (yen).
(iii) More details will be given in Lecture 8, Table 8.2.

Table 4A.3
Export and Production of Machinery Industry: Four Subsectors in Selected
Years, 1951–81

(%)

	1951	1961	1971	1981
1) General Machinery				
i) Ratio: Export/Production	11.5	6.5	12.4	25.1
ii) Share of Export	50.8	24.3	20.0	21.4
iii) Share of Production	34.9	31.7	28.9	25.2
2) Electric Machinery, Equipment and Supplies				
i) Ratio: Export/Production	4.3	7.5	15.9	26.3
ii) Share of Export	12.6	28.1	28.0	29.6
iii) Share of Production	23.9	32.2	32.0	33.1
3) Transportation Machinery				
i) Ratio: Export/Production	5.9	10.5	24.5	35.1
ii) Share of Export	28.5	40.0	46.3	43.2
iii) Share of Production	36.9	32.0	34.7	36.5
4) Precision Machinery				
i) Ratio: Export/Production	7.8	8.5	18.2	29.7
ii) Share of Export	7.9	7.7	5.7	5.8
iii) Share of Production	4.3	4.2	4.3	4.9
Total				
i) Ratio: Export/Production	7.8	8.5	18.2	29.7
ii) Share of Export	100.0	100.0	100.0	100.0
iii) Share of Production	100.0	100.0	100.0	100.0

Sources: 1951: Trade Yearbook of Japan, Ministry of Finance, 1951 edition.
1961–81: Kikai Yushutu Sanju-nen-shi [Thirty-Year History of Machinery Exports] (Tokyo: Japan Association of Machinery Exports, 1981).
Remarks: Between the series of LTES (Vol. 14, Table 1, Part III) and these data, some discrepancies are found, but they are judged to be minor.

In the case of export substitution our view is the same. In this case, a by-use approach is not possible due to lack of available data, so the commodity approach is adopted. Its advantage is its direct connection with industry.

To reflect, albeit roughly, the aspect of "by use," the columns in the table are arranged so as to be used in two ways: one is a comparison between two groups of commodities (subtotal of machinery, metals, and chemicals vs. subtotal of textiles and others) and the other a comparison of single commodities (machinery vs. textiles). These can roughly correspond to a comparison of durable goods with nondurable goods. Additionally, a comparison within the former group (machinery vs. sum of metals and chemicals) is tried.

The following are noted. i) If the subtotal of machinery, metals, and chemicals (4) is compared with subtotal (7), the date at which export amounts were nearly equal is 1960–61. In a comparison of machinery (1) with textiles (5), the corresponding date is the same, 1960–61. ii) The trends of increase in (4) and (1) and decrease in (6) and (5) are shown to continue to the 1980s. In fact, the end of this trend should be demarcated somewhere. The mid-1970s seems to be a plausible point if we apply both a subtotal and a commodity approach. In both sectors (7) and (5) the shares tend to be much smaller. iii) However, for the three components of (4), the performance differs: machinery (1) increases steadily, reaching over 70% in 1984. In the cases of metals and chemicals, the trend is toward a decreasing share in the mid-1970s. Thus, in 1984 the role played by these two commodity categories became minor. In the future, this differential between major and minor will continue to widen.

Now, how do we interpret these findings in confirming the dates of the phase of secondary export substitution? An answer can be given as follows. There is no doubt about the date at which the two approaches coincide. For dating its end, the different performance within subtotal (4), in our view, should be considered important. It strongly supports dating the end of the process at the mid-1970s because metals and chemicals ceased to substitute for (5) and/or (7) at that time. We conclude that the phase of secondary export substitution starts at the beginning of the 1960s and ends in the mid-1970s.

A new phenomenon emerges, however: machinery substituting for metals and chemicals, changing the export composition, since the mid-1970s. One may be tempted to define this as the beginning of what we call tentatively a "tertiary subphase" of export substitution. Such a phenomenon may be peculiar to Japan, whose exports intensively tend to concentrate on machineries.

Although further scrutiny is required, for the time being, our view can be stated as follows. i) Japan's phase of secondary export substitution started around 1955–60 and ended in the mid-1970s. ii) The process of export replacement of metals and chemicals by machinery may better be categorized as a property of the fully industrialized phase. iii) However, it is of categorical significance in demarcating the mid-1970s as the end of the phase to identify the point at which the share of metals and chemicals began to decrease.

The second topic is the sustained trend of increase in machinery exports observed above. Corresponding to the conventional four machinery industry subsectors treated in the production analysis, the export data are arranged in Table 4A.3, which aims at clarifying the relation between exports and domestic production. Since the amount of imports is minor, the table can indicate roughly the relation between export and domestic demand.[18]

The following trends are noted. i) For manufacturing as a whole, the ratio of export to domestic production appears rather smaller (30% in 1981) than expected from its dominance in total exports of manufactured goods. This is of course due to the large dimensions of domestic demand, a characteristic of Japan and a feature of a "medium-sized" economy. Analytically, the production analysis developed in the main text seems to have an even greater significance here than elsewhere, though the changes in the comparative advantage of this industry were not examined. ii) As we go back to earlier years, this feature becomes stronger. During the decade 1951–61, the ratio was lower than 10%. This is consistent with our demarcation of the start of the phase under review, stated earlier. The pace of enhancement of the export ratio was remarkable through the 1960s and the 1970s. This implies that export substitution depended on much more than expansion of domestic production. iii) In subsector observation, this trend appears to be broadly uniform, although for transportation machinery (3) and precision machinery (4) the rate of acceleration was particularly rapid. As of 1981, the export ratio was higher (30–35%) for these two than for general and electric machinery (25–26%).[19] Still, we are inclined to stress the broad uniformity in pattern of the four subsectors.

---

[18] For example, the ratio of import/production for machinery was 3.6% in 1971 and 2.5% in 1980.

[19] The characterization of each subsector in this regard would need further scrutiny. For instance, highly advanced electronics is included in (2) and machine tool production, in (1). These require special treatment.

II
Major Factors and Activities

5

Capital Investment:

Pattern, Allocation, and Efficiency

In Lectures 5 and 6, the two basic production factors, physical capital and human resources, will be discussed. The phase approach in Part I treated capital and human resources as the major factors in shaping development—first in the conceptual framework in Lecture 1, and second in its application to individual phases of development in the latter part of Lecture 1 and Lectures 2, 3, and 4. In Lectures 5 and 6, we attempt to discuss them in depth, examining the behavior of each factor *per se*. We hope this will contribute to combining a phase approach with a factor approach.

In this lecture, capital formation is discussed using the conventional term *gross domestic investment* (I, hereinafter). Its proportion to GNP (or GDP), I/Y, is one of the "great" ratios used in measuring economic performance. Economic history tells us that I/Y tends to increase over the long term through the entire process of development. Investment increases effective demand on the one hand and enhances production capacity on the other. Of these two activities, the focus here will be on the latter, as it is more relevant to longer-term performance of the economy. Over-time pattern, allocation among sectors (institutional and industrial), and efficiency are the major topics. As was touched upon in Lecture 2, long swings and spurts are features of Japan's investment pattern in the secondary phase. These need further scrutiny. Investment allocation between public and private sectors, between direct-production industries and infrastructures, is another important concern. Because technical discussions are necessary for understanding the problem of infrastructure, it is treated extensively in an Appendix to this lecture. Particular emphasis will be placed on efficiency.

Incremental capital-output ratio, $I/\Delta Y$ (ΔY = incremental increase of output, hereinafter ICOR) is a conventional term often used, as in the Harrod-Domar formula. Its over-time performance (unchanged, increasing, or decreasing) will be examined in detail. Its use as an investment efficiency criterion is controversial. After decomposing ICOR into several terms, we will discuss its legitimate use by examining the performance of the industrial sector, and attempt to apply it to development planning.

I. The Overall Picture: Long-term Performance

Let us begin by looking at Table 5.1 to grasp the overall picture of investment performance. The phase demarcation is from Lecture 1, for convenience, with notations I and II for major phases and a and b for subphases. IIb is divided into two intervals, b_1 and b_2.

The investment proportion increased steadily during each phase, from a minimum of approximately 10% to a maximum of nearly 30%, in parallel with accelerating GNP growth rate and per capita GNP until IIb_1. A long-term trend of an accelerating rate of output growth was seen throughout all phases, although interrupted by occasional slowing down as the performance of latecomers caught up with that of leaders. Deceleration with higher I/Y in phase IIb_2 marks the end of the accelerated growth period, as will be discussed later. Two points

Table 5.1
Investment Performance by Phase (average annual rate of change, %)

		GNP (Y)	Total Popu- lation	GNP Per Capita	Investment Proportion (I/Y)	Incremental Capital-Output Ratio (I/ΔY)
Ia	(1887–1904)	2.6	1.1	1.5	9.7	3.7
Ib	(1904–1919)	3.3	1.2	2.1	14.8	4.2
IIa	prewar (1919–1938)	4.9	1.4	3.5	18.4	3.8
IIb_1	postwar (1954–1965)	9.6	1.0	8.6	27.0	2.8
IIb_2	(1965–1975)	6.2	1.1	5.1	33.4	5.4

Sources: Kazushi Ohkawa and Miyohei Shinohara, eds., *Patterns of Japanese Economic Development: A Quantitative Appraisal* (New Haven: Yale University Press, 1979)—hereafter, *PJE*. Postwar data are from Economic Planning Agency, *Annual Report on National Economic Accounts*.

Remarks: Average annual rates of change are calculated by a simple bridge procedure based on smoothed series. Investment (I) excludes military investment.

should be noted regarding the investment proportion I/Y. First, in the early 1960s the 30% investment proportion drew attention since such a high level had never been attained in a market economy. However, since that time other developing countries have also shown similar highs, and this is no longer considered a feature unique to the Japanese economy. The other point is the very low proportion of I/Y in the initial phase, which is not often found even in contemporary developing countries.[1] It is not true that Japan's investment proportion and savings ratio were initially high, as is often assumed. I/Y increased gradually along with a moderate output growth rate in the beginning; the rate per capita was as low as 1.5% despite the smaller rate of population increase compared with contemporary developing countries. This low I/Y is understandable in light of the analysis in Lecture 1, section II.

The long-term trend of increasing investment proportion can be called "trend acceleration," and is a "normal" pattern in successful developing economies. Asian developing countries generally followed this pattern until the semi-industrialization phase. The argument that this is a normal pattern requires qualification because controversial issues are involved. A sharp increase in the initial phase was particularly emphasized by W. W. Rostow and other economists of the "big push" school, as mentioned in Lecture 1. Such initial investment spurts strongly affected development planning by developing countries after the early postwar period, and the investment proportion increased in almost all developing economies during that period, with a few exceptions.[2] Present data indicate that investment patterns are better assessed from a longer perspective than the initial "take-off" period. Thus, special emphasis on the initial investment spurt is misplaced, and in fact no such initial spurt occurred in Japan. As discussed later, during the long-term process of development, the Japanese investment spurt took place later when impacts emerged and conditions allowing response to it existed.

Capital-Output Ratio: Change Over Time

The trend acceleration pattern of investment comprises a number of issues, among which investment efficiency is most important. What efficiency is and how it is measured are elaborated later. But as a

---

[1] In Asia, investment proportions for the 1970s averaged as follows: Nepal, 9.5%, Bangladesh, 14%, Pakistan, 17%, India, 21%, and Sri Lanka, 28%. In a number of African countries the proportion surpassed 20%.

[2] On average, from the 1960s to the 1970s the investment proportion I/Y increased as follows: in Asia (15 countries), from 17% to 22.3%; in Africa (22 countries), from 16.4% to 18.6%; and in Latin America (13 countries), from 18.7% to 20.1%.

preliminary approach, the incremental capital-output ratio, ICOR, is useful.[3] It is a simple ratio of investment amount, I, over the incremental increase in output, ΔY. If ΔY is planned for a five-year period, for example, by a 6% rate of output growth ($\Delta Y/Y$), if the required I/Y is 18% (or 24%), ICOR is expected to be 3 (or 4). The ratio thus simply indicates the relation between investment and output. For the time being the term "efficiency" is used in this loose sense, although in section III it will be defined in a more rigorous way.

The numerical value of ICOR is presented in the last column in Table 5.1. From Ia to Ib it increased, but in subsequent phases it decreased. In other words, ICOR is high and tends to increase during earlier phases, but toward the semi-industrialization phase it decreases. This tendency was sustained until IIb$_1$. We call this an "inverse U-shape," and the figures in Table 5.1 were calculated to show the ICOR shape. Without greater scrutiny it would be premature to fix the dates of the turning point of ICOR increase to decrease. This will be examined in the following section. Nevertheless, the shape itself does indicate the basic characteristics of the long-term ICOR performance. This is important because previous studies have not elucidated this shape explicitly, focusing instead on other aspects.

Economists often make judgments based on comparisons. When ICOR is smaller (larger), the rate of output growth will be higher (lower), given the same investment proportion I/Y. Japan's high rate of output growth can be explained by a low ICOR value with a high investment proportion (and/or savings ratio). This is a cross-sectional country comparison. Actually, the variation of numerical ICOR values among countries and their comparison may have some significance, although the factors responsible for determining the actual value differ from one country to another and the reasons for such differences are not clear. Estimates of average ICOR values for contemporary developing economies over the two decades 1960–80 are: Asia (15 countries), 3.5; Africa (22 countries), 4.2; and Latin America (13 countries), 4.1. The data and method of computation are comparable to those used for Japan in Table 5.1. These figures are strikingly similar to those for Japan except in the last postwar phase. ICOR values for individual countries sometimes differ widely, for example, the value for India and Sri Lanka tends to be high (over 5), while that for Pakis-

---

[3] The incremental capital-output ratio, $I/\Delta Y$, is calculated by the formula $I/\Delta Y = I/Y$ (investment proportion) $\div \Delta Y/Y$ (growth rate of output). This term is often called "marginal capital-output ratio," but "incremental" is better since it is not marginal in the conventional sense.

tan is low (around 3). Therefore, in international terms Japan's ICOR value is not especially low.

In assessing historical ICOR patterns, Kuznets's view[4] is suggestive. Based on a comprehensive examination of the historical experience of industrialized countries, he concluded that it is impossible to identify any historical regularity in ICOR performance internationally. However, Japan was a latecomer to industrialization after the Western countries, and it may not be inconsistent with Kuznets's findings that its ICOR pattern has not been identified in the West. Some economists have observed a pattern similar to that of Japan in Eastern Europe.[5]

It should also be noted that a number of development models often assume a constant ICOR; in fact, governmental development plans are based on its constancy. Analytically, such an assumption is a highly simplified sort of production function. Because most development plans are of relatively short duration (five years or less), the assumption of constant ICOR may appear valid in the short term, although it is not over the long term. Long-term changes in ICOR values are more important in analysis.[6]

The reasons for the inverse U-shape of ICOR values require lengthy discussion, in which there are two main components. One is the role played by industrialization and the other the infrastructure requirement. Successful industrial development with appropriately selected level and type of technology will contribute to maintaining a low level of macro-ICOR. If the operation of this force is not interrupted, it will cause a long-term declining trend. On the other hand, infrastructure establishment needs lump-sum investments, and the expected output is over a long duration. During earlier development phases, the pressure stemming from this is particularly strong. This may be a major reason for the relatively large value of ICOR and its tendency to increase in phases during which the force of industrialization is not yet operating fully.

[4] Simon Kuznets, "Quantitative Aspects of the Economic Growth of Nations: Long-Term Trends in Capital Formation Proportion," *Economic Development and Cultural Change*, Vol. 9, July 1961.

[5] Although such reports in the literature are limited, see Rudulf Bicanic, "The Threshold of Economic Growth," *Kyklos*, Vol. XV, 1962.

[6] In economics textbooks, the Harrod-Domar model is explained by using ICOR as a parameter to treat the I-S (investment vs. savings) relationship to examine the stability or instability of a growing economy. Furthermore, to define the type of technological change, constancy of ICOR is given specific content by calling it "neutral." This is often misunderstood to mean that ICOR is historically "typical" when it is unchanged. Note that the present approach is quite different from such a model framework.

The factors and phenomena relevant to this hypothesis are as follows. Fixed investment by type includes producer durable equipment (hereafter PDE), structures, and buildings (residential and nonresidential). All three components are indispensable for production promotion, although their combination varies according to each sector's technological properties. Here the significance of PDE is for manufacturing, whereas structures are significant for infrastructure investment. Actually, PDE is part of the infrastructure, for example, railway vehicles, and its proportion tends to increase over time, particularly in relation to the increase in electricity supply facilities. Nevertheless, it depends mainly on structures.

The ratio of PDE to structures is thus important. In Japan's case, change in the ratio over time distinctly shows an increasing trend. Using the phase demarcation in Table 5.1, the ratio on a phase average was 0.74 (Ia), 1.17 (Ib), and 1.51. (IIa). In the semi-industrialization phase, it became two times higher than its initial value in earlier years. Such a change in the type composition is involved in the investment performance previously discussed at the macro level. This drastic tempo of the ratio change cannot be expected for all developing economies. A more moderate pace may be set according to the circumstances and policies of each country. For latecomers in economic development, however, catching up may necessitate a fairly rapid increase in the ratio. Actually, compared with that in the U.S.A., for example, Japan's ratio rose much faster.

What are the effects of this performance on the ICOR? Table 5.2 provides some evidence. In terms of gross capital stock, the capital-output ratio (COR) is given as K/Y, but in long-term observation, the performance must be essentially similar to that for $\Delta K/\Delta Y$ or $I/\Delta Y$. What we call "facilitating industry" is actually very close to the infrastructure sector (see the Appendix to this lecture). The magnitude of the capital-output ratio shows a very big difference between the two subsectors despite its considerable variance over time. In earlier years, the difference of COR (and ICOR) must have been similar. This is the explanation for the greater value of ICOR in the earlier phases. These data are not sufficient to show changes over time precisely, but the general tendency for the COR in manufacturing to decrease fits the present hypothesis. During the primary phase, COR of the manufacturing sector was nearly unchanged in light of ICOR performance for the silk-reeling and cotton-textile industry examined in Lecture 1. The PDE is most directly related to industrial technology. In Lecture 2, imported PDE was called a carrier of technological knowledge to be transferred. If COR of manufacturing is large in the initial phase, as

Table 5.2
Capital-Output Ratio: Manufacturing vs. Facilitating Industries, Selected
Years 1908-38

	Manufacturing	Facilitating	Industry
1908	1.55	4.40	2.73
1910	1.61	4.67	2.83
1915	1.57	4.87	2.95
1920	1.33	7.30	3.34
1925	1.10	5.14	2.79
1931	0.90	7.09	2.88
1934	0.93	7.92	2.91
1938	1.16	6.37	2.75

Source: From IDCJ worksheets prepared by Nobukiyo Takamatsu, "Tentative Estimates," 1985, Supplement to LTES.
Remarks: (i) Mining is included in manufacturing. Public utilities, transportation, and communications compose "facilitating industries" (construction is included).
(ii) Industry covers manufacturing and facilitating industries.
(iii) In terms of 1934-36 prices.

in India, the economy will experience greater pressure to increase investment efficiency.

To discuss the subject more specifically, additional explanations are in order concerning the function of government during earlier phases. During the initial phase, in any developing economy, governmental decisions on physical infrastructure are most important. The problem of allocating investment between the public and private sectors is a topic discussed in section II. Here the discussion is confined to one specific dimension. As mentioned above, government investment in infrastructure is "structured" by type classification, and its performance is examined by its relation to the total investment in the private sector, excluding residential buildings. Numerical values are given in Table 5.3.

One would expect the ratio (1)/(2) to increase toward the end of the initial phase. In fact, it did increase except for period (7), which was clearly influenced by a private investment spurt during World War I. To compare these figures with the phase averages presented above, an average of the ratio for phase Ib excluding period (7) is calculated as 40.0%, compared with 32.6% for phase Ia. Government investment in structures covers such major items as harbors, repair work, roads, water works, irrigation-drainage facilities, and railroads. It is our conjecture that this is most responsible for the increase in ICOR from

Table 5.3
Investment in Earlier Phases: Government Structure Investment in Relation to Total Private Investment (five-year averages)

(unit: million yen, 1934–36 prices)

		(1) Government investment in structures	(%)	(2) Total private investment	(%)	(%)
(1)	1885–1889	42	(24.2)	173	(75.8)	(100.0)
(2)	1890–1894	62	(26.8)	232	(73.2)	(100.0)
(3)	1895–1899	98	(30.0)	323	(70.0)	(100.0)
(4)	1900–1904	133	(49.4)	269	(50.6)	(100.0)
(5)	1905–1909	171	(37.8)	451	(62.2)	(100.0)
(6)	1910–1914	259	(42.1)	614	(57.9)	(100.0)
(7)	1915–1919	169	(15.6)	1,080	(84.4)	(100.0)

Source: Ohkawa and Shinohara, eds., *Patterns of Japanese Economic Development* (*PJE*), Table A39, pp. 354–60.
Remarks: (1) excludes military investment; (2) excludes residential buildings.

Ia to Ib, as shown in Table 5.1. Thus the basic tendency for ICOR to increase is strongly endorsed by this evidence.

Japan's ICOR pattern in the initial phase is normal performance for developing economies in a broad sense. Currently a number of developing economies face difficulties in dealing with similar pressure for required infrastructure investment. Today public utilities are much more important. To make a shift to the next phase of semi-industrialization, the total amount of investment required to build up the infrastructure is so enormous that no government can accomplish it in a short period. Japan had the advantage of irrigation facilities and roads inherited from the Tokugawa Era. Nevertheless, toward the latter part of the primary phase a greater portion of total investment was required for infrastructure buildings. Some developing economies may be able to maintain the macro-level of ICOR nearly unchanged, avoiding a distinct increase in the primary phase. For example, a country with abundant natural resources can maintain ICOR at a low level in the primary commodity production sector. In agriculture, rich land resources can lower it. As long as the output share of this sector remains fairly large, the macro-ICOR may be affected and thus not increase. Pakistan presents such a case. As stated in Lecture 1, Japan lacked land resources, and the agricultural sector ICOR was comparatively large (4.5–5.0 in the primary phase and even larger in the secondary phase). Such country-specific differences should be taken into account. From the viewpoint of industrialization, however, the possibility of an initial increase in ICOR may be fairly general.

Finally, in addition to these empirical findings, the "interactive mechanism" that is supposed to operate between the infrastructure and direct production sector, particularly the industrial sector, must be emphasized. The direct production sector needs infrastructure to develop and make technological advances, while the infrastructure needs to maintain efficiency by keeping its rate of utilization above a certain level. Otherwise, investment in these facilities would not be beneficial. This relation is called the interactive mechanism. A lack or weaker operation of one element would hamper the effective work of this interactive mechanism and affect ICOR. Recognizing this mechanism is generally valid for the long-term performance of ICOR in the inverse U-shaped curve, we can interpret it in a specific conceptual framework. During the earlier phases of development the mechanism operates with a positive function of the infrastructure, especially that invested in by the government, whereas in the later phases of semi-industrialization the mechanism works with the leading function from private investment. In some countries, the turning point is reached earlier, whereas in others it is later. These important points are discussed in depth in the Appendix on infrastructure.

II. Investment Swings: The Private and Public Relationship

Long Swings and ICOR Trends

Having discussed long-term investment performance, let us now focus on its swings. "Swings" mean ups-and-downs in investment either in terms of its proportion to output (I/Y) or in the rate of change in the investment itself (GI). The ups-and-downs of investment in the short term are a feature of business cycles. "Swings" here are defined as being of longer duration, usually 15–20 years. Kuznets called them "long swings." Originally, this notion pertained to changes in the rate of output growth rate, but here it is used for investment. It is often called a "Kuznets cycle," and the possibility of regular repetition of upswings and downswings has long been a topic of academic research to explain the historical experience of industrialized countries. Here we are not concerned with analyzing the mechanism, but with examining empirically Japan's pattern of up- and downswings in relation to long-term investment performance. For developing countries

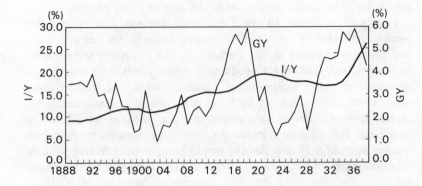

Figure 5.1(A)
Investment Proportion (I/Y) and Rates of Output Growth, 1887–1938
Source: LTES, Vol. 1. I/Y from Table 35, p. 241; GY from Table 38, p. 244.
Remarks: i) Smoothed series (7-year moving averages except 1887 and 1938, which are 5-year averages, all in 1934–36 prices).
  ii) I is gross domestic investment, excluding inventory changes.

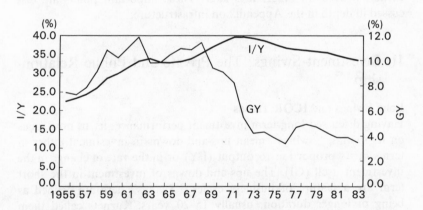

Figure 5.1(B)
Investment Proportion (I/Y) and Rates of Output Growth, 1955–83
Source: For 1954–65, LTES, Vol. 1, Table 18-A, p. 214. For 1966–84, EPA, National Income Accounts.
Remarks: i) In 5-year moving averages (3-year for 1983) of deflated series (1965 prices).
  ii) I includes inventory changes.

the postwar years were largely upswings, but in the 1980s they faced downward pressure on growth. This may not be a short-term problem of the business cycle type, but a long-swing one and thus a matter for concern.

Figure 5.1 (A, prewar; B, postwar) presents an overall picture of changes in investment proportion, I/Y, with the average annual rate of output (GNP) growth, GY, in the entire period. Both are 7-year (postwar, 5-year) moving averages in order to eliminate business cycles and *ad hoc* effects, and yet the range of variation remains considerable in GY, especially for prewar years. For I/Y, however, we can see a long-term moderately increasing tendency until around the turn of the century (preliminary upswing), followed by a preliminary downswing of shorter duration, which indicates the operation of depressing factors in the initial phase. A moderate upswing started after the Russo-Japanese War, 1904–5, and was accelerated by the World War I boom, forming the first upswing. Its termination, the peak of which was around 1920 (I/Y was still smaller than 20%), was followed by a long-lasting I/Y decrease. The trough of this first downswing was around 1931, and I/Y dropped as low as 16%. This coincided with the Great Depression. The second upswing began slowly in the early 1930s and accelerated toward its end. The third upswing in the postwar growth period was very sharp (I/Y near 40% at its peak) and was sustained until the early 1970s, followed by another decline.

We are not concerned with a history of Japanese investment, but instead would like to show that the eventual successful trend acceleration pattern of investment had to overcome the pressures of drawback forces (the war-affected 1945–52 period excluded in our calculations marked the biggest downswing). This is not an inevitable phenomenon for all developing economies, although the effects of external factors, such as World War I and the Great Depression, as well as those of internal factors, such as wartime resources mobilization in the 1930s, are important. Operation of external and internal factors differs among individual developing economies. The unfavorable world economic situation in the interwar period should not be expected to be repeated. Nevertheless, attention must be paid to downswings rather than assuming implicitly that upswings experienced by most postwar developing economies are "normal" phenomena.

Although GY varies more than I/Y, its performance also shows a distinct long-term pattern. Of interest is the relation between the two—swings of investment proportion and those of the rate of output growth. As seen in Figure 5.1, in upswings I/Y becomes higher but the rate of GY acceleration is more impressive, while in downswings, the decline of I/Y appears slow and the deceleration of GY is more drastic. If the incremental capital-output ratio is assumed to be constant, I/Y and GY should change in parallel. Therefore, it is obvious that under the swing-unit observation the numerical value of ICOR must change considerably.

What are the reasons for this? First is the demand aspect. For a similar performance of business cycle the usual answer is the effects of demand variation and hence of the changes in the rate of utilization of production factors, in particular, capital stock. Therefore the conventional method is to adjust the rate of utilization change by use of a "normal" value of ICOR defined as nearly the full rate of utilization. An analogous application of this method may be useful for swing-unit observations. Table 5.4 lists the swing-unit figures calculated as

Table 5.4
Investment, Output Growth, and Incremental Capital-Output Ratio in Swing Averages, 1881–1965

(%)

Period	No. of years	GY	I/Y	ICOR	
1. U, 1888–1897	(10)	3.31	8.34	2.53	
					3.76 (1+2)
2. D, 1898–1904	(7)	1.85	9.87	5.34	
					4.74 (2+3)
3. U, 1905–1919	(15)	3.32	14.63	4.41	
					5.39 (3+4)
4. D, 1920–1930	(11)	2.27	15.63	6.88	
					5.14 (4+5)
5. U, 1931–1938	(8)	5.01	14.98	3.00	
6. U, 1953–1965	(12)	9.43	26.18	2.56	
7. 1965–1975	(10)	7.86	36.43	4.63	

Source: The same as for Figure 5.1 except for 1953–65 (period 6), for which the original data are from LTES, Vol. 1, Table 18-A, p. 214, and Table 38-A, p. 245.

Remarks: (i) Averages are calculated in the same way as for Figure 5.1 except for period 6 (1953–65), for which 5-year moving averages (3-year for 1963 and 1965) of the series in 1965 prices are used.

(ii) Demarcation of upswings (U) and downswings (D) identifies peaks and troughs in the rate of investment changes. The number of years' duration for each is shown in parentheses.

(iii) Because of its abnormal performance and lower data reliability, the period affected by the war, 1940–52, is excluded.

(iv) GY is period average of the annual rate of growth of GNP calculated from smoothed series. I/Y is also a period average of annual figures.

perliminary averages. As expected, ICOR is smaller for upswing periods (U) and greater for downswings (D). The investment proportion I/Y shows a long-term trend of increase despite swings. One exception, in period 5, is caused by allocating resources for military purposes. On the other hand, GY shows a typical pattern of swings. These two forces shaped the swingwise changes in ICOR. In the last column, the value of ICOR is shown for periods covering U and D in overlapping averages for reference. The value tended to increase until periods 3 and 4, 1904–30, and then began to decrease toward the next interval, 1919–38. This appears to be a confirmation of the long-term trend. But the "average" approach, although convenient, does not yield a clear picture.

A comparison over time through the U periods (1, 3, 5, and 6) reveals the pattern of ICOR throughout the entire period: first there was an initial increase (from 2.5 in period 1 to 4.4 in period 3), and then it began to decline through the long semi-industrialization phase (from 4.4 in period 3 to 2.6 in period 6). It is meaningful to observe a long-term trend through upswings because the numerical values of ICOR indicate that changes in the relation between GY and I/Y in terms of productive capacity are little affected by changes in the rate of utilization. In theory, the ICOR defined in terms of production capacity is an acceptable notion, and the trend through U periods shows an inverse U-shape of the ICOR curve, which confirms the validity of the hypothesis in the preceding section.[7]

Beyond statistical measurements, what does the inverse U-shaped curve imply? To shift phases in development successfully, a trend acceleration of the investment proportion is necessary. This is why the "capacity to absorb investment" of a nation has been considered important. If this idea holds true, the trend acceleration pattern implies a parallel increase in the level of that capacity, first at a moderate and later at an increasingly accelerated pace. The applicability of this notion is doubtful, however. Without connecting it with the performance of investment efficiency, it is not realistic. A higher investment proportion with lower efficiency is not sufficient for a sustained development process. Nevertheless, the inverse U-shaped curve suggests that this "unfavorable" phenomenon is inevitable in earlier phases. Economic development is a challenge for all nations. If this curve is applied to all as it is to Japan, then combat with the forces of decreasing investment efficiency, stemming from investment proportion increase,

---

[7] An increase from period 6 to 7 presents a different problem related to reaching the terminal point (Lecture 1), and will be discussed later.

would have to occur to maintain the required level. If it fell below that level, a shift to the next phase would be impossible.

To talk about the ICOR performance of the postwar developing countries is not our primary concern, but a comparison is made for reference among selected Asian countries (Table 5.5). The figures are comparable to those for Japan, although U and D periods are not distinguished. The two decades of the 1960s and 1970s can be thought of as an upswing phase, although the 1970s were affected by less favorable effects of demand expansion in two oil crises. In Asia there was a general tendency for ICOR to increase, except in Indonesia, an oil-producing country. Some Asian countries experienced a decline in GY, while in others it increased; and yet ICOR increased because of a marked increase in investment proportion I/Y. This was particularly noticeable in the Philippines, Malaysia, and the Republic of Korea—countries near or in the semi-industrialization phase.

Thus a general increase in ICOR occurred from 1960 to 1980, possibly due to increased ICOR in production capacity. This conjecture is based upon a notable increase in the investment proportion toward the 1970s. Apart from group I, all the countries in group II increased I/Y in the 1970s to a level higher than the prewar high in Japan. In

Table 5.5
Growth Performance Related to Investment: Selected Asian Countries, 1960–80

(%)

		GY		I/Y		ICOR	
		1960s	1970s	1960s	1970s	1960s	1970s
I:	Bangladesh	3.7	3.9	9.0	14.0	2.4	3.5
	Nepal	2.5	2.5	7.0	9.5	2.8	3.8
II:	India	3.4	3.6	18.0	21.0	5.2	5.8
	Sri Lanka	4.6	4.1	17.0	28.0	3.6	6.8
	Pakistan	6.7	4.7	14.0	17.0	2.0	3.6
	Indonesia	3.9	7.6	11.0	18.0	2.8	2.3
III:	Thailand	8.4	7.2	21.0	26.5	2.5	3.6
	Philippines	5.1	6.3	18.5	25.5	3.6	4.0
	Malaysia	6.5	7.8	17.0	24.5	2.6	3.1
IV:	Republic of Korea	8.6	9.5	19.0	29.0	2.2	3.0

Source: World Bank, World Development Report, 1983, Appendix Tables; World Tables, 1978, Table 3.
Remarks: I includes inventory changes. I/Y is an average of 1960 and 1970 for the 1960s and an average of 1970 and 1980 for the 1970s.

all the countries in groups III and IV, the level of I/Y was close to Japan's postwar high. That a larger I/Y is characteristic of Asian developing countries cannot be denied, and although their higher ICOR value is often criticized as a distortion from the normal line of changing ICOR, this view is not legitimate in light of our earlier discussion. It is our view that these developing economies were facing difficulties in combating the forces of inducing inefficiency stemming from a rapid increase in the investment proportion, similar to Japan's experience in earlier phases. However, this observation is not without problems. When will a decrease in ICOR occur in these countries? Newly industrializing economics (NIEs) and near-NIEs are candidates for that point in the near future, and we look forward to observing their performance in the coming phase.

Unfortunately, after the early 1980s, GY in most developing countries dropped. In some, the deceleration has been serious and thus ICOR has tended to increase sharply (in most of them to 5–7). It is our view that this phenomenon will not be the short-duration, cyclical type, and thus the tendency for greater ICOR may become a sustained, serious problem because adjustment of I/Y to GY deceleration is extremely difficult.

Private vs. Public Investment

Let us look now at the role of investment and its allocation between the public and private sectors. During the secondary phase, the investment upswing was led by the private sector, whereas public investment played a greater role in the downswing. The performance during the primary phase, however, was different: the public sector played a stronger role almost completely throughout. These patterns are illustrated in Figure 5.2 in terms of average annual rate of fixed investment change.

In the initial phase, the greater role of public investment is evidenced by its larger rate of growth, as discussed in relation to infrastructure in the preceding section. The major point here is to discuss investment during the long phase of semi-industrialization. Two aspects are of major concern: one is private investment spurt, the core of upswings; the other is the public investment during downswings.

A notable private investment upswing was first seen during World War I, second, in the latter part of the 1930s, and third, during the early postwar growth period around the 1960s. The duration of a high level of investment longer than a business cycle (for example, the seven years of the Juglar cycle) is called a "spurt." Three types of

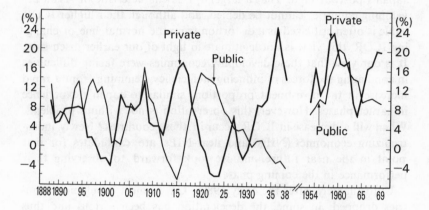

Figure 5.2
Rates of Change in Investment: Private vs. Public, 1888–1969
Source: LTES, Vol. 1, p. 33.
Remarks: i) Fixed investment, residential construction, and military investment excluded.
ii) Calculated from smoothed series based on the same procedure as for the series in Table 5.4.

spurt have been identified for Japan.[8] In Lecture 1, the investment spurt was characterized for its important role of demarcating phases. In Lecture 2, its significant role in bringing about demand expansion was identified in the process of industrial transformation. Now further discussion is in order.

The distinct occurrence of an investment spurt is discernible not in the primary phase, but in later years. In this respect, this is quite a different notion from the take-off concept discussed in the preceding section. In the postwar developing economies, especially the newly industrializing economies, investment spurts have recently been identified, and thus Japan's pattern is not unique. As discussed earlier, it is not necessary to limit the possibility of occurrence to "only once," since in Japan's case they have been multiple. It could be repeated if the economy enters a downswing and could act to recover acceleration. Private investment was responsible for Japanese spurts, except for the second in the late 1930s when public investment played a greater role through "military expenditure" (excluded in Figure 5.2). As will

[8] K. Ohkawa and H. Rosovsky, Japanese Economic Growth, especially p. 205.

be discussed further in Lecture 7, the first private investment spurt marks the beginning of independent operation of private activities. This is of great historical significance, as clearly shown in Figure 5.2. During downswings, the rate of increase in public investment increase surpasses that of private investment; typical examples were the 1920s and the downswing in the primary phase in the late 1890s. During postwar growth, public investment appears simply to follow private investment. During the dip (short-term downswing) around the mid-1960s, however, the usual pattern seems to have recurred.

With respect to public and private investment, one argument is that the relationship is that of leader and follower. In a market economy, the private sector should be the leader and the government the follower. This is too simple and rigid to be applied to the real process in developing economies. First, historically a distinct difference is witnessed between the primary and the secondary major phase: during the former, public investment generally took the leadership role, whereas during the latter private investment played the leading role. Second, with respect to long swings, the situation is different. The actual performance of investment, as seen from the viewpoint of leader-follower, is explained as follows. During downswings, the leading role played by government contributed to reducing the imbalance caused by the downswing in private investment. The slowness of the decline in the total investment proportion, I/Y, during the downswings noted earlier thus resulted, without which the downswing would have been much more severe. It is possible to say that generally the private and public sector investment operate in a complementary relationship to some extent. On the other hand, during upswings, private leadership is followed by public investment. A more competitive relationship did not develop except during the second upswing.[9]

"Complementary vs. competitive" may be too simple a description, but at least two aspects of this relationship are to be distinguished: one is commodity production and the other financing. As discussed in Lecture 2, Japan's case presents no serious problem resulting from negative effects of competition between the two sectors. From the point

[9] To supplement Figure 5.2, the same data expressed in terms of percentage proportion of private vs. public investment are added for the selected P (peak) and T (trough) years of prewar long swings.

	Private	Public		Private	Public
1887 (T)	78.6	21.4	1918 (P)	79.8	20.2
1894 (P)	76.6	23.4	1932 (T)	58.8	41.2
1901 (T)	64.0	36.0	1938 (P)	79.1	20.9

of financing, during the postwar upswing the government maintained a balanced budget policy. In principle, this was aimed at avoiding undesirable effects of investment competitive with the private sector. In the first investment spurt in the private sector, public investment did nothing positive. However, in the second investment spurt, government investment was accelerated by increasing its I-S (investment-savings) gap in the public account. This illustrates the competitive case which naturally leads to inflationary growth. On the contrary, during downswings the increase in public investment based on widening the I-S gap did not compete with private investment, but savings siphoned off by government borrowing acted as a complementary force.[10]

Actually, the alteration of negative $(I > S)$ and positive $(S > I)$ gap in the public account largely coincides with the long swing demarcation discussed earlier. It was moderately positive for 1885–92 but negative in 1893–1905 (including the wartime effects of the Sino-Japanese War, 1894–95, and the Russo-Japanese War, 1904–5). A positive situation recurred thereafter, especially during World War I. Particular attention is drawn to the period that followed, 1920–26, which sustained the $S > I$ position despite a severe downswing. During the 1930s, of course, it again became $I > S$.[11]

Finally, investment planning should be discussed. Up to the present, development economics has paid little attention to the problem of downswings, and our knowledge is limited on this important aspect of development for the years ahead. In Indonesia, Thailand, and Malay-

[10] Savings are implicitly treated as the domestic source for financing investment.

i) At the macro level, a trend acceleration type is broadly witnessed for savings ratio, S/Y, similar to I/Y. Actually, from the very low ratio (close to 10% in gross) in the initial phase, it increased to a high level close to 30%. The leveling up of income and the acceleration of its rate of growth, in our view, are most influential in determining the performance of savings over time.

ii) Sectorwise, apart from the government, the relation between private enterprise and households (including unincorporated enterprises) has long been similar to other developing Asian economies: savings of the latter finance the great part of investment of the former.

iii) With regard to the households sector, a savings function of the type $S_t = A + bY_t + cY_{t-1}$ is a good fit (1908–66). Y stands for disposable income. This is a test of the hypothesis mentioned in i), as this lag form implies the rate of income growth in addition to its level. For details, see Kazushi Ohkawa, "Chochiku-ritsu no Choki Hendo" [Long-term Changes in Savings], Chapter 7 in *Nihon Keizai no Kozo* [Structure of the Japanese Economy] (Tokyo: Keiso Shobo, 1974).

For the primary phase, savings of farm households are particularly important in forming "agricultural surplus." This will be discussed in Lecture 7.

[11] Based on the accounts presented in Tables 3 and 4 in Part III, *LTES*, Vol. 1. Government savings are estimated by the conventional definition (current revenue minus expenditure). Investment excludes military. See further discussion in Lecture 7.

sia, for example, recent five-year national development plans are compiled based on 5% annual rate of GNP growth. Their ICOR thus implied may be 5–7, a big increase compared with the levels in Table 5.5. Very much like the case of Japan's downswing, this is primarily due to the difficulty of adjusting the high proportion of investment to the slower rate of GNP growth. Strategies and policies to cope with downswings may differ from one country to another, and no general suggestion can be made. Yet, something relevant can be induced from Japan's experience.

First, from the viewpoint of long-term planning, a very high magnitude of ICOR in downswings should be distinguished from that realized during upswings. Japan's value of 5.3–6.9 during downswings may be a good reference value. It is much greater than the value during upswings (2.5–4.4), as shown in Table 5.4. It is now desirable to take a longer-term perspective, taking into account both downswings and upswings. Examination of Japan's experience indicates that the magnitude of ICOR in production capacity terms tends to increase during the primary phase and that from the earlier years of the secondary phase it starts to decrease. We are convinced that the inverse U-shaped pattern holds, although the dates of the turning point in Japan may not be directly applicable to other developing economies since the factors involved will differ from one country to another. In some cases the turning point can be earlier, whereas in others it may be later. To proceed along this line, a more intensive sectoral approach may be useful in arranging and improving a country's knowledge for sectoral investment allocation.

Second, in some countries, investment spurts supported by public sector leadership occurred, accompanying an unduly large gap $(I > S)$ in the public account. This would need reconsideration for the sound operation of market economies. Public investment can be planned to play a complementary role during downswings, although the actual situation may differ among the countries under review. In this respect, as suggested earlier, Japan's experience in the second downswing was unsatisfactory because the public account maintained the $S > I$ situation. Public investment should play a stronger role during downswings.

III. Investment Criteria and Decomposition of the Capital-Output Ratio

The objectives of development plans are characterized by sociocultural values as well as by the political system of each country and cannot be treated uniformly by a general theme. However, the means of fulfilling the objectives must be discussed generally in terms of criteria pertaining to the use and allocation of given resources. The criteria can be considered with respect to planning decision-making with respect to the input and allocation of production factors at three levels: macro, sectoral (including subsectoral), and micro (individual projects).

The criterion for capital investment was the incremental capital-output ratio, ICOR, in the early postwar beginning stage of macro (and major sectoral) development plan compilation. Since then, the development of technical procedures has made ICOR less useful, in particular in the demand-expenditure approach. Yet even now the use of ICOR, as discussed in preceding sections, continues especially in the compilation of long-term plans to which the demand-expenditure approach cannot usefully be applied. On the other hand, the project appraisal approaches recently developed at the micro level treat the criterion in terms of the rate of expected capital return, principally following the theory of microeconomics. They are developed in somewhat different ways, but are essentially the same in using the time discounting method in deriving "cash flow." From this aspect, the classic notion of ICOR is often rejected as being not useful and even misleading. Thus macro and micro approaches are divorced. In between, for the sectoral (for example, manufacturing) and subsectoral (electric machinery) approaches, no clear-cut proposition has yet been made with respect to the investment criterion: some use ICOR, others labor productivity and employment.

In light of this situation, in this section we would like to go one step further in forging closer conceptual links between these approaches at different levels by introducing the concept of a "residual" in decomposing ICOR. In doing so, we would like to clarify its meaning as the criterion for investment at the sector level.

Let us assume, for the sake of illustration, that we have two major objectives: augmentation of investment efficiency and labor employment. These two have often been considered to be in a "trade-off" relation: selection of technology yielding higher labor productivity results in poor employment effects and *vice versa*. This is valid in a static sense. Without taking further steps conceptually, however, such a proposition is not useful for solving the practical problems involved in setting economic development policies. The ICOR at the macro-sectoral level will be decomposed into two elements which basically correspond to the above-mentioned two objectives.

This attempt is to grasp the process of economic development of an innovative nature *à la* Schumpeter's original concept of "innovation." At the macro-sectoral level, the concept of a "residual" in the growth accounting approach is placed at the center of the framework in order to quantify the innovative process. At the micro level, through transforming all the project data into added-value terms, the concept of a residual can similarly be used. In practice, some authors use the term "residual" in project analysis.[12] At the same time, it is suggested that this type of project analysis should be reformulated in order to treat more explicitly the employment effects, in particular in relation to the residual appraisal. A detailed discussion of this is beyond the scope of this lecture, however.

Innovative Process: Residual Approach
Let us begin with a simple but important assumption with which an innovative process can be measured quantitatively. The assumption is indispensable for applying the conventional notion that the residual is the value added obtained over and above the prevailing input costs.[13] In comparison with the base year, a development plan aims at a certain increase in the output in the coming year. This is expressed by ΔY, the incremental output increase. Actually all development plans expressed it in a growth formula, $\Delta Y/Y_0$, where Y_0 stands for the output in the base year. In the preceding sections we have discussed it as GY. Below, however, comparison with the base year will be dropped. This changes nothing substantively. The input costs at the incremental level are given by ΔC. For simplicity, let us take up production factor capital, K, and labor, L, excluding land, which is especially important in agriculture. Their incremental increases, ΔK and ΔL, are evaluated by their market prices, r (rate of capital return, or interest rates), and w (wage rates, with differentials due to skill differences), respectively. This assumes a near-competitive factor market.[14] We have

$$\Delta C = r\Delta K + w\Delta L.$$

The main content of this simple procedure is as follows. We can conceive ΔY^*, the incremental output, which is equal to ΔC, for the hypothetical case of no innovations, or no technological-organiza-

[12] J. Price Gittinger, *Economic Analysis of Agricultural Projects* (Baltimore: Johns Hopkins University Press, 1972), p. 66.

[13] In application, this is well described by John W. Kendrick, "A Perspective on Partial and Total Productivity Measurement," in Yujiro Hayami, Vernon W. Ruttan, and H.W. Southworth, *Agricultural Growth in Japan, Taiwan, Korea and the Philippines* (Honolulu: East-West Center, The University of Hawaii, 1979).

[14] In project appraisal, r and w are "opportunity costs" of capital and labor in concept. As for their application to actual cases, we have to make approximations of various kinds.

tional changes between the base period and the period to be compared. Under this assumption we define the incremental increase in the residual, ΔR, as the difference between the two kinds of output increase, that is

(1) $\Delta R = \Delta Y - \Delta Y^*$, where $\Delta Y^* = r\Delta K + w\Delta L$.

In other words, it is assumed that the output effects of technological-organizational changes can be measured by the incremental increase in what we call the residual.

This is the simplest statement of the methodology. Its possible distance from reality requires more qualifications. In concept one may naturally suspect that ΔY^* is not possible in the real world. This is legitimate, but it represents an approximation by conceiving that the comparison pertains to a very short interval. In addition, the residual thus estimated would include all the effects of nonconventional factors (other than capital and labor), such as economies of scale, reallocation effects of conventional factors, changes in the natural endowment effects, and so forth. Finally, as in the previous discussion of ICOR, measures in shorter-term dimensions would show considerable distortions of the numerical value of the residual from that in the capacity concept. An appropriate interval is required to obtain meaningful values of the residual.

These are the actual problems we face. Actually, in the application of the growth accounting formula to analysis of the experience of industrialized countries, great efforts have been made with respect to the decomposition of the residual itself.[15] Decomposition of the residual, however, is beyond the scope of this lecture. Changes in technology and organization have been referred to as illustrating the major elements of innovations, and we would like to interpret them in a wider scope without decomposing them. As will be discussed in Lecture 6, in interpreting the residual estimated we will pay special attention to the function of human capability. At present the magnitude and change in the residual in relation to capital investment is of major concern. Let us transform formula (1) into (2) in terms of the ratio to capital investment, I, as follows:

(2) $\Delta Y/I = \Delta R/I + r + w\Delta L/I$.

This is the formula that decomposes the ICOR (actually its reciprocal, output-investment ratio or investment productivity) into three

---

[15] Among a number of works, the best knownis Edward F. Denison, assisted by J.P. Poulier, *Why Growth Rates Differ: Postwar Experience in Nine Western Countries* (Washington, D.C.: Brookings Institution, 1967).

terms: the incremental increase in the residual per investment, the rate of investment return, and the incremental increase in the wage payments per investment. The implication of this formula is interpreted as follows.

First, the incremental change in the capital stock is ΔK. It can be linked with I by introducing the rate of capital replacement, δ, simply as $\Delta K = (1 - \delta)I$. δ can be approximated by use of capital depreciation allowance. For simplicity of conceptual explanation, δ can be assumed constant and we have formula (2) for ΔK. Second, given the prevailing rate of capital return, changes in the magnitude of ICOR are composed of two elements: residual changes and employment changes at the incremental level (both negatively related to ICOR). That is, ICOR can be reduced by an increase in the residual and the increase in the employment evaluated by wages, both per investment unit. The former relation is naturally expected, and therefore ICOR has often been used as the criterion for measuring investment efficiency, as we did loosely in Section I. Third, however, the latter relation is not usually expected. The term $w\Delta L/I$ is the incremental term of Lw/K, which was explained in detail in Lecture 3. It is defined as "factor-input ratio (FIR)," the economic indicator of technological property of industries. The incremental term has essentially the same meaning. In other words, it is not merely an employment term, but represents the technological property of the industry under consideration. If this term is greater (smaller) or more labor-intensive (capital-intensive) in our sense, investment productivity ($\Delta Y/I$) will be higher (lower). Thus ICOR cannot be treated independently from the technological type involved. In order to grasp this idea more clearly, Table 5.6 is arranged to present a numerical illustration using hypothetical figures.

The incremental residual per investment is very high for cases 1 and 2 in Table 5.6: investment of 100 units produces around 20 units (hereafter "unit" is not repeated) of ΔR after paying the capital cost 12 and the labor cost, which is 9.5 for case 2 and 5.2 for case 1. Although the wage rates are higher in case 1 than in case 2, because of its labor intensiveness (a greater increase in the labor force for investment), labor cost is greater for the former. Therefore, if we define $\Delta Y'/I$ as the incremental output-capital ratio, deducting the rate of interest (12%), it is 27.1 for 1 and 33.4 for 2, and we note that in case 2 both $\Delta R/I$ and $w\Delta L/I$ are greater than in case 1. Toward the 1970s in Korea (case 3), however, both $\Delta R/I$ and $w\Delta L/I$ decreased and $\Delta Y'/I$ dropped to 21.0.

Thailand (case 4) and Pakistan (case 5) illustrate the case of smaller values of $\Delta Y'/I$: 15.8 for the former and 15.5 for the latter. If r is ac-

Table 5.6

Hypothetical Illustration of ICOR Decomposition: Selected Asian Countries
(%)

	ICOR (I/ΔY)	ΔY/I	wΔL/I	ΔR/I	I/Y	GY	(GL)
Japan							
1 (1953–65)	2.6	39.1	5.2	20.8	26.2	9.4	2.0
Republic of Korea							
2 1960s	2.2	45.4	9.5	21.5	19.0	8.6	3.0
3 1970s	3.0	33.0	5.8	16.5	29.0	9.5	2.8
Thailand							
4 1970s	3.6	27.8	6.8	9.0	26.5	7.2	2.9
Pakistan							
5 1970s	3.6	27.8	8.3	7.5	17.0	4.7	2.5

Sources: Japan, the same as for Table 5.4. Korea, Thailand, and Pakistan, the same as for Table 5.5.

Remarks: r in formula (1) is assumed to be 12%. w · ΔL/I is calculated by assuming β (labor's income share) is 0.60, except in Japan where it is 0.70. The formula is GL β · Y/I (GL being the rate of growth of labor force). This means Lw/Y·ΔL/L = w·L/I = w·ΔL/Y·Y/I. The 0.60 is drawn from Japan's prewar data, and there is no realistic evidence for the reliability of data for other countries. Together with the use of 12% for r, these are hypothetical elements.

tually higher, these estimated values would be lower to the same extent. As compared with cases 2 and 3, cases 4 and 5 are characterized by lower values of ΔR/I although there is not much difference in wΔL/I. Particular attention is drawn to the comparison of 4 and 5 with case 2: both the residual term and technology-employment term are higher in the latter.

The illustration may shed more light on our understanding of the performance of ICOR over time. The residual term is really a direct indicator of investment efficiency. No doubt a greater residual, representing stronger innovative activity, creates a tendency for ICOR to decrease. Apart from the changes in the rate of interest, on which we will not dwell here, the effects of another term, the indicator of the technological type, are also influential on ICOR changes. This is quite different from the usual notion of investment efficiency. The increase in the labor-employment per investment certainly reduces the value of ICOR. In other words, viewed from the standpoint of investment criteria, the ICOR per se cannot give any definite information. In order to obtain useful investment criteria in the framework of an innovative process, the only legitimate way is to know more about the relationship between the residual and the technology-employment term. We believe this proposition is extremely important.

At present, however, we do not have any systematic theory to clarify this important relationship. For example, what type of the factor inputs combination will create greater residuals? No definite answer can be given. What we can do is identify possibilities of varied relationships instead of assuming *a priori* that one type of relationship or another definitely holds. For instance, if it is assumed that a smaller wΔL/I creates a greater ΔR/I, more capital-intensive technology should be adopted to realize a more innovative process. However, another possibility is that a greater wΔL/I would create a greater ΔR/I. This means that more labor-intensive (quality betterment included) technology can realize a more innovative process. In our view, to be operational, only empirical studies on these possibilities could shed more light on this problem.

Measurements to Identify Investment Criteria
Taking further steps along this line, let us examine Japan's historical experience of private industrial sector development using actual data listed in Table 5.7. In the three columns on the right-hand side, relevant terms are added for reference. The second postwar period, 7, is not a downswing in the same sense as for the preceding intervals. Its features were explained in Lecture 1, section I. The table is arranged to present both swingwise and phasewise observations. The swingwise performance is the direct issue, but we want to clarify its relation to phasewise performance as well. In developing economies with surplus labor, industrialization is expected to contribute to both productivity increase and labor absorption because the majority of surplus labor exists in agriculture and services, the other two major sectors (refer to the formula used in Lecture 1). Formula (2) is intended to be applied to this framework. It is of course desirable to examine the performance of manufacturing in this way as well, but the data are less reliable for long-term analysis, and we do not intend to touch upon it below.

The findings are impressive in elucidating the relation between investment efficiency enhancement and employment-technology augmentation. First, to begin with swingwise performance, ICOR shows a historical performance similar to the macro ICOR presented previously in Table 5.4: as expected, its variation (low in U, high in D) is exactly the same. For the long-term performance through U periods in the production capacity sense, the significance of its long-term decline is distinctly elucidated through intervals 1, 3, 5, and 6.

Table 5.7
Decomposition of Incremental Capital-Output Ratio: Private Industrial Sector, Japan, 1891–1974

Intervals with phase reference		ICOR $(I/\Delta Y)$	$\Delta Y/I$	$\Delta R/I$	$w\Delta L/I$	r	I/Y	GY	GL
1 1891–97 (7), (U)		3.40	29.4	5.1	5.8	18.5	22.1	6.5	2.0
2 1898–1904 (7), (D)		4.10	24.4	2.9	3.3	18.2	17.2	4.4	0.8
1–2	Ia	3.75	26.9	4.0	4.6	18.4	19.7	5.5	1.4
3 1905–19 (15), (U)	Ib	3.24	30.9	8.0	6.6	16.3	22.9	7.5	3.0
4 1920–30 (11), (D)	IIa$_1$	4.12	24.2	7.7	3.3	13.2	19.6	4.6	0.7
5 1931–38 (8), (U)	IIa$_2$	3.09	32.4	12.6	7.5	12.3	22.3	7.2	2.9
4–5	IIa	3.68	27.6	9.8	5.1	12.8	20.7	5.7	1.1
6 1955–65 (11), (U)	IIb$_1$	2.82	35.5	14.8	9.0	11.7	37.3	15.5	4.7
7 1966–74 (9)	IIb$_2$	3.62	26.7	10.3	5.1	11.3	34.4	9.6	2.3

Sources: IDCJ Work Sheets prepared by Nobukiyo Takamatsu. Data for years before 1891 are not available. The basic data are *LTES* volumes for prewar years and EPA National Income Statistics for postwar years. Neither give the necessary data directly for the private industrial sector. Takamatsu made great efforts to estimate these by use of relevant materials. The term w $\Delta L/I$ is estimated by use of βGL. The value of r is similarly estimated by use of αGK ($\alpha = 1 - \beta$). But for earlier intervals the data for GK are preliminary. $I/\Delta K = 1.3$ is flatly assumed for all intervals. The major source for β, labor's income share, is Ryoshin Minami and Akira Ono, "Factor Incomes and Shares" in *PJE, op. cit.* The data are used with some modifications. Another way is a direct use of r and w data.

Remarks: i) "Industry" here covers manufacturing, mining, construction, public utilities, transportation, and communications.
ii) The annual original data are smoothed by five-year moving averages. The numerical values of all terms are presented in their period averages.
iii) Because of rounding and averaging procedures, some inconsistencies remain.
iv) The number of years are shown in parentheses for each U (upswing) and D (downswing) interval. The war-involved period, 1941–52, is exluded in the original series. Phase reference is shown for each interval. The number is the same as for Table 5.1. IIa and IIb are divided into two intervals.
v) All prewar years are in 1934–36 price series. For postwar years period 6 in 1965 prices and period 7 in 1970 prices.
vi) The magnitude of r appears too high for earlier periods, but this is not directly comparable with the interest rates, because of conceptual differences. However, a trend of its decline toward later periods is broadly consistent with that of interest rates, as follows (%, indices in parentheses):

	Bank Loans	Bank Deposits	r
1891–1904	9.51 (100.0)	6.44 (100.0)	18.3 (100.0)
1931–38	6.75 (71.0)	3.99 (60.0)	12.3 (67.6)

Source: Shinichi Goto, *Nihon Zaisei Tokei* (Japan's Financial Statistics), (Tokyo: Toyo Keizai Shimposha, 1970), Table 110 on the Tokyo area.

Such performance of industrial ICOR is caused by its higher output growth rate, GY (in GDP terms), with its somewhat higher investment proportion, I/Y, as compared to the macro case. One of the two elements of our hypothesis on the inverse U-shaped curve of ICOR is thus confirmed: the industrial sector sustained its positive power of decreasing ICOR throughout the entire period except the last interval, 7. This exception is important in relation to phasing, and we will come back to it later.

The two terms decomposed from $\Delta Y/I$, the reciprocal of ICOR, that is, $\Delta R/I$ and $w\Delta L/I$, present a distinct pattern of changes over time. Both terms seem to show a general tendency to increase, with swingwise variations making them relatively greater in upswings and smaller in downswings. This pattern appears fairly regular. The sharp drop in both $\Delta R/I$ and $w\Delta L/I$ in period 7 again deserves particular attention. We believe these are important findings. Their substantive meaning can be interpreted by introducing phasewise observations as follows.

First, a trend of increasing the residual per investment is witnessed through phases Ia–IIb$_1$. This is strongly indicative of an augmenting innovative process. The method of decision-making for investment by enterprises cannot be clarified by such a simple approach, but the expected rate of return is widely recognized as its major determinant. In our formula, it is represented by the magnitude of $\Delta R/I$. Its decline during downswings discourages investment enhancement. Despite this drawback, in the phase-unit observation, a trend of increasing $\Delta R/I$ sustained the incentive for investment enhancement by enterprises.

Second, the performance over time of $w\Delta L/I$, the incremental factor-input ratio, deserves particular attention. In phase-unit observations, it does not show a straightforward tendency to increase, with the notable exception of phase IIa when its value was lower than in Ib, despite the increase of $\Delta R/I$ between the two phases. We know that this is due to the sharp drop in $w \Delta L/I$ to the very low level of 3.3 during the downswing (interval 4). A similar but weaker drop was seen in the earlier downswing (interval 2). A parallel increase in both $\Delta R/I$ and $w\Delta L/I$ appears to be a stronger trend, as suggested earlier, but two types of relation between the two terms should better be identified categorically: one is residual growth with augmented labor employment and the other residual growth with decreasing labor employment. This is an answer to the proposal made earlier. What is clear in Japan's experience is that innovations of the capital-intensive type are adopted during downswings, whereas the augmenting labor employment type are adopted during upswings. In the former, the level of $\Delta R/I$ could thus be maintained for enterprises in the industrial sector, but socially this contributed to forming the differential structure discussed earlier in Lecture 1, section I. More strongly, the latter case implies an important positive suggestion. Technological-organizational progress can be made *with* augmenting employment. It is confirmed that the trade-off between productivity increase and employment enhancement is merely of a static nature and cannot be accepted for the innovative process.

Third, the performance of IIb_2, 1966–74, is quite different, as pointed out earlier, from the long-term trend. All the key terms, $\Delta Y/I$, $\Delta R/I$, and $w\Delta L/I$, show a distinct decline from IIb_1, 1955–65. The reasons for this can be explained as follows. In our phasing, the terminal point is identified in the mid-1970s (Lecture 1, section I). The interval 1966–74 actually covers the major part of the phase of secondary export substitution. Substantially, two basic changes emerged, as pointed out in Lecture 4: increased difficulties in technology borrowing due to the narrowed technology gap and less flexibility of labor supply. These will be discussed further in Lecture 7. The enterprises' response to these is indicated by our measurement. The lowered value of $\Delta R/I$ was still fairly high, but there was a sharp drop in the level of $w\Delta L/I$.[16] The meaning differs from that identified regarding IIa, the prewar phase of secondary import substitution.

Finally, concerning the original problem of investment criteria, our conclusion is as follows. Static criteria, such as the marginal rate of return, cannot be recommended for an innovative process of development. Realizing the incremental increase by investment enhancement, $\Delta R/I$, must be the major criterion for private enterprise investment. In terms of social criteria, more discussion is needed of various value judgments. In our narrowly defined framework, at least, labor employment augmentation is an important criterion. Appropriate use of ICOR for an investment criterion should be based on these points. Its decomposition analysis, we hope, may contribute to providing useful knowledge for that purpose. With the assumption of unchanged opportunity costs of capital, the following conclusions can be stated. i) Incremental residual increase is the criterion for private investment. ii) ICOR is the social criterion for investment allocation, with options for alternative combinations of the residual per investment and factor inputs ratio. There is no single, absolute criterion.

[16] This does not imply, however, that the positive association of $\Delta R/I$ and $w\Delta L/I$ ceased to operate in this last phase. Instead it continued to work. The results of subsector analysis of manufacture in Lecture 4 (Table 4.2) is evidence. The value of $\Delta R/I$ is estimated at 26.1 for electric machinery and 8.2 for steel. The value of $w\Delta L/I$ for the former is 0.62 but for the latter -0.35. The machinery industry maintained its greater value of the factor inputs ratio in cross-sectoral comparison.

Appendix: Infrastructure: Facilitating Industries

1. Problems

"Infrastructure" is a conventional term, commonly used in economic development literature, including formal government documents. Its coverage and definition, however, are not necessarily clear, and major differences exist between the broad and narrow usages of the word. It often includes "social infrastructure" (facilities for human resource improvement), distinguished from the usual "physical" infrastructure which is used uniformly to mean public utilities, transportation, communications, and public works, although it is sometimes used more broadly to include such basic industries as steel and coal.

The infrastructure is a sort of system of social overhead facilities and originates not in an industry or sector dimension, but is treated for convenience as a sector (for example, vs. direct production sector including such industries as manufacturing and agriculture). Viewed from the "by-type" classification of capital stock, it is basically composed of "structures," although combined with the two other components of nonresidential construction and producer durable equipment. The usual capital stock and investment accounts do not specify structures by including them in "construction." Unfortunately, this obscures the features and problems of infrastructure.

Thus empirical analysis of infrastructure is not clear-cut and requires strategic focus to be operational. Social infrastructure will not be treated here (see Lecture 6). In the discussions that follow, first an industry approach will be presented, focusing on what we call "facilitating industries"; second, additional analysis will be presented by an assets-type approach. A facilitating industry is defined as an industry whose activity facilitates the productive activities of other industries. Examples are, as mentioned previously, public utilities, transportation, and communications.[17] This covers the major part of infrastructure, although some elements such as public works are excluded.

In compiling socioeconomic development plans, infrastructure has long been treated as a specific field, at both the macro sectoral and micro project levels, because of its lump-sum investment with a long-term duration and lower rates of expected return. For these reasons,

---

[17] When a three major sector classification (agriculture, industry, and services) is adopted, transportation-communication is often included in "services" and public utilities in "industry" (for example, World Bank, *World Development Report*, Annex Tables). Classification depends upon the objective of use. Here, these categories are combined.

infrastructure investment is mostly carried out directly by the public sector. In international economic cooperation, the greater portion of capital inflow for financing investment on a concessional basis to developing countries has been allocated to this particular field. In most cases, the existence of a "supply bottleneck" in infrastructure and the urgency of eliminating it are the rationale for such allocations. Thus, the technical experts play a major role in taking the "physical approach." In financial and economic appraisal of individual projects, the so-called indirect effects, i.e., the effects on the activity of the direct production sector as well as the consumption aspect, are generally recognized as an important part of the expected return. Its measurement, however, is difficult and allows room for arbitrary decision-making in investment allocation.

Economic analysis of infrastructure is necessary to shed more light on its characteristics. Like other sectors, the relation between the demand and supply of output, investment efficiency augmenting its capacity, and variation in the rate of utilization due to demand changes are essentially similar problems for infrastructure. Its peculiarities are better elucidated from the economic standpoint.[18]

This naturally leads us to emphasize the interrelationship of activities between infrastructure and other sectors of the economy. Hirschman's thesis of sequence in his theoretical framework of induced mechanism of investment is, we believe, a pioneering attempt in this area. Between social overhead capital (SOC) and direct productive activities (DPA), two kinds of sequence are proposed as investment allocation strategies: one is "development via excessive capacity of SOC" and the other "development via its shortage."[19] One may or may not support his thesis, but no one can deny its validity in assessing the core of the economic problem. Is there any possibility of presenting another approach along this line?

With regard to the relationship between the two activities or sectors, on the other hand, the notion seems to prevail among development economists in the long-term perspective that during the initial phase, infrastructure plays a greater role than in later phases of development. This notion leads to a policy of particular emphasis on infrastructure

[18] Actually, between the macro-sectoral approach and micro-project appraisal some technical problems of inconsistency and differences in output-benefit concept (time-saving benefit, for example) in transportation exist. These are, however, minor reservations.

[19] Albert O. Hirschman, *The Strategy of Economic Development* (New Haven: Yale University Press, 1961).

building in the initial phase, as illustrated by African experience until the 1970s. Sometimes this has resulted in the problem of underutilization of built capacity. In later phases of industrialization, can the role to be played by infrastructure be assumed to be less important?

A much larger ICOR is a well-known feature of infrastructure. When its macro value is large or becomes larger over time, this feature is often the problem at issue.[20] Recent discussions of the Indian Seventh plan are a good illustration. The problem pertains to the aspect of investment efficiency, as for other sectors of the economy, so that the technological-organizational level and its changes over time are involved. Despite its peculiarities, we must seek possible decreases in infrastructure ICOR as development proceeds. Is there any suggestion that this possibility could be realized?

The problems at issue cover wide fields, theoretically and empirically. Below, only selected aspects can be dealt with. First, observations on the empirical facts systematically arranged for the experience of Japan will be our topic; second, based on those, we will try to establish a conceptual framework with which to deal with some of the problems mentioned above.

2. Japan's Historical Experience

Japan's experience is discussed because of the availability of long-term data. The data are arranged to follow the framework expressed by the formula $\nu = I/Y \;/\; GY$ ($\nu = ICOR$). For facilitating industries (F), it is $\nu_f = I_f/Y_f \;/\; GY_f$. These are used for statistical measurements, without assuming any theoretical setting in this section.

Comparison of Growth Rates of Output. Figure 5A.1 presents a long-term comparison of GY_f with GY (macro); GY_m (manufacturing and mining) is added for reference. First let us compare GY_f and GY. GY_f is distinctly larger than GY, a pattern sustained for a long period from the beginning until 1913, when GY_f and GY became equal. Since then the pattern has changed to an alteration of inequality: $GY_f < GY$ and $GY_f > GY$.[21] In a comparison with GY_m, the alteration is much more distinct from 1911. Before that, the same pattern of $GY_f > GY_m$ was sustained, although the difference became narrower because $GY_m > GY$. Two long segments are clearly demarcated: during the first, the

---

[20] Because of the longer duration of capital stock in infrastructure, adjusted annual amount of output with time discounting would give a different picture. This is an aspect of linkage between the macro and micro approaches.

[21] These coincide with the leader-follower relationship between public and private investment, as discussed in section II.

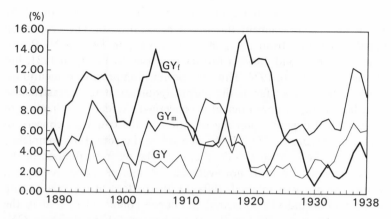

Figure 5A.1

Growth Rates of Output: Comparison of Facilitating (F) and Manufacturing (M) Sectors and Macro Economy, Japan (1888–1938)

Source: LTES, Vol. 1, National Income, Part III, Table 40, p. 247.

Remarks: i) Average annual growth rate of output (GDP and its components), estimated by smoothed series (7-year moving average), in 1934–36 prices.

ii) M includes mining. F is a sum of transportation, communications, and public utilities.

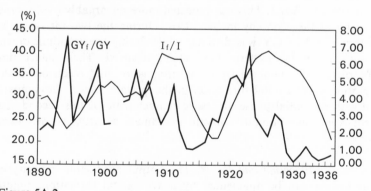

Figure 5A.2

Share of Facilitating Industry in Capital Formation and the Ratio of Growth Rates of Output, Japan (1890–1936)

Source: i) For development, LTES, Vol. 4, Capital Formation, Part III, Tables 1, 2, 4, 5, 6, 10, pp. 224–257 rearranged at IDCJ.

ii) Output growth rates are the same as for Figure 5A.1.

Remarks: i) Smoothed (5-year moving average) series of current prices.

ii) Because of the abnormally high value, the value of GY_f/GY_1 for 1902 is not presented.

output of F industries is required to be greater in proportion to Y, but in the second segment this is not necessarily so. The proportion actually increased from 2.6% in 1888 to 6.1% in 1913 in NDP estimates; in the second phase it further increased to 13.9% in 1931, but decreased to 8.2% in 1938. Thus, the proposition previously mentioned seems to be valid so far as the output requirement for infrastructure in earlier phases of development is concerned. Actual periodization of "earlier" will depend upon the situation of the countries concerned.

The initial phase, 1885–1900, defined in Lecture 1 is completely covered by the interval of $GY_f > GY$. In the second subphase of the primary phase, 1904–19, however, careful interpretation is needed. During the previous interval, 1904–13, the pattern of the relationship between GY_f and GY appeared to change compared to that in the previous phase: despite the almost unchanged GY (and GY_m), GY_f began to decrease. This can be interpreted as a transitory process in the formation of the new pattern of the second long segment. Thus, we believe the specific function played by infrastructure is confirmed to be generally consistent with the framework of development phasing; in turn, this supports the significance of phase demarcation. As discussed earlier, the dynamic role played by the industrial sector was still not sufficiently positive in the second subphase. A change occurred in the latter part of this subphase, 1913–19: the upswing of the economy during World War I. This was repeated more remarkably by a second upswing of the economy in the 1930s. During the two intervals the pattern of $GY_f < GY$ was distinct, while during the economic downswing the reverse pattern, $GY_f > GY$, recurred. These alternating patterns clearly stemmed from the progression and recession in the performance of capital formation in the private sector. In comparison with the initial phase, the basic characteristic of this second segment is an "autonomous" private investment activity, as mentioned earlier.

Investment Allocation and ICOR. The output production capacity of F industries can be augmented by heavy capital formation. Figure 5A.2 shows the long-term pattern of I_f/I: the share of investment for F industries in the gross domestic capital formation, a basic indicator for investment allocation. The ratio of output growth rates, GY_f/GY, is shown also in the figure for comparison.

First, the share of infrastructure investment appears to present two long waves: one from around 1904 to 1918 and the other from 1918 to 1936. The long segment of development path covered by these two waves corresponds to the second long segment demarcated earlier with respect to the growth rates of output. On the other hand, for the first segment (initial phase), it is hard to identify a distinct wave, although a dip occurred around 1894. The upward part of the wave implies that the share of infrastructure investment was increasing and its downward part was decreasing. It is our view that these were basically caused by the leading positive role played by private investment performance during the downward parts of the waves. During the upward parts, because of its recessionary performance, infrastructure investment sustained an increase.

The ratio of output growth rates, GY_f/GY, may help in interpretation. If the ratio of incremental capital-output ratio between F industries and the aggregate remains largely unchanged, the two curves in Figure 5A.2 should move in parallel. Actually, the ratio of output growth rates is much more volatile than the investment share. This is because of the changes in the rate of utilization of capital stock and *ad hoc* causes, for example, in earlier years, crop variations in agriculture and the earthquake of 1923. Despite these effects, it changed broadly parallel with the waves of investment share. The previous discussion on the output growth comparison, therefore, can roughly be understood as referring to the performance of output producing capacity.

Second, the rate of output growth and the investment proportion are combined in terms of ICOR for F industries. The estimated figures are listed in Table 5A.1. In light of the preceding discussions, we know that the magnitude of ICOR is close to the production capacity concept. Adequate averages of suitably selected intervals are attempted for convenience: four intervals are demarcated (the third one has two subintervals). The high rate of output growth of F industries was generally sustained with the notable exception of phase IIa$_2$, as expected from Figure 5A.1. The variance of ICOR thus stems mainly from that of the investment proportion, fluctuating along a trend of decline. The following points are noted. (i) During the initial phase (I), the ICOR level was high—2.5 times the aggregate value of 3.7 (see section I). A very conservative view is that Japan had no special advantage of low-level ICOR for infrastructure as an initial condition. Together with education, the major part of the social infrastructure (see Lecture 6), it has often been asserted that favorable initial factors such as low ICOR might have been crucial for Japan's success in initiating modern economic growth. We do not share this view.[22] (iii) Worthy

_____

[22] International comparison is beyond the scope of our research. But, for example, for two periods, 1974/75–1979/80 (I) and 1980/81–1983/84 (II), ICOR is estimated

Table 5A.1

Performance of Facilitating Industries: Output Growth Rates, Investment Proportion, and ICOR, Japan, 1888–1938

		GY_f (%)	I_f/Y_f (%)	ICOR
I	1888–1902	8.62	78.6	9.09
Ib_1	1903–1913	9.63	57.7	6.00
	1914–1930	8.29	49.1	5.93
Ib_2	(1914–1919)	8.35	34.6	4.15
IIa_1	(1920–1930)	8.25	51.6	6.18
IIa_2	1931–1938	3.57	34.9	9.18

Sources: For I_f, the same as for Figure 5A-2. For Y_f, NDP from LTES, Vol. I, National Income, Part III, Table 12, p. 206, is converted to GDP terms by use of capital depreciation allowances in Table 7–1, p. 148, Part III.

Remarks: ICOR is estimated by $I_f/Y_f/$ GY_f for interval averages. The number of phases follows the previous tables, but Ib is divided into Ib_1 and Ib_2, and IIa into IIa_1 and IIa_2.

of attention is the decline over time of ICOR in later phases. (The notable exception of phase IIa_2 will be discussed later.) The implication is that the increased requirement for the output of F industries was met by capacity growth by investment augmentation with increased efficiency. Otherwise, the problem of investment allocation between infrastructure and the direct production sector would have been more serious, as was realized toward the second subphase.

A closer look at Table 5A.1 reveals the following. The performance of ICOR decline in Ib_1 was strengthened in Ib_2, the period of the first investment spurt. Its investment proportion distinctly decreased from 50% to 35%, indicating that capacity augmentation in F industries was retarded by the shift of investment allocation to the direct production sectors. Nevertheless, the rate of output growth of F industries did not decline much, because of the greater rate of utilization of in-

as follows for India:

	I	II
F industries	10.8	7.1
Aggregate	5.6	3.5

Japan's value appears closer to the Indian ICOR on average. The ICOR value of electricity is very high in India and in view of the lack of electricity in Japan's case, Japan's value can be judged comparatively higher. The Indian ratio F/aggregate is 2.0.

frastructure during Ib_2. Thus the measured ICOR for this interval is notably low. A similar pattern is expected for IIa_2, during the latter part of which the second investment spurt took place, and this was actually realized. However, during the former part the remnants of the Great Depression remained (note the smoothed 7-year moving average). The rate of output growth of F industries was extremely small (see Figure 5A.2), being greatly affected by underutilization of the infrastructure. The average figures in the table are mixed, indicative of a depressed state.

Types of infrastructure in capital stock require additional explanation. In the preceding discussions, we have used the term "capacity," which is basically composed of facilities defined as "structures" by type classification of capital stock. Conventional national income accounts, however, use a dichotomy—equipment or producer durable equipment (PDE) and construction. The structure is not specified, being included in construction. Below, a few aspects of infrastructure will briefly be reviewed so far as data are available for structures in order to clarify the implication of the performance of ICOR and related terms.

First, the ratio of structures to PDE in capital stock is found to have undergone a distinct trend of decline throughout the entire prewar period in Japan; averages were 1.35 in the period 1886–1905, 0.85 in 1905–20, and 0.66 in 1921–40.[23] During the initial phase it was high, but the pace of decrease is remarkable. Industrialization halved the ratio. Structures are entirely for infrastructure, while PDE is mainly for manufacturing, although smaller portions go to other sectors. The ratio trend might be understood to imply a decreasing role played by infrastructure capacity. However, the facilitating capacity works with the function of PDE (vehicles in railways, ships in navigation, machinery in electricity). As industrialization proceeds, the proportion of PDE also tends to increase in F industries: it was 3.5% in 1886, 8.1% in 1903 (18.3% in 1905), 18.3% in 1921, and 27.4% in 1940.[24] These changes in the proportion of PDE in all infrastructure investment is estimated as the composition of the infrastructure's facilitating capacity contributes to form a trend of decline of the ratio of structures to PDE.

Japan's empirical values for earlier years may not be directly relevant to contemporary developing countries because the infrastructure did not include electricity and other modern facilitating industries. In ad-

[23] Ishiwata estimates in *LTES*, Vol. 3, *Capital Stock*, 1966.
[24] Source: The same as for Figure 5A-1, estimated at IDCJ.

dition, "telescoping effects" may work on these industries with the possibility of technological-organizational progress in this sector. If this is generally the case, the average service life of infrastructure would be somewhat shorter.

Second, the ratio of investment (I) to capital stock (K) is taken as a crude indicator of the interval of service duration (life). Capital stock estimates have recently become available in some developing countries, and Japan's case may be relevant in comparison. For the selected years, the ratio K/I (both in gross terms) had a range of 6.4–16.3 for PDE, while for construction (sum of structures and nonresidential buildings), the range was 20.2–30.8. These are crude, as "new" investment (corresponding to ΔK) to replace capital stock is not counted. Even such rough measures are not possible for F industries. Nevertheless, some useful suggestions can be drawn. For example, a longer service life of structures than PDE (say, 2.5 vs. 1) cannot be the sole explanation for the far greater ICOR often observed. Note that the efficiency problem of infrastructure remains. A tendency of decreasing ICOR found earlier for Japan's case may at least partially be explained by its compositional changes, with a greater proportion of PDE. It is contended that a long trend of efficiency augmentation was perhaps realized.

3. Interrelationship between Facilitating and Direct Producing Activities

Sequential Development Path. Let us begin by observing the time sequence of the relationship between facilitating and direct producing activities. What was found in Japan's historical experience can be summarized as follows. When the direct producing sector expands its capacity at a faster pace, the facilitating sector falls behind in increasing its capacity. In light of Hirschman's category, the pattern appears to be a case of "development via the facilitating sector shortage." When the producing sector stagnates or is in a recessionary process, the capacity of the facilitating sector expands at a faster pace than that of the direct producing sector. The pattern appears to be a case of "development via excessive capacity" of the facilitating sector (Figure 5A.3).

The dotted line in Figure 5A.3 shows a long-term path of the "balanced" relation (ratio) between the two capacities. For the typical case, its slope should be sharper for the initial phase, as facilitating capacity is required to expand at a faster pace than direct producing capacity. However, for simplicity, the line is drawn without a kink. The intervals 0–I and II–III appear to be development via excess, while the other intervals, I–II and III–IV, are development via shortage.

What we see regarding investment swings, however, differs in nature

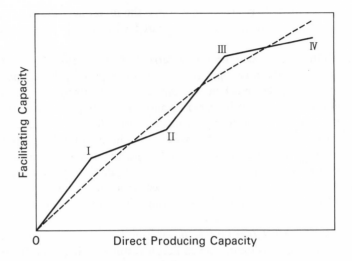

Figure 5A.3
Time Sequence of Relation between Facilitating and Direct Producing Capacity

from Hirschman's thesis despite the similarity on the surface. The difference is basically shown by the time sequence of alternating succession of the two patterns. The faster growth of the direct-producing sector cannot be thought as "induced" via the shortage of facilitating capacity. Instead, it was due to an investment spurt, which is of an "autonomous" nature as viewed from the facilitating sector. This fact suggests that the interrelationship of the two sectors cannot be treated by setting them on an equal footing with the notable exception of the interval which we call the initial phase (this will be discussed later). However, we must recognize that an important function of infrastructure is its capacity for facilitating investment spurts of the direct production sector. Its shortage is covered to a considerable extent by the facilitating capacity accumulated during the preceding interval, in which its "excessive" situation prevailed. Why does the excessive path of development take place? This is again created by the downward swing of investment in the direct production sector "autonomously."

The underlying assumption for these interpretations is that the capacity of the facilitating sector tends to expand at a relatively steady pace, while that of the direct production sector is more subject to swings. This is acceptable when public investment plays the major role in expanding facilitating capacity. Even when the private sector participates in it, it is acceptable, since the investment depends upon longer-term decision-making as compared with the direct production sector.

The initial phase can be characterized by the weaker investment performance of the direct production sector, especially for economies based on the market mechanism. But, even with stronger public participation in investment in general, and particularly for basic industries, the initiating task needs stronger efforts. A "via shortage" case is not usually conceivable. A greater role should thus be played by infrastructure building in order to facilitate the activity expansion of the direct-production sector. No past accumulation of infrastructure capacity occurred except for inheritances from the premodern period (for instance, railways in India, main roads in Japan).

Rationale of Public Infrastructure Investment. Because of the lower rates of expected return on lump-sum capital investment, physical infrastructure is treated as the major area of public investment. Let us discuss this aspect by use of our simple formula given in section III of this lecture. The decomposition of the incremental output per investment, $\Delta Y/I$, is applied to the two sectors, direct production and facilitating (no suffix for the former and f for the latter, $\Delta Y_f/I_f$), assuming greater ICOR for the latter ($\Delta Y_f/I_f < \Delta Y/I$). For simplicity, the employment term, $w\Delta L/I$, is dropped, and $\Delta R_f/I_f + r < \Delta R/I + r$ is assumed. This simply means that $\Delta R_f/I_f < \Delta R/I$ as the opportunity cost of capital, r, must be the same for the two sectors: the residual per investment in the facilitating sector is smaller than that of the direct production sector. (Discounting by time is needed in a more rigorous discussion.) If this situation is maintained in a sustained manner, it is a sort of "unbalanced path" of development, because it is our view that a balanced path of innovative development between sectors requires $\Delta R_f/I_f = \Delta R/I$.

Usually, however, no distinction is made between the residual term and the opportunity cost of capital; only the sum of the two is measured, and the gap of rate of return (ε) between the two sectors is considered (e.g., 7% vs. 15%). Despite the gap ε, (8%), public investment in infrastructure is justified because of its social "indirect effects." In our formula, the indirect effects can simply be treated by the incremental magnitude of $\Delta R/I$; that is, the contribution of the facilitating function in augmenting an innovative path. Otherwise, it must be lower: that is, $\Delta R/I - \Delta R^*/I = \delta$ (* denotes the incremental residual in the case of a lack of facilitating capacity increase). The rationale is $\varepsilon I_f = \delta I$. The amount of cost paid by the government, εI_f, should be equal to the amount of benefit (specifically defined), and δI is expected to increase.

An important and difficult problem here has two aspects: one is to make a legitimate judgment on the effects on $\Delta R/I$, and the other is the policy options for developing the facilitating sector, which pertains to the degree of imbalance discussed earlier.

Let us first discuss the latter aspect. Facilitating industries can be developed by the private sector. In favorable conditions, electricity and railways, for example, are actually operated by the private sector, although often supported by government in various ways. In our formula, this depends upon the possibility of realizing $\Delta R_f/I_f = \Delta R/I$. The variation range is wide, from the case of balanced growth to a negative growth, or even zero value. As the degree of imbalance widens, private enterprise cannot participate. Broadly, its participation possibility will become larger as industrialization proceeds toward later development phases. At a given phase, however, there is a policy option in a long-term perspective.[25]

The first aspect is more directly relevant to assessing the problem at issue, but it is more difficult to deal with. A highly simplified approach is unavoidable. We assume that due to government policy decisions the facilitating function is completely carried out by the public sector with no residual increase, $\Delta R_f/I_f = 0$. The rationale stated above can be applied in aggregate form. Using two quantitative relationships, let us try to explain the implication of the equality between εI_f and δI derived earlier. The first relationship is between facilitating capacity expansion and the amount of input costs required; this relation is simply assumed to increase. The second is between the facilitating capacity augmentation and a possible increase of the residual in the direct production sector ($\Delta R^*/I$). This is again simply assumed to be a "decreasing return." Figure 5A.4 illustrates these two relationships by two hypothetical curves (ε and δ', for simplicity $\varepsilon' = \varepsilon I_f'$, $\delta' = \delta I$).

[25] The average proportion invested by the public sector (general government and public corporation) in total infrastructure investment in prewar Japan is estimated at 63.4% for 1885–1903, 56% for 1904–19, 55.4% for 1920–30, and 59.5% for 1931–40. In the initial phase it was naturally higher, but not so drastically changed throughout the later phases. The role of private investment took a considerable part. The determining factors other than financial and economic operate in any country. For example, in 1906, the nationalization of railways took place because of political reasons (defense and others). What we are concerned with here is that "public investment" is not a fixed theme for building and expanding facilitating activity. In the socialistic scheme, together with the basic industries, F industries are in the public sector. Even in such cases, the government cost should be counted by the expected residual increase in the direct-production sectors, in particular in competition with the basic industries.

The cost of expanding infrastructure may not increase or may increase at a moderate pace. At any rate, it can be assumed to face less favorable conditions as its expansion goes on. With respect to curve δ', we know little quantitatively. However, we believe the difference of absorptive capacity of the direct production sector is important: beyond a certain level, the rate of increase in the "indirect effects" may begin to decrease. Curve δ'_1 is described as a schedule hypothetically described at dimension 1. Another curve δ'_2 is inserted in the figure at dimension 2 to show the possibility of a higher level of residual increase than δ'_1 for the same amount of facilitating capacity. The recognition of the difference is important because the augmentation of the same physical capacity will bring forth differential effects, depending upon the level of capability of the direct-production sector. The sectorwise concept of social capability, pertaining to technology and organization, is discussed in Lecture 6. If this is higher (lower), the effects will be greater (smaller). The difference of technological capability is illustrated as follows. Introduction of a high-yielding variety of rice has greater effects on irrigation facility augmentation. An improved level of mechanical technology has greater effects on electrical facility expansion.

Even if one does not accept the assumed shape of these curves, the realistic implication of their use at two different dimensions can be

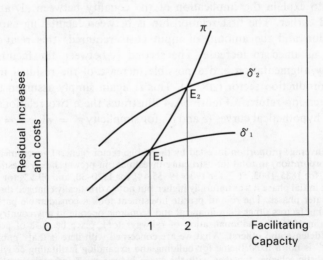

Figure 5A.4
Relation between Facilitating Capacity and the Residual Increase in the Direct Production Sector: A Hypothetical Case

recognized. At a higher level of capability, the point of equality between costs and benefits, E_2, is located at a higher level than E_1. In other words, the rationale can be met at a higher or a lower level. This illustrates the aspects of what we have called the "interaction mechanism" between the two activities, facilitating and direct production (section I in the main text).

Lecture

6

Technology Borrowing and Human Resources:
Capability, Education, and Utilization

In the last section of Lecture 5, we dealt with the residual in order to quantify the effects of technological-organizational innovations. Although the main argument in Lecture 6 will be along the same lines, the topic will focus on human resources. First, the conceptual framework will be presented focusing on technology (section I). Japan, as a latecomer to development, presents a typical example of an industrialization process mainly based on borrowed technology. From the very beginning of its modern economic growth until quite recently, manufacturing depended heavily on technological knowledge transferred from abroad. It is often said that such borrowing was an economical process, but how did it occur? What kinds of difficulties were encountered? For contemporary developing countries, the problem of achieving technological advances is of the same nature as for latecomers. Our conceptual framework will specifically deal with this aspect, instead of technological progress in general. R&D activity is crucial for making technological advances. For latecomers it is also necessary for the adaptation and assimilation of borrowed technologies, but it is not a central issue as it is in technologically advanced countries. In our framework the central function is assumed to be played by a nation's capability for absorbing advanced technological knowledge from forerunners. Conceptual clarification of such capability and empirical analysis will be made.

Facile arguments have often been heard that the reason for Japan's success in economic development is its educated population. A relatively high level of education was inherited from the premodern Tokugawa Era, and a primary education system was quickly established by the Meiji government. Assertions of such uniqueness of Japan's educational system and its role cannot be accepted without careful examination. Undoubtedly education is most important in upgrading human resources, but at the same time an appropriate evaluation should be

204

made of its benefits and costs in enhancing human capability. Our approach is narrow, confined to institutional education and leaving out other important components, including "learning by doing." Nevertheless, a trend of increasing education expenditures in relation to physical investment, together with the results, merits particular attention as a normal requirement for latecomers (section II).

What we call "utilization" requires explanation. "Human resources at a certain level of capability" is certainly understood in terms of a stock, instead of flow, concept. The rate of utilization of this stock may differ according to demand variation in terms of the conventional notion concerning the production factors employed. This notion can also be applied more widely. For example, in determining the realloca- tion effects of the labor force shifting from a lower-productivity to a higher-productivity sector (e.g., from agriculture to manufacturing), we apply the same concept analogously, because the productivity con- tribution of the same labor force is enhanced by raising the rate of its utilization. Actually, reallocation effects are of considerable import- ance in forming the residual amount in a macro setting in an economy with a dualistic structure. It is our view that advances in the rate of utilization of human resources is an important aspect of industrializa- tion.

The type of technological progress is also relevant. It has often been said that labor-intensive technology has greater effects in augmenting the rate of labor utilization than the capital-intensive type. In bor- rowing technological knowledge from advanced countries the factor- proportion is always an issue. This is better discussed from a wider standpoint, including the rate of utilization aspect (section III).

I. Technology Transfer and Social Capability

Concept of Social Capability

In Lecture 1, section I, our major hypothesis was that an upgrading of social capability is required to shift the economy successfully from one phase to the next. This was stated more explicitly by Ohkawa and Rosovsky:

> By *backlog* we mean the difference between the average state of technology within an industry or in the aggregate of all industries and international best practice. Thus the existence of a *backlog* within a country represents an opportunity for a particular indus- try or for all industries to bring the level of technology closer to

international best practice. The bigger the backlog, the greater and more obvious the opportunity. For most industries and countries, and clearly for Japan, the main way to explain this opportunity lies in the importation of more advanced techniques from the few leaders of world technology. This process is called *inflow*. However, the presence of a backlog describes only the possibility of progress, and inflow can only be an *ex post* measure. What needs to be explained is why inflow varies in magnitude from time to time, and this will eventually be considered in terms of social capability, i.e., the capacity of various sectors of the society to absorb technical advances.[1]

We will test the validity of this proposition in this lecture, since the problem is relevant to all latecomers. Today we know that the inflow varies in magnitude from one country to another in the developing world, and this implies a varied level of social capability among countries.[2] The components of social capability are complex and cover a wide range of economic activities. To be comprehensive is beyond our present scope. Yet, viewed from the constraints on possible technology transfer, the following are major issues: financing capital investment; differences in factor prices implied in the technology to be transferred and those in the local factor market; differences in organizations and institutions pertaining to technology; and human capability (technical, managerial, and entrepreneurial). Let us discuss these in order.

First, capital investment, in our view, is a means of using the stock of social capability, instead of being a capability itself. The concept of "absorbing capacity" is often used as pertaining to capital investment. This is closely related to our meaning but is not the same. As explained in the preceding lecture, technological advancement requires capital investment. The two interrelate, and the capital-embodied thesis even argues that the two are inseparable: no distinction can be made between "investment absorbing" and "technology inflow absorbing" capability. In our view, the two should be distinguished and treated separately in the backlog-inflow framework. In developing economies,

---

[1] Kazushi Ohkawa and Henry Rosovsky, *Japanese Economic Growth: Trend Acceleration in the Twentieth Century* (Stanford: Stanford University Press, 1973), p. 91. As will be illustrated later, the absorbing capability includes functions of choice, adaptation, and assimilation of foreign technologies.

[2] The term "social" has sometimes been misunderstood to pertain only to noneconomic factors, but, as is obvious in the original statement, it means the society's or nation's capability consisting of sectorwise components. It does not imply a specific emphasis on "noneconomic" aspects.

the problem of supplying required technicians is a different one from that of importing capital equipment and production plants. Viewed from the financing aspect, too, the problem of providing the capital source is different in nature from the problem of transferring technology for augmenting investment efficiency. In Lecture 5 we discussed the change over time in investment efficiency in Japan. The capacity for absorbing investment showed an increasing trend, but the performance of investment efficiency, which pertains to social capability, appeared different from it.

Second, the factor price difference is a well-known problem in determining the possibility of technology transfer. This concerns all aspects of choice, adaptation, and diffusion of technology under consideration. In the preceding lectures, a number of illustrations were presented, ranging from textiles to steel. The possibility of successful technology transfer is the most important component of social capability, particularly in its sectorwise connotations. The restraint on technological transfer is usually discussed mainly from the viewpoint of factor prices. In our view, the speed of technological progress is basically determined by the operation of this capability.

Third are other important aspects. Human capabilities in both individual and organizational-institutional settings play a role in forming the level of social capability. For example, education contributes to upgrading human resources on an individual level, while on the other hand, the possibilities of adapting, modifying, or creating new institutions and organizations are also issues. In Japan's case the permanent employment system and subcontracting arrangements are often cited as examples of such new institutions. The former is a device to adapt to the needs of the modern enterprises' company-factory system, by encouraging job training through "learning by doing." The latter, as discussed earlier, relies on the technical features of the machinery industry (parts production), to change the factor proportion to a much less capital-intensive one. These examples are found in private enterprise; in industrial organizations in general, the discussion should be extended to include the *zaibatsu* and *sogo-shosha* (general trading companies), which we will not discuss here.[3] In absorbing modern technologies, the function of individual human capability is often car-

---

[3] For *zaibatsu*, see "Some Aspects of Institution Building" in Ohkawa and Rosovsky, *Japanese Economic Growth*, pp. 218–28. For general trading companies, see Lecture 8, section III, in this volume, and Ippei Yamazawa and Hirohisa Kohama, "Trading Companies and the Expansion of Foreign Trade: Japan, Korea, and Thailand," in Kazushi Ohkawa and Gustav Ranis, eds., *Japan and the Developing Countries* (Oxford: Basil Blackwell, 1985).

ried out through certain institutions or certain forms of organization, as illustrated above. In this sense, we would like to treat the institutional-organizational factors as inseparable components of social capability. If their transformation contributes to absorbing technologies from abroad, it is understood as a leveling-up of social capability.

Now, the content of our hypothesis concerning shifting phases through the improvement in social capability can be explained in depth. In the framework of backlog-inflow, between latecomers and forerunners the *relevance* (or irrelevance) of technological knowledge for the former requires our attention. Some of the stock of technological knowledge accumulated in forerunners may be less relevant or entirely irrelevant to the requirements of latecomers, while other parts of its stock are relevant. The difference is due to the level of development phase of the latecomers concerned. When it is not entirely irrelevant, the technology stock of forerunners cannot easily be borrowed because the gap between its level and the given social capability is too wide. Unless special efforts are made latecomers may not gain from borrowed technology. Special efforts are often made by governments, as illustrated by the cases of steel and shipbuilding in historical Japan.

For private-sector activity, it is of utmost importance to have a legitimate perspective in evaluating the degree of relevance. The problem pertains not to the macro economy but to individual sectors. With time, the level of social capability will be raised. Regarding the stock of technological knowledge accumulated in the forerunner countries, what was once relevant will become less relevant, and what was once less relevant will become more relevant to the latecomer countries. In Japan's case, in the broad terms of major phase demarcations, the sector of relevance was the textile industry during the primary phase, and the machinery industry was less important. During the secondary phase, however, machinery became the major sector. This is the reason why the shift of phase is realized by the leveling-up of social capability by choice, adaptation through modification, and diffusion toward full assimilation of the relevant technology. The actual process of operation of these activities was explained in Lecture 1, section II for the textile industry and in Lectures 2, 3, and 4 for engineering and heavy industries. A shift of subphase, from import substitution to export substitution (of both nondurables and durables), can be viewed as a shift from a process of introduction to a move toward full assimilation of the borrowed technological knowledge.[4]

---

[4] For the original concept of relevance, see Simon Kuznets, "Notes on Japan's Economic Growth," in Lawrence Klein and Kazushi Ohkawa, eds., *Economic*

Human Capability and the Residual: The Concept

Now, let us discuss the relationship between social capability and the residual approach developed earlier in Lecture 5. It is our view that social capability is the basic factor producing the residual in an innovative process of development. The reason is explained as follows.

The stock of social capability can be decomposed into two parts: one is "embodied" in individual human resource and the other is not. The effects of education and learning by doing illustrate the former, while the function of organization and institution is in the latter category. The former category is called "human capability" (HC hereafter). For the sake of simplicity, let us assume that HC is enhanced by the nonmarket (for example, government) activity and the private sector uses HC as the input for production combined with capital and a certain technology. Note that enterprises use not HC itself but its flow, paying wages and salaries at "opportunity costs" determined competitively in the factor market, as explained in Lecture 5.

Can we expect that the market evaluation of the input of HC does reflect its "potential" value? The answer varies depending upon the actual situation of each developing economy. In a situation in which the market presents undervaluation of HC, the government allocates education expenditures for enhancing the HC level on the one hand, and the capacity of demand for it in the private sector is not sufficient enough to use it fully on the other. The capacity pertains particularly to the level of capital and technology, which may not be sufficiently high. Such a situation is not merely an arbitrary assumption. The level of salaries and wages paid by private enterprises is basically determined by the workers' "contribution" to production in competitive markets. That contribution, however, depends upon the level of capital accumulation and technology used in each phase of developing economies. Nobody can evaluate the potential value of HC precisely, yet it is clear that a gap does exist between the HC potential and its evaluation by the market. The idea of *potential* is useful to understand the significance of the gap: the contribution of HC would be higher if it were combined with capital and technology of a higher level. Even the same level of HC may imply a higher (lower) potential according to lower (higher) level of market evaluation.

For applying the framework of backlog-inflow of technological knowledge, in our view, potential is one of the key concepts. A fuller use of potential, by paying the opportunity costs prevailing in the

---

Growth: The Japanese Experience since the Meiji Era (Homewood, Ill.: Richard D. Irwin, 1968), pp. 391–92.

market, is a necessary condition for transferring advanced technologies from forerunners. The residual will thus be augmented. To understand this process, recognition of the differential of the potentials among various human resources seems important, instead of assuming a homogenous magnitude of potentials. As will be discussed later in connection with education, two categories of HC level can be distinguished: one is a limited pool of human resources engaged specifically in transferring technology, and the other is a mass of workers participating in its realization by engaging in the production process.

In light of Japan's experience, the potential of the first category seems greater than that of the second. In fact, data for the 1960s show that the differential of wages and salaries by education level have been narrower in Japan than in Western countries. Graduates of colleges and universities are paid less because their activity occurs in a setting with a lower level of capital and productivity.[5] We suppose a similar situation may prevail in most contemporary developing economies. We do not deny the important function of human resources in the second category, but would like to focus on the greater potential of the first category.

Within our simple framework, a number of qualifications are needed, including the following. First, conceptually, the augmentation of HC through education can also be pursued by the private sector, but the results vary to a considerable extent. The process of learning by doing is particularly influential. The possibility of improving organizations and institutions is relevant to making fuller use of the potentials in this regard.

Second, historically, a few words are needed to draw attention to the indigenous technological knowledge and human capability inherited from the premodern era. Many latecomer nations possess these before embarking upon modern technology transfer. This is an important element in the initial conditions. Artisans' activity in the primary phase is, as described in Lecture 1, section II, a notable illustration of the level of engineering expertise. Minami shares our view:

> Carpenters copied and sometimes modified imported modern machinery. For instance, carpenters in weaving districts reproduced the batten apparatus soon after it was introduced in Japan. Wooden machine filature technology was also produced. Without these artisans, rapid and wide dissemination of machine filature tech-

---

[5] Ohkawa and Rosovsky, *Japanese Economic Development*, Chapter 3.

nology and the improved handloom would not have been possible during the Meiji period.[6]

Not only the level of education, as will be discussed in subsequent sections, but technical expertise as well is based on the initial level of human capability, which mostly pertains to the adaptation and dissemination of borrowed technologies. Potential, as discussed above, should be assumed to be this indigenous capability. Actually this operated significantly during the primary phase.

Third, according to the conventional classification, the present discussion concerns technicians and skilled workers. A complementary relation is often pointed out between skill and capital equipment because a higher level of technology requires augmentation of both factors. As discussed in Lectures 2 and 3, this is not necessarily true in sectorwise comparison. For broad trends over time, however, we may not be able to reject this relationship. As the economy develops, the part having such a relationship may increase its weight because of upgrading of technology. What we have discussed above on the gap between potentials and market evaluation of HC, therefore, can be thought to increase its significance over time. In order to maintain the gap, the HC stock must be enhanced at the same speed as capital increases, with which higher technology has a complementary relationship. On the other hand, the social costs required for augmenting the HC stock cannot directly be measured, but an increase in its ratio to the total physical capital accumulation is quite possible because the actual expenditures for increasing the level of HC appear great for institutional education at higher levels. This problem requires empirical clarification.

Human Capability and the Residual: Measurements and Interpretation
Now, let us re-examine the findings by residual measurements presented in the last part of Lecture 5 from the viewpoint of HC: a comparison of the residual and employment increase in relative magnitude in terms of Japan's historical experience. A preliminary discussion is needed for the explanation of the conventional procedure to clarify the features of our formula.

In the private industrial sector, the primary mover is assumed to

---

[6] Ryōshin Minami, "Industrialization and Technological Progress in Japan," in *Asian Development Review*, Vol. 2, No. 2. This paper cites a number of impressive examples of technological progress.

be private investment. This was indicated by a trend of increase in I/Y as shown in Table 5.7, creating the residual and employment. Therefore, $(\Delta R/I) \times (I/Y) = \Delta R/Y$ is a measure of the result. This is the ratio of residual to the output of the base year. In the conventional growth accounting formula, $\Delta R/Y$, instead of $\Delta R/I$, is used as the "rate of residual growth," often expressed by GR.[7] Viewed from this standpoint, our formula decomposes into two terms: $\Delta R/I$ and I/Y. As shown in Table 6.1, panel A, the performance of $\Delta R/Y$ both in trend and in swings is broadly similar to that of $\Delta R/I$, but with wider variations. Through upswing intervals, it tends to increase at a distinct pace during the prewar period, followed by a drastic upsurge in the postwar period (period 6). In the downswing intervals (periods

Table 6.1.
Residual and Incremental Factor Inputs Ratio: Private Industrial Sector.

(%)

Period	$\Delta R/I$ (1)	$\Delta R/Y$ (2)	$w\Delta L/I$ (3)	$\Delta R/\Delta Y$ (4)
(A):				
1 1891–1897 (U)	5.1	1.10	5.8	17.4
2 1898–1904 (D)	2.9	0.49	3.3	−11.1
3 1905–1919 (U)	8.0	1.84	6.6	24.5
4 1920–1930 (D)	7.7	1.16	3.3	25.2
5 1931–1938 (U)	12.6	2.81	7.5	39.0
6 1955–1965 (U)	14.8	5.37	9.0	34.7
7 1966–1974	10.3	3.54	5.1	36.8

	$\Delta R/I$ (1)	$w\Delta L/I$ (2)	$\Delta R/\Delta Y$ (3)
(B):			
I 1 (U)–2 (D)	−2.3	−2.5	−6.3
II 2 (D)–3 (U)	5.1	3.3	13.4
III 3 (U)–4 (D)	−0.3	−3.3	0.7
IV 4 (D)–5 (U)	4.9	4.2	13.8
V 5 (U)–6 (U)	−2.2	1.5	−4.2
VI 6 (U)–7	−4.5	−3.9	2.1

Source: The same as for Table 5.7.
Remarks: (1), (2), and (3) are reproduced from Table 5.7.

[7] In the growth accounting formula, GR = α(GY–GK) + β(GY–GL), the residual increase is a weighted sum of the rate of growth of partial productivity of capital and labor. The weights α and β are the output elasticities of capital and labor, respectively. Thus this is called rates of *total productivity increase*.

2 and 4) it drops, as would be expected. These fluctuations are caused by a wider range of change in the investment proportion. Finally, the distinct decline of $\Delta R/Y$ from period 6 to 7 is caused not by I/Y, but by $\Delta R/I$.

The relative magnitude of the rate of residual growth, GR, to that of output growth, GY, or GR/GY, is a conventional term used in evaluating the role played by the residual. This is equivalent to $\Delta R/\Delta Y$, ($\Delta R/Y$ / $\Delta Y/Y$) the contribution of the residual to output growth at the incremental level. As is shown in the table, the ratio $\Delta R/\Delta Y$ shows a fairly clear tendency of increase throughout the entire period, and again it is followed by a postwar drop (in period 7). This can be said to be significant because $\Delta R/\Delta Y$ is essentially the measure of technological-organizational advance in relation to output growth. Particular attention is drawn to its marked increase. As is shown simply by $\Delta R/\Delta Y$ = ($\Delta R/I$) × ($I/\Delta Y$), this is a product of our two familiar terms $\Delta R/I$ and ICOR. Our formula actually decomposes these two terms in order to analyze investment performance specifically. HC is assumed to be used in the private sector through capital formation. The notion of $\Delta R/I$ is much more relevant than $\Delta R/Y$: how to increase investment efficiency is crucial. This is one interpretation of the relation of our formula to the conventional accounting approach.

Now, to return to the main thread of our argument, first, we believe that the trend performance of the residual per investment identified in Lecture 5 confirms the validity of our hypothesis of backlog-inflow. The technological gap between Japan and the West narrowed as Japan's industrialization proceeded. Why did the residual increase despite the narrowed gap? If the gap of technological knowledge itself is assumed to be the reason for technological advance in latecomers, as is often hypothesized, the value of $\Delta R/I$ should have a tendency to decline. Its trend of increase, therefore, does imply that some other positive factors were operating. Our answer is that there was a trend of increase in social capability. Despite the narrowed range of technological level, the magnitude of inflow increased as a function of this capability. This is the essential explanation of the residual performance; a more detailed explanation will be given below of the actual performance.

Table 6.1, Panel B, shows the changes over time in the residual and related terms between successive periods. If we look at $\Delta R/I$ and $\Delta R/\Delta Y$, a swing variation is notable. From U (upswing) to D (downswing), $\Delta R/I$ decreases, whereas from D to U it increases. But the magnitude of change is far greater in the latter than in the former, resulting in a long-term trend of increase through phase shifts except during phase

VI, when it declined, as will be discussed later. For reference, $\Delta R/\Delta Y$ is added, and its general performance over time is similar to that of $\Delta R/I$, but with distinct differences (for instance, in phase III). It increases from period 3 to 4, in contrast to a slight decrease in $\Delta R/I$. Surely this is the effect of ICOR variation. A large increase in $I/\Delta Y$ in the downswing is not counted in measuring $\Delta R/\Delta Y$, or GR/GY in the conventional approach.

Why is $\Delta R/I$ smaller in the downswing intervals? Was the level of capability reduced? The answer is "No." The smaller $\Delta R/I$ resulted from the smaller rate of utilization of the stock of social capability. A weaker current of inflow thus created is the reason for the residual tending to be smaller in downswing intervals. This interpretation implies that the process of increasing the capability level is sustained steadily through both upswings and downswings.

Why did the magnitude of the residual show a distinct upsurge in the first postwar interval? Was it caused by a drastic increase in the capability level? The answer is essentially "Yes." The early postwar economy possessed the considerable benefit of "spillover" from Japan's own activities carried out during the war-affected period from the latter part of the 1930s through the war's end in 1945. As described in Lecture 5, the development of engineering and heavy industries had been "artificially" encouraged by the government for military purposes, and these industries achieved a spurt of output growth. The point here is that this government activity produced as a result a large pool of technically trained manpower, together with some technological inventions,[8] and this spilled over to the subsequent intervals. Human capability in dealing with advanced technological knowledge was thus enhanced greatly by such spillover.

During the war interval, Japan was almost completely isolated from the West, and the backlog widened despite Japan's own internal advances in technological knowledge. Was the widened gap or stronger inflow the cause of the higher value of the residual? The answer is related to what we called "simultaneous technological infusion" in Lecture 4. It cannot be denied that the widened backlog gap provided greater opportunity for upgrading the technological level. However, we are inclined to state that this was a supporting factor, instead of being the major reason for the greater residuals. It is very difficult to give evidence for such a judgment, although between the older,

---

[8] How to evaluate the effects of Japan's own devices invented during the war-affected interval is another problem of spillover analysis, discussed in Lecture 4 in relation to simultaneous technological infusion.

well-established technologies for heavy and engineering industries and the new ones for television, varied synthetics, and most other science-based goods production (not yet electronics), the spillover effects of trained manpower must have operated similarly.

Finally, why did the magnitude of the residual show a drastic decline near the 1970s? This was not caused by a decline in the stock of capability level. As suggested earlier in the framework presentation, the essential cause was the very narrow range of the technological gap between Japan and the West, although the gap between best practice and Japanese levels had not yet been eliminated. Again, evidence for this assertion is difficult to cite, although the second export substitution drive implies that Japan's technological level in manufacturing had become sufficiently high to be nearly competitive internationally. Detailed discussion will be given in Lecture 7. The problem at issue thus changes: the social capability should be defined in terms of creating new technological knowledge, instead of absorbing it from abroad.

Performance over Time of Factor-Input Ratio
Looking at the term $w\Delta L/I$ in Table 6.1, how did Japan succeed or fail in solving the dilemma between the requirement of borrowing foreign technologies and the requirement of employment stemming from the dualistic structure of the domestic economy? The former requires capital intensity, while the latter requires labor intensity. As pointed out previously, the difference in factor prices is the essential problem. Much discussion has been devoted to methods for reconciling the dilemma. The historical performance of $w\Delta L/I$ in relation to $\Delta R/I$ (Table 6.1) is a measure of actual results of the responses made to this challenge in modern sectors, and a variety of factors are involved.

Our hypothesis in the simple framework presented earlier emphasizes the significant role played by the gap between the market evaluation and the HC potential. $w\Delta L/I$ is an incremental term of Lw/K, the factor input ratio, which indicates the economic property of technology used in industrial production. If the hypothesis is applicable to the process of assimilating technological knowledge borrowed, the human capability employed by enterprises may have a higher potential than the level indicated by its market evaluation (Lw) in combination with an increase in the amount of capital (K). The use of human resources will contribute to augmenting the residual in this way. A comparison of $w\Delta L/I$ with $\Delta R/I$ in their changes over time reveals broadly associated performance: a decline in the period from U to D, but an increase in the period from D to U. Taking these together with their trend of long-term increase identified earlier, we can say the hypothesis is applicable to Japan's case insofar as the aggregate industrial sector is concerned.

A sectorwise approach, however, is desirable. Two elements are to be distinguished: one is the performance of individual sectors and the other changes over time in the weight of structural changes within the industrial sector. As technology advances, Lw/K is generally expected to become smaller, so that the first element appears to counter the empirical findings mentioned above. However, if the second element operates to cancel this, Japan's pattern would be a possible result.

To begin with the second element of the effects of sectorwise changes in the industrial structure, as has been discussed in the preceding lectures, sectorwise changes are notable in the entire process of industrialization. In order to treat them simply but adequately, three subsectors of manufacturing are distinguished in terms of the composition of Lw/K: subsector A with greater K/L and higher w (heavy industry); B with smaller K/L and higher w (engineering industry); and C with smaller K/L and lower w (light industry).[9]

The actual average values of Lw/K for these groups between 1957 and 1966, roughly corresponding to period 6 in Table 6.1, are 33.2 for A, 57.6 for C, and 98.3 for B. The rank of magnitude is distinct. A simplified proposition can be made historically. In earlier phases when subsector C dominates, Lw/K has moderate values. In subsequent phases the greater weight of subsector A makes its aggregate value smaller, and such a shift is usually assumed to take place in latecomers. However, our findings are to the contrary. Actually, in Japan's case the effects of subsector B occurred simultaneously, and this operated to increase the aggregate value of Lw/K. The average performance of the manufacturing sector in general depends upon the relative weights of A and B.[10]

According to the first element, the magnitude of Lw/K for each subsector should decrease over time as capital intensification proceeds. This is illustrated by the change between 1957 and 1966 in the same data used in Lecture 3: A, from 41.2 to 25.2; C, from 61.2 to 54.0; and B, from 121.0 to 75.6. This general tendency implies that the rate of K/L change is greater than the rate of wage change. Although no direct data are available, a similar tendency is assumed to have oc-

---

[9] Calculated from Table 3.2 in Lecture 3. A—Petroleum, chemicals, steel and iron, pulp-paper, nonferrous metals; B—machines and metals; C—food, ceramics, textiles, and rubber. Traditional industries are excluded as they are not directly relevant to testing our hypothesis.

[10] The weight is capital, as is shown by

$$L_1 w_1/K_1 \cdot K_1/K + L_2 w_2/K_2 \cdot K_2/K = Lw/K.$$

curred between the periods demarcated in Table 6.1. The widely prevailing view that the magnitude of Lw/K should tend to decrease
over time appears to be endorsed by this tendency.[11] Actually, however,
in Japan's case the effects of sectorwise structural change dominated.

The industrial sector under consideration includes such nonmanu-
facturing industries as mining, construction, and facilitating industries.
Therefore, changes in the weight as well as the value of Lw/K in these
industries should be examined. Facilitating industries can be treated
similarly to subsector A and mining similar to subsector C, although
its weight is very small.[12] Using the preliminary data on investment
allocation in private industrial subsectors, the percentage distribution
of facilitating industries and manufacturing (including mining) can be
roughly estimated. For the years corresponding to the period demarcation in Table 6.1, the percentages for facilitating industries (construction is excluded because of its minor weight) were: 1905, 43.3; 1919,
79.0; 1930, 70.1; 1938, 49.6; 1954, 50.1; 1966, 47.6; and 1970, 36.4.

From 1905 to 1919, the share of facilitating industries increased;
nevertheless, the magnitude of $w\Delta L/I$ increased from 3.3 in the preceding
period to a high of 6.6 in this interval. The effects of this subsector
were apparently overwhelmed by those of the manufacturing sector
due to the continued expansion of textiles and a new growth spurt
in the machinery industry during the latter part of this period. During
1920–30, the share of facilitating industries was maintained at a
high level. This combined with the depressed performance of manufacturing resulted in a smaller value of $w\Delta L/I$. Since then the share of
facilitating industries has decreased and remained low, and manufacturing has contributed to a greater extent.

A lengthy explanation is necessary to understand the substantive
implications involved in the historical performance of the term $w\Delta L/I$.
In essence, it reveals that so-called labor-intensive technology and
industry developed simultaneously with the capital-intensive sector,
represented by heavy industries such as iron/steel and chemicals and
by the facilitating industries, such as utilities, particularly in the private
sector. Thus our conclusion on this topic is as follows. In establishing

---

[11] This relates to the argument that the rate of residual increase is associated with
the rate of capital intensity increase. In the growth accounting formula, we have
GR = GY − GK + β(GK–GL). For simplicity, if Y/K and β are assumed constant, this appears to take place. This argument ignores the effects of sectorwise
changes.

[12] Lw/K of private corporate sector in 1958, taking the value of manufacturing
as 100, is 46 for facilitating, 124 for mining, and 349 for construction (Ohkawa and
Rosovsky, *Japanese Economic Growth*, Table A.3, p. 256).

the long-term tendency of increase in the incremental factor-input ratio (FIR), the effect of structural change was more influential than the effects of capital intensification in individual subsectors. This implies that subsectors with higher FIR can develop more rapidly by assimilating borrowed technologies. However, this was not sustained at a steady pace but was interrupted by downswings of the economy.

Much has been said about the rigidity or flexibility of factor proportions, that is, the technological property of industries, and a number of "classical" examples of possibilities for mitigating the incongruity between required factor proportions and domestic factor prices have been cited in Japan's case. A well-known method of mitigation is the fuller utilization of capital through the more intensive use of labor. The multishift system in the textile industry is a notable example. The subcontracting system, first developed in the 1920s, also showed a possibility of substituting labor for capital in the machine industry where parts productivity was possible. This system developed more widely in the postwar period. Flexibility has recently been found to offer greater possibility in Japanese textile industries than had previously been thought.[13] In later phases the remarkable development of subsector B, characterized by a higher quality of labor, is actually a furtherance of this line of development. Our assertion depends on all these facts and arguments. However, if one understands all these solely in terms of substitution of labor for capital (in comparing latecomers with forerunners) and states that this is the core element in assimilating borrowed foreign technology, important qualifying comments must be made. Cheap labor must substitute for expensive capital in the latecomer economies. Modifications of technology and organization actually realized in Japan's case are indicative of the active functioning of HC. If we incorporated this line of thought into our framework, social capability would be interpreted simply as the capability for substituting labor for capital in transferring foreign technology.

Our viewpoint differs in placing the possibility of technological catch-up at the center. The possibility of making a success of technology transformation depends primarily on the gap between the potential and cost of HC irrespective of the type of industry. Actually, even with regard to heavy industry and facilitating industries for which the level of Lw/K is low, technology transfer could go on utilizing the potential, although with greater difficulties. This advantage was realized more in industry with a high level of Lw/K because the re-

---

[13] Ohkawa and Ranis, eds., *Japan and the Developing Countries*, Part III, Technology Choice in Industry.

sidual expected by enterprises is greater per investment unit. This is beyond factor substitutions because the pace of technological advance can be accelerated even without accompanying factor substitution. Between the thesis of factor substitution and our argument, however, we suspect there is no substantial contradiction. The difference stems from the emphasis in the framework of factual observation.

Finally, Table 6.1 shows a broadly associated performance of the two terms $\Delta R/I$ and $w\Delta L/I$. As a long-term tendency, as noted earlier, both show a general increasing trend. If the increase in $w\Delta L/I$ is simply called a movement toward greater labor intensity, one is tempted to say that the increase in the residual was created by this type of technological advance. One may say that the thesis of factor substitution is evidence of its validity. This may sound attractive, but our interpretation differs. No causal relationship can be identified in an approach of this kind. What we can identify is a sustained association between the movements of the two terms, strongly influenced by structural changes. If a broad comparison is made between the two major phases (periods 1, 2, and 3 vs. 4, 5, 6), the magnitude of $\Delta R/I$ increased remarkably, from 5.9 in the primary phase to 13.7 in the secondary phase, (excluding period 7). However, $w\Delta L/I$ increased only slightly, from 5.6 in the former to 6.2 in the latter. In such a broad phasewise comparison, it becomes difficult to treat labor intensification as the cause of the residual augmentation. Actually, capital intensity did increase from the primary to the secondary phase. What is really suggested by Japan's experience is that even in the secondary phase the level of $w\Delta L/I$ did not decrease in the aggregate industrial sector, contrary to expectations. The residual increase, in our view, is caused by raising of the HC level, which is not measured directly by $w\Delta L/I$. Much has been said about labor intensification with respect to Japan's classical example, but less has been recognized concerning the function of human resources improvement. Without identifying its role, performance in the semi-industrial phase cannot be fully understood.

II. Education: Effects and Costs[14]

In the simple framework proposed in the preceding section, human capital is assumed to be enhanced by public activity. School education is most relevant to its empirical examination. In this field both macro

[14] This section depends heavily on Kazushi Ohkawa, "School Education in Modern Japan's Economic Evaluation and Possible Relevance to Contemporary Less Developed Countries," IDCJ Working Paper No. 33, March 1986.

and micro approaches have been developed. The theoretical and empirical studies on human capital, mainly developed by Theodore Schultz and John W. Kendrick for the United States, are widely known as representing the macro approach. As a micro approach, project analysis using benefits-costs appraisal has recently been advanced for dealing with education. Our simple framework does not allow direct application of either of the two, but its principal idea is similar in aiming at an evaluation of the effects and costs of school education. Before discussing this major topic, however, a preliminary review of the facts in Japan's case is necessary because we suspect *a priori* thinking may impede an understanding of the reality of Japan's historical performance in education.

First, in the literature on the education policy of governments in terms of socioeconomic development, Japan has often been cited as a classical example of success. What is especially emphasized is the crucial role played by such policies in the initial phase. Second, its unique characteristic of a relatively high level of traditional education inherited from the premodern Tokugawa Era has often been cited as a factor in that success. Relevance or irrelevance to contemporary developing countries, in our view, cannot be legitimately judged by either of these two. The scope of our treatment is confined to school education from the viewpoint of its economic aspects, and yet it is our view that Japan deserves attention because it performed as a typical latecomer, not because it was unique.

Let us begin with the argument regarding the initial difficulties of the government's education policy implementation. It actually did not start in a well-established way: the plan was not systematic and policy implementation met with a reluctant response in the case of primary school education. In 1872, immediately after the Meiji Restoration of 1868, the government started its modernization plan by proclaiming a new educational system. Its implementation, however, was a trial-and-error process. This is illustrated by the successive revisions of primary school age. Initially, under the general proclamation of 1875 the age of compulsory education was set at "6–14 (eight years)." But soon it was revised to three years for the first grade, to be followed by two higher grades of three and two years. Again in 1886, the primary school system was revised to be composed of two grades: compulsory regular primary) education of four years, followed by another four years (higher primary). At that time school fees were levied for the first time, instead of depending solely upon community expenditures as before. In 1890, school age was made more flexible:

three or four years of compulsory and two, three, or four years for higher primary schooling. In 1900, the duration of compulsory education was fixed at four years, and school fees were entirely abolished. Eventually, in 1908, the revised system of six years for compulsory and two years for higher primary school was introduced. This proved to be a stable system, and was maintained during the entire prewar period.

In retrospect, the difficult problem for the government was how to narrow the gap between its education policy goals and the people's response to the government's requests. Our estimates of enrollment and dropout ratios to the total school age population are evidence of the problem. The enrollment rate in 1881 was poor: males (m) 69%, females (f) 34.3%. It took rather a long time to make it much higher: in 1900, m 90.6%, f 58.8%; in 1905, m 97.7%, f 93.1%; and in 1913, m 98.7%, f 97.5%. A more or less acceptable enrollment rate was reached toward the end of the primary phase. Note that female enrollment lagged behind the male percentages. The enrollment rate is more meaningful if the dropout rate is taken into account: it was m 28.8%, f 57.8% in 1895—a fairly high rate for males and remarkably high for females. This rate tended to decrease gradually. In 1913, it is estimated to have been m 16.8%, f 27.8%; in 1930, m 8.7%, f 19.3%.[15]

A rough comparison is made with enrollment rates for Asian developing countries in Table 6.2. Dropout rates are not available, although they were high in a number of them. The enrollment rate differs from one country to another. For example, between the two neighboring countries of India and Pakistan, the rate differs considerably. Generally, however, the rate in Japan during the initial phase of development appears similar to that in other countries. In particular, there was a slow start and lower female enrollment. Thus, although government education policy in Japan did have remarkable influence on human resource improvement, it actually resulted in only average performance during the initial development process. To identify a unique feature in Japan's case is rather difficult as far as primary education is concerned.[16]

No doubt a relatively high level of basic education was provided by the traditional system, and Dore's well-known argument is acceptable, although some overestimation may be involved due to urban

---

[15] The two ratios, from Ohkawa, "School Education in Modern Japan's Economic Evaluation," are estimated by Nobukiyo Takamatsu.

[16] The problem of professional education for higher-level technicians is another matter and requires separate analysis.

Table 6.2
Enrollment Rate among the Population of Compulsory School Age: Asian
Developing Countries   (%)

Country	Male		Female	
	1965	1982	1965	1982
Group I				
Nepal	36	102	4	42
Burma	67	68	31	51
Bangladesh	76	87	65	81
Group II				
India	89	83	57	64
Sri Lanka	98	106	86	101
Pakistan	59	57	20	30
Indonesia	79	124	65	116
Group III				
Philippines	115	107	111	105
Thailand	82	98	74	94
Malaysia	96	93	99	99
Rep. of Korea	103	102	84	91

Source: World Bank, World Development Report, 1985, Appendix Table 24.
Remark: Rates over 100% are due to the mechanical calculation of the
   school-age population.

bias.[17] No reliable data can be incorporated systematically into our
estimates; the problem, however, is conceptual. Assume that the initial
level of education was higher than the data on the new school system
tell us: how can we judge the effects of the "revised" initial condition
(discussed in Lecture 1) on the subsequent development process? It
is our view that the initial level of social capability in Japan was high
relative to its economic level. The traditional education effects as well
as other HC, including that of farmers and artisans, are important in-
gredients. Based on our framework described in the preceding section,
however, the real problem is how and to what extent the level of HC
increased during the subsequent periods. From this point of view, we
do not evaluate highly the effects of the traditional education per se.
Its effects on the initial start should be appreciated, but it cannot explain
the continuous process of ugrading human capability during subsequent
development.

[17] R.P. Dore, Education in Tokugawa Japan (Berkeley: University of California
Press, 1965). See data on rural districts (p. 9) in Ohkawa, "School Education in
Modern Japan's Economic Evaluation."

School Education: Effects

First, our topic is the effects of school education in general. Basic information on the changing educational level of the working-age population (aged 15–64 years) is presented in Table 6.3. In 1900, the year of the end of phase I_a (1887–1900), the majority (86%) of the working-age population was not educated by the new school system. This may appear astonishing at first glance, but it is quite natural because (i) most of the working-age group were born before the start of the new system and even after that children were not satisfactorily enrolled; and (ii) there was a time lag in reaching working age. During phase I_b, until around 1920, the new system began to exert stronger effects. The percentage in category (1) declined to less than half in 1915 (males) and in 1925 (females). However, remnants in category (1) lasted even through phase II_a of semi-industrialization (1919–38). In 1940, some 10% of males and more than 20% of females still did not complete compulsory education.

While category (3) was very minor during the primary phase, it showed a rapid rate of increase, to nearly 10% in 1940. A detailed discussion on its breakdown into middle school, college, and university is beyond the scope of this section. However, a few words are needed concerning vocational education. The supplementary continuing educational system started as early as in 1893, but it began to operate substantively after the system was expanded in 1920 to include two years for the students who had completed both regular and higher primary school. Category (4) in Table 6.3 indicates a faster pace of increase over category (3) during phase II_a, 1919–38.[18]

It would be desirable to evaluate these effects of school education from the standpoint of manpower planning and/or policy, with which contemporary developing economies are concerned. A systematic approach is beyond our scope, but an intuitive view is possible of the broad pattern of the supply-demand relationship in relation to investment swings. At the time of World War I, for the first time, there was a shortage of skilled and semiskilled workers. This tempted private enterprises in the modern sector to devise an institutional adaptation to conduct enterprise-oriented education and training on their own responsibility. This was an initial step in the establishment of the "permanent employment system." The government increased its expendi-

---

[18] The government did make efforts to inaugurate education for vocational purposes. In 1899, a special school system was proclaimed for middle-school level, including agriculture, fisheries, manufacturing, commerce, and navigation. These are contained in category (3) in Table 6.3.

Table 6.3
Changes in the Composition of Working-age Population by School Education Level, 1900–40

Year	Compulsory Education Not Completed (1)	Primary Education Completed (2)	Education Beyond Primary (3)	Supplementary Continuation (4)	Working-age Population (Total, thousands) (5)	(%)
Total:						
1900	85.5%	14.3%	0.2%	0.0%	26,674	(100.0)
1910	66.2	32.1	1.1	0.6	29,266	(100.0)
1920	47.8	44.8	2.9	4.5	30,960	(100.0)
1930	29.3	56.1	5.8	8.8	37,804	(100.0)
1940	16.2	62.9	10.0	10.9	41,897	(100.0)
Males:						
1900	78.3	21.5	0.2	0.0	13,435	(100.0)
1910	56.7	40.7	1.5	1.1	14,720	(100.0)
1920	37.8	50.9	3.6	7.7	16,374	(100.0)
1930	20.5	59.9	6.6	13.0	19,179	(100.0)
1940	9.8	64.1	10.0	16.1	20,392	(100.0)
Females:						
1900	92.8	7.1	0.1	0.0	13,212	(100.0)
1910	75.7	23.3	0.7	0.3	14,546	(100.0)
1920	58.0	38.6	2.1	1.3	16,664	(100.0)
1930	38.4	52.2	5.1	4.3	18,626	(100.0)
1940	22.3	61.8	9.9	6.0	21,505	(100.0)

Source: Ohkawa, "School Education in Modern Japan's Economic Evaluation," Table 3 at five-year intervals, with method of estimates description.

Remarks: (i) Data include all public and private schools under the jurisdiction of the Ministry of Education. Schools under the jurisdiction of other ministries were a minority.
(ii) If Category (2) contains "higher primary," in addition to the "regular" compulsory, its percentages are 14.8% in 1900, 25.8% in 1920, and 34.2% in 1940 for the total of males and females.

tures in order to create a number of special colleges for industry, commerce, and agriculture with the purpose of increasing the supply of technicians, as well as the expansion of vocational education mentioned above.

As discussed in Lecture 5, the magnitude of the investment spurt at the time of World War I was unprecedented, so the response to the shortage of educated manpower by the government followed with a short time lag. During the investment downswings, the supply of educated manpower thus increased above the shrunken demand, and the unemployment problem became serious in the early 1930s. Again, however, the demand surpassed supply in the next investment spurt in the latter part of the 1930s. In summary, a trendwise increase in education supply vs. swingwise demand for educated workers seems to have been the broad pattern Japan experienced historically. We will come back to this when discussing the education expenditure approach.

Beyond the swingwise variations, a few words on longer-term observations are needed. During the primary phase the government could not produce manpower of sufficiently high capability to meet the demand hike by the private sector resulting from the first investment spurt. As will be discussed later, increasing education expenditures were a continuing burden on the government's fiscal situation. In particular, public education at the higher level was extremely costly. In the physical infrastructure, as discussed in the Appendix to Lecture 5, fuller utilization of the capital stock accumulated during the primary phase was a possible means of meeting the demand hike at that time. Here we distinguish between the "hard" (physical) infrastructure and "soft" (social) infrastructure.

The purpose of education is so general that evaluating its overall effects is impossible. However, confined to its economic effects on the labor market of the private sector, it provides an indicator, that is, differentials of salaries and wages by education level. The basic notion assumes an equality between wages and marginal productivity of labor at equilibrium. In our framework, this was treated as "opportunity costs" determined through the market. The effect of education on HC is conventionally evaluated by the opportunity costs by means of a "quality index." Our approach also depends upon this conventional one, but in addition the contribution of enhanced HC is treated as relevant to augmenting the residual. This will be discussed later. To apply the conventional approach, a careful selection of the actual data is required so as to avoid distorted effects of the demand-supply situation. For prewar Japan, such data are available only for 1935, the most stable year of that period.[19] The index of labor quality by education thus estimated is as follows, taking 1900 = 100 for the total of males and females: 1910, 104.2; 1920, 109.2; 1930, 114.2; and 1940, 118.7. The average annual rate of increase was 0.47% for 1900–1920 and 0.43% for 1920–1940. These rates may appear extremely small. Actually the magnitude is substantive relative to the average rate of increase in the total working-age population: 0.67% in 1900–20 and 1.18% in 1920–40, yielding a relative rate of increase of 70.2% for the former and 36.5% for the latter period. Due to limited data we have reservations about evaluating HC using this approach. Nevertheless, the effects of widespread school education were significant, particularly in the prewar phases of development. This proposition is further endorsed by circumstances in the earlier postwar years. In 1955–65, the average annual rate of increase of the quality index by similar estimates was 0.38%, lower than the prewar values, while the rate of increase in the labor force was 1.5%, much higher than prewar values. The relative rate of increase in the quality index was 25%, and the composition became much more stable.[20]

Education data on the compositional change are not directly available for the labor force. An approximate value of the relative rates calculated using the same values as above was 88.6% for 1900–1920 and 48.3% for 1920–1940. Use of the same standard of education-wage differentials for the former period may give conservative estimates since the differentials might have been wider for earlier years. We think the rate of change in the effects of education was greater in earlier years and tended to be smaller for later years, basically due to the slower rate of compositional changes, as shown in Table 6.3. From 1900 to 1920, the proportion of (2) in the total working-age population increased by more than three times (from 14.3% to 44.8%), but from 1920 to 1940 the pace of increase slowed to 1.4 times (from 44.8% to 62.8%). The proportion of (3) increased from 0.2% in the period 1900–20, to 2.9% in the period 1920–40, and this accelerated further

[19] For details, see Appendix III, Ohkawa, "School Education in Modern Japan's Economic Evaluation." The standard wage differential index is catculated taking category (2) excluding "higher" primary education (category number from Table 8.3) as 100.

Males	(1) 90	(2) Regular 100, higher 120	(3) 150	(4) 125
Females	(1) 90	(2) Regular 105, higher 110	(3) 125	(4) 115

[20] Based on wage differential data for 1954. Ohkawa and Rosovsky, *Japanese Economic Development*, pp. 52–54.

to 10% in 1940. Most of the compositional change, however, was due to the rapid acceptance of primary school education.

Public Education Expenditures

Let us now turn to the costs-expenditure aspect. For education in general, expenditure payments cannot be approached easily because of their complexity. Both public and private sectors participate in school education. Households and even enterprises pay fees for it. Actually, all these pertain to the education effects estimated earlier. Our working assumption is that only public expenditures can be treated as costs without gaining direct benefits. This boldly assumes that the costs essentially correspond to the benefits in all private sectors. Private school education is essentially self-paid, although subsidies are also involved. For the fee payments of households, it is simply assumed that they obtain corresponding benefits in terms of higher educational levels for pupils.

Our estimates are rough with these simple assumptions, yet we intend to elucidate the performance of public education expenditure. This is consistent with the framework presented in the preceding section, which assumes that the government education expenditure is for the nation, the benefits of which are largely gained by use of improved human resources in the private sector.

The implementation of the government's education policy discussed earlier is thus grasped by its cost-expenditure aspect, covering both central and local activities. Its performance in relation to capital investment is taken up. Much has been said about "human capital" in relation to physcial capital. Because of the conceptual difficulty of incorporating human capital into our framework, we do not follow this line of approach. Instead, at the level of investment (I), the specified public education expenditure (E_g) is observed in relation to it (additionally I_g, public investment). However, this does not imply our rejection of human capital approach. In principle the two are complementary.

As a preliminary, the data are presented in terms of rates of growth in Table 6.4. E_g shows a strong trend of increase: its rate of growth is sustained much larger than that of GNP, with swings, except in period 5 when resource mobilization for military purposes distorted it. The rate of capital formation has remarkable swings, as identified in Lecture 5. In its rate relative to investment (E_g/I), therefore, drastic swings emerge counter to investment swings.

The sustained pattern of a high rate of government education ex-

Table 6.4

Government Education Expenditure in Comparison with GNP and Investment: Average Annual Rate of Growth, 1887–1982 (%)

(%)

Period	GE_g (1)	GY (GNP) (2)	GI (3)	GE_g-GY (4)	GE_g-GI (5)
1 1887–1897	6.7	3.2	6.0	3.5	0.7
2 1897–1904	7.6	1.9	1.5	5.7	6.1
3 1904–1919	4.8	3.6	7.0	1.3	-2.2
4 1919–1930	5.6	2.1	1.2	3.5	3.4
5 1930–1938	2.1	5.2	10.9	-3.1	-8.8
6 1954–1964	5.2	9.4	14.8	4.2	-5.6
7 1965–1974	5.5	8.4	11.2	-2.9	-5.7
8 1975–1982	4.7	4.1	2.4	0.6	2.3

Sources: E_g from LTES, Vol. 7, Finance Expenditure, Appendix Table 12, pp. 197–98. The data are "net," adjusting duplication between central and local governments. In 1934–36 prices, deflated by government consumption expenditure price indices available from LTES, Vol. 1, Appendix Table 30, p. 232.

Remarks: (i) Prewar years: inclusion of construction investment such as school building and maintenance in E_g presents a problem of duplication with I. However, overlap is not large. Its percentage of total education expenditure is mainly in the range of 10–20 through public primary and middle school and government university. (Statistics since 1890 are available in Ministry of Education, Japan's Growth and Education, Appendix Table 11, pp. 208–9; Y and I (1934–36 prices) from the data of PJE.)

(ii) Postwar years: E_g from Ministry of Education, Survey Report of Local Education Expenditures, 1985. Y and I (in 1965 prices) from Economic Planning Agency, Annual Report on National Accounts, 1986.

penditure deserves particular attention.[21] It was witnessed not only in the primary phase but also in the semi-industrialized phase. Its per-

[21] Education expenditure of private schools (E_p) is not treated in the main text. The ratio E_p/E_g(%) for selected years was

1904	3.5	1930	10.2	1950	17.4
1913	4.2	1938	14.5	1965	11.5
1919	4.4			1970	15.4

The ratio shows a broad trend of increase and E/I (E = E_g + E_p) tends to increase faster than E_g/I. Incidentally, by the annual data an increase is particularly witnessed after 1919 toward the phase of semi-industrialization.
(Data source: Ministry of Education, Japan's Growth and Education, Appendix Table 13, and Statistical Yearbook of the same ministry for the postwar years.)

formance relative to capital formation requires careful scrutiny. The difference, column (5), fluctuates in a wide range. However, a broad long-term trend of increase is confirmed as the major tendency. Substantive interruptions were caused by investment spurts, but these were of very short duration. As presented in the table, a tendency of substantive increase through periods 1, 2, and 4 existed, with short-term interruptions first in the World War I period and second near the end of the 1930s. In these intervals, the level of E_g in relation to GNP remained almost unchanged (period 3) or slightly declined (period 5) (column 4).

In postwar performance, because of a sustained high rate of investment increase, the increase in education expenditure, although not slowed down substantially, fell far behind investment through periods 6 and 7. In the latter its rate of increase lagged behind GNP increase. This might have been a repetition of the performance in upswings. However, an almost equal rate of increase in E_g and Y in period 8 deserves attention, although it is too early to say anything definite about a shift to a new pattern.

Detailed comparisons with contemporary developing countries are beyond our scope, but a general comparison is given in Table 6.5 for selected Asian countries. The data are for central government expendi-

Table 6.5
Central Government Education Expenditure vs. Gross Domestic Investment and GNP, Asian Developing Countries, 1981–82

(%)

Country	E_g/I	I/Y	E_g/Y	I_g/Y
Nepal	10.1	14.5	1.45	1.49
Burma	7.6	23.5	1.79	1.78
India	1.3	24.0	0.31	0.28
Sri Lanka	8.7	29.5	2.57	2.57
Pakistan	3.0	17.0	0.51	0.52
Indonesia	9.3	22.0	2.05	2.05
Thailand	10.1	24.5	2.46	2.82
Philippines	7.2	29.5	2.12	1.43
Malaysia	13.9	33.0	4.49	4.61
Rep. of Korea	13.1	26.0	3.41	3.40
Singapore	10.5	44.0	4.62	4.63

Source: World Bank, World Development Report, 1983–1985, Appendix Tables. I/Y from 1983, 1984 issues and others from 1984, 1985 issues.
Remarks: All in 1981, 1982 averages.

tures only, since local government plays only a limited role in most countries.[22] The ratio E_g/I varies rather widely in the range of 3.0 (Pakistan) to 13.9 (Malaysia), excluding India, for which the exclusion of state (local) education expenditure creates an exceptional underestimate. The difference does not necessarily appear to be associated with different phases of development or income level. Nepal, Burma, and Sri Lanka rank high, perhaps corresponding to the greater enrollment ratio shown in Table 6.2, despite being in the primary phase, while the ratio is relatively low for the Philippines despite its semi-industrialization. We know that the low ratio for Pakistan presents the actual situation, because local government education expenditure is negligible. This also corresponds to its poor enrollment ratio shown in Table 6.2.

Despite these differences among individual countries, which must be caused by government policy, we see a broad tendency for a greater value of the ratio E_g/I in later-phase countries as compared to earlier-phase countries. A similar pattern is witnessed for E_g/Y. These correspond broadly to its trend increase seen in historical Japan. It should be noted that investment proportion to GNP (I/Y) in contemporary LDCs is greater than that in historical Japan, and thus its value and related ratio, I_g/Y, are listed in the table for reference.[23] Again with considerable variance, the broad tendency is for a greater value of I/Y in semi-industrialized countries. Generally speaking, the higher value of I/Y does not appear to lower the ratio E_g/I compared to that in historical Japan, except for such countries as Pakistan and the Philippines. Whether Japan's pattern is also found in other developing economies or not is a problem to be examined further by use of time series for individual countries. Nevertheless, the long-term tendency of increase in the proportion of educational expenditure to gross domestic capital formation, as confirmed for Japan, presents the important suggestion that this may be characteristic of successful latecomers.[24]

---

[22] Emi's data used for E_g for Japan implies the major part (in net accounting) was accounted for by local government. In million yen for selected years it was as follows:

	1885	1895	1905	1915	1925	1935
Central	0.9	1.7	7.0	13.9	115.9	180.3
Local	6.8	12.2	36.7	77.3	379.2	462.4

Source: LTES, Vol. 7, Appendix Table 12, pp. 196–198.

[23] For reference, I_g/Y in Japan was 0.6% for 1885–1904, 1.9% for 1904–1919, and 2.9% for 1919–1938.

[24] Despite the actual existence of variance in the rate of increase in the labor force, both over time for one country and for cross-sectional comparisons of countries, why is the performance of the ratio E_g/I of such significance? The answer is simple.

We have no systematic data on the historical experience of industrialized countries. If they show similar tendencies, as some of the U.S. data suggest, Japan must have had a faster rate of increase in the proportion. This is our conjecture.[25]

Education and the Residual

How are these findings and suggestions linked with what we have stated in the preceding section? First of all, the performance of E_g/I has a tendency to increase with $\Delta R/I_i$ measured for industrial sector (I_i is investment for this sector). In Table 6.6 two terms are reproduced for convenience, together with other relevant terms. The demand for and the use of HC enhanced by school education of course pertain to the national economy, and are not confined to the industrial sector. The residual will be produced in the nonindustrial sectors as well. But the residual measurement of the macro economy is not available. The positively associated performance of the two terms suggests that an augmented source of HC was supplied in a sustained way to meet the increased demand stemming from the innovative development of industry.

ΔC stands for the sum of opportunity costs of labor and capital. ε, column (4), is a crude hypothetical measure of opportunity costs of public education expenditure based on the assumption that its alternative can be represented by investment in the industrial sector. This may roughly suggest the limit of increasing the amount of E_g. In period 2 in the table, ε is estimated to be greater than the value

---

The incremental increase in the labor force, ΔL, is included in both E_g and in I. Let e and i stand, respectively, for E_g per unit labor and I per unit labor, E /I = $e\Delta L/i\Delta L = e/i$. Therefore, we do not need to worry about the variance of the magnitude of ΔL.

[25] The fee payment for schools by households is estimated by Miyohei Shinohara in *LTES*, Vol. 6, *Personal Consumption Expenditure*, Table 96, pp. 252–53. The ratio of total fee payments to government education expenditures (E_g) in current prices is as follows for selected years (%) (numbers in parentheses are for government and public schools):

1887	22.8 (20.3)	1904	17.2 (14.0)
1891	26.8 (23.3)	1919	9.4 (6.1)
1897	20.5 (18.5)	1930	16.7 (9.7)
		1838	17.2 (10.1)

The ratio was greater in the initial phase. In particular its decrease toward the phase of semi-industrialization is distinct in the case of government and public schools. This may be against usual expectations. The trend of increase in E_g relative to capital formation does imply such an important aspect. It is conjectured that the education costs were much heavier in earlier years for the government budget as well as for households.

Table 6.6
Comparison of Government Education Expenditure with the Components
of Investment Productivity: Macro Economy, 1891–1938

(%)

Period	E_g/I (1)	R/I_i (2)	C/I_i (3)	ε (4)=(1)×(3)	Amount of E_g (5)	
1 1887–1897	10.8	5.1	24.3	2.6	1891	37.7
2 1897–1904	14.5	2.9	21.5	3.1	1897	72.7
3 1904–1919	15.3	8.0	22.9	3.5	1904	120.5
4 1919–1930	17.3	7.7	16.5	2.9	1919	243.3
5 1930–1938	22.3	12.6	19.8	4.4	1930	485.1
					1938	569.7
6 1955–1965	19.6	14.8	20.7	4.1	1955	7,775
7 1966–1974	9.4	10.3	16.4	1.5	1965	13,935
					1974	23,684

Source: E_g, the same as for Table 6.4; others from Table 5.7.
Remarks: Column (5): three-year average centering on the year mentioned.
Prewar: million yen in 1934–36 prices. Postwar: billion yen in 1965 prices.

of $\Delta R/I_i$, although for all other periods $\Delta R/I$ is far greater than ε. E_g partially contributes to enhancing the residual as it includes the parts irrelevant to economic activities. Nevertheless, this suggests that a possibility of increase in public education expenditure depends upon a sustained process of residual augmentation in the private sector.

With the above qualifications, in our view the human resource improvement by school education does have dynamic relevance to the residual augmentation beyond increasing the quality of the labor force measured earlier. At least it can be said that the trend of increase in the ratio E_g/I was a necessary condition for upgrading the residual growth by enhancing social capability.

To continue along this line of argument is difficult, but the paragraphs below may deepen our understanding. Greater expenditure on education per physical investment unit is required to enhance the potential of HC in the long process of innovative development based on borrowing foreign technologies. As noted earlier, the proportion of those receiving higher school education gradually increased. The cost of higher education per person is far greater than that of primary schooling. Therefore, a total education expenditure increase is inevitable.

The cost differential per student varies between countries and between development phases, but it is always high, particularly in earlier

Table 6.7
Cost Differential by Educational Level

Period	Public Middle School	Government University
1890–1900	11.5	53.3
1900–1920	6.2	33.6
1920–1930	4.1	30.9
1930–1940	3.3	30.2
1950–1960	2.2	10.9
1969–1971	1.1	7.3
1979–1981	1.2	4.5

Source: Ministry of Education, *Japan's Growth and Education*, Appendix Table 11, pp. 208–9.

years. In Japan's case it was as shown in Table 6.7 for selected years, taking public primary school education costs as 1.0.

The degree of the differential and its narrowing trend is remarkable, particularly in the postwar years. Since a substantial part of education expenditures is teacher salaries and expenditures tend to decrease over time, we suspect that a sort of scale economy operates more at higher levels of education. The tendency to allocate increasing proportions to higher education was encouraged by this cost-saving activity.

This differential, combined with changes in the student distribution, gave rise to the expenditure distribution by school level among the working-age population groups classified by education level in Table 6.3. Table 6.8 summarizes the changes in education expenditure distribution by school. Such points as a higher proportion for higher-level education (due to high costs) and for teacher education (due to the urgent need for teachers) in earlier years, and a postwar jump in the middle school proportion (due to longer compulsory education) need no explanation. The shift to higher school level in allocation of education expenditures was induced by economic expansion of the private sector as fuller industrialization was realized. It is, however, impressive that in the postwar phase, middle school eventually began to receive a higher proportion, corresponding to its greater magnitude of $w\Delta L/I$ in our formula.

Such increases in the cost of school education are not directly evaluated by the labor market. The wage differential in terms of educational level dealt with earlier is much narrower than the cost differential observed here. The larger part of its revenue is gained socially through technological advance. This is one of the important reasons

Table 6.8
Changes in Education Expenditure Distribution by School Level for Selected
Years, 1887–1960

(%)

	Primary	Middle	Higher	Teacher education*	Total
1887	79.1	3.6	8.8	8.5	100.0
1897	74.3	10.7	8.0	6.0	100.0
1904	64.8	17.2	10.3	7.7	100.0
1919	67.3	17.3	11.5	3.9	100.0
1930	59.4	20.3	16.5	3.8	100.0
1938	59.2	20.1	18.4	2.6	100.0
1953	44.5	43.9	11.6	–	100.0
1960	42.4	44.5	13.1	–	100.0

Source: Ministry of Education, *Japan's Growth and Education*, Appendix
Table 10, pp. 206–7.
Remarks: Private schools included. In three-year averages centering on the
year given.
* Classification for teacher education in the postwar years is not available.

why we associate it with residual augmentation.

Before completing the discussion of school education, at least two mutually related aspects must be considered in evaluating Japan's situation. Both concern the problem of resource allocation within the total education expenditure. First, if our hypothesis is extended, the function of enhancing HC can be classified into two categories: one pertains to the leading activity of educated personnel in technology and the other to the activity of the mass of workers educated at the common level who engage in actual production of goods and services using that technology. Between the two categories, intermediate ranges exist, although distinctions cannot be made easily. This conceptual classification may be useful to discuss the effects of education on HC as development proceeds. For instance, in the primary phase, primary school education mainly pertained to the second category, but near the end of the secondary phase most of the second category consisted of secondary and primary school education.

Because of a lack of international comparisons, our evaluation of Japan's case is speculative, but what follows is our impression. i) The expenditure allocation for higher education in the first category was very high in the early years and this largely continued throughout the prewar period. ii) For middle school education in the intermediate category, the allocation proportion was rather poor. This was certainly influenced by the inevitable allocation of a considerable proportion of expenditure for the education of teachers. As pointed out earlier, relatively high costs for first (and intermediate) category augmentation was one reason for this, and yet this creates a problem in evaluating Japan's education policy.

The second point specifically concerns "technical education." We could not examine this aspect, but in our opinion there is no evidence endorsing the argument that Japanese education policy emphasized the importance of technical, in particular engineering, education in the primary phase. We are rather inclined to the view that it was inferior compared with European technical education.[26] As mentioned earlier, a shortage of technicians was a serious problem when Japan experienced its first private investment spurt. How was the problem tackled? First, with respect to the primary phase, the HC was enhanced and accumulated by the development of traditional technology and contributed a great deal to forming the potential. Second, in borrowing and assimilating foreign advanced technologies, local organizations and institutions played an important role as well, beyond a mere increase in the number of technical experts. As explained in the preceding section in presenting the notion of social capability, what Japan did in this regard deserves attention. Technical education cannot be the sole explanatory variable. Discussion along this line leads to the learning-by-doing aspect, which will be discussed at the end of the following section.

III. Reallocation and Utilization of Human Resources

This section discusses two topics regarding reallocation and utilization of human resources using a sectorwise approach. One is an extended examination of the subject "Sectoral Reallocation of the Labor Force" in Lecture 1. Japan's case will be examined in more depth. Since we have clarified the concept of HC and the problem of enhancing it through education, some new light can be shed on that subject. In practice, educated human resources cannot be fully utilized on the demand side, and underutilization is often an important problem. The other topic concerns the quantitative measurements of the effects of capital accumulation on industrial employment and the sectoral reallocation of human resources in relation to augmenting the residuals.

---

[26] David S. Landes, "Japan and Europe: Contrasts in Industrialization," Chapter 3 in W.W. Lockwood, ed., *The State and Economic Enterprise in Japan* (Princeton: Princeton University Press, 1965).

These discussions will clarify the problems for developing economies with dualistic structures. Examination of Japan's case, we believe, is relevant to other developing countries in which underemployment of labor is a serious problem.

Sectoral Reallocation of Labor: Trends and Swings

How to utilize human resources more fully is a big problem of development. Apart from short-term demand fluctuations, structural transformation in a long-term process with swings will be the focus below. The dualistic structure of the economy will be treated in terms of the industrial sector (Sector I) vs. the agriculture-services sector (Sector II). Given the supply performance of the labor force with various quality levels, capital formation with varied types of technological advance operates as the demand for labor. Through such a supply-demand mechanism, the rates of human resource utilization are determined.

The conventional two-sector model is agriculture vs. nonagriculture, with the latter including services. In light of the explanation in Lecture 1, this model is less suitable in dealing with labor reallocation problems, because "surplus labor" exists not only in agriculture, but also in services. Actually, some modern subsectors, such as banking and insurance, that are included in the service sector are minor in terms of labor employment. Even in 1969, some 90% of establishments in the service sector in Japan employed 1–9 workers and mainly consisted of small proprietors and family workers. A similar situation is found in most developing economies.[27]

Table 6.9 summarizes the historical changes in the sectoral distribution of the labor force as a result of the reallocation process.

The morphological pattern follows the international tendency found and clarified by Clark and Kuznets; nothing is unique to Japan except that its reallocation process was faster than in Western countries. In our two-sector approach, starting from an industrial labor force of some 15% in 1892, it increased to 26% in 1936 and further increased to over 40% in 1969. Correspondingly, the labor force gainfully occupied in Sector II (sum of S and A) decreased from some 85% in 1892 to 74% in 1936 and to less than 60% in 1969.

The working-age population has been dealt with in the preceding section with respect to effects of education. A link between the labor force and the working-age population can be made by using the "par-

---

[27] Another kind of two-sector approach often used is agriculture vs. industry, excluding services. For theoretical treatment, this is convenient, but not practical.

Table 6.9

Changes in the Sectoral Distribution of the Labor Force, 1892–1979

(%)

Year	Industry (I)	Services (S)	Agriculture (A)	Total (ten thousand)
1892	15.2	14.9	69.9	2,341 (100.0)
1904	18.1	17.0	64.9	2,495 (100.0)
1916	18.1	21.9	60.0	2,664 (100.0)
1925	25.8	23.0	51.2	2,810 (100.0)
1936	26.1	26.4	47.5	3,161 (100.0)
1952	27.7	27.1	45.2	3,706 (100.0)
1961	34.8	34.0	31.2	4,515 (100.0)
1969	40.2	39.5	20.3	5,142 (100.0)
1979	41.4	47.6	11.0	5,477 (100.0)

Sources: For prewar years, Umemura and Takamatsu data in LTES, Vol. 2, Labor Force, 1988. For postwar years, the official Labor Force Survey.

Remarks: In five-year moving averages. The discrepancy due to the conceptual difference between prewar "gainfully occupied" and the postwar "labor force" may be minor in such a broad observation. This is comparable to Table 1.1.

ticipation ratio," or the ratio of the former to the latter. The ratio tends to become smaller over time mainly due to a longer "loss" (to the labor force) due to higher school education. From a ratio of 71.3% in 1905, it decreased to 60.2% in 1940 and to 57.9% in 1950. Since then, however, the tendency to decrease has slowed due to increased female participation. The effects and costs of education discussed earlier pertain to the labor force in such a reallocation process. Let us first examine the reallocation performance itself.

An overall picture is presented in Figure 6.1, which reveals the employment performance in terms of average annual rates of changes specifically designed.[28] The total labor force (L) is a sum of L_1, em-

---

[28] Visible unemployment data are not reliable for the prewar period. It is, however, thought to be minor except in depressed years such as the early 1930s. For simplicity, we do not deal with visible unemployment explicitly, assuming the entire labor force "employed" including those categorized as "underemployed" in terms of either shorter time or lower productivity in Sector II.

Some economists have coined the term "total employment." This means that instead of being fully unemployed, workers employed less than full time who are engaged in some job in Sector II are "employed" in addition to the "really" employed, and thus total employment is realized. An assertion that this is uniquely Japan's case cannot be accepted. A similar situation can be found in many contemporary

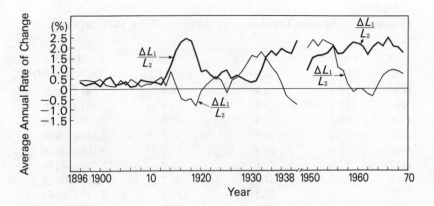

Figure 6.1
Labor Reallocation in Japan, 1896–1970
Source: Kazushi Ohkawa, *Nihon Keizai no Kozo* (*Structure of the Japanese Economy*) (Keiso Shobo, Tokyo: 1974), Chapter 3, p. 60.
Notes: All the data are in five-year moving averages. Notations: L, total labor force; L_1, industrial sector; L_2, for agriculture-services; ΔL_1 and ΔL_2, incremental changes.

ployment in Sector I, and L_2, employment in Sector II (L = L_1 + L_2). The incremental changes ΔL_1 and ΔL_2 are expressed in terms of their ratio to L_2. The specific ratio is derived in order to incorporate changes in the structural weights. Usually $\Delta L_1/L_1$ (or GL_1) is taken for Sector I, although the structural changes in the two sectors indicated by L_1/L_2 is a basic element labor reallocation process. This is taken into account by $\Delta L_1/L_2 = \Delta L_1/L_1 \cdot L_1/L_2$. For example, in an earlier phase (L_1 20%, L_2 80%), an 8% rate of increase in employment Sector I would only have an impact of 2% on $\Delta L/L_2$, while in a later phase (L_1 50%, L_2 50%), the same 8% would have a much greater impact of 8% on $\Delta L_1/L_2$.[29] Thus the demand-supply relation is close to the real situation.

Our analysis reveals the following. i) Until 1913, i.e., immediately before World War I, both $\Delta L_1/L_2$ and $\Delta L_2/L_2$ changed slightly. The process of labor reallocation had begun, albeit very slowly during the

---

developing countries. Greater rates of visible unemployment statistically shown in those countries should be dealt with separately from the phenomenon mentioned above.
[29] $(\Delta L_1/L_1) \cdot (L_1/L) + (\Delta L_2/L_2) \cdot (L_2/L) = \Delta L/L$ is applied for the total labor force, ignoring the unemployed for the sake of simplicity.

primary phase, with a slight increase in employment in Sector II. Incidentally, in the conventional two-sector model of agriculture vs. nonagriculture, the labor force engaged in agriculture began to decrease around 1903. ii) The first major change took place during World War I when a sharp contrast was seen between the remarkable increase in the rate of employment absorption by the industrial sector and the first recorded decrease in the labor force engaged in Sector II. This marks the first "turning point," as explained in Lecture 1. It is of historical significance that the labor demand surge in the industrial sector resulted in the first decline (in absolute terms) in the labor supply source for Sector II. It thus marked the beginning of the semi-industrialization phase. iii) The rate of labor demand increase by the industrial sector thereafter began to decrease, continuing until approximately 1930, during the long-lasting downswing of the Japanese economy discussed in Lecture 5. What is most noticeable is a remarkable upsurge in the labor force engaged in Sector II. Thus, surplus labor that had existed during the primary phase was exhausted, but again accumulated in the late 1920s and early 1930s.

iv) The second investment upswing in the 1930s repeated exactly the same pattern of increase in $\Delta L_1/L_2$ with a decrease of $\Delta L_2/L_2$, as in the previous upswing, and surplus labor again disappeared. v) World War II devastated the Japanese economy. Repatriates from the former Japanese empire aggravated the surplus labor situation in Sector II. Even with a sustained high value of $\Delta L_1/L_2$ (2%) for the industrial sector, a negative value of $\Delta L_2/L_2$ appeared at the end of the 1950s. This marked the second turning point in the Japanese economy. During the 1960s, the labor force engaged in agriculture decreased distinctly, but that employed in services began to increase. The upsurge in the $\Delta L_2/L_2$ curve in the 1960s, however, does not imply a recurrence of a surplus labor pool. Instead, it represents a basic change in economic structure, shifting employment from industry to services.

Three explanatory points should be made. First, surplus labor is usually defined as the working condition of the labor force, whose marginal productivity is smaller than the prevailing wage rate. We share this view theoretically.[30] As applied to the self-employed prevalent in agriculture and services, such a condition may be supposed to be of a voluntary nature as seen in the household behavior of utility maximization, while obtaining some nonlabor income from small assets. We recognize this aspect, but many of the self-employed be-

---

[30] In Lecture 1, because of the difficulty of measuring the changes over time in the marginal productivity of labor, this concept was not used.

came so involuntarily. Viewed from the macro standpoint, the reallocation of labor to modern sectors resulting from demand increase means a fuller utilization of the labor force, and the social product is increased to the same extent (a bigger increase in Sector I than the decrease in Sector II). The overall picture presented in Figure 6.1 shows the historical process of such reallocation. Through these long-term trend and swings, fuller utilization of the effects of education were realized.

Second, concerning the motivation for migration from Sector II to Sector I, it is not necessary to dwell upon the controversial aspects in an academic analysis. The problem at issue here is not people's motivation, but the factual macro-sectoral phenomena of labor force reallocation. What is indicated impressively by the overall picture is the demand performance of the industrial sector. When investment provides labor demand through increased numbers of jobs, the reallocation process tends to be accelerated, and *vice versa*. The job-opportunity thesis in this sense seems valid. Of course the basic situation includes sustained differentials in the real income level of workers in the two sectors, although the income differential is not the direct cause of sector migration. The differential is narrower in upswings and wider in downswings, whereas the degree of job opportunity is the reverse. In this sense, the mechanism of the labor reallocation process is essentially demand-determined. As stated in Lecture 1, the labor force not in demand by the industrial sector remains as "residue employment" in Sector II, forming surplus labor.

Third, the basic rationale of the macro-sectoral approach is the sustained existence of differentials of marginal productivity of labor between the modern and traditional sectors. Readers familiar with the method of project appraisal can understand the problem in connection with the notion of "shadow prices" (shadow wages in this case) used in "economic analysis," which deals with essentially the same phenomenon. Investment in industry is appraised to produce more revenue or residual in hiring underemployed labor than employed labor. Likewise, in our formula given in Lecture 5 the productivity difference should be dealt with by modifying the term $w\Delta L/I$ so as to increase $\Delta R/I$ to the same extent. These pertain to the policy aspect of the labor reallocation problem to increase the rate of human resource utilization and will be discussed below.

Capital Accumulation, Labor Utilization, and Reallocation Effects

Lecture 1, section I, emphasized Japan's much smaller rate of increase in the labor force supply than that in contemporary developing economies. Keeping this feature in mind, the following also deserve investigation: i) clarification of the industrial demand pattern through capital accumulation; ii) estimates of labor reallocation effects by applying the formula developed in Lecture 5; and iii) discussion of policy implications.

First, the labor demand can simply be assumed to be determined by capital accumulation in the industrial sector. In terms of the rate of growth, it is GL = F(GK). Its crude approximation can be obtained by use of crude elasticity ($\eta' = GL/GK$) estimates. A similar approach using $\eta = GL/GY$ was critically reviewed in Lecture 1, section I. η' is an elasticity term with regard to the input relation, while η pertains to the input-output relation. In our view, the former is a more acceptable notion than the latter. Enterprises make decisions on employing workers in relation to their plans for increasing capital stock. When adopting capital-intensive technology, η' is smaller, while for labor-intensive technology η' is larger. In Table 6.10, numerical estimates are illustrated for Japan's case.

The three prewar periods present two sharply contrasting cases: large elasticity during periods of upswing (1 and 3) versus very small elasticity during downswings (period 2). The adopted technology was labor-intensive in the former and capital-intensive in the latter. During the postwar periods, the value of elasticity tended to decrease from fairly labor intensive to more capital-intensive. In addition to the crudeness of the measurement, these are also affected by variation in the rate of capital utilization (in particular for period 2), so that the

Table 6.10

Employment Increase with Capital Accumulation: Private Industrial Sector, 1913–74

			(%)
Period	η'	GL	GK
1 1913–1920	0.54	4.8	9.0
2 1921–1930	0.14	0.7	4.6
3 1931–1938	0.55	2.7	5.0
4 1954–1963	0.40	4.6	11.7
5 1963–1969	0.28	3.5	12.6
6 (1964–1974)*	0.22	2.6	11.7

Source: The same as for Table 5.7.

Remarks: * The postwar deflator is 1965 base for periods 4 and 5, but 1970 base for period 6.

numerical values of η' represent the effects of technology type only in a loose sense. Nevertheless, the rate of human resource utilization appears affected by technology choice.

As expected from Lecture 1, section I, the magnitude of the rate of growth of captial, GK, itself is influential in determining the rate of labor demand. For example, in period 6, which mainly represents the phase of secondary export substitution, if GK were assumed to be 5%, GL would be just 1.1%. However, for developing economies the restraint on increasing the rate of capital formation is so severe that the problem of choice of technology type is a problem in the fuller utilization of human resources with enhanced capability. In this respect, how can we evaluate Japan's experience? It is our impression that despite the fast rate of industrial growth in its prewar secondary phase (semi-industrialization), Japan is not unique in enhancing its power of labor absorption from the low-productivity sector. During upswings the performance was good, but during downswings poor. This is expected in all developing economies. The magnitude of crude elasticity (η') cannot be evaluated in comparison with other developing economies (for which only the value of η is available). Nevertheless, we suspect it is not especially large for Japan even during upswings. In saying so, we are not referring to the tendency of decrease in η' toward the 1970s. Capital intensification is natural because of the required substitution of labor due to the upgrading of wages as full industrialization was realized. This is less relevant to other developing economies, except for the so-called newly industrializing economies (NIEs).

The second topic is the relevance of the labor reallocation performance so far observed to the dynamic activities of residual formation. According to the conventional approach of growth accounting, the residual growth measured at the macro level is understood to include the so-called effects of structural change. As mentioned earlier, reallocation of labor from lower-productivity to higher-productivity sectors (in the present case, from Sector II to Sector I) raises productivity measured at the macro level even without technological advance. Therefore, the total productivity growth (weighted average of labor productivity growth and capital productivity growth) must be broken down into two terms: nonstructural and structural.

The implication of the two terms is important. The formula for measuring the residual given in Lecture 5 pertains to the industrial sector. Viewed from the growth of the macro economy, it concerns the "nonstructural" part; the "structural part" is not included. But how can productivity increase even without technological advance? The answer lies in the enhancement of the rate of utilization of the same person reallocated to Sector I from Sector II. The amount of capital and the level of technology combined with a worker in Sector I are greater than those with the same worker in Sector II. In other words, there was a certain underutilization of the potential capability of human resources in Sector II. In reality the situation is not so simple; training and other costs may be needed for reallocation. Yet if we were able to estimate the magnitude of the contribution of the "structural part," it would be useful in determining the significance of the residual growth.

Estimates consistent with our two-sector approach are presented in Table 6.11 together with the relevant terms. The structural part of productivity increase realized in the industrial sector (Sector I) is shown in column (5). Its value per unit of investment transformed by use of I/Y is shown in column (3) as $\Delta R^*/I$, to be compared with $\Delta R/I$ which is by now familiar. For the two-sector model, the opportunity cost of labor is not w, but w*, which represents the lower marginal value product of labor produced by engaging in Sector II. Therefore our term, shown in column (2), is now $w^*\Delta L/I$; through the difference $(w - w^*)$ $\Delta L/I$, the residual per investment is increased.[31] This can be called the "additional residual" $(\Delta R^*/I)$ for lack of a better term. The ratio of ΔR^* to ΔR (column (3)) is around 20% on average: a significant magnitude. Because of the high underutilization rate in downswings, judgment on productivity activities cannot be reasonably made. As for

Table 6.11
Additional Residual Growth of the Industrial Sector

(%)

Period	R/I (1)	$\Delta R^*/I$ (2)	Ratio (3) (2)/(1)	Sum (4) (1)+(2)	Structural Part (5) (6)/(7)	I/Y (6)	$w\Delta L/I$ (7)
1 1908–17	6.7	1.9	0.22	8.6	0.24	21.9	6.8
2 1918–31	5.7	1.1	0.18	6.8	0.20	18.9	4.1
3 1932–38	11.7	2.2	0.19	13.9	0.47	21.0	9.7
4 1955–64	12.5	2.9	0.23	15.4	1.27	38.0	9.6

Sources: Columns (4) and (7) from Kazushi Ohkawa, "Effects of Structural Change in Productivity Growth: A Long-term Measurement," in Richard Kosobud and Ryoshin Minami, eds., Econometric Studies of Japan (Champaign: University of Illinois Press, 1977). Others the same as for Table 5.7.

the upswing intervals, the contribution of the effects of structural change, or reallocation of human resources, appears to be around 26–35% of the total productivity growth.

This is merely an extension of our original formula developed in Lecture 5. The method is simple. The estimated magnitude may differ according to data reliability and procedures. Nevertheless, quantitative identification of the additional residual growth is important since the industrial sector contributes to augmenting residual growth additionally to the same extent. Through the entire semi-industrialized phase, all developing economies may experience this phenomenon, as the differentials of the marginal product of labor characterize the structure of the economy. Two factors are involved. One is the speed of increase in the labor-absorbing power of the industrial sector, and the other is the degree of productivity differentials. Taking the two together brings out one important mechanism in the catching-up process of latecomers to industrialization. The two aspects involved in measuring crude elasticity and the structural term in labor reallocation treat only part of the whole problem, covering mainly the second category of human resources mentioned earlier. Nevertheless, its important aspect in terms of policy implication is elucidated. It appears that the policy of developing labor-intensive industry-technology is a desirable choice for realizing fuller utilization of human resources. This is rather obvious. The real problem is searching for an optimum in meeting the two objectives of enhancing both productivity and employment. Between our two terms $\Delta R/I$ and $w\Delta L/I$ no rigid *a priori* relationship exists. It can vary to a considerable extent through policy options.

For example, in order to increase the additional residual ($\Delta R^*/I$), the choice of labor-intensive industry is desirable. The same is recommended by use of shadow wages in economic analysis of individual projects. But what about the major residual, $\Delta R/I$? If greater ΔR^* accompanied smaller ΔR, as compared to the alternative, one would have positive and the other negative effects. If capital-intensive industry were chosen, the reverse would hold. Here lies the real problem at issue. Japan's case can be evaluated fairly well in meeting both require-

---

[31] For a two-sector model, the actual formula used is $\Delta L_1(w_1 - w) + \Delta L_2(w_2 - w)$, where w is average of the wage (marginal value product) of two sectors. Actually, the structural part of increased productivity is often measured by application of conventional growth accounting to measure total productivity growth. In a simple case of a two-sector model, for the labor term we have $Y_1/Y\beta_1(GL_1 - GL) + Y_2/Y\beta_2(GL_2 - GL)$. As $\beta_1 = L_1w_1/Y_1$, $\beta_2 = L_2w_2/Y_2$, we can derive $1/Y\{\Delta L_1(w_1 - w) + \Delta L (w_2 - w_1)\}$. For details, see Kazushi Ohkawa, "Sangyo Kozo Henka to Makuro Seisansei Josho [Change in Industrial Structure and Macro Productivity Growth], in Ohkawa, *Nihon Keizai no Kozo*, Chapter 4.

ments as far as the upswing intervals are concerned, but in downswings its performance was poor.

A number of factors are involved in such performance. Beyond the choice of type of technology, the function of organizations and institutions is an important factor. In our simple framework education is assumed to function to supply HC, but in practice learning by doing plays an important role through the process of dealing with borrowed advanced technology.[32] This is mainly carried out on the demand side, through the private sector. The efficiency of the activity of learning by doing is influenced by organizational and institutional set-ups. Labor-management relations in general, and permanent employment arrangements, particularly in Japan's case, illustrate this. Its positive effects tend to raise $\Delta R^*/I$, along with $\Delta R/I$, during upswings of the economy. To balance this view, however, we must mention that during downswings enterprises are apt to maintain $\Delta R/I$, sacrificing labor employment, especially short-term contracts, as suggested by the smaller crude elasticity observed earlier during economic downswings.

[32] "Learning by doing" is an important problem area, which has hitherto been discussed but not clarified by empirical studies. The association of its effects with visible factors, such as capital formation, output of production, or even passage of clock time, has been proposed and tried. None appears satisfatory in grasping its real function. It is thus a factual challenge and requires further research, including "training" (as distinguished from education) activity planned and financed by private enterprises, often supported by government. Insufficiency of school education is often supplemented and improved by this activity, and there is much evidence of its success in many developing economies.

Industrial Policy:
Interaction of Public and Private Sectors

I. Framework of Approach

In the preceding lectures, government activity in specific fields has been discussed: in Lecture 2, basic industries such as iron-steel and shipbuilding; in Lecture 5, a capital-investment approach to infrastructure building; in Lecture 6, public school education as a way to increase human resources. In this lecture these public activities will be discussed in a more systematic way within a framework of "interactions" between public and private sectors.

To be successful in fostering development, what kind of role should the government play? Answers differ with the political structure of the country involved. In the light of Japan's case, we believe a legitimate answer cannot be given by the government performance in itself, but must include the possible responses of the private sector and, in turn, public reactions to them. Conceptually, interactions between the public and private sectors must thus be assumed, and their changes over time should be explored. Historical reality is, however, so complex that we are not qualified to apply a theoretical model and arrive at any meaningful answer. In this lecture we intend to use a narrowly specified framework to describe the interactions, integrating the relevant parts of the other lectures.

The performance of enterprisers in the private sector is understood in terms of their innovative ways of augmenting capital formation, and of technological-organizational advances essentially through the competitive market mechanism. The magnitude of the residual growth per unit of investment ($\Delta R/I$), in the formula developed in Lecture 5, is the core indicator to be used for *ex post* observation of the performance in private industries. Note that the formula is derived using the opportunity cost—a basic concept pertaining to the operation of a free market mechanism. The magnitude of the residual thus realized in private enterprises, however, depends upon the effects of government activities. As discussed in connection with school education, the level of human capability used by private enterprise depends upon the government's education expenditures. In the development plans of contemporary developing countries, government expenditure on human resource improvement—a broader concept than education—is an important issue. No doubt these expenditures (often called human capital investment) contribute to building a base for the creation of residuals, even though it cannot be easily quantified (Lecture 6, section II).

A similar function of the government is recognized in physical infrastructure building. Its higher costs compared with benefits are socially acceptable so long as its contribution is at least equal to the residual to be augmented in the direct production activities of the private sector. This is the essence of what was discussed within a hypothetical framework in the Appendix to Lecture 5. We can say also that investment allocation to infrastructure is relevant to realizing the residuals in the private sector.

In evaluating these two activities of the government, disagreement among economists is not an important problem, although there is disagreement about the criteria for optimum allocation of investment sources among sectors. The basic consensus is that the innovative process in the private sector based on a market mechanism needs such public (non-market) activities. However, with respect to other participation of the government in direct-production sectors, the situation differs. Some economists assert that the government participation in this field differs from its activities in human resources and physical infrastructure augmentation, and they are conservative regarding its intervention in the free operation of the market mechanism.

Except for the well-known case of "infant industries," governments' industrial policies draw less systematic analytical attention than their macroeconomic policies—fiscal, monetary, and trade. Actually, however, for the latecomer countries, strategies and policies for industrial development have long been a matter of high priority. All the medium and long-term development plans of contemporary developing countries contain sectoral (and often subsectoral) versions together with the macro-frames of their plans and/or perspectives. The intensity and selection of government participation (direct and indirect) in various sectors differ from one country to another, but what is common to all of them, including those based on market mechanisms, is the basic recognition of the necessity of government activities for industrial development.

This question is an investigative challenge for us. The nature and characteristics of "industrial policy" should be clarified and evaluated more systematically. To do so, technology should first be treated inseparably in terms, say, of an "industry-technology" mix. Second, the approach should bear a close relation to the country's macroeconomic policies. For latecomers, modernization of industry depends upon being able to "borrow" technological knowledge from economically advanced countries. In fact, in developing a specific industry the options available in selecting the type of technology are rather limited in a number of cases: individual policies are faced with the usual macro-restraints on resources, externally and internally. There are some interactions between the two. For example, externally, import substitution by an expanding domestic machinery industry is expected to narrow the resource gap, but if it provokes greater imports of capital goods, the results would be the opposite of expectations. Internally, in the case of direct production of machinery by public enterprises, an investment–saving gap increase in the public sector would be a serious constraint on growth, and actually this is often the case.

Within such a framework Japan's case can be discussed as an illustration of the dimension of development phasing. Success in shifting the economy from a lower phase to a higher phase of development means a transformation in industrial structure to be realized by improved technological-organizational capability. Let us remember that investment spurts distinctly mark the dates of phase-shifts. In Lecture 5 we discussed the leader-follower relationship between public and private investment. The private investment spurt in 1913–19 marked the first break in the pattern of government leadership in capital formation, sustained throughout the primary phase. This in turn implied what we call an "early start" in secondary import substitution. Particularly speedy development in shipbuilding and some machinery industries was noted. Why was the private sector capable of taking the lead in investment at that time? Any answer must take into account the government's concentration on military buildup, especially after the Russo-Japanese War of 1904–5. This example, together with the case of iron and steel mentioned in Lecture 2, illustrates the initial leading role of the government in developing such industries. In large part the private sector followed.

The concept of leader/follower-ship, however, cannot be uniformly applied to all industries. For example, in the case of textiles the government's lead was limited to an initial kick. Development and primary export subsitution in these industries were mainly pursued by the private sector.

The initial move by the government was of particular importance in the engineering industries because of the higher level of technological and organizational capability required to establish them. The local adaptation and absorption of modern technology borrowed from advanced countries required a lengthy period of learning by doing and attaining economies of scale. In terms of the residual approach, the point is explained as follows. Viewing these industries in the given time framework, $\Delta R/I$ would be expected to be zero or even negative for private enterprises unless an initial move was made by the government. The type of policy required for taking the inital step and for the continuation of support, if necessary, may differ case by case, but at any rate the policy has social costs in subsidies, higher prices for protected products, and so on. The process is essentially analogous to the infrastructure sectors mentioned above, though accounting and measurements are more difficult in heavy industries and engineering because of the dynamic processes involved.

What the example does show is that government participation in the private market mechanism cannot be evaluated without setting certain criteria. A shift to a new phase of development within a certain period of time can be assumed to be the objective of industrial policy. The criteria should be set independently for each sector, instead of in aggregate, in order that the complex actual processes can be interpreted in a historical perspective as consistently as possible. To achieve the objective, the core criterion is how and to what extent public participation can contribute to enhancing the innovative development essentially carried out by the private sector.

Two comments should be made before this framework is applied. First, the market mechanism of the private sector cannot be assumed a priori to operate always in the same way in its scope, structure, and intensity. It changes over time: usually it is weaker in earlier phases of development and becomes stronger in later phases. This recognition is particularly important when we emphasize the significance of the market mechanism in a dynamic, instead of static, sense—that is, in the innovative process. Innovative enterprisers facilitate technological and organizational progress and their followers are active in its diffusion on the one hand, while on the other, losing competitors drop out of the market; these phenomena are assumed for the process of realizing the residuals produced by the industry under review. In this context, it is not so easy to define precisely the so-called "failures" of the market mechanism, as it is in the case of the static approach. To be more realistic, though less rigorous, perhaps we should depart from a failure-versus-success dichotomy and take up the aspect of intensity and the time dimension in evaluating the function of the market mechanism. The significance of government participation through industrial policy can be discussed more realistically from this point of view.

Second, and similarly, it may not be realistic to draw a sharp line *a priori* between the scope of public and private activities insofar as their economic aspects are concerned. To a certain extent, there is overlapping between the two. For instance, school education—the quintessential public activity—has partially been carried out by the private sector in a number of countries. With industrial policy, too, there are certain areas of overlap between private and public activities. In Japan's case, the iron and steel industry is a notable example of the direct participation of government in what are essentially private production activities.

In contemporary developing economies, public enterprises are major factors. Apart from political and/or strategic reasons, there is a question of economic options—whether private or public activity is more suitable for encouraging innovative development. Recent debates on the movement toward liberalization have dealt with this aspect of the problem. Our framework assumes that public production activity, if any, should be evaluated by the same competitive criteria used for the private sector.

II. Initial Policies for Industrialization

Transitional Measures
During the period of transition 1868–85 (Lecture 1), the industrial policy of Japan's new government was not carried out in a systematic way. Rather, it was implemented through "trial and error." The resistance of forces opposed to the revolutionary changes and the heavy task of institutional innovation required for "liberalization" from feudal restraints, among others, prevented a systematic policy approach. The governments of a number of developing countries were placed in a similar situation during the transition interval that followed their gaining of political independence in the early postwar years. Nevertheless, the initial industrial policy deserves our particular attention. This is not the place to describe the historical details of "trial and error." In what follows the discussions will be focused on the process of change in the means and measures of initiating industrialization: a shift from direct participation by government to indirect participation.

Japan's government initially spearheaded industrialization by pioneering new undertakings directly, not only in the facilitating sector (for example, railways and telegraph lines), but also in a wider variety of direct production activities, focusing on the "heavy" industries: opening new coal mines and establishing iron foundries, shipyards, and machine shops. It set up "model" factories to manufacture cement, paper, and glass. In the light industries, too, the government directly participated in importing machines and employing foreign technical experts to modernize raw silk reeling and cotton spinning. It set up a special department, the Ministry of Industry, in 1870 to carry out the major part of these activities. This direct participation, however, was short-lived. At the beginning of the 1880s, the Ministry became less active, and in 1885 it was dissolved. Direct participation was abandoned in favor of a new style of indirect participation, as will be discussed in greater detail below.

What we are concerned with is the government's objectives and the merits and demerits of its efforts. Views differ among economic historians. Some see the government's role as merely an extension of the activities of the *han* (feudal clan) governments, while others stress the significance of new undertakings. Our view is in accord with that expressed by Ohkawa and Rosovsky:

> Many scholars have attributed considerable importance to the establishment of certain modern Western industries by a few *han* during the first half of the nineteenth century. Since these were frequently connected with a desire to produce armaments, E.H. Norman [in *Japan's Emergence as a Modern State*, 1940] went so far as to suggest that the "normal" pattern for an industrial revolution was reversed in Japan, with heavy industry preceding the development of light industry. This is, we believe, a misunderstanding of the implication of an industrial revolution.[1]

Two aspects need further discussion: one is the usefulness of the initial moves of the government; the other, the factors responsible for its financial failures. In evaluating the government's efforts, one could argue that some of the factories established were useful investments. However, in our view, the defect was that an inappropriate distinction was made between "heavy" and "light" industries with respect to the usefulness of borrowing and assimilating Western ad-

[1] Kazushi Ohkawa and Henry Rosovsky, "A Century of Japanese Economic Growth," in W.W. Lockwood, ed., *The State and Economic Enterprise in Japan* (Princeton: Princeton University Press, 1965).

vanced technologies. A model factory, for example might be more suited to the economic needs of the initial development phase in silk reeling, an exemplary light industry, than in heavy industry, where the government built such factories. For the latter, strategic rather than economic needs were most pressing because of the need for security defense, internally and externally. This element of strategic needs was strongest in the 1930s, and one could argue that it "artificially" distorted (if not reversed) the "normal" course of industrialization. In this regard, the phenomena mentioned above as occurring in the transition interval cannot be viewed as one-time in nature.[2]

Regarding the financial failure of these policies, it is widely assumed that most of the public enterprises faced financial difficulties, with costs exceeding benefits, although detailed accounts are not available. The government finally decided to sell them to private enterprises. Why did they fail? Technical and managerial inefficiency are often blamed—as they are also in contemporary public enterprises of this kind in some developing countries. However, the unfavorable macroeconomic conditions prevailing during most of the transition interval deserve more attention than they are usually given.

The constraint of an international trade gap became especially severe in 1873, most directly through outflow of specie. Under the pressure of the unequal treaties with the Western powers, Japan had not been permitted to rely upon protective tariffs on imports. The real economic objective of the government's "industrial promotion policy" (*shokusan kogyo seisaku*) was clear. It aimed at achieving quick import substitution by expanding domestic production in order to counter the increasing pressure of the widening external resource gap. The direct participation policy implemented by the Ministry of Industry was the core of the wider industrial promotion policy that included textiles, apparel, livestock farming (wool production), agriculture, and sugar production. Export promotion was of course another aim of the policy, with raw silk and tea as the main items. But because of the depressed international market, the situation was unfavorable for a country ex-

---

[2] Quantitative evaluation of the direct participation of the Ministry of Industry is difficult. Most economic historians say that the Ministry's public expenditure was not large except for infrastructure investment. However, viewed in terms of the amount of PDE (machinery and equipment) production, it is not so small either. For example, in 1880, PDE production of the Ministry of Industry amounted to 908,000 yen. If this is added to production by the army (193,000 yen) and the navy (488,000 yen), the total amount of PDE production was 1.55 million yen—roughly a quarter of total production. *LTES*, Vol. 4, *Capital Formation*, by Koichi Emi: Table 4–63 (p. 108) and Table 6–8 (p. 199).

porting primary goods, in much the same way as it is today for developing economies in the primary phase.

The expectation of quick yields as a result of these measures was not fulfilled, despite accelerating public investment at the expense of the sound fiscal policy required for the new government. The result was an acceleration of the inflation caused by distorted monetary and fiscal policies. Although only rough statistical data are available, we suppose that overinvestment of a large I–S gap in public accounting was responsible.[3]

In sum, two points are noted. First, the objective of the government's direct production activities was achieving quick import substitution, but it was pursued without paying due consideration to the different technological levels required for "heavy" and "light" industries. Second, an unstable macroeconomic situation was responsible for aggravating the financial failures of these public enterprises.

Initial Development Plan

In retrospect, it is obvious that the initial "industrial promotion policy," despite the government's great efforts, was carried out without benefit of a normal path of development: no sound institutional set-up, with widening resource gaps both internally and externally. Therefore, fiscal and monetary austerity was recommended together with institutional adjustments to cope with the difficult situation. A drastic deflation policy was thus adopted—a policy widely known as "Matsukata deflation" after Masayoshi Matsukata, the new Finance Minister, who was responsible for it. The program was carried out from 1881 to 1884 with great sternness and determination, resulting in a genuine start toward modern economic growth.

The quantity of money was reduced by some 20%, and commodity prices fell by 75% from 1881 to 1884. Interest rates also declined. Deflation affected government revenue favorably because the land tax, its major component, was fixed in the revised system. Foreign

---

[3] Data on public investment (including military investment) are available in *LTES*, Vol. 4, thanks to Emi's contribution (Part III, Table 9). By use of the series of 1934–36 constant prices, the rate of average annual increase of public investment is as follows in 3-year periods:

1871–73 to 1874–76	16.9%
1874–76 to 1877–79	10.1
1877–79 to 1880–82	15.2
1880–82 to 1883–85	5.6

Through the 1870s and at the beginning of the 1880s, no doubt there was a spurt.

payments, with the exception of a small deficit in 1881, went into the black for the first time since the Restoration. As a result of these achievements the government could now move toward reforming the banking system: the Bank of Japan was founded in 1881 and took the place of the previously built national banks as the issuer of currency. Thus the Japanese economy now had a modern currency system and a public budget structure.

The unfavorable social and economic effects of the deflationary policy were of course severe. For example, the disposable income of landowners (most of them owners on a small scale, as now in Japan) fell sharply, with almost disastrous repercussions on the rural economy. In macro performance, the rate of output growth and capital investment were slowed down considerably. In retrospect, one could recommend less drastic measures than the Matsukata policy, as one could for contemporary developing economies. However, in light of the sound economic performance during the initial phase that followed it, we judge that this stringent strategy was essentially unavoidable in order to embark on a normal path of industrial policies conducive to augmenting the activities of the private sectors.

The last point leads us to a discussion of the *Kogyo Iken* (Recommendations for Economic Development), which was presented by Matsukata and officially approved in 1884. This was the first long-term (ten-year) development plan in Japan; it provided both macro and sectoral perspectives, with detailed information surveys. But the plan was not widely known, perhaps because government policies in subsequent years did not explicitly follow the Recommendations. Nevertheless, we share the view that actual subsequent policies were largely along the lines drawn by the Recommendations and that therefore this is an extremely important document for understanding nature and characteristics of industrial policy of the new government.[4] The following points deserve particular attention.

First of all, the Recommendations recognized the necessity for the plans and activities of the government to be considered within the framework of the market mechanism, in conjunction with private activities. The plan recommended is basically similar to those which today we call "indicative." Industrial policy is proposed from a long-term perspective, similar to some of the development plans of contemporary developing countries. The Western idea of laissez-faire had already been introduced into Japan by that time. According to his-

---

[4] For details, Ichiro Inukai, "The Kogyo Iken: Japan's Ten-Year Plan, 1884," in *Economic and Business Review*, No. 6, May 1979 (Kyoto Sangyo University).

torians, Matsukata himself was a believer in this Western idea, which was implemented by trial and error during the transition intervals. A policy of total laissez-faire with a minimum of government intervention could not have been implemented at that time because private enterprises were not confident enough to proceed automatically with the capital investment that accompanies technological and organizational advance. Based on this basic recognition, the primary objective of the indicative plan was to provide and upgrade the confidence of the private sector for the future. In the Recommendations, this point is repeatedly emphasized by use of the term "people's willingness."

Second, the problem of allocating resources among various sectors was dealt with through industrial policies. Recently it has been revealed that there was some disagreement within the government; the original unpublished version of the position paper written by Masana Maeda, another leader in government policy-making, took a perspective opposite to Matsukata's. Inukai interpreted the disagreement as follows, in his paper cited above:

In its essence the policy aims at an identification of key products of industries and puts all resources together to increase the production of identified commodities, with the view that a rise in production of these goods will have a significant spill-over effect on the rest of the national economy. Raw silk and tea for export promotion and sugar for import substitution were taken up strategically as the most important commodities, and Maeda intended to utilize available loan funds [from the proposed Industrial Bank] intensively on the production of these goods. Maeda then considered projects related to infrastructure to be given the lowest priority. This order of priority, however, was completely contrary to Matsukata's; he gave the highest priority to infrastructure projects from the point of view of defense, while he thought the private sector should be left alone with the least possible [direct] intervention of the Government.

Some experts may modify or even disagree with Inukai's interpretation. For example, Takamatsu seems to amplify Maeda's sectoral priority by placing more emphasis on the time dimension, dividing it into (i) short-term and (ii) long-term priorities. With regard to the traditional commodities, (i) is the same as in Inukai, but (ii) includes a variety of indigenous commodities such as marine products, paper, tobacco, porcelain, lacquer, rapeseed, livestock, and cotton textiles.

Infrastructure, too, can be divided on the basis of the time dimension. The short term (i) includes forests, roads, irrigation, reclamation, and land improvement, and the long term (ii) includes canals, shipbuilding, seaport construction, and river banking. In this interpretation, infrastructure is not necessarily the lowest priority; nor is it undertaken solely for defense purposes.[5]

We are not qualified to comment on the historical interpretation of different views. What we are interested in is the fact that the final, official version took a certain direction and identified several characteristics of the Meiji type of sectoral resource allocation which are relevant to contemporary problems.

(i) The dualistic nature of industrial policies. Latecomers' economic development can be categorized in terms of traditional (or indigenous) and modern (or Western) elements (see Lecture 1, section II), in particular with respect to technology and organization.[6] The Recommendations in its policy proposals, including that of a regional development plan, paid due attention to both the modern and the traditional sectors. Of course modern-style manufacturing was to be developed. What was at issue was how to improve indigenous sectors: agriculture, handicrafts-manufacture, and services. Maeda's proposal which Takamatsu evaluated was actually to a large extent contained in the final version, and Inukai also emphasized this aspect. Supporting the indigenous sectors also laid the basis for the phase of primary product exports. Agro-industry, in the form especially of raw silk and tea, was the major participant in early exporting. In agriculture, the hasty decision to introduce Western technology, in particular that of mechanization, made in the transition interval was recognized as a failure, and emphasis was switched to the policy of improving traditional small-scale farming by encouraging labor-intensive technology of a biological-chemical nature—what we call BC technology, for short.

(ii) Investment allocation between infrastructure and direct production sectors is always a great problem for developing economies. The final version of the Recommendations gave priority to both fields (i) and (ii) above. Both pertain to development activities in general, but (i) is more relevant to traditional direct production activities and (ii) more to modern direct production activities. As has been discussed

[5] Nobukiyo Takamatsu, "Notes on Kogyo Iken," mimeographed manuscript, IDCJ, June 1980.

[6] Kazushi Ohkawa, "Dualistic Growth and Economic Backwardness—Introduction" in *Differential Structure and Agriculture*, Economic Research Series No. 13, The Institute of Economic Research, Hitotsubashi University (Tokyo: Kinokuniya, 1972).

in some detail in Lecture 5, the government investment in infrastructure in Meiji Japan draws our particular attention for its leading role in conducting private investment. The basic policy framework was given in the Recommendations. It is interesting to see that the allocation percentage of subsidies, an indicator of indirect government participation, was highest for both construction and transportation-communications during the earlier years, but for the later years of the initial phase, the former declined in importance while the latter increased its weight a great deal. Subsidies were not the major means of channeling resources among sectors in prewar Japan, and yet this is symbolic of the dualistic policies and the shift from the traditional to the modern sectors.[7]

Concurrent Growth Policy

With regard to the direct production sectors, the policies actually adopted are briefly described below for the subsequent years of the primary phase before World War I. Agriculture and industry (textiles, heavy machinery, and engineering industries) and the relationships among them are the topic. The leadership role taken by the government was through indirect participation of a conducive nature, with the notable exception of steel manufacture. Within this framework, however, its style and intensity differ among sectors with respect to whether resources were channeled via fiscal or credit (loan) policies or technology-organization policies. However, it is possible to characterize them in general as a "concurrent growth" policy for agriculture and industry in the dualistic structure discussed earlier (Lecture 1). For latecomers, the sequential development pattern (first agriculture and then industry) based on British history cannot be repeated. Instead, both major sectors are required to develop concurrently. We believe Japan's development strategy and policies were conducted largely along these lines.

---

[7] According to *LTES*, Vol. 7, *Government Expenditure*, by Koichi Emi and Yuichi Shionoya (Table 5-3, p. 42), for selected years, the distribution percentages of central government industrial subsidies are estimated as follows (in five-year averages centering on the years selected):

	Construction	Transportation & Communications	Percentage of Subsidies in the Total Government Budget
1880	71.8	12.2	4.0
1890	43.9	40.2	5.3
1900	2.0	83.4	2.5
1910	–	92.7	2.1

Note: The last column is from Table 5-2, p. 41, of the same volume.

Agricultureal development policy was focused on the technological-organizational support for establishing the so-called "Meiji farming system," which produced an early type of "Green Revolution" in rice cultivation, although financing support through special banks was not missing. The measures include experiment station building (including the national station in 1893), technology diffusion through the Farmers Association, establishment of an inspection and control system, and expansion and improvement of irrigation-drainage facilities in the later years of this phase.[8] The essential problem was to develop land-saving technology without drastic organizational changes in the traditional system based on cultivating landowners.

Productivity increases in agriculture provided the basis for levying a land tax, the major source of government revenue. According to our research, in general, in terms of sectoral resource flow, net outflow of resources (savings) from the farm household sector to the non-farm household sector was sustained almost throughout the primary phase. The dependence on agricultural surplus in Japan's case is often pointed to as "atypical." However, other kinds of agricultural surplus, such as the export taxes on primary commodities which are levied in a number of contemporary developing countries, are essentially of the same nature. Agricultural surplus provided the fiscal foundation for conducting a concurrent growth policy under a limited amount of foreign capital inflow except during wartime.[9]

Modernization of the indigenous raw-silk industry was a well-considered choice; the government even established a model factory with invited French experts. Its technological contribution was undoubted, but financially it failed. Its most important contribution was indirect: encouraging technological improvement in sericulture—the raising of cocoons. The succeeding expansion of private activities was vital in the complementary development of silk-reeling and sericulture. In cotton textiles, the story was similar: following an initial move by the government, private activities became paramount. But an important difference was the serious adverse effects of international trade on domestic cotton cultivation. Under the pressure of imported cotton from China, India, and the U.S.A., local production was discontinued

[8] For details, see "Measures for the Encouragement—Control and Protection of Agriculture," chapter 8, in Takekazu Ogura, ed., *Agricultural Development in Modern Japan* (Tokyo: Japan FAO Association, 1963).

[9] For details of estimates and interpretation, see Kazushi Ohkawa, Yutaka Shimizu and Nobukiyo Takamatsu, "Agricultural Surplus in Japan's Case: Implication for Various Possible Patterns in the Initial Phase of Development," IDCJ Working Paper Series No. 19, 1982.

because of its inferiority in both quality and price. The government's readjustment policy was to lead the shift from cotton cultivation to sericulture.

The adverse effects of imports were apparent also in indigenous manufacturing of such products as sugar, paper, and metals. The unequal treaties on tariffs deprived Japan of the power to impose tariffs larger than the extremely low rate of around 3% (formally 5%), and these treaties continued in force until the early years of this century. Competition from imported goods was very hard on traditional manufacturers. In the metal industry, for example, indigenous nails were driven out of the domestic market in the 1880s as a result of a rapid increase in imports of nails from Europe. The production of European-type nails started with the transfer of modern production methods in 1896. Former nail production facilities were converted to the production of other goods such as pipe, files, and copperware, so as to put to use the workers' traditional technical experience. Here we see an example of the private sector's response to the adverse effects of government policies.

From the point of view of the government, which had no means of protecting industries from overseas competition, the problem was making what we call today "structural adjustments" in traditional manufacturing and services. In the light of bitter experience during the transition interval, the style of government participation also changed in this field. In 1885, the first of a series of "trade" associations" by commodity and by region was established. Through these associations the government provided technological guidance by convening seminars, dispatching technical experts, and providing direct technical guidance for domestic manufacturing and other areas. The response of the private sector was favorable, and the associations eventually spread nationwide. This style of government participation is analogous to that in agriculture, where Farmers' Associations, as discussed earlier, were the link between public and private activities.

It is not easy to evaluate the merits and demerits of the government policy of structural adjustments to meet the need to modernize these traditional production activities. Nevertheless, it is clear at least that adjustment makes more sense than the alternative, a policy biased toward government participation in the modern industries and depending almost solely on transferred technologies, with the only benefits for traditional industries those of a possible spillover.[10]

---

[10] The non-factory production share in total manufacturing output is estimated at 68.5% in 1890 and 53.8% in 1909, the year the Factory Law first came into effect.

The final topic in this section is the modern sectors of the heavy and engineering industries. Their "early start" in the primary phase was discussed in section I. The case of steel will be treated in the section that follows. Here shipbuilding is taken up as a typical case. The government actively promoted development in this industry from an early stage. In 1896 it enacted a measure for shipbuilding promotion and another for marine transportation promotion. The former was intended to give subsidies to private shipbuilding yards for producing steel ships of larger than 7,000 tons capacity. The latter was intended to encourage the activities of Japanese enterprisers engaged in marine transportation by providing subsidies for manufacturing or purchasing ships of larger than 1,000 tons.

These legislative measures were aimed at enlarging the size of Japanese ships, but because of the weakness of Japan's competitiveness, foreign boat purchases increased, so that the 1899 subsidies were cut to half of those for domestic production. This direct measure of import substitution was proved effective: total tonnage of shipbuilding did increase from 500 in 1895 to 32,000 in 1901, compared with a total import tonnage of 20,000. The domestic shipbuilding industry adopted higher-level technologies, enabling it to respond to the demand thus created. During the years after the Russo-Japanese War, it developed further, and by 1910 appeared to be close to self-sufficiency. In that year the Ocean Transportation Subsidy Act was enacted. The effect of this measure was to exclude imported ships from navigating designated ocean routes, and its ultimate goal was full dependence on the domestic shipbuilding industry.

Some economic historians point to this as a "typical" successful case of promoting an infant industry. We do not disagree with this view. However, we emphasize its significance as a typical case of an "early start" secondary import substitution as defined in section I. Actually, during the first investment spurt interval, domestic shipbuilding capacity expanded a great deal, resulting in a bilateral agreement with the U.S.A. on the exchange of ships for steel: mutually advantageous for one country with a steel shortage and one with a ship shortage. In 1919, the year of the shift to the next phase of industrialization, the Shipbuilding Promotion Act was discontinued.[11]

Incidentally, the distribution of workers in manufacturing is estimated for that year as follows: 74.5% for small-scale (1–4), 20.2% for medium-scale (5–499), and 5.3% for large-scale (500 and over).

[11] To show roughly the quantitative significance of the subsidies given by the government, the ratio of the amount of subsidy to total freight revenue is estimated for three big companies (Toyo Kisen, Nihon Yusen, and Osaka Shosen). The aver-

III. The Unstable Interwar Period

The major part of the phase of secondary import substitution was characterized by two factors: externally, an unstable international environment, and internally, military expansion toward the end of the prewar period. The style of interaction between public and private activities was very much affected by these factors. External restraints combined with internal strategic requirements characterize government industrial-technological policies. The first investment spurt is symbolic of the emergence of private sector activities, and one may be tempted to say that government leadership tended to fade away by that time. However, in the second investment spurt, which took place toward the terminal years of this period, the government again played a leading role in shaping the industrial transformation toward military mobilization. Therefore, this period is sometimes characterized as "military capitalism" or "state capitalism," with colonial expansion policies of course being implied.

We believe the effects of militarism in Japan should be treated as distortions of the long-term process of industrialization basically relying upon the private market mechanism. Even during the second investment spurt, private activity was mobilized a great deal, although the industrial structure was "artificially" greatly distorted in order to build "heavy" industries for strategic purposes. During the early interwar period, the government did not expand or strengthen its direct participation, with the exception of the nationalization of railways. Even in the steel industry government's direct participation was limited, and electricity generation was left in private hands for most of the interwar period.

Because of the distortions and biases thus arising, Japan's industrial policy of secondary import substitution should be interpreted with careful qualification. Below, three specific topics are discussed: first, the case of the iron-steel industry to illustrate the government's policy on heavy industries; second, protection policies and measures in general; third, the discontinuation of concurrent growth which resulted in the formation of what we call a "differential structure" by the 1930s.

A Representative Case: The Iron-Steel Industry

The iron and steel industry is another case of an early start with a stra-

---

age is 32.7% in 1900 and 31.9% in 1910. This amazingly big proportion decreased drastically by the end of World War I; for example, it was 1.7% in 1918. Drawn from the original data in *Kokusei Soran* [*Overall State of Japan*] (Tokyo: Toyo Keizai Shimposha, 1926).

tegic purpose, but it differs from shipbuilding: direct participation by the government was the initial move, followed by "coexistence" of public and private production during the major import substitution period. The initial move was made as early as 1891, to establish a state mill, and in 1901 furnace operation was commenced. It is often thought that there was a revival of short-lived direct participation by the government during the transition interval, but actually this was not the case. Long-term planning was undertaken by the government.

The initial difficulties, both technical and financial, that the mill management encountered were discussed in Lecture 2. Here we are more concerned with the policies which resulted in sustaining the coexistence of public and private production activities. After heated debate,[12] the final decision was formalized in the Act for Promotion of the Iron-Steel Industry, which was enacted in 1917. Its purpose was to undertake various new measures to encourage and promote private activities as well in this industrial area.

Through expansion and amplification, first in 1906 and then in 1911, the state mill took advantage of the most advanced technology borrowed from abroad to solve the difficult problems of coke production. The private enterprisers in this area also stepped up production in view of the emphasis on strategic industries in the light of the Russo-Japanese War. This was not part of government policy. However, the private sector concentrated on the production of finished goods such as pipe and cast iron, rather than on the entire process of steel and iron production. There was no competition between public and private activities: before 1917 the major activity was in the public sector and private activity was supplemental.

This situation changed completely at the beginning of World War I, when the cessation of iron and steel imports from abroad and the serious supply deficit that resulted induced an expansion of domestic production of steel in both public and private sectors: the upsurge of private enterprises' investment in this area was notable, and led for the first time to a competitive relationship between the public and private sectors. The 1917 Act was the first official recognition of the private sector's joint participation with the government—a recognition made with strategic purpose. If it wanted the nation to be self-sufficient in steel, the government was obliged to recognize the role to be played by the private sector. The alternative was to further augment the ca-

---

[12] These debates took place in the deliberation council and/or committees in which representatives of private sectors participated as well as in the parliament.

pacity of the state-run mills by a then-proposed third expansion plan. However, there was strong resistance from the private sector to this expansion. The result of the debate on this proposal was a sort of compromise in the form of the 1917 Act.

The substantial content of the Act was the setting of a protective tariff and tax exemption measures for private enterprises engaged in steel production. In 1921, the first amendment to the Act enlarged the scope of the tax exemption and converted the tariff to an *ad valorem* system. In 1926 a second amendment set subsidies for pig iron production and raised the tariff rate for steel products.

What was the result of this policy? In answering this question a distinction should be made between steel and pig iron.[13] Despite the government's support policy, a complete production system was not firmly established. Competition from imported Indian pig iron at cheaper prices was strong, and many private enterprises judged that it was more profitable to rely on pig iron imports insofar as import was possible. Thus the process of import substitution vacillated between the two modes of thought. The import dependency ratio for steel rapidly decreased to a low of 9% in 1936, but that for pig iron was far behind, being some 30% in the same year. Further steps thus had been taken by the government in order to combat the increasing pressure of imports. The first one was the formation of a cartel of domestic major producers in both public and private sectors. The cartel kept the domestic price equal to the low price level of imported goods in 1927–31, but the effort was a costly one for most of the private enterprises because the cartel-fixed price was too low to cover their production costs.[14] The yen devaluation policy (by 43% against the U.S. dollar) in 1932 actually remedied this difficult situation. A trust was formed eventually by Yawata and six major *zaibatsu* enter-

---

[13] Ippei Yamazawa, "Tekko-gyo no Ganko Keitaitei Hatten" [Wild Geese Pattern of the Iron-Steel Industry], chapter 5 in *Nihon Keizai no Hatten to Kokusai Bungyo* [Japanese Economic Development and International Trade] (Tokyo: Toyo Keizai Shimposha, 1983).

[14] In general, the cartelization movement of the 1930s was a direct outgrowth of the Depression. The government and private business jointly attempted to control "excessive competition" through schemes to control output and prices and through market allocation and sales quotas. The coverage was wide: some 45 industries were affected. As is illustrated by the case of iron-steel, cartelization was not necessarily successful. Yet it deserves particular attention because, in our view, the cartelization movement initiated the style of "administrative guidance" based on the notion of "excessive competition" that has become the backbone of government participation in carrying out postwar industrial policy. This will be discussed in the section that follows.

prises, which built Nippon Steel Company. Its share of total production was 95.2 % of pig iron and 43.9 % of steel.[15]

The entire process consisted of the following steps: (i) government leadership by direct participation; (ii) a compromised competitive coexistence of public and private enterprises, with the latter in the ascendant; (iii) an eventual merger of the two under government leadership. This long process was carried out with the strategic goal of achieving self-sufficiency. Such industrial policies cannot be "neutrally" discussed, however, independently of defense strategy. Even so, what concerns us is the technological character of this industry. In order to complete the process of import substitution, and eventually to be internationally competitive, economies of scale must be fully achieved. This requires institutional innovations as well as ability to absorb the necessary borrowed technological knowledge. Even with these features, one could think of an alternative type of indirect participation of the government, a neutral approach. However, in our view, the first two steps—government leadership and coexistence—are inevitable, but the third—merger of public and private enterprises—is a distortion.

External Restraint and Protection Policy
The gold standard was inaugurated in 1897, partly in response to the indemnity received from China after the Sino-Japanese War; the exchange rate fixed at that time remained in effect until 1917, when a gold embargo took place. Japan, however, continued to face foreign payments deficits despite its success in primary export substitution. The resource gap, further aggravated by the Russo-Japanese War, was to a considerable extent filled by financial borrowing from abroad, leading to a long-term capital inflow in national accounting. After an abnormal bonanza during World War I, the situation returned to the "normal" condition of increasing resource shortages: in 1919 a decrease in the amount of specie held abroad and a drastic drop in the exchange value of the yen took place. The trend was aggravated by a drastic increase in foreign borrowing after the Great Kanto Earthquake of 1923, which dropped the exchange value of 100 yen to 38 dollars—less than half of the initial rate set in 1897. Foreign capital borrowing continued.[16] After a short-lived period of trial and error,

---

[15] This section heavily depends upon the work of Ippei Yamazawa and Yuzo Yamamoto in both research and interpretation. *LTES*, Vol. 14, *Trade and Balance of Payments*, in particular Chapter 4 and related Appendix Tables.

[16] The current account deficit, including net transfers from the rest of the world, amounted to a maximum of 640 million yen in 1924, which was approximately equivalent to three-month exports of goods and services.

including a one-year return to the gold standard and measures pegging the yen to the pound sterling, eventually in 1939 a devaluated rate of 23 dollars to 100 yen was set—at which rate the yen was valued at less than one-third the original value. Therefore, broadly speaking, during the interwar period the resource gap was met by both capital inflow and yen devaluation.

More factual description should not be needed to convince readers that Japan, like many contemporary developing economies, had long suffered from the chronic deficit in foreign payments. Both foreign capital borrowing and yen devaluation were aggravated in particular by the unstable international environment, but this was not the sole cause. It is often said that Japan was self-reliant, depending almost solely on domestic finance for investment capital, but this is a distorted view when Japan's performance in combating resource shortages is considered.

A few words are in order on the investment–savings (I–S) gap. Except during wartime, the government kept it largely to a minimum. A great exception, however, is noted in the 1930s. The I–S gap estimated in the conventional way (but with military investment included in I) had begun to increase in 1927 (the I/S ratio was 1.32 in that year), and reached 7.78 by some estimates in 1940. This is a rough figure, but it can be an indicator of the government's direct participation in investment and can show us the financial aspect of the artificial industrial policies discussed earlier. Apart from this period and wartime, government can be said to have been rather conservative in its direct investment activities—a different story from that of some of the contemporary developing countries whose I–S gaps are intensified by the public sector.

Our second topic, protectionist policies with tariffs, requires that we look back to the primary phase. The unequal treaties with the Western powers were discontinued, though not fully, in 1899. In return for allowing goods to be imported from major Western countries, a special low tariff rate, 5–15%, was applied until 1911, when complete independence was eventually established. Therefore, a sharp distinction can be made between the primary phase and the subsequent semi-industrialization phase. Some economists have taken advantage of hindsight to note that Japanese private enterprises were "encouraged" to augment their competitive power by adversity in the form of this long-sustained unequal treaty relationship with the West, particularly in comparison with the high tariffs in the contemporary developing countries. What we are concerned with is quite a different aspect. As discussed in the preceding section, the importing of goods of the West-

ern type was actually detrimental to the domestic producers of traditional goods in competition with them. Imports tested domestic makers' ability to make quick shifts. Perhaps sociocultural factors were
important: long-standing traditional preferences in consumer goods
and the force of inertia vested in traditional technology for their production gave Japan an advantage over economies in which modern
goods were already influential in the colonial period.[17]

After attaining tariff policy independence, Japan adopted tariff
measures in line with an industrial policy that was "protective" and
whose protectist tendencies had increased during the interwar period.
This is confirmed by Yamazawa's detailed research by commodity
(LTES, Vol. 14, Part III), which indicates that Japan's import tariff
rates were moderate in comparison both with Western countries at
the same stage of development and with contemporary developing
countries. What we are concerned with here is the "escalating tariff
structure" in which rates increased for goods manufactured by more
sophisticated production methods. Virtually no distinction is made
between products of light and heavy industries, but clear-cut differences are identified by end-use classification (refer to Lecture 5), as
is shown by Table 7.1.

We wish to add two points to Yamazawa's clarification. The first
pertains to the import of producer durables—the carriers of technological knowledge to be borrowed. As was touched upon in Lecture
2, special lower tariffs were adopted especially for absorbing advanced
technologies. This is a sort of specific import promotion policy. The
government was keenly concerned with this aspect, in particular during
the 1930s. For example, the tariff rate for machine tools, a most backward sector of the machine industries, was kept relatively low and
dropped sharply in the 1930s as the nation moved toward military
mobilization. Actually machine tool imports were sustained almost
at the level of domestic production until around 1934. A far higher
import dependency ratio was maintained than the total PDE (producer
durable equipment) import dependency ratio mentioned in Lecture 2.

The second point concerns the evaluation of tariff policy in the
general context of industrial promotion and protection. Since export
tariffs were minor and import control by quota was adopted only
after 1937 as an emergency measure, the major policy tool was import
tariffs, and their purpose gradually shifted from revenue to industrial

[17] Henry Rosovsky and Kazushi Ohkawa, "The Indigenous Components in the
Modern Japanese Economy," Economic Development and Cultural Change, Vol.
IX, No. 3, April 1961.

Table 7.1
End-Use Classification of Import Tariff Rates, Selected Years, 1893–1938

(%)

	Capital Goods (1)	Inter-mediate Goods (2)	Raw Materials (3)	Consump-tion Goods (4)	Food (5)	Total Commodities (6)
(A):						
1893	3.8	4.1	4.0	4.0	2.9	3.9
1889	3.9	4.1	2.8	4.1	3.0	3.7
1903	8.6	9.6	5.7	17.3	10.8	9.9
1908	13.8	8.9	8.7	31.2	29.8	16.2
(B):						
1913	17.3	17.0	6.4	30.1	33.6	19.8
1918	7.0	5.1	3.3	20.6	20.4	10.7
1924	10.6	6.7	1.8	20.4	14.9	10.9
1928	14.3	17.9	4.0	41.4	34.2	22.6
1933	16.9	14.6	7.6	41.6	39.6	23.8
1938	7.3	10.9	4.2	63.1	44.7	29.2

Source: *LTES*, Vol. 14, Table 4–2, p. 81.
Remarks: i. Data are simple rather than weighted averages to avoid possible distortions from tariff effects on import volumes.
ii. (2) is an average of goods produced by both light and heavy industries.
iii. (A) is added for reference and comparison.

protection. Yamazawa and Yamamoto contend (*LTES*, Vol. 14) that other industrial policies might have had stronger effects than tariffs on Japan's industrialization. We share their view with much more firmness in the light of our analysis of the direct as well as indirect participation of the government, including its various measures of fiscal and financial policies. The considerable inflow of foreign funds discussed earlier should be included in the discussion. For example, the loan raised in the U.S. for promoting electricity generation by private sector was strongly backed up by the government. Industrial policy thus requires target-setting, specifically in the form of investment fund channelling and guiding technological advance. In this sense, tariff measures are too broad despite the qualifications mentioned above.

Toward Internal Instability
Industry-technology policy cannot be evaluated legitimately without

a discussion of its effects on social aspects of the economy, in particular labor employment. The trade-off between productivity and employment is a great problem in most of the contemporary developing countries. The controversy involved in choosing capital-intensive or labor-intensive industrial technology is well known.

During the interwar period the Japanese economy moved toward forming what we called "differential structure" (Lecture 1), with increasing differentials of productivity and labor income between the modern and traditional sectors. This implies discontinuation of the concurrent growth that largely characterizes the growth pattern of the primary phase. If the "employment problem" is grasped in a broad sense, including self-employment in the traditional sector, the differential structure means deterioration in the employment situation toward internal instability of the society.[18]

The point here is how and to what extent industrial policy was responsible for the instability. The question is not easy to answer with quantitative evidence. Our speculative observation, however, is that government industrial policy was responsible to a considerable extent, if not totally, for setting levels of both demand for and supply of labor. To begin with the demand side, let us refer to our earlier discussion pertaining to Figure 6.1. During the downswing interval of the interwar period, the incremental increase in labor employment in the industrial sector declined drastically. This was caused by two factors, mutually related: one is an investment downswing in the economy and the response of the private sector; the other, a capital intensification in the private response. For the latter, let us remember our discussion of Table 5.7 on the private industrial sector. The magnitude of the term $w\Delta L/I$ for 1920–30 was estimated to be less than half of those for other intervals, despite the favorable value of $\Delta R/I$. No doubt, capital intensification was of major importance in the industry-technology equation. Government industrial policy was responsible for capital intensification in the light of its leading role in this area of modernization. In the light machinery industries using labor-intensive technology, no explicit guidance had been extended by the government, leaving this area almost entirely in private hands. The same is true for medium- and small-scale enterprises. Unlike the postwar case, no

---

[18] Income distribution is not taken up here, but its increasing inequality during this period was also relevant. See Lecture 1, section I, and Toshiyuki Otsuki and Nobukiyo Takamatsu, "An Aspect of the Size Distribution of Income in Prewar Japan," IDCJ Working Paper Series No. 9, June 1978.

attempt was made explicitly to protect or encourage medium and small-scale enterprises.

On the supply side, agriculture and services were the major source in the context of dualistic structure. Figure 6.2, referred to earlier, tells us that reproduced "surplus labor" accumulated as residues in these sectors in addition to the natural increase in the labor force supply due to demographic causes. A widening differential of output value per worker between agriculture and manufacturing was mentioned in Lecture 1 as a symbolic indicator of the differential structure.

The government's agricultural policy is responsible to a considerable extent, if not totally, for this situation. Two mutually related factors are at issue. First, after the "rice revolt" of 1918, the government began to promote rice production in Korea and Taiwan to fill the supply deficit in Japan proper. The success of rice imports from these colonies, however, resulted in a decline in rice prices that discouraged domestic farmers. A drastic price decline in raw silk due to the global depression aggravated the difficulties of the rural economy. The second factor was the almost stagnant state of technological advance in agriculture, as described in Lecture 1. Innovation had slackened and per-capita income disparity widened. The government bore considerable responsibility for the situation. Its sectoral allocation of subsidies began to show a heavy bias toward i) agriculture and ii) construction related to rural infrastructure. As a percentage of total industrial subsidies, agricultural allocations increased from 22.2% in 1920 to 58.4% in 1940; infrastructure investment increased from 26.6% in 1920 to 32.6% in 1935.[19] This subsidy policy was not a positive, dynamic one, but rather of the nature of a rescue operation in the drive toward food self-sufficiency. It contributed little to raising the level of the supply price of labor in the private sector, even while reversing the sectoral resource flow from industry to agriculture.

Taking into account both demand and supply sides of the labor force, the industrial policy during the interwar period, in our view, could not solve the problem of trade-off between augmentation of productivity and employment. The unstable international environment externally and the drive toward military mobilization internally seriously distorted the "normal" path of Japan's secondary import substitution phase. We can conceive of an alternative policy laying more weight on employment in the broad sense. Some of the contemporary developing economies in the semi-industrialized phase face a problem

[19] Emi and Shionoya, *LTES*, Vol. 7, *Government Expenditure*, Table 5-3, p. 42.

of similar nature. The relevance of Japan's experience for these economies may be as a negative example.

IV. Toward Fuller Industrialization

Nothing positive for enriching our knowledge about development policies can be drawn from Japan's experience during and immediately after World War II. What we are concerned with is the war's influence on industrial policy in the subsequent years. Having suffered disastrous damage in the War, Japan's GNP in 1946 was reduced to the levels of the World War I years. Until around 1953–54, Japan was at the transit interval of reconstruction and rehabilitation. Strong government leadership and foreign aid were required because the market mechanism could not work well. After being more or less normalized, however, the economy soon moved toward an investment spurt and a high growth rate—the "Japanese miracle."

In discussing the postwar interaction between public and private activities, perhaps the significance of three aspects should be emphasized: internationally, a long-term isolation; domestically, abnormal government intervention during the early postwar years; and increased activity in the private sector in the subsequent years. Japan's economic isolation from normal international contacts continued for all of 15 years, from the time of military mobilization in the 1930s to the beginning of the postwar 1950s. During most of these years, government intervention continued to be abnormally strong, particularly in the years of a "controlled" economy. This must have had a sort of spillover effect on the style of active government participation in the private sector in the subsequent years.

The third investment spurt, however, emerged as a landmark phenomenon. In our view this is vital evidence of a wider sphere of activities in the private sector. It emerged in the latter part of the 1950s and was largely sustained over the 1960s. Investment proportion of GNP increased to well over 30% (Lecture 5). Historically, interaction between public and private activities was first led largely by the government through the initial phase of industrialization. This pattern was broken for the first time by the first private investment spurt in the bonanza of World War I, but this step could not be followed in a sustained way; it was interrupted first by the downswing in the 1920s and then toward the late 1930s by the government's stronger intervention aimed at military mobilization: the activity of the private sector was distorted, though it did not lose its vitality (section III).

The democratization of institution-organizations—dissolution of the *zaibatsu*, undertaking of land reform, etc.—contributed much to enhancing the postwar vitality of the private sector. Some economists argue that it was the sole cause. We do not share this opinion. The distortions due to institutional and organizational restraints on free operation of market mechanisms mainly took place during the prewar phase of secondary import substitution, as observed earlier. The democratization contributed much to remedying these distortions. However, from a longer-term historical perspective, the nation's potential, in our view, had been accumulated during the long prewar development experience. What we call social capability had been developed. This potential was augmented by the emancipation from government control and other restraints on the operation of market mechanisms.

These aspects taken together may appear ironic: the government tries to lead the private sector, on the one hand, while in the private sector more activities are now being handled independently. Actually, however, such a situation, in our view, was very close to the reality. The interaction mechanism worked positively for both sectors, public and private, in combating the widened technological gap due to international isolation—that is the problem of first priority of this phase.

The Economic Planning Agency (EPA) was newly established. This agency is responsible for compiling medium-term macroeconomic plans of an indicative nature with the Economic Council, most of whose members represent the private sector. One may have the impression that this marked quite a new direction taken for the first time by the government. Actually, however, it was a sort of extension of the less formal planning that took place during the rehabilitation period. In the milieu of active interaction between public and private sectors, the plan primarily aimed at providing people with "confidence" for making future judgments about the economy.[20] Historically, it was along the same lines as the early Meiji Recommendations discussed earlier. Actually, postwar growth exceeded the planned rates, and the plans were revised to follow the performance of the private sector.[21]

[20] The Ministry of International Trade and Industry (MITI) is responsible for incorporating the industrial plan in its broad framework with the macroeconomic plan developed by the EPA, but its major task is its sectorwise implementation of industrial policy in close contact with the private sector.

[21] Some economists from the perspective of hindsight contend that the government deliberately intended to keep the rate of growth slower in order to minimize the adverse effects of excessive competition among private enterprises. We believe this is a misjudgment. No evidence for it is found in the process of deliberation and compilation of the plans.

Protection from Foreign Competition

Protection policies with the aim of shifting the economy to the phase of secondary export substitution deserve particular attention. In the first half of this process of making a shift, the Japanese government's policies of protecting domestic industries from international competition were strong, and its attitude toward liberalization was hesitant and reluctant. The measures of protection were direct control, a quota system, tariffs on commodity trade, and foreign capital inflow regulation. These in themselves deserve no particular attention as they are essentially the same as those used in many contemporary developing economies, and there is no need of a detailed description. What we describe below is the significance and evaluation of each measure, viewed for each dimension of development.

The first topic is commodity import regulation. A quota system continued to be the major import regulation measure at the beginning of the 1960s, even after the end of the total regulation system adopted in the rehabilitation period. During the 1960s the deregulation continued, but the process was not smooth and was highly selective: more than 100 commodities remained import-regulated even in the latter part of the 1960s. A speed-up of import deregulation in the 1970s had been implemented deliberately, commodity by commodity, on the basis of the government's judgment of the possibility of attaining international competitiveness. As would be expected from our analysis in Lecture 4, machineries are the earlier candidates—to begin with, buses and trucks (1961), color television sets (1964), and passenger cars (1965). However, even in the late 1980s, 20-odd commodities remain import-regulated; most of them are farm products, including rice.

Tariff measures became increasingly dominant as the process of deregulation continued. It took the form of an escalating system, and the nominal rate of tariff difference by commodity category is very similar to the prewar structure in the 1920s and 1930s (Table 7.1). Viewed from the standpoint of industrial policy, this is not so important.

At the same time several export promotion measures were set up during the early postwar years. Among them were the tax exemption system, in force 1953–63, additions to the special credit treatment for exports, 1946–72, and the export insurance system started in 1950. These indirect measures, however, were rather moderate in their effects in comparison with the direct regulation of imports.

Second, and even more important than commodity regulation, was the firmly established policy of regulating direct investment from abroad. The legal basis was given by the *Gaishi Ho* (Foreign Investment Act), proclaimed in 1950. Such direct investment control was unprecedented in Japan's long development history, except in the prewar years leading toward military mobilization and war. Actually, control was implemented as an extension of the emergency measures taken in the rehabilitation period. Internally, the industrial policy had also the aspect of being an extended version of the administrative intervention originating in the wartime and rehabilitation period. Actually, the criteria for permitting direct foreign investment did include the stipulation "when recognized to have adverse effects on the rehabilitation of the Japanese economy." The Act was in operation until immediately before 1964, when Japan became an Article 8 member of the International Monetary Fund. As is often the case in contemporary developing countries, the actual procedure of applying the criteria of the Act to individual cases was not made public. But judging from the factual results, it was carried out strictly, as cases of permitted investment are limited. A complete liberalization eventually took place in the first half of the 1970s—for passenger cars in 1971, integrated circuits in 1974, and computers in 1975.

The pace of liberalization was kept even slower than that of commodity trade liberalization. Clearly the government adopted a protection policy to minimize competition with foreign capital in the domestic market for the industries which were judged to "be behind." The Ministry of International Trade and Industry (MITI) worried about the danger of being dominated by foreign enterprises in these industries. An alternative would be to make use of the advantage of inducing direct investment from foreign enterprises with the expectation of promoting the competitiveness of domestic enterprises more quickly and efficiently through diffusing advanced technologies directly. This alternative strategy has been adopted in a number of contemporary developing countries, although not without the framework of certain regulating measures.

The experience of receiving direct foreign investment was not lacking during the prewar period—for heavy industries, including electricity, in the 1920s and some even before World War I; later even for the automobile industry—although the total amount was moderate. With a few exceptions, joint ventures were the dominant type, but the management leadership was kept on the Japanese side. The major purpose was to transfer advanced technology, and in particular to speed up the pace of its absorption. This policy was successful in accelerating the process of secondary import substitution. However, the government favored domestic producers in purchasing goods and in granting tax exemptions, as well as providing subsidies to the enterprises whose share of foreign capital was below a certain percentage. As a result of these discouraging policies, together with direct regulation, foreign investment faded away in the 1930s.[22]

The prolonged postwar regulation of direct foreign investment was implemented in a different international environment. In the 1920s, big multinational corporations had not yet emerged. What was common to both cases is the favorable attitude of the government toward accelerating the pace of technological advance. However, compared with the early prewar phase of secondary import substitution, the situation differs: in the later postwar phase, the technological gap between firms was much narrower in most of the major industries. The possibility of catching up to the most advanced level appeared to be much closer. MITI thought that severe direct competition in the domestic market with earlier liberalization would retard the pace of catch-up. Some economists argue, to the contrary, that the catch-up process might actually be retarded by prolonged regulation, particularly in new industries such as computers production. If this were the case, an alternative policy of earlier deregulation could be a wiser one.[23] A "neutral" post-evaluation, however, is almost impossible. What is clear in Japan's case is that the government had a firmly established target of catch-up within a certain time period for selected industries, and this was the major priority in carrying out its industrial policy. Some observers call it a "nationalization policy." We think this is a misleading term. The aim is to eliminate a technology gap. The intention of avoiding possible domination of the industry in question by foreign enterprises is not a matter of nationalization *per se* but one of technological catch-up. Nationalization is of course an attractive target for latecomers. However, we have to apply economic standards. If it is done too early, it can result in increasing the social costs that stem from prolonged low productivity, high domestic prices, and low quality levels, in the protected products of domestic industry. Technological catch-up and nationalization should be differentiated categorically, though actually the two are interrelated. The crucial

[22] Yamazawa's observation. Ippei Yamazawa, *Nihon Keizai no Hatten to Kokusai Bungyo* [Japanese Economic Development and International Trade], pp. 158–160.

[23] A good source on this aspect is Philip A. Trezise with the collaboration of Yukio Suzuki, "Politics, Government and Economic Growth in Japan," chapter 11 in Hugh Patrick and Henry Rosovsky, eds., *Asia's New Giant* (Washington, D.C.: Brookings Institution, 1976), in particular the section on industrial policy.

elements in making the catch-up target realistic in Japan's case were (i) efficient operation of a competitive market and (ii) technological level of knowledge and capability hitherto acquired.

Despite the enormous physical damage Japan sustained in the war, the nation's technological knowledge and human capability survived almost intact. More than that, technological knowledge was greatly improved and widely diffused during wartime, over a wide range of industries. Even in backward areas such as machine tools, special efforts were made to catch up. The spillover effects cannot be underestimated in discussing technological progress in the subsequent peacetime years. The "artificial" distortion of the pace of industrialization by military mobilization had been tremendous. The share of net output of manufacturing (mining included) to NDP was as high as 39.7% in 1940. This share was never surpassed by postwar records: 24.4% in 1955, 30.5% in 1970, and 31.8% in 1980.

As mentioned earlier, one should of course count the adverse effects of Japan's isolation on technological knowledge, but the spillover effects should also be duly evaluated.[24] Not only for government policies, but also for the performance of the private sector, these legacies had considerable relevance. They meant that private enterprisers could make their investment plans while taking into account the improved engineering capability not only for old but also for new industries.

Interaction through "Administrative Guidance"

Along with the measures protecting industries from international competition, the government pursued domestic measures of industrial policy for the areas it considered "strategic," covering industries both in "old" and "new" categories of simultaneous technological infusion (Lecture 4). The means were those conventionally used today in a number of developing countries, including channeling allocation of financing through special banks (particularly the Japan Development Bank), incentive measures such as corporate tax exemptions and special capital depreciation allowances, direct subsidies from the budget of the central government, licenses for importing foreign technologies, and so on. These were in principle backed up legally by Special Acts, mostly

---

[24] There are many examples. Most of the wartime aircraft producers entered the automobile and motor scooter businesses. A number of munitions manufacturers started to make sewing machines. Many of the leading companies in the optics industry were direct descendants of makers of optical war equipment and relied extensively on what they had learned during the war in making gunsights, bombsights, and so forth.

of a provisional nature—for example, the Laws on Temporary Measures for the Promotion of Electronics Industry (1957) and the Laws on Temporary Measures for the Promotion of Machinery Industry (LTMP) (1965).

The reader may be interested in "administrative guidance," as the term has widely been used to characterize Japan's bureaucrats' function in what is sometimes described by the facile phrase "Japan, Incorporated." Administrative guidance is of course not unique to Japan, but its historical significance in Japan draws our attention, as was pointed out in the preceding section. Let us discuss it with regard to implementing industrial policy, which aims at technological catch-up in the context of interaction. Under the legal framework, the above-mentioned conventional measures were actually implemented through "administrative guidance." The guidance specifically aimed at directing the industrial structure, technology, and organization in a certain direction. It started with basic industries, with the notion of "bigness" prevalent in the 1950s. The notion of "excessive competition" followed it in the 1960s: in the opinion of MITI, "There are too many automobile and computer firms, and we can expect the requisite reductions to take place soon"—a process that had already occurred in other industries. Spurred by the inevitability of the trade liberalization, MITI in the 1960s was especially concerned with arranging these mergers. Their purpose was clear: to control effectively the expansion of capacity and to form strong (large) and technologically up-to-date firms that could compete with the best foreign producers.

A few preliminary words are needed to avoid misunderstanding. The scope of the industrial policy formulated by MITI bureaucrats was actually not so wide, but was limited to particular industries. There are a number of industries on which industrial policy had no direct influence and yet whose pace of technological advance deserves our attention. Let us recall our finding in Lecture 4 that "general machinery" (transportation and electricity excluded) is the industry with the highest rate of total factor productivity increase per unit of investment. Yet for this industry, government policies of protection and promotion were rather weak. Actually, it is not hard to list many prosperous industries with which the government had no direct concern: cement, paper, glass, bicycles, optical goods, motorcycles, and others.

The actual type of MITI intervention and the reaction of private enterprises vary among industries in intensity and time dimension. Two representative cases are selected for the discussion below: iron-steel and machine tools.

As we have described in the preceding lectures, iron-steel has long been the industry of highest priority. During the period of postwar reconstruction, together with coal and electricity, the so-called priority production policy was applied for this basic industry, aiming at its quick recovery. Special allocations of financial resources and domestic supplies of coal, as well as subsidies for purchases of imported materials (the difference between production cost and controlled price) were provided to ensure stable steel supplies for other industries, even though they placed a heavy fiscal burden on the government general account. By around 1953, production had recovered to the prewar level. The interaction between public and private activities in this industry in the subsequent years was greatly affected by the notion of industry thus established.

During the 1950s, "rationalization" was carried out. First, after subsidies were discontinued, low-interest loans and special depreciation allowances were provided. These contributed a great deal to providing the large amounts required for investment. Special allocations of foreign currency and import tariff exemptions were adopted for machinery and technology imports in the iron-steel industry. The rolling process was completely modernized. In the latter half of the decade, further steps were taken toward establishing new integrated mills with top-level technologies. These were mostly financed by private funds supported by World Bank loans. Thus, in this decade, production concentrated in the big enterprises with full-scale production facilities. An oligopolistic system was established, systematizing the enterprises based on open-hearth furnaces. The technologies newly introduced included methods of operating strip mills, development of a pure oxygen revolving furnace, and continuous casting.

There is little disagreement among experts about the economic success of the rationalization policy. The process of lowering production costs enabled the industry to strengthen its international competitiveness. According to certain data, the cost of steel production in Japan was lower than that in the U.S. at the beginning of the 1960s. As we have observed elsewhere, steel played a pioneering role in secondary export substitution with its early export expansion. The government policy of export promotion supported the industry's growth and expansion, and the rapid expansion of the domestic market under the influence of the third postwar investment spurt was another important factor. However, we share the view that the basic cause of the expansion was the investment acceleration accompanying the ambitious borrowing of advanced technology within an oligopolistic structure of competition.

In the 1970s, some change took place in the oligopolistic structure, particularly with the merger of two major producers, Yawata and Fuji, to form the new Nippon Steel Company. MITI did not participate directly, but it supported the merger, based on its confidence in the great competitiveness of "bigness." As will be discussed later, this notion operates in MITI policy on other industries as well. Competitiveness within an oligopolistic market is not easy to evaluate for a specific industry, but we can generally say that mergers tend to make the structure of an industry less competitive. In the case of steel, there is some evidence that this is the case.[25]

Second, the administrative guidance offered by MITI was not necessarily followed by private enterprises, either as associations or as individual companies. It had more effect through the interactions between the public and private sectors. It is important to avoid overestimation of the effects of guidance.

The case of machine tools is selected as an illustration.[26] As was discussed often in the preceding lectures, machinery producers are characterized by their high value of Lw/K—that is, they are labor-intensive with high labor quality, the enterprise scale being relatively evenly distributed. These producers are not characterized by "bigness," unlike basic industries with small Lw/K. The machine tool industry represents this size spread well because of its high level of technology and multiple specialization; transportation machinery, in contrast, shows more concentration, and government concern for the latter industry was much greater.

The government's policy for the machinery industry was based on the 1956 temporary promotion measures for the machinery industry, mentioned earlier. The government was authorized to compile a basic plan for rationalization and to recommend the implementation of cooperative actions necessary to achieve the target of the plan. However, the government was requested to take into consideration the opinions of the Deliberation Council of the Machinery Industry as the representative of the private sector. The Act itself was less restrictive than in other cases.[27] Nevertheless, administrative guidance followed in principle the same rationale as that for basic industries—

[25] The description of the iron-steel industry is based on Yamazawa, *Nihon no Keizai Hatten to Kokusai Bungyo*, Chapter 4, and on Hideki Yamawaki, "The Steel Industry," Part IV, chapter 11, in Ryutaro Komiya, Masahiro Okuno, and Kotaro Suzumura, eds., *Industrial Policy in Japan* (Tokyo: Academic Press, 1988).

[26] Based on Toshimasa Tsuruoka, "The Rapid Growth Era," Part I, chapter 3 in Komiya, Okuno, and Suzumura, eds., *Industrial Policy in Japan*.

[27] Tsuruoka, "The Rapid Growth Era."

that is, "the establishment of concentrated and specialized production systems" in individual industrial sectors.

In line with this policy, the private producers' committee discussed the measures and reached "agreement" on the actions to be taken. But the agreements were non-compulsory, leaving decision-making in the hands of the private enterprises concerned. More specifically, in 1968, MITI announced a Basic Machine Tool Industry Promotion Plan in response to requests for foreign capital liberalization. It included directives (i) to determine the optimum scale of production of twelve kinds of machinery for general use, such as an all-gear lathe; (ii) to establish a specialized production system for which the scale of firms should be larger than the above-determined optimum standard; (iii) to discontinue the production of machineries by firms too small in scale. Private producers responded by implementing general "agreements" in line with this specific guidance. But the measures were not compulsory, and the number of new production areas and kinds of machines developed strongly reflected the opinions of private enterprisers.

Having described this process in detail, Tsuruoka expressed the view that the machinery industry's development should not be attributed to the industrial policy of the government; rather, it was achieved in spite of the policy.[28] Of course the machine-tool industry cannot be generalized to other cases: the situation differs from one industry to another.[29] As we understand it, however, Tsuruoka emphasizes that the failure of guidance was caused by inappropriate application in an area where private enterprisers could deal well with the problem by themselves.

Having touched upon the achievement of rapid growth in the machine tool industry under the initiative of private activity, the question may arise: "Why?" We want to point out two aspects: one concerns

[28] Regarding technology promotion policy for the machinery industry, see Lecture 8, section II.

[29] In the automobile industry, for example, which also features oligopolistic competition, the circumstances are more complex: limited numbers of large-scale enterprises with widespread subcontract arrangements. On the one hand, despite MITI's original administrative guidance that established two big firms, several others actually also survived and developed. On the other hand, ancillary parts production firms were supported and promoted under the measures mentioned earlier. The amounts of loans given by the Japan Development Bank and the Small Business Financing Corporation were considerable, being more than half the total amounts of loans in 1966–74, the major weight being given to this industry. Refer to Lecture 4, section III.

demand; the other, technological capability. The first aspect is simple in nature, but deserves attention. The effective demand for machine tools stems from the demand for producer durable equipment, and the latter in turn is provoked by investment expansion. The third investment spurt contributed a great deal to increasing the demand for machine tools and hence to production expansion. This accelerated the pace of import substitution.

The second aspect is indispensable to interpret the last point. This industry was an area of technological backwardness despite the fact that the Japanese Industrial Standard (JIS) had been initiated much earlier, in 1921. According to Kiyokawa,[30] a "technological turning point" in quality improvement was reached in 1939–40 due to the strategic requirement of standardization. Such technological catch-up certainly spilled over into machine tool production for peaceful uses in the early postwar years. This, combined with the first demand spurt, formed the actual competitive conditions that worked for this industry. This environment was called "excessive competition." It was reminiscent of a similar phenomenon at the time of the first private investment spurt. Together with other areas of the machinery industry, production expansion in this area was remarkable, and the severe competition among a larger number of producers turned out to be "excessive" at the time of the downswing in investment activity in the 1920s. The "excessive competition" assumed by MITI's postwar industrial policy was a problem at a time of liberalization and increased international competition. A sympathetic view might support it as an advance guide to efficient operation of market forces, in view of bitter prewar experiences. However, we are concerned with the fact that this is a symbolic case, in which private activity is vigorous enough on its own.

Taking these two representative cases together and considering cases of other industries, we share the view that administrative guidance had a bias toward "bigness": firms of bigger scale have stronger competitiveness, the official thinking went, and therefore the number of firms should be controlled. In a capital-intensive industry in which economies of scale have a distinct advantage, guidance based on this notion worked in interaction with the private sector to a certain extent. However, in a technology-intensive industry in which economies of

---

[30] Yukihiko Kiyokawa and Shigeru Ishikawa, "The Significance of Standardization in the Development of the Machine-Tool Industry: The Cases of Japan and China," Discussion Paper Series No. 123, Institute of Economic Research, Hitotsubashi University, 1985.

scale are much less significant, it could not have a positive effect. In developing economies in general, the lesson drawn from Japan's case is to avoid a sweeping application of this notion irrespective of the different economic and technological properties of industries.

Eliminating the Technology Gap

No doubt the control of technology imports was a major instrument of industrial policy in the 1950s and 1960s, almost two decades before liberalization. In a number of contemporary developing countries, likewise, the regulation of technological imports is a major policy instrument. Appropriate evaluation of government intervention in this area should be undertaken not *a priori*, but based on the actual development phase of the country under consideration.

In 1950, MITI issued a list of 33 desired technologies, most of which were for the heavy-chemical and engineering industries. The list was only a guide and was used to review applications for import licenses under the Foreign Capital Law mentioned earlier. Actually, the average annual number of permits issued for foreign technology import did increase, from 103 in 1950–59 to 469 in 1960–67, during the subsequent interval of partial liberalization. Still, controls apparently suppressed the demand for foreign technology. The number of import applications jumped to 1,061 in 1968 and 1,154 in 1969, the years immediately following the liberalization.[31]

What was the effect of this measure? Experts give different answers: one view argues that it actually was not an effective means of suppression, at least of large-scale enterprises, while another view thinks it had significant effects. We are inclined to share the former view of the allocation of technology imports as a policy tool. The controls gave priority to the technology for producing producer durables (the major investment goods) and to intermediate goods, suppressing the demand for consumer goods technology (except that for new consumer durables such as automobiles). If the statistics are divided by type of industry, technology import agreements (in percentage of the total) are actually dominated by the machinery industry. Its share, including non-electric, electric, transport, and precision machineries, amounted to 56.6% in 1945–56 and 49.0% in 1965–72. The second most prominent is the heavy-chemical industry: its share, including chemicals, iron and steel, petroleum, and coal, was 23.0% in 1949–56 and 21.2%

---

[31] Akira Goto and Ryuhei Wakasugi, "Technology Policy," Part I, chapter 6 in Komiya, Okuno, and Suzumura, eds., *Industrial Policy in Japan*.

in 1965–72.[32] Although this is just a number, it still corresponds consistently to what we have clarified in the preceding lectures: the fast development of the machinery industries was the core of the notable growth performance during this interval. More detailed discussion will be presented below.

Selected technology imports have often been used as a major instrument in pursuing industrial policy. In an economy where private activities are dynamic, it is difficult to measure quantitatively the effects of such measures. Qualitative evaluation can, however, estimate their effects on the speed of technological advance. In postwar Japan, the catch-up process was handicapped by the long-continuing isolation. The time element was extremely important. The government considered that speeding up or retarding the use of a particular technology was crucial even it it only made several years' difference. In fact, it will be recalled that in the preceding lectures, with respect to the "early start" of Japan's heavy and engineering industries, we emphasized the significance of the time dimension in importing and diffusing foreign technologies in shifting phases of long-term development. For the final phase of a narrowing gap in technological levels, the time dimension becomes an especially crucial factor in government decision-making during the interval leading toward liberalization.[33]

With respect to the process of eliminating the technology gap, private activity was vigorous, and conventional measures can be used for making a judgment—indicators based on statistical data on payments and receipts of royalties in technology trade and R&D expenditures. In the Appendix, the results of our measures for postwar Japan are presented with a breakdown into representative subsectors of manufacturing. The concept of "technological parity" is defined to designate the situation of an industry for which the technology gap has been perfectly eliminated. The gap is assumed between two levels: one is the top-level technology domestically used; the other, the top-level technology available from the forerunners. There are no precise measures directly available for this definition. The data on technology in trade, however, can serve as a rough proxy in a sectorwise approach: they should be dated in bands of years instead of in a single year. In the Appendix this will be examined and discussed in greater detail. Broadly

---

[32] Merton J. Peck with the collaboration of Shuji Tamura, "Technology," Chapter 8 in Hugh Patrick, ed., *Asia's New Giant*, Table 8–5, p. 539.
[33] A similar view is found in Merton J. Peck with Shuji Tamura, "Technology," p. 553.

speaking, the point is reached in the beginning of the 1970s for steel and chemicals and somewhat later for machineries. The goal of eliminating the technology gap has sometimes been talked about in terms of the macro economy or the industrial economy as a whole. The concept of technological parity, however, is sectorwise *par excellence*. It cannot be applied meaningfully on a macro or aggregate scale. Rather, its sequence over time is significant, as in the typical sequence of first textiles, second steel, and third machinery.

R&D activity in Japan, as is shown in the Appendix, has been widespread in recent years, particularly in the private sector: some three quarters of the nation's total R&D expenditure is paid by private enterprises, in cooperation with MITI for a limited number of large projects. As has often been pointed out, this distribution pattern of research expenditure biased Japan's technology development toward research areas sensitive to market signals, chosen to bring benefits directly and quickly to the enterprises and industries concerned. This implies that Japan has been behind in support for basic research aimed at augmenting social benefits over the long term.

From the point of view of economic development, Japan's pattern was seen as "economical," because actually research on market-sensitive areas pertains mostly to what we have called "improvement engineering" based on the technological knowledge originally imported. As was pointed out in Lecture 4, in the shift to full industrialization, Japan was newly required to conduct its own research on technology, facing much greater difficulties. From this viewpoint, in the Appendix the results of a special survey on recent R&D performance are summarized. A tendency toward increase in the ratio of receipts to payments of royalties on leased technology and the tendency toward rapid increases in R&D expenditures, more than replacing the royalty payments, are visible. These are indicative of a shift from dependence on borrowing to independence in obtaining technological knowledge. What we are concerned with specifically here are the different patterns and characteristics of the transition process in representative industries (in particular, machinery and iron-steel). Borrowing the data arranged by Tahara,[34] Table 7.2 shows these tendencies.

The ratio of R&D to investment is calculated corresponding to our formula of the ratio of incremental residual to investment $(\Delta R/I)$.

---

[34] Kenji Tahara, "Postwar Manufacturing Technology in Japan: A Shift from 'Borrowed' Toward 'Independent,'" IDCJ Working Paper Series No. 38, March 1987.

Table 7.2
R&D Expenditure and Royalty Payments and Their Ratio to Gross Domestic
Investment: Selected Years in Machinery and Basic Metal Industry

(%)

	Manu-facturing	Electric Machinery	Transportation Machinery	General Machinery	Basic Metals
(A) R&D/Investment					
1970	3.1	8.7	2.8	1.6	0.5
1973	5.2	19.3	7.8	3.5	1.1
1977	14.4	43.6	24.6	11.7	3.5
1981	22.8	51.4	33.9	12.4	5.2
1984	34.9	54.4	55.9	23.8	9.8
(B) Payments of Royalties/Investment					
1971	8.5	28.1	42.5	3.4	9.7
1973	6.6	11.9	23.9	1.6	4.7
1977	3.9	5.7	10.1	0.5	2.2
1981	5.9	12.4	15.4	1.0	4.6
1984	3.5	4.5	8.7	0.5	2.2

Sources: Royalty payments from Science and Technology Agency, White
Paper of Science Technology, 1986.
Remarks: Deflated by 1980 prices.

People often talk about "technology-intensive" industry. The two
ratios shown in Panels (A) and (B), are input ratios, so they can be
indicative of technology intensity relative to investment in a similar
way to the term $w\Delta L/I$. For manufacturing as a whole, the ratio in
(A) has increased at a fast pace, especially since the latter part of the
1970s, beyond the level at which the ratio in (B) is replaced. Electric
and transportation machinery show a remarkable performance: in
the mid-1980s, the ratio in (A) exceeded 50% and that in (B) decreased
to less than 10%. These industries at the beginning of the 1970s had
relied intensively on borrowed technology. In contrast, for basic metals
the replacement process was much less impressive. This is mostly
because of the much greater amount of investment required to make
technological advances in basic metals. In this sense, the industry is
capital-intensive. General machinery seems to be in between, but its
ratio in (A) increased much faster than the decrease in the ratio in (B).

R&D expenditure cannot be the indicator of real invention of technology, but it can show the degree of effort directed toward independence in advancing technology. In this regard, it is interesting to recognize a positive association between the magnitude of $\Delta R/I$ (measured

in Lecture 4) and sectoral R&D/I in the machinery and basic metal industries. The implication is important. Human resource-intensive sectors, for which w∆L/I is larger, do correspond to the R&D-intensive sectors. At least the efforts in Japan's transition process appear distinctly to move toward strengthening this association. Further observation which breaks down electric machinery into high-technology subsectors such as electronics, integrated circuits, and semiconductors would reveal this characteristic more clearly. This may be an indication of what Shishido calls the "era of miniaturization."[35]

Two remarks should be made. First, the rapid increase in R&D expenditures is a factual challenge for us, requiring an analytical interpretation of what is sometimes called "technological competition." Both theoretically and empirically, the problem is complex and its solution is beyond the scope of this lecture. However, what is clear is that the conventional notion of "product competition" (price and non-price factors included) is not enough for understanding the market mechanism at issue, because enterprisers' performance in improving and developing technologies is the most important element in pursuing competition—that is, technological competition of an innovative nature.[36] In addition, the industrial policy of the government, in our view, envisages this type of competition in its measures on foreign investment and technology import control and/or regulation of the number of firms through administrative guidance.

As was mentioned earlier, an oligopolistic structure in varying degrees has been established through interactions between government and firms. Following the well-known classic notion of Schumpeter, the possibility of technological innovation has been discussed intensively in relation to the organization and structure of the market. Today nobody believes simply in the superiority of a monopolistic structure for technological innovation; often the market structure is thought to be the determinant of technological innovation. No doubt the former does influence the latter. But this aspect does not hold priority in our

[35] Toshio Shishido, "Japanese Technological Development," chapter 15 in Toshio Shishido and Ryuzo Sato, eds., *Economic Policy and Development: New Perspectives* (AH Publishing Company, 1985).

[36] A simple illustration can be given by the case of car export competition between two countries, A and B, with equal strength regarding price and product quality. However, the engine is produced domestically in A, whereas in B it is imported and thus supply depends upon foreign technology. In the area of technological competition, country A is superior to country B. In evaluationg secondary export substitution, the distinction between the two categories of international competitiveness is significant.

view. What we want to identify is the fact that technological competition has occurred along with the process of replacing the technological knowledge borrowed, and that this has mostly taken place in the oligopolistic structure of the market for many subsectors concerned, particularly the machinery industries. The dominance of R&D expenditures in these specific subsectors is a result not of the oligopolistic structure itself, but of the determination of entrepreneurs.

Note that the importance of a competitive market is emphasized within the framework of interaction. It implies that if government intervention stifled the activity of the private sector by restraining competition, the innovative process would be discouraged. Identification of this possibility would require detailed examination of individual cases. An encouraging tendency pointed out by Sato may deserve attention.[37] Efforts to produce new technology, Sato points out, can often be made cooperatively rather than competitively among enterprisers. The government can guide such cooperative activity by selecting firms with suitable qualifications. The use of newly created technology is, however, then guaranteed by the government not to be open to all parties involved in its development. Such a relationship between the public and private sector, according to Sato, is found in Japan. This is a case when creation and use of technology can be pursued separately. It is our understanding that such a pattern, if it exists on a wider scale, can be incorporated into the framework of interaction in which the innovative process is essentially carried out in the private sector with some modification of technological competition by government participation.

Second, we are concerned with the substantial contents of the pattern and process of eliminating the technology gap. It is true that technological advance is becoming more costly, as reflected in increasing resource allocations for R&D. But this does not necessarily mean that greater amounts of resources are channelled to promoting more basic scientific research. The expenditure of private companies for R&D still composes the greater share of research spending, and the major fraction of that is developmental research (DR). In terms of composition of total R&D expenditures, DR ranged from 84.8% to 92.4% during the years 1971–83. The other two items, basic research and applied research, are minor: the former 1.6%–7.9%, the latter

[37] Ryuzo Sato, "Nothing New? An Historical Perspective of Japanese Technology," chapter 20 in Shishido and Sato, eds., *Economic Policy and Development: New Perspectives* (Dover, Mass.: Auburn House, 1985).

6.0%-15.2% in the same interval. Japan is still rather weak in basic and applied research.[38]

If these data are to be believed, the question that naturally arises is why Japanese industry technologically advanced at a fairly rapid pace during the interval under review. The answer is found in the augmentation of *development capability*, as illustrated by the case of semiconductors, in which scientific knowledge was borrowed but efficient development for industrial use was Japan's achievement. Such capability is, we believe, an extended version of the capability of absorbing borrowed technology. A weaker current of inflow causes weaker operation of potential based on borrowing capability. If another kind of capability, that of developing technology independently, cannot supplement the defects thus produced, the slowdown of technological advance will be drastic. An intensive shift from the absorbing capability to the capability of self-development of technology is significant: greater improvement and wider and quicker application of the technological and scientific knowledge already acquired seem to be the major, if not total, determinants of the fast increase in R&D expenditures. What we have called "improvement engineering" activity works more systematically and intensively to compensate for the weaker inflow of foreign technological knowledge. The effects of dissemination and diffusion through competition are also substantive, as was illustrated by the scale-organization analysis in Lecture 4.

These activities were not utterly absent in the preceding phase of secondary import substitution. What draws our particular attention is its stronger intensity and quicker operation in the period of movement toward technology parity. The other side of the coin is the nonbasic nature of research, mostly pertaining to process rather than product advancement. Without basic breakthroughs in technological frontiers through scientific discovery, there may be a limit on development capability for making further technological advances in the future.

Finally, let us briefly look at public-sector activity. Governmental incentives for R&D are conventional ones such as subsidies, special tax treatment, and credit at low interest rates. Goto and Wakasugi[39] estimated the ratio of total public expenditures for these incentive measures to the total amount of private expenditures on R&D payments for technology imports annually for 1957–1980. According to

---

[38] The data are from Management and Coordination Agency, 1984. For details see Tahara, "Postwar Manufacturing Technology in Japan."

[39] Akira Goto and Takahira Wakasugi, "Technology Policy," Table 6–1, p. 168.

their estimates, the ratio was more than 5% during 1957–65, around 3% during 1966–75, and 2.0–2.8% in 1976–80. The decrease in this ratio indicates that the private R&D activity became more independent. It is beyond the scope of our research to examine the real content of government R&D expenditure. But at least until the 1970s, we have the impression that the government made no new move toward stronger leadership to guide private R&D in the direction of initiating more creative research. Its objective seems to have been to support private activities by complementary interaction working toward technological catch-up.

Concluding Remarks: Focus on Technological Advance
Combining the relevant points in the preceding lectures, our concluding remarks summarize the discussion of technological advance.

1) The hypothesis presented in section I of Lecture 6, regarding technology transfer and social capability, has been tested, focusing on human resources. The process of technological-organizational progress and related aspects were dealt with in the preceding lectures: in particular, what was discussed in Lectures 4 and 5 is more relevant to the test of the hypothesis. The central finding is a long-term tendency toward increase in the residual per unit of investment, $\Delta R/I$, and in the human resource input per unit of investment, $w\Delta L/I$ (incremental magnitude of factor input ratio, FIR). Insofar as the inflow was not restricted, the process of borrowing technological knowledge from forerunners continued through the operation of the potentials. Acceleration of this process, though with some drawbacks, is a result of structural changes in the industrial sector that widened the operating area of the potentials.

A decrease in both $\Delta R/I$ and $w\Delta L/I$ between the two decades (1955–65 and 1966–74) draws our particular attention. Its cause is the weaker inflows, according to our hypothesis. Technology trade performance (payments vs. receipts of royalties) as presented in the Appendix endorses this view. There is no doubt that between these intervals the royalty payments declined distinctly relative to domestic expenditures for R&D, even though payments applicable to past commitments are included.

In Lecture 4, the significance of a fundamental change from borrowed technology to self-invention was mentioned as taking place at the beginning of the 1970s, and the difficulties Japan will face in the coming decades were discussed. The analysis in that lecture revealed that through the 1970s, residual growth per investment unit was maintained at fairly high rates—at least higher than we expected—especially in the engineering industries. This suggests that technological progress owed to the rapid increase in domestic expenditures for R&D, although Japan still did not get out from under its dependence on the inflow of foreign advanced technological knowledge. The point of technological parity was defined and its dates approximated by use of the data on trade in technology and R&D expenditures by sector. In Appendix II to Lecture 4, the terminal point is found to be near the mid-1970s. The process of eliminating the technology gap appears to have ended around that date: steel a bit earlier, machinery a bit later.[40] The long secondary phase essentially based on borrowed technological knowledge eventually ended with arrival at the point of technological parity for these advanced industries.

2) A related problem is how to interpret the mechanism of completing secondary export substitution. As was stated in Lecture 4, the risk in eliminating the technology gap was that of losing the advantage of cheap labor. As is indicated by a decline of $w\Delta L/I$, capital intensification through replacing labor with capital appears to be imperative on the one hand. On the other, the need to technologically advance by their own efforts is a great pressure on enterprisers. The former requirement appeared to limit the type and direction of possible technological advance, and a breakthrough seemed to be difficult to make.

In-depth observation of Japan's case (Lectures 4 and 5), however, reveals that technological-organizational advance was made possible with modest changes in Lw/K in the engineering industry. Capital intensification took place just to meet wage increases, essentially keeping the same technological property with high dependence on human capability in most machinery industries. In other subsectors, Lw/K decreased a great deal. With increases in the weight of machinery in pursuing secondary export substitution, the dilemma mentioned above was solved. The type and direction of technological advance was not drastically changed, but further improvement and invention were made broadly along past lines. We did not discuss the aspect of comparative advantage. But actually, productivity in the machinery industry constituted the bulk of Japan's export expansion. It is clear that secondary export substitution was essentially completed by techno-

---

[40] The end of secondary export substitution and the point of technological parity took place at almost the same time in Japan's case. Is this a necessary condition for all developing economies for completing this phase? At present no answer can be given based on empirical evidence. Our speculative observation is as follows. The newly industrializing countries have hitherto had the competitive advantage of cheaper labor compared with industrialized economies. To the extent that this advantage is maintained, the need to narrow the technology gap is less urgent.

logical advance in the engineering industries, in the absence of both the traditional advantage of cheaper labor and "bigness" in the high capital-intensive sectors. During this phase the economy arrived at the point of technological parity sector by sector, eliminating the long technology gap.[41] In this regard, we emphasize the significance of the association between human capability and technology in relation to capital investment.

3) All the processes of technological advance characterized above have been realized through interactions between public and private activities. The essential element is the sustenance of competition in the private sector during the innovative process of development. The possibility of technological advance is the key element for success through technological competition. The role played by the government through industrial policy in postwar Japan has often been over-estimated. We do not share the view that the innovative process was led by public policy guidance. Despite government intervention, technological competition has basically been kept efficient. Sometimes it was even promoted by the government guidance.

Through our review from a historical perspective, we identified the necessity of government participation in the market mechanism in a latecomer developing economy. The importance of a long-term perspective on industrial transformation in shifting the economy from one phase to another has been particularly emphasized. The scope and style of industrial policy accordingly change through the long-term process of phase-shift. No "ideal" pattern exists *a priori*. Nevertheless, the central criterion is the degree of public policy contribution to augmenting the residual creation in the private sector subject to the option of improving employment performance.

The public performance in the final phase of secondary export substitution, viewed in historical perspective, is essentially the same as that in pursuing residual augmentation, though the latter is not always successful. But it is characterized by setting the target of final technological catch-up in order for specified industries to be internationally competitive within a specified time period. The final phase was com-

---

[41] We do not imply that this is always an inevitable pattern and mechanism of secondary export substitution. For instance, the rapid progress of the Asian newly industrializing economies (NIEs) is characterized by a combination of cheaper wages and speedy technological advance, supported by telescoping effects. How will they eventually complete this phase? This is a challenging problem. Some countries in Latin America appear to put much more emphasis on the role to be played by heavy industries in accelerating the pace of secondary export substitution. The possibility of shifting more emphasis to engineering industries seems to be a problem to be examined at the policy option level.

pleted in less than 15 years, in contrast to the prolonged phase of secondary import substitution. However, here again the significance of government leadership has often been overemphasized, confusing its function in the innovative process of competitive mechanism with its function in setting the target of eliminating the technological gap. Full industrialization could not be realized merely by the government's administrative leadership. Sometimes its bias toward "bigness" even had negative effects. The problem is not government policy itself, but maximizing its effects through interaction with private activities.

Appendix: Trade in Technology and R&D Expenditures

This Appendix is intended to provide data in a compact form to support what has been discussed on technology transfer and domestic activity to enhance Japan's own technology. From the statistics on trade in technology, receipts and payments of royalties are used as indicators of outflow and inflow of technological knowledge. This is the conventional method and is useful for determining the broad currents of technology trade, although certain qualifications are needed for the interpretation.

The expenditures for R&D are the total sum of expenditures by companies (1), research institutions (2), and universities (3). In 1984, the proportion accounted for by each type of institution was (1) 65.1%, (2) 13.1%, and (3) 21.8%. The proportion of (1) shows a tendency to increase over time. In 1961 the proportions were (1) 59.0%, (2) 16.1%, and (3) 24.9%; and in 1970, (1) 60.7%, (2) 12.3%, and (3) 27.0%. The data give no precise breakdown into private- and public-sector institutions. However, private activity is dominant.

Table 7A.1 gives an overview. Because it includes long-continuing

Table 7A.1
Technology Trade and R&D Expenditures: All Industries, 1953–1984

(%)

	Receipts Payments (1)	Payments R&D (2)	R&D GNP (3)
1953–55	1.5	22.6	0.6
1961–64	6.9	13.0	1.5
1972–74	13.6	7.9	2.0
1982–84	29.8	6.9	2.5

Source: Bank of Japan, *Annual Economic Statistics*.

payments for commitments made in the past, the ratio in column (1) appears too small even for recent years. Yet the tempo of its increase is impressive: it more than doubled in the intervals measurements. The ratio in column (3), a conventional one for international comparison, indicates that Japan now ranks in the top group of countries in its relative magnitude of R&D expenditures to GNP. This achievement was made possible by an impressively fast increase in the postwar years. During the 1970s its share of gross domestic investment increased steadily: from 4.9% in 1970 to 5.4% in 1975, 6.2% in 1980, and 7.8% in 1984. Thus ratio (2) in the table shows a distinct tendency to decline.

Technology trade and R&D expenditure heavily concentrated in manufacturing. For instance, in 1974 (1984), the proportion of receipts in manufacturing was 93.2% (87.7%); in payments, 96.7% (98.4%). For R&D, the manufacturing proportion was 91.6% (93.3%). Table 7A.2 attempts to provide some information on the eight subsectors which were selected as representative in Lecture 4. Panels (A) and (B) present sectoral breakdowns of ratios (1) and (2) in Table 7A.1 and Panels (C) and (D) sectoral composition percentages. These are not direct indicators of the performance of the technology gap, but they do provide useful information for our observation.

The ratio in Panel (B) suggests that at the beginning of the 1970s, the majority of these subsectors arrived at the threshold of what we have called "technological parity" in the main text, and that at the beginning of the 1980s parity had largely been achieved for the majority. Some royalty payments, mostly for past commitments, remain to be paid, but these are moderate or minor relative to the expenditure on R&D. Sectorwise, a tendency for the ratio to decline seems uniform except in textiles and food (although this may be coincidental). The fast tempo in general machinery is particularly impressive.

Of course expenditure for R&D cannot be a precise indicator of improvement of technology itself, but we consider that it can be used as a rough proxy. Panel (B) in the table shows average annual rate of R&D expenditures in real terms. This corresponds to Table 4.1 in the main text. It is deflated by the output prices by subsector shown in Panel (E) in Table 4.1. It is higher for the three machinery subsectors 3, 4, and 5 and low for chemicals, textiles, and food; general machinery and steel are in between. In referring to the rate of total productivity growth shown in Table 4.2, the contribution of R&D expenditure to technological progress can broadly be recognized by sector for manufacturing.

The ratio in Panel (A) suggests somewhat different aspects. In terms

Table 7A.2
Technology in Trade and R&D Expenditures: Manufacturing, 1969–1984 (%)

	Manufacturing (1)	General Machinery (2)	Electric Machinery (3)	Transportation Machinery (4)	Precision Machinery (5)	Steel (6)	Chemicals (7)	Textiles (8)	Food (9)
(A) Receipts/Payments									
1971–74	25.2	11.1	11.6	12.9	25.1	88.9	55.0	45.5	32.0
1975–79	44.5	16.9	25.4	29.6	17.2	212.0	88.0	82.4	25.6
1980–84	64.7	30.8	45.7	55.5	60.0	309.4	81.6	116.2	39.9
(B) Payments/R&D									
1971–74	19.1	36.1	14.8	13.5	8.8	10.2	14.5	16.9	8.6
1975–79	10.6	20.0	9.2	11.2	7.4	7.4	8.3	20.8	24.0
1980–84	7.5	11.8	6.7	7.4	3.2	6.0	6.2	11.4	11.4
(B′) Rates of Increase in R&D Expenditure (1971–1981)									
In current prices	15.8	12.7	16.3	18.8	21.0	15.4	12.3	10.6	12.6
In real terms		8.2	12.7	13.9	18.5	8.9	4.7	5.4	5.4
(C) Composition of Payments									
1971–74	100.0	15.3	27.2	15.3	1.6	3.6	19.3	1.5	1.6
1975–79	100.0	13.0	24.7	20.0	1.8	4.1	15.8	1.8	3.6
1980–84	100.0	10.8	29.7	18.9	1.5	4.0	15.3	1.7	3.8
(D) Composition of R&D Expenditures									
1969–74	100.0	7.1	30.6	16.5	2.0	5.5	22.5	1.4	2.8
1975–79	100.0	6.9	28.5	19.2	2.6	5.8	20.3	1.0	2.7
1980–84	100.0	6.8	32.3	18.5	3.6	5.0	18.2	1.1	2.5
(E) Receipts/Payments (Annual new contract)									
1971–74	115.4	64.5	78.0	32.2	133.6	147.9	348.8	371.4	50.0
1975–79	146.3	134.8	51.1	74.9	42.9	597.5	530.3	598.6	115.8
1980–84	142.0	125.5	63.3	348.5	112.2	435.5	218.6	336.6	80.5

Source: Science and Technology Agency, 1986 White Paper.

of three groups, several features of subsectors are observed: (i) Steel, textiles, and chemicals have superior positions in technology export. (ii) General machinery and food are inferior. (iii) The other three machinery subsectors are intermediate. Of course all export figures are relative to their import amounts. Group (i) marks a situation beyond the point of parity. Among them, steel is most impressive. Let us note that the machinery subsectors, despite fast increases in the ratio, lag behind Group (i) in this respect. General machinery is especially slow, perhaps because of its greater component of domestic industrial use. Arrival at the parity point thus requires widely varying amounts of time.

The ratios in Panels (C) and (D) are simple, indicating the distribution of payments and R&D expenditures of representative subsectors within manufacturing. Attention is drawn to the higher percentages for four machinery industries. These are much greater than the distribution percentage of sectoral GDP, as shown in Table 7A.3 for the sum of the four subsectors.

The high values of both ratios, (1)/(3) and (2)/(3), endorse what has been described above regarding the rapid technological advance of this sector.

Finally, for reference, the ratio of receipts/payments, in terms of annual new contracts, is shown in Panel (E). Although the range of variation is wide for annual data, the averages shown in the table appear reasonable except in a few subsectors. The following findings are particularly noted. (i) For manufacturing as a whole, the ratio became slightly over unity at the beginning of the 1970s; since then, it has been near 1.4. (ii) Steel, chemicals, and textiles compose a group with the highest ratios throughout the entire period, and transportation machinery appears to join this group in the 1980s. (iii) Particular attention is drawn to electric machinery, the high-technology subsector. Its ratio is definitely under unity, showing no sign of a tendency to increase.

Table 7A.3
Payments and R & D Expenditures, Machinery Industry

(%)

	Payments (1)	R&D (2)	GDP (3)	(1)/(3)	(2)/(3)
1969–74	59.2	56.2	35.0	1.41	1.61
1975–79	59.5	57.2	34.6	1.72	1.65
1980–84	60.9	61.2	38.4	1.57	1.59

Although these cannot be a direct indicator for the level of the technology gap, they may suggest over-time changes in technological positions. Depending upon these data on annual new contracts for total manufacturing, some observers assert that Japan's technological gap disappeared at the very beginning of the 1970s. We do have reservations about sharing this view because of the different performances in different subsectors; larger values over unity of the ratio in total manufacturing at the beginning of the 1970s were largely accounted for by textiles, chemicals, and steel, not machinery.

Export Expansion and Economic Development

In previous lectures export performance has been discussed in relation to the major subjects. However, we believe this important activity needs a more systematic treatment.

The purpose of this lecture is to analyze the role played by exports in developing economies, based on Japan's experience. When Japan started modern economic growth in the 1880s, it was an exporter of primary products. In the 19th century, Japan's major export goods were raw silk, coal, copper, and tea. If we regard raw silk and copper as primary products, more than three quarters of Japan's exports were primary products before 1890. However, the share of primary products export declined sharply, to less than 50% around the turn of the century. This lecture mentions the export expansion in the prewar period, but major analysis is devoted to rapid economic growth in postwar Japan.

Some argue that Japan's economic development was led by export expansion. This is not true. Japan's domestic market is not small. In the 1880s, the total population was less than 40 million, but it grew fast, to more than 50 million in 1912, 60 million in 1926, 70 million in 1936, 80 million in 1948, 90 million in 1957, 100 million in 1967, and 110 million in 1974. We cannot underrate domestic demand. It has played an important role, and export expansion was not the sole dominant factor in explaining Japan's economic development.

We will focus our analysis on the role of exports, especially manufactured exports, in the process of rapid industrialization. It is our view that technological progress was the most important factor in rapid economic growth in the postwar period and that this can be attributed to the severe competition among private companies in Japan's protected and oligopolistic market. All manufacturers, government officials, and economists knew in the 1950s that Japan would have to open the domestic market to import from foreign countries in the 1960s. This scheduled trade liberalization in part explains the severe competition in the protected domestic market.

I. Trade and Development

The export/GNP ratios of Japan and Korea are presented in Table

Table 8.1
Export/GNP Ratios of Japan and the Republic of Korea

(%)

Year	Japan		Rep. of Korea	
	(A)	(B)	(A)	(B)
1885	5.2	2.6		
1890	6.2	2.9		
1895	9.7	3.9		
1900	10.7	5.8		
1905	13.0	6.2		
1910	15.0	8.5		
1915	20.1	13.1		
1920	18.8	10.7		
1925	20.1	12.4		
1930	16.9	15.6		
1935	22.7	23.2		
1940	19.5	18.5		
1955	12.1	6.5	1.7	1.4
1960	11.5	8.0	3.3	2.4
1965	10.9	9.8	8.6	5.2
1970	11.3	11.7	14.0	14.7
1975	13.7	15.7	27.1	21.8
1980	15.1	14.6	33.7	33.7
1985	16.4	18.9	36.4	37.1

Sources: Kazushi Ohkawa and Miyohei Shinohara, eds., *Patterns of Japanese Economic Development: A Quantitative Appraisal* (New Haven: Yale University Press, 1979) (hereafter, *PJE*), Tables A1 and A2; Economic Planning Agency, *National Accounts Statistics Yearbook*; IMF-IFS, *Korea Statistical Yearbook*.

Notes: (A) in current prices; (B) in constant prices.
Prewar Japan: 1934–36 prices;
1955–70, 1970 prices;
1975–85, 1980 prices.
Korea:
1955–70, 1970 prices;
1975–85, 1980 prices.

8.1. In 1885 Japan's export/GNP ratio was a low 5.2%. It increased somewhat, but remained lower than 10% throughout the 19th century, at levels comparable to Korea's export/GNP ratio until the mid-1960s. The ratio fluctuated, but it did not exceed 25% in prewar Japan. In the postwar years the ratio has been between 10% and 20%. Although the ratio increased in the 1980s, it was less than 15% in the 1950s, 1960s, and 1970s in current price series, showing no tendency to increase. In constant prices, we find a slight increasing trend in the 1950s and 1960s. Japan's export/GDP ratios are slightly lower than those of other industrialized countries. According to World Bank estimates, Japan's ratios in 1965 and 1986 were 11% and 12%, respectively, while the average ratio for industrialized countries was 12% in 1965 and 17% in 1986 (World Bank, *World Development Report 1988*).

Korea's export/GNP ratio shows a tendency toward sharp increase. The ratios in current price and constant price series show almost no differences. The ratio was less than 10% in 1965, but exceeded 20% at the beginning of the 1970s. In the 1980s it was higher than 30%.

In order to make the contrast in the contribution of export expansion to GNP growth clear, the export contribution ratio (Δexport/ ΔGNP in current prices) is calculated. Although export contribution in Japan was very high in the 1920s and 1930s, it was less than 25% throughout the postwar period, and less even than 12% in the rapid-growth years of the 1960s. This simple indicator tells us that Japan's rapid economic growth was not led solely by the export expansion. In the beginning of the 1960s, Korea began its industrialization. Although export contribution for Korea was less than 20% in the 1960s (10.9% for 1960–65, 16.2% for 1965–70), it became larger than 30% in the 1970s (32.0% for 1970–75, 36.1% for 1975–80) and as high as 45% for 1980–84. Comparing the export contribution ratios of Japan and Korea makes the difference clear. As far as the demand aspect of export expansion is concerned, Japan's postwar economic growth was much less export-led than that in Korea.

Table 8.2 shows the export/production ratios of the manufacturing subsectors. In prewar Japan the export/production ratio for manufacturing as a whole was more than 20%, but it was less than 10% in postwar Japan. The ratio for textiles was larger than that for manufacturing as a whole. It was as high as 42.6% in 1915, but declined to less than 20% in the 1960s. The ratio of machinery increased slightly in the 1960s, but it was less than 15% in 1968. These export/production ratios of manufacturing subsectors constitute further evidence that Japan's postwar rapid economic growth was not led solely by export expansion.

Table 8.2
Export/Production Ratio of Japan: 1880–1968

	Processed food	Textiles	Wood products	Chemicals	Ceramics	Metals	Machinery	Other manufactures	Total manufactures
1880	0.5	14.3	0.3	2.9	6.4	12.7	0.0	6.9	5.6
1885	0.5	19.9	0.6	5.2	17.2	23.4	0.3	10.7	8.6
1890	0.5	19.8	1.4	8.0	17.6	37.2	0.9	17.2	11.2
1895	0.7	19.0	1.7	10.7	16.3	36.3	1.6	28.5	12.4
1900	1.4	28.2	2.9	12.7	16.0	45.3	2.3	32.8	15.5
1905	3.2	40.6	10.0	15.2	26.9	46.7	4.9	40.2	20.9
1910	3.2	38.0	12.9	14.6	19.6	42.9	4.7	34.3	19.8
1915	5.3	42.6	15.2	20.2	24.3	29.4	5.7	38.8	23.5
1920	4.3	35.2	10.1	15.3	20.2	14.3	5.0	26.3	19.0
1925	4.0	40.6	7.2	13.3	18.9	9.9	5.3	19.1	20.5
1930	5.4	37.5	7.4	12.8	24.1	11.5	8.0	19.9	19.2
1935	7.8	35.8	9.1	13.6	25.6	12.4	10.3	25.5	19.4
1955	2.3	19.9	3.9	2.4	12.3	8.9	9.9	14.0	8.5
1960	2.6	20.0	3.5	2.5	9.7	7.4	9.7	17.3	8.3
1965	1.6	16.0	2.4	3.5	8.5	9.6	12.1	14.6	8.7
1968	1.5	16.6	1.9	3.9	6.9	9.7	13.9	11.2	9.2

Source: Ohkawa and Shinohara, eds., PJE, Tables A19 (pp. 298–300), A20 (p. 301), A26 (pp. 315–318).
Remarks: Figures are 5-year averages.

II. Changes in Industrial and Trade Structure

It is a widely prevailing view that Japan started its "heavy industrialization" in the 1950s. "Heavy industry" includes metals, chemicals, and machinery, but from the technological point of view, it can also be decomposed into two subsectors. The required level of technology for "traditional heavy industry," such as steel and shipbuilding, is different from that for "new industries," such as computers and "mechatronics." The latter can be called a "technology-intensive industry," consistent with our notion developed in Lecture 3. Rapid change in the industrial and trade structure of postwar Japan will be reviewed in this section.

Patterns of Structural Changes

Changes in the shipment value shares of the manufacturing total are shown for 21 subsectors in Table 8.3. In 1984 the shares of only three subsectors (food, electric machinery, transport equipment) were larger than 10%. In 1955, in the early phase of rapid economic growth, the shares of textiles and of iron and steel were 16.2% and 9.6%, respectively. Textiles' share decreased sharply, to a low of 3.2% in 1984. The share of iron and steel was larger than 9% of the manufacturing total until 1970, but started to decline in the 1970s, to 6.8% in 1984.

We clearly witness rapid structural change in postwar Japan. In the latter half of the 1950s, the contribution of iron and steel, general machinery, electric machinery, and transport equipment exceeded 10% of total manufacturing growth. These four subsectors accounted for 44.3% of manufacturing shipment growth for the period. In the 1960s the contribution ratio of iron and steel slightly declined, to 7.5% for 1960–65 and 9.8% for 1965–70. The key industries for Japan's industrial development in the 1960s and 1970s were the machine industries. The contribution ratio of three subsectors of the machine industry—general machinery, electric machinery, and transport equipment—for the 1960s and 1970s was between 6% and 13%. Although iron and steel maintained its contribution ratio of more than 7% in the 1970s, an absolute decline in shipments was recorded for 1980–84. Five more subsectors—wood products, furniture, petroleum and coal products, leather products, non-ferrous metals—also show absolute decreases in shipment values for 1980–84. In contrast to these subsectors, the contribution of electric machinery increased remarkably in the 1980s: it rose to 44.3% in 1980–84.

Table 8.4 shows export structure. Textiles were the largest export items in the early postwar phase. Textile export share was 37.3% in

Table 8.3
Structure of Manufacturing: Postwar Japan (Value of Shipments)

(%)

	1955	1960	1965	1970	1975	1980	1984
Manufacturing total	100.0	100.0	100.0	100.0	100.0	100.0	100.0
Food	17.9	12.4	12.5	10.4	11.9	10.5	10.8
Textiles	16.2	11.2	8.8	6.4	5.1	3.8	3.2
Apparels	1.3	1.2	1.5	1.4	1.7	1.4	1.3
Wood products	4.0	3.5	3.6	3.2	2.8	2.5	1.6
Furniture	1.0	1.0	1.4	1.5	1.5	1.4	1.1
Paper and pulp	4.2	3.9	3.8	3.3	3.3	3.2	2.9
Publishing and printing	3.3	2.5	3.1	2.9	3.3	3.3	3.3
Chemicals	11.0	9.4	9.5	8.0	8.2	8.4	8.0
Petroleum and coal products	1.9	2.4	2.8	2.6	5.9	7.1	5.4
Rubber products	1.4	1.5	1.3	1.1	1.1	1.2	1.1
Leather products	0.6	0.5	0.6	0.5	0.5	0.5	0.4
Ceramics	3.4	3.5	3.6	3.6	3.8	3.9	3.5
Iron and steel	9.6	10.6	9.1	9.5	8.9	8.3	6.8
Non-ferrous metals	4.1	4.3	4.0	4.4	3.1	3.8	2.8
Metal products	3.3	3.9	4.7	5.4	5.2	5.0	4.7
General machinery	4.6	7.8	7.8	9.9	8.3	8.2	8.8
Electric machinery	3.7	8.3	7.8	10.6	8.5	10.4	15.4
Transport equipment	5.5	8.5	9.7	10.5	11.6	11.6	12.7
Precision instrument	0.8	1.1	1.3	1.3	1.4	1.6	1.6
Ordnance	0.0	0.1	0.0	0.0	0.0	0.0	0.0
Others	2.0	2.5	3.3	3.6	4.0	4.1	4.5

Source: MITI, *KTH*, various issues.

1955 and 30.1% in 1960, but it declined to 12.5% in 1970, 4.8% in 1980, and 3.6% in 1985. In the latter half of the 1950s, about one-fourth of Japan's export expansion was explained by textile export increases. Its contribution ratio to total export expansion was 23.1% for 1955–60, but it decreased to about 8% in the 1960s, 2.5% in the 1970s, and less than 1% for 1980–85.

Steel was the leading export industry until the mid-1970s. Steel exports' share was less than 10% in 1960, but it increased to more than 15% in 1965 and to 18% in 1975. However, it started to decline in the mid-1970s. Export share of steel decreased to 11.9% in 1980 and 7.8% in 1985. Change in the export contribution ratio of the steel

Table 8.4

Export Structure of Manufactures: Postwar Japan

(%)

	1955	1960	1965	1970	1975	1980	1985
Total	100.0	100.0	100.0	100.0	100.0	100.0	100.0
Foodstuff	6.2	6.3	4.1	3.4	1.4	1.2	0.8
Textiles	37.3	30.1	18.7	12.5	6.7	4.8	3.6
Textile fibers	2.9	2.0	1.8	1.0	0.8	0.5	0.4
Textile yarn	29.1	22.7	13.5	9.0	5.2	3.9	2.8
Clothing	5.2	5.4	3.4	2.4	0.6	0.4	0.4
Chemicals	5.1	4.5	6.5	6.4	7.0	5.3	4.4
Non-metallic minerals	4.7	4.2	3.1	1.9	1.3	1.4	1.2
Metals and metal products	19.2	14.0	20.3	19.7	22.4	16.5	10.6
Iron and steel	12.8	9.6	15.3	14.7	18.2	11.9	7.8
Non-ferrous metals	3.3	0.6	1.4	1.3	1.0	1.5	0.8
Metal products	3.0	3.8	3.6	3.7	3.2	3.0	2.0
Machinery	na	25.5	35.2	46.3	53.8	62.7	71.8
General machinery	na	na	7.4	10.4	12.1	13.9	16.8
Electric machinery	na	na	9.2	12.3	11.0	14.4	16.9
Transport equipment	na	na	14.7	17.8	26.1	26.5	28.0
Precision instruments	na	na	3.9	5.7	4.7	7.9	10.1
Others	na	15.3	12.1	9.9	7.4	8.1	7.7

Sources: Ministry of Finance, *The Summary Report, Trade of Japan* (Tokyo, Japan Tariff Association), various issues, Statistics Bureau, Management and Coordination Agency, *Japan Statistical Yearbook* (Tokyo, Japan Statistical Association), various issues.

industry clearly tells us the rise and fall of steel industry in postwar Japan. It was just 6.4% for 1955–60, but rose to more than 20% for 1960–65 and 1970–75.

Japan's crude steel production exceeded 10 million metric tons in 1956. It increased to 22 million in 1960, 41 million in 1965, 93 million in 1970, and more than 100 million MT in 1973. Japan's steel industry began export expansion in the 1930s. But the nation's share of world steel exports was still low in the early postwar years: in 1960 Japan exported 2,242,000 MT of steel, 5.7% of total world steel exports.

In the same year, West Germany was the world's largest steel exporter, with a 20% share. In the 1960s steel exports from Japan increased sharply. In 1970 Japan exported 17.6 million MT, 20% of the world total; and, in 1985 Japan exported 31.5 million, MT, a 19.7% share of exports. In the same year Korea exported 5.9 million MT of steel, and the share was 3.7%. Japan is still the world's largest steel exporter, but it seems to us that the steel industry is not the leading industry in more fully industrialized countries as it is in newly industrializing economies. The catch-up speed of steel-exporting NIEs such as Korea and Brazil is very high. Korea started an integrated steel mill in 1973 in Pohang. Pohang Steel Company (POSCO) completed the first stage of its second plant in Kwangyang in May 1987. Consequently, POSCO's crude steel production capacity increased to about 11.8 million MT. It took more than 50 years to exceed the 10 million tons of steel production achieved since the establishment of the first integrated steel mill in Japan, but only 14 years in Korea.

In the latter half of the 1970s, the contribution of iron and steel exports declined sharply, to less than 4% of Japan's total export expansion. For 1980–85, iron and steel exports decreased absolutely in value. Machinery, as mentioned in Lecture 4, became the leading export industry in postwar Japan. Machinery's export share was 25.5% in 1960, 46% in 1970, 63% in 1980, and 72% in 1985. Since the mid-1960s more than half of Japan's export expansion has been attributed to the expansion of machinery exports. For the latter half of the 1970s, about three-fourths of Japan's export expansion is explained by machinery export expansion. For the period 1980–85, the percentage increased to 93%. When compared with the export contribution ratio of 1965–70, the 1980–85 contributions of total machinery, general machinery, electric machinery, transport equipment, and precision instruments had increased by 38.2, 10.8, 8.1, 11.3, and 8.2 percentage points, respectively.

Transport equipment, mainly automobiles, accounted for the largest share of machinery export in 1985. In 1955 Japan exported only two passenger cars; 30 years later, more than four million. The export/ production ratio of passenger cars was less than 5% in 1960, but increased to 22.8% in 1970, 40.4% in 1975, 56.1% in 1980, and 57.9% in 1985. The export/production ratio of the electronics industry, one of the major subsectors of the machinery industry, is also very high: about 25% in 1970, more than 30% in 1974, and 50% in 1982. If we compare the export/production ratios of consumer electronics (television sets, video recorders, audio equipment), industrial electronics (telecommunications equipment, computers, electronic measuring equipment), and electronic parts (semiconductors, integrated circuits), consumer electronics had the highest ratios: 40% in 1970 and more than 70% in 1981. The ratios of industrial electronics and electronics parts are lower than those of consumer electronics: about 15% in 1970, rising recently to about 40% for industrial electronics and about 50% for electronics parts.

Comparative Advantage and Trade Balance

Net export ratio (NER) is one of the simple *ex post* indicators of international competitiveness. Net export ratio is defined as $(X-M)/(X+M)$, where X and M are exports and imports. It ranges from -1 to $+1$—negative when the country is a net importer, and positive when it is a net exporter. An increase in NER indicates improvement in international competitiveness. Long-term trends in NER for manufacturing as a whole, as well as for textiles, metals, and machinery, are shown in Figures 8.1 and 8.2.

The NER of manufactured goods shows a continuous tendency to increase. Japan became a net exporter of manufactured products around the turn of the century. The long-term pattern of NER for Japan's textiles shows a typical case of rise and fall of consumer non-durables. Japan became a net exporter of textiles in the 1890s. Textile exports increased sharply, leading Japan's export expansion. NER of textiles

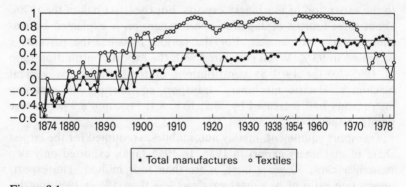

Figure 8.1
NER of Manufactured Total and Textiles: Japan, 1874–1978
Sources: Ohkawa and Shinohara, eds., *Patterns of Japanese Economic Development*, Tables A26 (pp. 315–318), A27 (pp. 319–322); Ippei Yamazawa, *Japanese Economic Development and International Trade*, Appendix Tables 1–1 and 1–2 (pp. 240–243).
Note: Five-year averages.

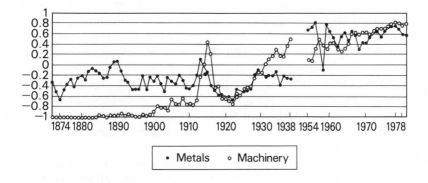

Figure 8.2
NER of Metals and Machinery: Japan, 1874–1978
Source: The same as for Figure 8.1.

reached +0.8 in the 1910s. It ranged between +0.8 and +1.0 until
the 1960s, but declined sharply in the 1970s. It was as low as 0.044
in 1979, and probably has continued to decline.

NERs of metals and machinery are shown in Figure 8.2. Japan was
a net importer of metals in the prewar period, but the postwar period
saw a rapid expansion of steel exports, as mentioned earlier. Japan was
also a net importer of machinery until the beginning of the 1930s,
except during World War I. The NER of machinery started to increase
in the 1920s, and continued to increase in the postwar period with
the rapid expansion of exports of automobiles, electric machinery,
and other products. NER of metals has not increased in the postwar
period, But that of machinery continues to increase, and the trend
of NER of machine tools in postwar Japan shows rapid improvement
in the international competitiveness of this industry. Though not shown
in the figure, NER of machine tools varied between −0.9 and −0.6
for 1953 to 1963, but it started to improve after 1963. Japan became
a net exporter of machine tools in 1972. Its NER continues to increase,
reaching more than 0.8 in the mid-1980s. Machine tools are often
called mother machines because they produce industrial machinery.
Thus the quality of machine tools is very imporant for industrialization, and their manufacture requires a high level of technological development.

As mentioned earlier, Japan was a net importer of machine tools
in the 1950s. In 1955 more than half of domestic demand was depend-

ent on imports. In 1951 the government introduced a subsidy system for promoting machine tool imports, subsidizing half of the cost of importing specified high-quality machine tools. Subsequently another subsidy system was developed, this time for import substitution, under which the government bore half the cost of producing machine tools rather than subsidizing imports. This policy was adopted in order to promote the domestic machine-tool industry and to save foreign currency. The quick shift from import subsidy to domestic production subsidy is very important: if the government had continued to subsidize machine tool imports, Japan's machine tool industry might not have developed.

Progress in Japanese machine-tool manufacture has been remarkable in the past 20 years. The import dependency ratio (import/domestic demand), with a high 58% in 1955, declined to less than 10% in the late 1970s. Introduction of new technology is important to the machine-tool industry. Since the microelectronics revolution, numerical control (NC) machine tools have become the mainstream of machine tools. Data on NC machine tool exports since 1969 are available. The ratio of NC machine tool exports to total machine tool exports was less than 10% before 1975. The ratio exceeded 50% in 1980, and 70% in 1984.

A change in trade balance is the result of change in the comparative advantage structure. Trade balance ratios for the prewar and postwar periods are presented in Figure 8.3. The ratio is the ratio of the trade balance to the sum of exports and imports (NER, discussed above). In prewar Japan the trade balance was almost negative. The ratio became positive around the mid-1960s and has increased recently, reaching nearly 0.3 in 1986.

III. Postwar Export Promotion Policy

Institutions, Systems, and Organizations

Postwar export promotion has been carried out by establishing various institutions, systems, and organizations backed up by legal provisions. They include policy measures for financing and taxation; systems of insurance, inspection, design promotion, marketing information, and services; and export trade organization. A brief explanation of their functions follows.

Japan's foreign trade, which was directly controlled by the government just after World War II, was completely transferred to the private sector in January 1950. A series of laws and regulations were intro-

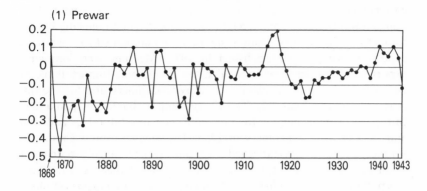

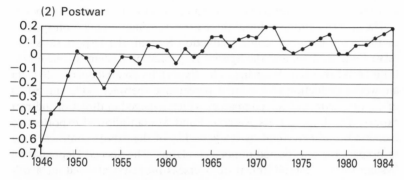

Figure 8.3

Trade Balance Ratio: Japan 1868–1984

Sources: Ohkawa and Shinohara, eds., *Patterns of Japanese Economic Development*, Tables A31 and A32 (pp. 332–336); IMF, *International
Financial Statistics Yearbook*, various issues.

Note: Five-year averages.

duced: they include the Foreign Trade Control Law (1949), Export
Credit Insurance Law (1950), Special Taxation Measures Law (1953),
Export Goods Design Law, and Export Inspection Law (1958). Export
promotion systems such as export financing (1950), export inspection
(1950), foreign exchange function (1953), and export promotion taxation were also introduced. In addition to these laws and systems, trade-
related organizations such as the Japan Export Bank (1950—later the
Export-Import Bank of Japan, 1952), JETRO (1954), and the Export
Council (1954) were established.

The Bank of Japan introduced the export advance bill system and
the import settlement bill system to finance foreign trade through

commercial banks at preferential interest rates (1 to 3 percentage points lower than the commercial rate) in 1950, and a financing system for export bills in 1953. These systems, which amounted to short-term export financing, were abolished in 1972. Medium- and long-term export financing has been provided by the Export-Import Bank of Japan for the export of plants and heavy machinery and for the import of basic raw materials. The Export-Import Bank of Japan added to the list of items eligible for financing: consumer durables and iron and steel in 1962, machinery in 1965. The Small Business Credit Insurance Corporation established a special export financing system for small and medium enterprises in 1961. The Small Business Financing Corporation also established a financing system to modernize small and medium-scale companies and equip them to expand into exports.

The government introduced three export promotion taxation systems in 1953: the Export Income Deduction System, the Export Loss Reserve Fund System, and the Special Depreciation System for the establishment of overseas branches. The Export Income Deduction System allowed a deduction of a certain percentage (between 50% and 80%) of export income of the companies which engaged in direct or indirect export. The Export Loss Reserve Fund System allowed exporters to increase the reserve fund by 0.5% to 1% of the export contract value to prepare for unexpected importers' claims. The Special Depreciation System for the establishment of overseas branches allowed an accelerated depreciation. The tax reform of 1964 introduced the following export promotion measures: (i) establishment of an overseas market development reserve, (ii) overseas investment loss reserves, (iii) overseas market development reserves, (iv) expansion of depreciation allowances for exports, (v) continuation of technology export income deduction, and (vi) special permission for inclusion in losses of entire overseas social entertainment expenses.

In addition to direct export promotion policy measures, the government introduced an export supporting policy. Its major component measures include the following.

i) Export Insurance. The export insurance system was introduced in March 1950. This system covered only the risk during the preshipment period. In addition to this ordinary export insurance, new types of insurance systems were introduced in subsequent years: an export payment insurance system (1951), export financing insurance (1952), overseas advertising insurance (1952), export bill insurance (1953), consignment sales export insurance (1954), overseas investment insurance (1956, 1957), exchange fluctuation insurance (1974), and export guarantee insurance (1977).

ii) Export Inspection System. Japan has a long history of export inspection. The government established the raw-silk export inspection system in 1895. In the postwar period the government recognized that a rational third-party inspection system was necessary for quality improvement of export products. For this reason the Export Inspection Law was enacted, in 1958. Under this law, 176 items are to be inspected for export. Among them, 60 items are machinery and metal products, 51 sundries, 40 textiles, 23 agricultural products, and 2 types of medical equipment. The export share of these items in Japan's total exports was some 50% in the late 1950s, then decreased to 30% in the 1960s and 20% in the 1970s. At present it is less than 10%.

iii) Design Promotion System. The Good Design Mark Products (G-mark) system was stared in 1957, and a Design Division was created within MITI in 1959. In order to promote good craft articles, the Japan Superior Handicraft Articles Export Promotion Plan began in 1960. The Japan Export Design Exhibition has been held once a year since 1963. Trial production of general merchandise was carried out at the Industrial Craft Laboratory, and of pottery at Nagoya Industrial Engineering Laboratory. Four design centers were established for the improvement of industrial design: the Japan Textile Design Center (1955), the Japan Pottery Design Center (1956), the Japan General Merchandise Design Center (1956), and the Japan Machinery Design Center. In 1960 a Japan Design House was established within JETRO, the Japan External Trade Organization, as an exhibition hall for superior design products. Later the Japan Design House was dissolved and the Japan Industrial Design Promotion Organization established, in 1971.

iv) International Marketing Information System and Trade Supplement Services. An international marketing information system is very important for export promotion. Without such an institution, rapid export expansion is not possible even if the products of a country are internationally competitive in price and quality. General trading companies and large manufacturing companies have these capabilities on their own. JETRO also serves this function.

MITI established the Japan Export Trade Research Organization in 1951, the International Trade Fair Council in 1952, and the Japan Trade Center in 1953. These organizations merged in 1954 as the Japan *Export* Trade Organization (JETRO), which was reorganized in 1958 under the present name, Japan *External* Trade Organization (JETRO). JETRO's major functions are research on overseas markets and trade products, export market surveys, trade information services, hosting overseas trade fairs, publications on the Japanese economy and products, trade consulting services, consultation on improved export product design, and helping Japanese businessmen traveling abroad for market surveys and business negotiations.

JETRO has (as of 1983) 31 domestic offices and 78 overseas offices. All are connected by facsimile links, and enormous amounts of information are being sent to JETRO headquarters, where a daily bulletin based on the information sent from all over the world is published. This bulletin is sent directly to subscribers every day except Sunday, providing easy access to information on the general economic and political situation, trade policy changes, and new products in every country in the world.[1]

Trading Companies

Japanese general trading companies such as C. Itoh, Marubeni, Mitsui, Mitsubishi, and Sumitomo played an important role in export expansion of Japan. GTCs, which have no counterparts elsewhere in the world, enjoy the benefits of economies of scale because they handle a wide variety of products and conduct exports, imports, and offshore and domestic trade utilizing a worldwide information network. They have been devoted to export expansion and industrialization since the Meiji Era. With an advantage over foreign trading companies in their proximity to domestic manufacturers and consumers, they were able to find new export goods and develop new export markets. These activities are very important for rapid export expansion.

Let us look at some postwar changes in the composition of exports handled by the general trading companies. A sharp decline in foodstuff and textile exports took place. The rate of increase in exports of heavy industrial goods is much higher than that for exports as a whole. Although the GTCs handled over three quarters of Japan's total metal exports in 1970, their share of machinery exports was much lower because many manufacturers of electrical machinery and motor vehicles export directly, without going through GTCs. In spite of direct export by machine manufactures, however, GTCs machinery export share had increased to more than half in 1985. This reflects the recent changes in the industrial and trade structure.[2]

---

[1] Information from JETRO, *A History of Japan's Postwar Export Policy*, 1983.

[2] For more details on the role of GTCs, see Ippei Yamazawa and Hirohisa Kohama, "Trading Companies and the Expansion of Foreign Trade: Japan, Korea and Thailand," in Kazushi Ohkawa and Gustar Ranis, eds., *Japan and the Developing Countries* (Oxford: Basil Blackwell, 1985), pp. 426–446.

Industrial Policy and International Competitiveness

Many non-Japanese economists argue that the Japanese government, especially MITI, played a crucial role in the rapid postwar industrialization of Japan. The "Japan, Inc." argument is based on this view. The government did promote industrialization with various policy measures. But the most important factor in rapid economic growth was not industrial policy, but the dynamism of the private sector. In our view, private dynamism—in other words, efficient operation of the market mechanism—is much more rational and powerful than policy orientation, as emphasized earlier. It seems to us that even in the reconstruction phase just after World War II, the government never interfered in private-sector decision-making. The following is a good example. When Toyota and Nissan applied for financing to the Reconstruction Financing Corporation (1947–52), one of the board members was opposed to financing these companies. It was quite difficult at that time to foresee the present prosperity of Japan's automobile industry. It was rational, in terms of the static notions of conventional economic theory, not to promote the growth of an automobile industry in Japan. But the Reconstruction Financing Corporation finally decided to finance Toyota and Nissan.

The major function of the Reconstruction Financing Corporation and the Japan Development Bank was to finance basic industries such as electricity, coal, ocean transportation, and steel. In addition to this basic function, these banks helped to promote industrialization for utilizing new technology. SONY is a good example. When SONY developed the first transistor radio, commercial banks were reluctant to finance the company. The Japan Development Bank financed SONY in order to promote technology-intensive manufacture in Japan. Tax policy also operated flexibly in order to promote the manufacture of new products such as transistor radios, television sets, and photo film. Transistor radios were exempted from the commodity tax for two years in the initial phase of development.

We think industrial policy and export promotion policy played a role to a certain extent in rapid industrialization and export expansion in postwar Japan. But these policies were not the necessary condition for rapid economic growth. Japan's economic management has been efficiency-oriented in the long run. In the previous lectures, we saw that protectionist policy can be justified from the long-run standpoint of industrialization. With this orientation, Japanese manufacturers have competed strenuously even in the protected and oligopolistic domestic market.

A good example of the harsh competition is the petrochemical industry. When this industry began to develop in the late 1950s, ethylene production capacity was 10,000 or 20,000 tons per year. In order to benefit from economies of scale and improve the international competitiveness of petrochemical products, MITI set minimum capacity requirements for ethylene plants in 1967. Only an ethylene plant whose capacity is more than 300,000 tons per year was eligible to set up as a new establishment. Before the announcement of this policy, MITI officials thought that only three or four petrochemical companies could fulfill this criterion because of the enormous amount of capital necessary for investing in a large-scale ethylene plant. However, all 12 of the integrated petrochemical companies managed to clear this hurdle.

Japanese manufacturers have been very eager to improve and import technology. Before trade liberalization, they had faced the pressures of competition with foreign companies. They were eager for technology improvement in order to enhance their international competitiveness.

Protection policy can be rationalized when the protected industry is in its infancy. However, it is very difficult to identify a specific "infant industry" *ex ante*. Protection policies in the course of import substitution tend to be prolonged, as many examples in Latin American countries show. In the early years of postwar rapid economic growth, domestic industries in Japan were heavily protected and promoted. However, businessmen, economists, and government officials all knew that trade liberalization was inevitable in the 1960s and would be followed by capital liberalization.

Even if protection in certain development phases can be rationalized from an economic standpoint, the crucial issue is how to maintain and promote efficiency-oriented economic management in a protected market. For this purpose the government should announce a schedule for liberalization. Gradual and step-by-step liberalization is desirable, but the liberalization schedule should not be substantially changed by political pressure once it is announced. Private manufacturers should make every effort to improve their competitiveness by the time of the scheduled liberalization.

These experiences of Japan—efficiency-oriented economic management, competition in a protected and oligopolistic domestic market, and the consciousness of international competition externally—have important implications for the contemporary developing countries.

Epilogue: The Post-Development Phase

Japan's export performance, particularly its fast expansion to a huge surplus over imports in recent years, poses the difficult problem of adjusting international trade imbalances. This volume attempts to analyze developing economies, and the problem of "developed" economies is beyond its scope. However, because of the importance of this problem, it will be treated briefly here in the framework of the final subphase before full industrialization, as defined in Lecture 1, section I. Actually, this is a post-development phase. This approach is essentially based on our view that the recent export surge does show the structural characteristics of this particular phase. The short interval of time that has passed since the mid-1970s makes it difficult to characterize such a specific phase because of unknown factors in the future. It may be thought that this is a temporary phenomenon of adjustment to the shocks of the oil crisis. The reason we do not share this view will be clarified through the discussions that follow.

Let us recall that manufacturing output was growing faster than GDP ($GY_m > GY$), growth of which was sustained even after the Japanese economy passed through the end of secondary export substitution (Table 1.1). This seemingly "atypical pattern" needs further clarification here through the analysis of relevant factors other than the export surge. What is observed for the years between 1975 and 1985 cannot be interpreted satisfactorily without considering the remnants of the long process of development as a latecomer. Japan's eventual success in completing development, though not without drawbacks, was essentially achieved by sustaining the pattern of $GY_m > GY$. The productivity level of modern manufacturing had risen at a rapid pace. Its continuation in this phase is the basic cause of the recent export surge, as explained earlier. However, on the other hand, weaker sectors such as agriculture, mining, construction, and services remain at comparatively lower productivity levels despite their considerable growth. Medium and small-scale enterprises in manufacturing belong to this category. In Kuznets's terminology this is the pattern of "divergence," as opposed to convergence,[3] which is identified for the post-development phase in general. This is not the place to discuss it in detail beyond the figures given in the footnote. We are concerned with the over-time change rather than the level of the ratio. In constant prices the ratio distinctly decreases; changes in relative prices, including the effects of government policy, operated against it.

[3] "Diverge or converge" is measured simply in terms of product per worker in major sectors. Simon Kuznets, *Economic Growth of Nations: Total Output and Production Structure* (Cambridge: Harvard University, Press, 1972). A turn from divergence to convergence was recognized for most Western industrialized countries during the postwar period. However, Japan was placed on the path of divergence

The international problems of trade imbalances and the resulting foreign payments imbalances is widely known and do not need further explanation except to say that Japan's export surplus is a recent phenomenon, reversing the chronic trend of export deficit over imports.[4] Now, the path of long-term development is characterized by two imbalances, one external and the other internal. The particular phase under review is thus characterized by the reversal of the trade imbalance externally but with sustained remnants of the pattern of divergence of industrial structure internally.

Below, the recent phenomena will be examined in greater detail and possible performance in the next 10 or 15 years will be discussed.

Let us begin by noting that the performance of GY_m vs. GY in current prices differs distinctly from what has been observed earlier in constant prices (Table 1.1). The ratio Y_m/Y does not show a tendency to increase, but rather to decrease from the 1960s to the recent interval under review.[5] The achievement of full industrialization in Japan could be identified as conforming with the international pattern. Such a distinct discrepancy between the two series is of course brought forth by a drastic decline in the prices of manufacturing output. Taking the average of 1961–65 as 100, the price index of GDP increased to 303 on average for 1981–85, but that of manufacturing increased only to 169. This suggests the significance of the drastic changes in relative

---

by Kazushi Ohkawa, "Keizai Hatten to Kozo" [Economic Development and Structure], Chapter 8, in Kazushi Ohkawa and Ryoshin Minami, eds., *Kindai Nihon no Keizai Hatten* [Economic Development of Modern Japan] (Tokyo: Toyo Keizai Shimposha, 1975).

For the intervals comparable to those in Table 1.1, the ratio (%) of output per worker of agriculture (A) and services (S) to that of manufacturing (M) in 1980 prices (in current prices in parenthesis) is

	A/M		(A+S)/M	
1970–75	28.8	(26.8)	82.7	(74.0)
1976–80	25.8	(27.2)	79.1	(79.5)
1981–85	23.1	(28.6)	74.9	(80.0)

Source: EPA, *Annual Reports on National Accounts*.

[4] Because of the required linkage to the industrial approach, merchandise trade balance is adopted, with a narrower scope than the conventional "resource gap," in current national accounts in order to illustrate the latest reversal. The ratio (%) of exports (X) and imports (M) to GDP (Y) in current yen is as follows on average for the intervals:

	1961–65	1966–70	1971–75	1976–80	1981–84
X/Y	9.3	9.3	10.3	10.9	12.3
M/Y	10.9	10.2	11.7	11.3	11.8
Balance	–1.6	–0.9	–0.4	–0.4	0.5

[5] The ratio of Y_m/Y in current prices in five-year averages is 31.9 in 1961–65, 33.2% in 1966–70, 32.5% in 1971–75, 28.2% in 1976–80, and 28.3% in 1981–85.

sectoral prices in treating the problem at issue. A faster rate of technological progress and effects of economies of scale in manufacturing,
particularly the machinery subsector, are the most responsible factors.
Supply prices could become lower with a favorable demand situation.
But, as a matter of fact, domestic demand increase was rather limited,
and the major part of supply increases was for export (in 1984, 99.2%
of total merchandise exports was manufactured goods and 70.2%
was machinery). On the other hand, the relative increase of output
prices in the non-manufacturing sector was the effect of a combination
of various factors which differ from one subsector to another, but
basically its slower rate of technological advance and the decreasing
favorable effects of scale economies are the major factors, along with
protective government policy. The symbolic case is that of farm products, particularly rice. As observed earlier, output per worker in current prices in this sector tended to increase, despite its decrease in
constant prices, relative to that of manufacturing. This was a way of
solving the problem of labor employment in the broad sense, which
included small proprietors and family workers.

We cannot have precise knowledge about the changes in the domestic demand for output in these two sectors thus broadly demarcated, because demand is complex, including not only final demand
(consumption, investment), but also that for intermediate goods. Nevertheless, a rough conjecture is possible. If $GY_m = GY_n$ (Y_n = non-
manufacturing) can be assumed for an economy in terms of domestic
demand, we can say that crude elasticity of demand with respect to
income is equal for the two. Actually, the pattern close to $GY_m = GY$
presented earlier is often explained in this way. During the development process, demand elasticity of Y_m is sustained at a level greater
than that of Y_n. With full industrialization, it tends to decrease to be
closer to the elasticity of Y_n. Greater value of elasticity of demand
for services is the major element in the latter. In Japan's case such a
demand performance certainly operates, perhaps with considerable
price effect on Y_m demand. Rough estimates by adjusting the $Y_m \cdot Y$
relation in output production to the domestic use term show the ratio
in constant price series: 21.3% in 1970–74, 19.0% in 1975–79, and
20.2% in 1980–84. It is hard to expect a trend of distinct increase
for the latter part of the phase under consideration.

In considering the future, we do not attempt to forecast or to make
policy recommendations. Instead, our intention is to clarify the structural characteristics of the present phase, which we expect to continue
until the end of this century, from a long-term perspective under certain assumptions which are unavoidable. In the short run, Japan's rate

of growth will be sustained at a level somewhat higher than the average of other industrialized market economies, as in the past, but toward the end of the 1990s, this moderate difference will disappear. In comparison with the growth rates of Asian industrializing countries, the growth rate will be distinctly lower. These speculations assume that no drastic change will take place in the international economic environment.

Now, having made these observations, let us search for the necessary conditions, if not sufficient, which would lead Japanese economy to the structural pattern of $GY_m = GY$ at the end of the phase under review. What is crucial is the problem of how to perceive the mutually related performance of exports and domestic demand. The proportion of exports to GDP (X/Y), in our view, will and should be sustained almost unchanged at the level attained during the first half of the 1980s, immediately before the drastic yen appreciation (12.3% for merchandise trade). This is in disagreement with the widely prevailing view that the proportion (X/Y) should be lower in the future. The assertion is based on the biased observation that export dependency has long been the "intrinsic property" of Japanese growth, so that the contemporary trade imbalance can and should be remedied by changing this basic nature of past performance. As discussed earlier in this lecture, the export proportion varied widely in the historical process of Japanese growth. Particularly noteworthy is its negative correlation with the movement of domestic gross investment. For example, during the postwar investment spurt X/Y was 8–9%. The recent increase in this ratio is associated with a decrease in domestic investment proportion (I/Y). In an economy that has completed the development process, it is impossible to expect another investment spurt for some time. The policy of enhancing public investment, recently proposed particularly for social overhead capital, is aiming in the right direction as its shortcomings were brought out by concentrating investment in the direct production sectors. However, its effects should be evaluated in a short-term dimension. From a longer-term perspective, domestic investment enhancement, private and public, cannot be expected to replace contracted exports.

A more important aspect may be that of supply-production. The majority of Japan's export is now machinery—producer durables, transportation equipment, and consumer durables. As examined earlier in detail in Lectures 4 and 7, the recent advance of technology in this area has been notable. The nation's capability thus established is representative of the factors composing Japan's comparative advantage, and we cannot think about future performance without recognizing the significance of this advantage. The problem at issue is not export in general, but machinery in particular. Additional demand for producer durables to be filled by enhancing domestic investment will be limited as the majority of such investment (perhaps two-thirds) goes to construction and its materials (for example, steel and cement). A relative decrease in exports could be realized only by paying the high price of loss of the accumulated national advantage. Japan's machine exports will continue to increase. Qualified machinery is indispensable for industrialization. The level of technology required for producing industrial machinery and machine tools is much higher than for other industrial products. Therefore, it is difficult to produce industrial machinery and machine tools in countries still in the early phases of development. Japan's industrial machine exports have contributed to the industrialization of Asian developing countries. During their semi-industrialized phase, a considerable portion of these machines will continue to be imported from Japan. For example, the share of Korea's textile machine imports from Japan in total textile machine imports has varied between 50% and 84% since the beginning of the 1960s.

Another aspect of our view is that policies aimed at enhancing domestic demand in Japan's present situation may not be as effective as has often been expected in the conventional view based on macroeconomic concepts. The tight fiscal policy firmly adopted for several years certainly contributed to reducing the increase in effective demand. Therefore a change, even not a full-scale one, may increase the rate of growth. Some weakening of export incentive can be expected. However, short-term changes are not our concern. A number of commentators have pointed out the small value of elasticity of imports with respect to income. The majority of imports is minerals, fuels, and food items, the proportion of manufactured goods being quite small. This is the pattern established through the development path to industrialization, but it has been changing rapidly in recent years. Japan's trade balance can be simply expressed by $M_p - X_m$ (M_p = imports of primary products; X_m = exports of manufactured goods). Its deficit is caused by $M_p > X_m$ and its surplus by $X_m > M_p$. Changes in both quantity and terms of trade are influential. The ratio M_p/M_m tended to decrease rapidly through the postwar phases of secondary import and export substitution (from 0.92 in 1956–60 to 0.36 in 1976–80 in 1965 constant prices). The decrease in current prices, however, was interrupted after 1973 by the impact of the oil crisis: the lowest ratio of 0.60 in 1971–72 increased to a high of 1.00 in 1980, declining again to 0.60 in 1984.

During the latter years of this century, the trade balance performance will not be stable owing to possible variation in the prices of "non-competitive" import goods, despite sustained growth in export of manufactured goods with certain effects on energy-saving efforts.

The problem for the post-development phase is how and to what extent this pattern can be changed for the future. The assertion has often been made that Japan is taking its time in eliminating barriers to imports. With such a criticism we have no disagreement in principle. However, to be realistic in our response and also to be reasonable in our conceptual approach, we want to emphasize the importance of the time dimension. Increases in import promotion will and should proceed not in a short-term but in a long-term perspective, looking toward the end of the phase of full industrialization.

In saying so, we are not merely stressing the importance of structural adjustment through policies. Instead, the significance of price effects expected in the market mechanism, including the effects of changes in exchange rates, should be adequately recognized in increasing the proportion of imports in relation to exports in order to keep the resource gap at a manageable level. In recent years the drastic appreciation of the yen in value has tended to increase Japan's imports, heralding a possible longer-term trend. During the last part of this phase this international price mechanism is expected to operate to a fuller extent if the policy and institutional restraints on imports are eliminated in due course.

However, the comparative price mechanism cannot be expected to work automatically. When exports are more or less an unchanged proportion of growing GDP even at the current exchange rate, considerable efforts by private enterprises would be required to make the technological-organizational progress required. Japan will face greater obstacles in enhancing imports, because they are competitive with the production activities of weaker sectors of the economy; this presents a new challenge to industrial policy. Productivity enhancement in the non-manufacturing sector is one of the central problems. To the extent that this is carried out effectively, though it is difficult, Japan's domestic price structure will move closer to the international price system by the end of the century, when the pattern of $GY_m = GY$ will be more fully realized. A shift to convergence from divergence in terms of output per worker in the domestic production structure may be a possibility, if sectoral employment reallocation is successful.[6]

[6] In terms of $GY_m = GY_n$, it is $Gy_m + GL_m = Gy_n + GL_n$ (y and L stand for output per worker and the number of laborers employed, respectively). GL_m will be slightly negative, and GL_n will be postive mostly in services, though negative

The final point we want to discuss is a new dimension of industrial policy: substituting imports for domestic production—a reversal of the process of import substitution which is a part of the process of industrialization pursued by Japan and all other developing economies. In Japan, the process was almost perfectly completed in manufacturing: the import dependency ratio for producer durables dropped lower than 10%. In the light of this historical type of development completion, one can conceive of the difficulty of reversing because of inertia in both public and private sectors. Nevertheless, in our view, from a historical perspective the reversal is a natural and necessary step in proceeding toward full industrialization. Let us recall the phenomenon tentatively called "tertiary" export substitution in Lecture 7. Toward the end of secondary export substitution, the role played by steel and chemicals took the form of a decrease in export substitution by durables: another export substitution is thought to take place for durable goods. In the phase that follows, machinery comes to play the dominant role, revealing an increasingly higher comparative advantage for technology-intensive products over capital-intensive products. The recent appreciation in the yen's value has further weakened exports' competitiveness, and similar phenomena will emerge in a wider range of manufacturing industries. Imports to Japan from newly industrializing economies and even from industrialized countries have already begun to increase due to the operation of the market mechanism. The example can be generalized to a wider range of manufactured goods, including not only finished goods, but also their parts and components.[7]

While Japan's technological advance will proceed in the subsectors which require higher technological knowledge, machinery and equipment for common use should and will be increasingly imported from developing countries, which will come to have a comparative advantage in producing these goods with a standard level of technology and lower prices of labor.

---

in agriculture and mining. Thus $Gy_m > Gy_n$ is still a required condition during this phase, though its degree of inequality will gradually become smaller.

[7] Quantitative evidence cannot yet be given for such recent phenomena. However, from past experience, it is possible to identify signs of increase in the ratio of manufactured imports to domestic manufacturing output (GDP component). The average ratios were 8% in 1967–72, 9.3% in 1973–78, and 10.3% in 1979–84.

Index

321